Stoogeology

Stoogeology: Essays on the Three Stooges

Edited by
Peter Seely and
Gail W. Pieper

McFarland & Company, Inc., Publishers
Jefferson, North Carolina, and London

LIBRARY OF CONGRESS CATALOGUING-IN-PUBLICATION DATA

Stoogeology : essays on the Three Stooges / edited by Peter Seely and Gail W. Pieper.
    p.   cm.
Includes bibliographical references and index.

978-0-7864-2920-2
softcover : 50# alkaline paper

1. Three Stooges films. 2. Three Stooges (Comedy team).
I. Seely, Peter. II. Pieper, Gail W.
PN1995.9.T5S77 2007
791.4302'80922–dc22   2007008508

British Library cataloguing data are available

©2007 Peter Seely and Gail W. Pieper. All rights reserved

No part of this book may be reproduced or transmitted in any form or by any means, electronic or mechanical, including photocopying or recording, or by any information storage and retrieval system, without permission in writing from the publisher.

On the cover: Moe Howard, Larry Fine and Curly Howard (Columbia Pictures/Photofest)

Manufactured in the United States of America

McFarland & Company, Inc., Publishers
  Box 611, Jefferson, North Carolina 28640
    www.mcfarlandpub.com

Acknowledgments

From the editors

We acknowledge the following sources and individuals for their contributions: Leonard Maltin for his book *The Great Movie Shorts*, the first book that provided a roadmap to the Stooges; David Bruskin for his book *The White Brothers*, the best behind-the-scenes source about Stooges filmmaking; Moe Howard's autobiography *Moe Howard and the Three Stooges,* which gave us our first look at the Stooges' background; Ted Okuda and Edward Watz for their excellent book *The Columbia Comedy Shorts*; the Margaret Herrick Library of the Academy of Motion Picture Arts and Sciences for allowing access to the Jules White collection, containing many primary sources of script information; Jack Shaheen for his book *Reel Bad Arabs* and for his generous help in providing information for Chapter 16 when there was a dearth of research on the images of Arabs; Garth Jowett for his book *Film: The Democratic Art;* and the Three Stooges Fan Club, The Three Stooges Fan Club Inc., P.O. Box 747, Gwynedd Valley, PA 19437 for keeping the fire alive and providing a treasure trove of information.

From Peter Seely

I thank the following individuals for their contributions great and small: my beautiful wife, Mary, who encouraged me even though she lost me for months at a time to this book; my brothers Perry, Joe, and Jon, whose recollections and observations of Stooges films often surpassed my own; my parents, Philip and Bernice, who forced their sons to sharpen their critical defense of the Stooges; contributors Dr. Don Morlan of the University of Dayton and Dr. Lynn Rapaport of Pomona College, who not only contributed their chapters but also gave encouragement and direction when I needed it most; Dr. James Iaccino for his help with my vision and directing me to McFarland; Dr. Elizabeth Kubek for her help on feminist studies; and Timon Goode for his probing thoughts and his help in giving perspective to Chapter 17. I also thank the following individuals, who contributed even though they probably didn't realize it: James and Barbara Keck, Rita Mugg, Karin Hadley and Christina Wichmann. And finally I thank my coeditor, Dr. Gail Pieper of Benedictine University, who forced me to do tenth, eleventh, and twelfth drafts when I thought the first drafts were good, and whose contributions to the Communication Arts Department I cannot begin to enumerate.

From Gail Pieper

I was delighted to be asked to coedit this book, and I am grateful to Peter Seely for introducing me to the various aspects of Stooges comedies. His zeal and enthusiasm, even after I sent him back to the shorts yet another time to clarify a point, show him to be the finest of colleagues. I also thank my husband, Steven, for his support during this project. As he has done for more than 40 years, he patiently listened to my concerns and offered suggestions (when asked).

Contents

Acknowledgments — v
Preface — 1
Introduction — 3

I. THE AESTHETICS OF STOOGE FILMMAKING — 11

1. Casting Asparagus, Tunis Sandwiches, and *Moidering* the King's English: Puns, Wordplay, and Malapropisms in the Three Stooges Films   *Peter Seely* — 13

2. Surrealistic Stooges: The Supernatural and the Extraordinary in Slapstick Comedy   *Peter Seely* — 30

3. Discovered Treasures: The Three Stooges' Missing Scenes   *Brent Seguine* — 42

4. A Comedy of Errors: Mistakes and the Humorous Results in the Three Stooges Films   *Peter Seely* — 71

5. Hail, Columbia! A Deconstruction of the Columbia Studios' Style in the Three Stooges and Other Comedy Shorts   *Peter Seely* — 82

II. STOOGE PSYCHOLOGY AND RELIGION — 95

6. Deconstructing the Three Stooges: Freud's Concept of the Id, Ego, and Superego   *Tim Snyder* — 96

7. You Gotta Have Heart: The Pathos of Slapstick and the Three Stooges   *Peter Seely* — 101

8. Much Ado about Nothing: Violence in the Three
Stooges Comedies   *Don Morlan*   109
9. A Pie in the Face: The Three Stooges' Antiaristocracy Theme
in Depression-Era American Film   *Don Morlan*   118
10. Slap-*shtik*: The Three Stooges in the Context of Jewish
Humor and Vaudeville   *Faye Ringel*   128
11. Larry — the Existential Stooge   *Ted Levitt*   138

III. THE STOOGES GO TO WAR   145

12. The Three Stooges' Contribution to World War II
Propaganda: Moe Hailstone and Adenoid Hynkel's Race
to the Screen   *Don Morlan*   147
13. "Hang Hitler!" The Three Stooges Take Potshots at Nazis
Lynn Rapaport   156
14. Slapstick Satire: The Three Stooges' Portrayals of the Japanese
in World War II Comedies   *Don Morlan*   172

IV. RACE, ETHNICITY, AND GENDER IN STOOGE FILMS   179

15. The Image of the Negro in the Three Stooges Shorts
Peter Seely   181
16. Hassan Ben Sober: Images of American Indians, Latinos,
and Arabs in the Short Films of the Three Stooges
Peter Seely   198
17. Europeans and the Stooges: The Other "Other"   *Peter Seely*   217
18. "Hiya, Toots": Women and Gender in the Three Stooges
Kathleen Chamberlain   226
19. Dames, Babes, Battleaxes, and Tomatoes: Women and
the Three Stooges   *Peter Seely*   236

Appendix: Three Stooges Films for Columbia (1934–1959)   251
Bibliography   255
Contributors   261
Index   265

Preface

In the book *Tragedy and Comedy,* author Walter Kerr refers to the creation of comedy as "the royal twin that is born five minutes later [than tragedy], astonishing everyone and deeply threatening the orderly succession of the house. It is the mistake of nature." If comedy is in fact "the mistake of nature," then slapstick comedy is certainly the child nobody wanted.

Scholarship on slapstick comedy is a relatively new phenomenon. While the work of comics such as Charlie Chaplin, Buster Keaton, the Marx Brothers, and Laurel and Hardy has been studied and documented quite extensively, there remains a dearth of research concerning the lesser-known comics of the twentieth century, such as Andy Clyde, Wheeler and Woolsey, Clark and McCullough, El Brendel, and Edgar Kennedy, and better-known performers such as Abbott and Costello and even the Three Stooges. In the case of the lesser-known performers, the lack of definitive study of their work might be attributed to brief and fleeting popularity and the lack of interest in these subjects over 60 years later.

The same cannot be said about the Three Stooges, whose popularity has continued relatively unabated since the early days of television. One might be led to the conclusion that an academic and scholarly bias against the Stooges has prevailed. The fact that the Stooges, unlike Keaton and Chaplin, were not studied in their own day has established a tradition of considering the Stooges as too "lowbrow" and therefore unworthy of serious study.

But the Stooges' lasting popularity has made them difficult to ignore, even among stodgy academics who might feel more at home studying more esoteric topics. This popularity has undoubtedly been greatest among the Baby Boom generation, the first children raised with television. It was this group that bestowed upon the Stooges their greatest celebrity, thanks in large part to the predominance of Stooges short films on television beginning in the 1950s. The Boomers are largely responsible for the more positive light in which the Three Stooges are considered today.

Since the 1990s, the Popular Culture Association has become fertile ground for research on the Three Stooges. Scholars and authors such as Don Morlan of the University of Dayton, Kathleen Chamberlain of Emory College, and Jon Solomon of the University of Arizona have studied the influence of the Three Stooges from a multitude of different perspectives. Indeed, Morlan's study in 1991, included in this anthology, proved that it was not Charlie Chaplin, but rather Moe Howard, who gave audiences the first cinematic portrayal of Adolf Hitler.

This book is intended to fill the gap that exists in the serious study of the Three Stooges. The chapters included here expand on the efforts of the Popular Culture Association and reveal new insights into the work of the Stooges — including language, literary structure, politics, race, gender, ethnicity, and even psychology. Taken together, the chapters convincingly show that this comic trio whose popularity has lasted over 70 years has indeed had a lasting impact on art, culture, and thought.

This book is dedicated to Moe, Curly, and Shemp Howard, Larry Fine, Joe Besser, Joe DeRita, Jules White, Del Lord, Vernon Dent, Bud Jamison, Kenneth McDonald, Dick Curtis, Dudley Dickerson, Symona Boniface, Christine McIntyre, Emil Sitka, Richard Fiske, Dorothy Appleby, Clyde Bruckman, Hugh McCollum, Elwood Ullman, and Edward Bernds, and to the many, many other fine actors, writers, producers, and directors who contributed to the overwhelming and lasting legacy created by 190 short films of the Three Stooges and the hundreds of other short films produced at Columbia Pictures.

Introduction

The Three Stooges are, quite simply, the most popular and influential comedy group in the history of American film. Their impact on the world of popular culture is undeniable. Their unmatched popularity spans from their early years as a vaudeville act in the 1920s, through their black and white comedy films made between 1934 and 1959, and includes a series of color motion pictures and animated features made in the 1960s. Their popularity has long survived the deaths of the individual comics and continues well into the new millennium and the digital age.

Why has the popularity of the Stooges continued, unabated and undiminished, for so long, when all but a handful of the great and not-so-great films from the same era have been either forgotten or relegated to the domain of film studies and criticism? What is it about the Three Stooges films that cause them not only to endure in the public consciousness but also to remain beloved and vital in the present? Let us look first at the Stooges themselves for part of the answer.

A Brief History of the Three Stooges

Six different actors at one time or another were part of the Stooges team: Moe Howard, Larry Fine, Shemp Howard, Jerry (Curly) Howard, Joe Besser, and Joe DeRita. The genesis of the comedy team can be found in New York with the Jennie and Solomon Horwitz family. Harry Moses Horwitz (1897–1975), better known as Moe Howard, was to become the leader of this comedy group. His brothers Samuel (Shemp, 1895–1956) and Jerome (Curly, 1903–1952) each took a turn as the so-called third Stooge. Louis Feinberg (1902–1975), better known as Larry Fine, was a song-and-dance man from Philadelphia. Moe and Shemp began their careers as single acts in vaudeville and first teamed as a professional comedy act in 1916, doing a blackface routine. They continued to do a variety of comedy acts until 1922, when they teamed with another vaudevillian, comedian Ted Healy.

Larry Fine began his show business career while in his teens in his native Philadelphia. A versatile performer who played violin, sang, and did comedy, Larry had teamed with a number of comediennes in his early performing years. He was working as part of a comedy trio called "the Haney Sisters and Fine" when he was spotted by the Howard Brothers and Healy while they were all appearing in Chicago. Healy asked Larry to join the group on the spot. They were to be named "Ted Healy and his Three Southern Gentlemen," and later became "Ted Healy and his Three Stooges."

Healy and his Stooges did mostly stage performances in their early years, including a stint on Broadway in a Busby Berkeley production titled *A Night in Venice*. Healy and the Stooges' feature film debut came in the 20th–Century Fox picture *Soup to Nuts* (1930). Shortly after the film was made, Moe, Larry, and Shemp left to form the short-lived group of Howard, Fine, and Howard. Healy apparently begged the Stooges to rejoin him, but Shemp, who

Larry Fine, Shemp Howard, Moe Howard, and Curly Howard surround Jack Norton in the MGM film *Beer and Pretzels* (1933).

had tired of Healy and his alcoholic rages, declined to return. Instead he embarked on a solo career that started when he appeared as a supporting character in the *Joe Palooka* films for Vitaphone. Enter Jerry Howard.

When Shemp refused to return to Healy, Moe suggested his younger brother Jerry as a replacement. Jerry had had a variety of show business jobs, including a stint in the late 1920s as a comedy bandleader for the "Mickey Mouse" band of Orville Knapp. To fit in with the strange-looking Moe and Larry, Jerry shaved his moustache and his head and was thereafter known as Curly.

Healy and the Stooges signed a one-year contract with MGM for five two-reel subjects: *Nertsery Rhymes, Hello Pop, Plain Nuts, Beer and Pretzels,* and *The Big Idea*. Following their appearance in several features for MGM, Moe, Larry, and Curly split from Ted Healy for the final time in 1934. Later that year, the Stooges signed their first of several contracts with Columbia Pictures, a deal to make a two-reel comedy called *Woman Haters*, for the sum of $1,500.

Two-reel comedies, also called short subjects or shorts, were the staple of most major studios in the 1930s and 1940s. These films were intended mostly as extras to run with full-length feature films at motion picture theaters. Those produced by Paramount, RKO, and MGM tended to reflect the styles of their studios and the larger budgets available for making those films. Shorts made at other studios such as Republic, Vitaphone, and Educational were produced with smaller budgets and reflected the approach of independents. Columbia, while a major studio, had not had a long string of hit movies as had other "majors," and so their approach tended to be more similar to that of the independents than to the approach of the larger and more successful studios.

Nonetheless, Columbia Pictures developed an identifiable style that would remain relatively consistent over the years, largely because of their stable of writers, producers, directors, and sound people who remained with the studio for many years. Columbia's Short Subjects Department acquired a reputation for signing famous comedians who were on the downside of their careers, such as Buster Keaton and Hugh Herbert, and others who had not hit their peaks of popularity yet, including Andy Clyde and the Three Stooges.

During the Stooges' time with Ted Healy, it was he who was the boss, dishing out the slaps and other physical and verbal abuse. Once they left Healy, Moe was clearly the boss, both on- and off-screen. Off-screen, Moe had already been acting as the leader when it came to business decisions; Larry was not suited for the role, and Shemp had left the group. On-screen, while the Stooges showed some hint of becoming a democratic team in their first five films at Columbia, Moe had turned into the on-screen boss as well. His cruel demeanor and craggy face, his "sugar-bowl haircut," and his low-pitched, high-volume voice made him a natural for the role of the abusive, dictatorial headman.

On the other hand, Larry Fine's simplicity and happy-go-lucky demeanor (both on- and off-screen) made him the perfect comic foil. Labeled "the Stooge in the middle," Larry assumed the job of reacting to Moe's abuse, Curly's antics, and anything else that came along. However, one should not diminish the importance of Larry to the synergy and the humor of the group. In addition to his musical abilities, Larry was a visually striking performer. Thanks to a head of curly, frizzed-out hair, he was occasionally referred to as "Porcupine" or as the Stooge with the "mattress head." Moreover, while most of the best lines were written for Moe or Curly, the very humanity of Larry, along with his ability to occasionally deliver a hilarious line, made him a crucial part of the act.

Curly Howard was easily the most popular, and many would argue the most talented, of all the Stooges. He was an acrobatic man-child, an affable clown whose gifts of physical and verbal comedy made him a likeable protagonist in most of their films. His ever-present stupefying simplicity, which he personified even more than the other Stooges, was well suited to the variety of situations and environments created for the team. While probably the best looking of the Howard brothers, Curly nevertheless had a fat body, bald head, and joyous, expressive face that made him the most obvious focal point of the comedy.

The team of Moe Howard, Larry Fine, and Curly Howard ended up making 97 films between 1934 and 1947. The first Stooges films found the team searching for an identity, trying to assimilate with the type of short films being made at Columbia. But once they hit their stride, the Stooges developed a style that would be refined and maintained for the remainder of their career at Columbia. They became the most popular comedians at Columbia in their day, and that legacy grew with the passing years. Their style is perhaps best remembered today for the gratuitous eye pokes, face slaps, odd body mannerisms, obligatory pie fights, and a handful of mispronunciations and malapropisms.

But the Stooges films were actually much more layered than that, as the nineteen chapters in this collection of essays attest. Their films combined clever wordplay, acrobatic sight gags, quality writing, quick and deft direction, and integration of music and sound effects, to create a slapstick panoply that was unequaled, even by those generally considered the comic superiors of the Stooges.

Most Stooges fans consider the team's films in the Curly era to be their best work, and the humor they created came easier to the Stooges as the years went by. But a major problem loomed on the horizon. While Curly's on-camera demeanor was simple and happy-go-lucky, the actor himself was a more complicated person. Quiet and reserved off-camera, Curly was much given to life's excesses. Curly's vices led to a gradual deterioration of his health in the mid–1940s, and it noticeably affected his performances.

In 1945, Curly suffered a stroke. This caused the Stooge a great deal of difficulty in remembering lines, and his speech and physical actions lost much of their energy. The situation is abundantly apparent in the film *If a Body Meets a Body*, the first film where Curly is clearly a shell of his old self. He continued to perform and struggled through the next 18 months of filming. Curly suffered a debilitating stroke during the filming of *Half-Wits Holiday* that forced him to retire from the Stooges. He appeared for the last time in a Stooges film in a cameo role for the 1947 short *Hold That Lion!* He also apparently filmed a cameo for *Malice in the Palace* in 1949 that was never actually used. He passed away in 1952 at the age of 49.

After filming wrapped up on *Half-Wits Holiday*, Moe and Larry faced a decision of whether to retire the act or find a replacement for Curly. Moe proposed his older brother Shemp, who had been an original member of Healy's Stooges, for the role. Following his departure from the Stooges in 1933, Shemp had spent the next several years refining his craft as a contract player at Columbia, appearing in many non–Stooges two-reel comedies. He had been awarded a solo series in 1944, making nine films under his own name at the studio.

In spite of Shemp's previous experience as a Stooge, the suggestion was initially met with some resistance by Columbia. Shemp's comedy was much different from that of Curly. While Shemp had many physical talents, they were not nearly equal to those of Curly. Further, he bore a strong physical resemblance to Moe, and some at Columbia felt that this might create confusion among moviegoers. At Moe's insistence, however, the studio agreed to install Shemp as the new third Stooge, a role he held for 77 films made from 1947 to 1956.

To this day, controversy still surrounds the films Shemp made with the Stooges. A sizable number of Stooges fans and critics alike feel that the team should have disbanded following Curly's retirement. Others feel that Shemp's brand of humor infused new life and energy into a comedy team that had struggled over the final four years or so of Curly's career. And unlike the early years with Curly, the Stooges' first Columbia film with Shemp, the 1947 short *Fright Night*, showed the Stooges carrying on without missing a beat. Shemp fit in immediately, and long-time professionals Moe and Larry had an instant rapport with the "other" Howard brother.

Shemp's humor was quite unlike that of Curly. He was less overtly childlike than Curly, and he had a more assertive personality. While he did not possess the acrobatic grace of his younger brother, he nonetheless was a gifted slapstick comedian. Whereas Curly had an almost cherubic face, Shemp was quite homely by comparison (his agent once launched a campaign to have him named "the homeliest man alive"). Shemp was also a more adept ad libber than Curly, a skill that was to serve him well in later years, as tight budgets required more on-the-spot comedy. In spite of his physical resemblance to Moe, Shemp was clearly the "third Stooge," the one most likely to be on the receiving end of Moe's physical abuse, and like Curly he become the focal point of most of the Stooges' humor. The films made with Shemp also displayed a sharp upturn in the amount and degree of violence.

Coinciding with Shemp's Columbia years with the Stooges was an increasing level of austerity at the studio. Jules White, head of the Short Subjects Department and producer or director of most of the Stooges' later films, made an art form out of working with limited resources. While production costs during the Shemp years soared, the budgets for the Stooges films remained constant. Sets, scripts, and even footage were heavily recycled, climaxing with the last four Shemp films actually being made after the actor's death.

After the filming of *For Crimin' Out Loud* in 1956, Shemp suffered a heart attack and died instantly. The final four "Shemp" films were remakes of earlier films, while new footage was shot with Moe, Larry, and Joe Palma, who played the part of Shemp while his face was obscured.

Once again Moe and Larry faced the difficult decision of whether to retire the Stooges' act. Had Shemp been unavailable in 1947, the decision might well have been made to disband. But by 1956, television had replaced film as the primary visual medium, and the Stooges' old films were being newly revived for the cathode ray tube. This gave Moe and Larry an incentive to keep the act alive. They settled on Columbia contract player Joe Besser to succeed Shemp, and the trio made their final 16 two-reel comedies, released from 1957 to 1959.

While the Stooges films made with Shemp are not held in the same esteem as those of Curly by some Stooges' fans, others feel that much of Shemp's work equaled or even eclipsed that of Curly. But there is little disagreement from both camps that the Besser films represent the low point of the series. Like Curly, Besser was fat and childlike, but the resemblance ended there. Besser possessed neither the physical dexterity nor the comic timing of either Curly or Shemp. But the fault was not entirely Besser's. Moe and Larry had grown older; their skills had diminished somewhat by this time. Further, the scripts, while eschewing the extreme violence that characterized the Shemp years, now consisted of rehashing of old Curly or Shemp films or of highly implausible escapades involving reincarnation, space travel, and other unlikely scenarios. The end of the Stooges' two-reel career coincided with the closing of the Short Subjects Department at Columbia in 1958.

When the Stooges' shorts career ended, Joe Besser, who did not wish to travel, retired from the Stooges. A large portion of the Stooges' income came from nationwide public appearances, so another third Stooge was hired to replace Besser: Joe DeRita, dubbed "Curly Joe." Like Besser, DeRita had been a contract player at Columbia. He bore a strong resemblance to Curly Howard, which proved both a blessing and a curse, as the unfavorable comparisons were raised once again. While DeRita's shorts with Columbia showed him to be a capable and talented comedian, these skills were not very evident during his Stooges career. Ironically, it was while DeRita was a member of the group that the Stooges achieved newfound popularity, largely due to their increasing exposure on television. The boys finally had a chance to do feature films, making seven features from 1959 to 1970 and making appearances in three others. They also filmed brief appearances in a series of animated features beginning in 1965. When Larry Fine suffered a debilitating stroke in 1970, the Three Stooges act was retired for good.

The Stooges in Perspective

It is not difficult to understand why the Stooges became popular and have remained so, but the explanation is not nearly as simple as some might believe. Their lasting appeal to children is most readily apparent: the Stooges' bizarre appearance, the physical mayhem they created, and the nonsensical dialogues and situations made them the perfect living, breathing cartoon characters. However, one rarely hears of fans "outgrowing" the Stooges; they merely come to appreciate the many other layers they may have missed in the first 50 or so viewings.

What also emerges immediately when viewing the films of the Three Stooges and what endures and captivates upon repeated viewings are the many uses of clever dialogue and malapropisms. Curly's "I'm a victim of *soicumstances*" or his venerable and affirmative "*soiteny*" (not the commonly mistaken "soitenly") is still uttered by Stooges fanatics and dilettantes alike. If one uses an insult such as *nitwit, numbskull, lamebrain*, or *ignoramus*, the reference is immediately clear. There are in fact myriad examples of how the Stooges have wormed their way into American vernacular (or as Curly would respond, "Vernacular? That's a *doiby!*"). Even their verbal nonsense sounds have become legendary. Curly's "*Woo Woo Woo*" and Shemp's "*Bee-Bee-Bee-Bee*," even when used out of context, convey their intended meanings. Curly's "Nyuk Nyuk Nyuk" is still used as a rejoinder to a bad joke, much like the modern-day "rim shot."

Almost as identifiable as the Stooges themselves are the many noises and sound effects that are peppered throughout the Stooges films, each perfectly capturing the viewers' visceral reaction to the slapstick they are witnessing: the eye gouge (a high-pitched violin string pluck), a sock in the stomach (done with a kettle drum), and the various sound effects to accompany face slaps, punches, chugging of water and the aftereffects of rotgut alcohol that were regular parts of the Stooges' landscape, as well as that of most comedy two-reelers made at Columbia.

And there were other notable aspects of that Columbia style. While the

Stooges were very funny fellows in their own right, they would not have endured without the tight production, directing, and wonderful writing provided by the stable of creative regulars who worked on their films. One needs only to watch a live performance of the boys to see how much the sound effects contributed. Compare the average Stooges short with one of the non–Columbia features they worked on in the forties, and it becomes abundantly clear that the long-term success of the Stooges was a larger team effort.

Finally, one explanation for the endurance of these 190 films has to be with the Stooges and the situations in which they found themselves. A key element in comedy is to create a situation where the viewers feel superior to the characters they are watching. Viewers can't help but feel superior when witnessing the stupidity, unattractiveness, and naiveté of the boys. Even today, incompetent trios of politicians or businessmen are as likely as not to be referred to as "the Three Stooges." Perhaps this is why, unlike so many other slapstick comedians, the Stooges can be *placed* anywhere — because they didn't really *fit* anywhere.

This last point perhaps best explains the timelessness of the Three Stooges. If we were to bring Moe, Larry, Curly, and Shemp into the twenty-first century, they could still perform incompetently as plumbers, carpenters, doctors, dentists, dictators, or restaurateurs. But as a colleague of mine recently pointed out, the Stooges would also fit comfortably into new millennium humor. Imagine the Stooges as computer repairmen, getting into dot com businesses, or acting as CIA operatives. They could easily be dropped into the present day, which is probably why filmmakers such as the Farrelly brothers have sought for years to create a new Three Stooges.

Other comic contemporaries of the Stooges, such as W. C. Fields, the Marx Brothers, Laurel and Hardy, and Buster Keaton are generally thought to have been superior talents to the Three Stooges. So why is it that the Stooges have remained vital and contemporary while other comics are relegated to the occasional film festival or documentary? It is for all the reasons stated above, and more, as you will discover in this book.

You might say that Moe, Larry, Curly, Shemp, Joe, and Curly Joe were just "victims of *soicumstances*."

I. THE AESTHESTICS OF STOOGE FILMMAKING

As we begin our study of the short films of the Three Stooges, we consider two overarching themes. The first is how the Stooges used verbal and situational comedy in new and creative ways. (Their physical comedy is discussed elsewhere in this book.) The Stooges' verbal humor was unique, creating a whole lexicon of new words, expressions, and pronunciations that still echo in conversation in the twenty-first century. Chapter 1 gives a thorough accounting of the Stooges' use of puns, plays on words, and malapropisms.

Situationally, the Stooges traveled facilely through time, space, and reality. Indeed, as a result, the Stooges often created their own reality, where the past became the future, where violence became commonplace, and the supernatural was the norm. These phenomena are the subject of Chapter 2.

The second theme focuses on austerity in the Columbia Pictures Short Subjects Department. Unlike some other studios, such as MGM or RKO, Columbia gave its shorts fairly small budgets, as the studio felt justified in putting most of their resources into feature films. One apparent result of Columbia's austerity was that several of the scripts for the Stooges films had large sections that were never shot. Whether it was strictly for reasons of economy or whether there were other reasons why portions of scripts remained unfilmed is not clear. Chapter 3 provides the reader with a treasure trove of scenes and dialogue that never reached the screen and presumably were never filmed. The serious student of the Stooges films will discover new products from the boys' creative team.

The austerity with which the short subjects department was run had several consequences for the films of the Three Stooges. For one, it meant that the films were made relatively quickly, with little time for reshooting or pickups. Also, the remaking of several Stooges shorts and the extensive use of stock footage meant that continuity errors and problems with dialogue replacement abounded throughout the years of their films. Chapter 4 discusses this phenomenon in a study of the role of the mistake in the Stooges films.

This section establishes beyond a doubt that there was much more to the films of the Three Stooges than just face slaps, eye gouges, and pie fights.

Ironically, all these years later, it is the shorts of the Stooges and not the feature films that distinguish Columbia during the first three decades of talking pictures. The bevy of talented actors, directors, writers, producers, sound engineers, and special effects creators that were at Columbia ensured a recognizable identity for virtually all of the shorts produced during this period. Chapter 5 provides an analysis of this identity and challenges several commonly accepted assumptions that much of the dialogue, sound effects, and sight gags, as well as the use of certain scripts and character actors, were unique to the Stooges.

1

Casting Asparagus, Tunis Sandwiches, and *Moidering* the King's English: Puns, Wordplay, and Malapropisms in the Three Stooges Films

Peter Seely

While the Three Stooges are much better known for their particularly violent brand of slapstick humor, their films also left a lasting legacy of humor achieved through puns, plays on words, and malapropisms. This humor was often derived from a combination of wordplay and incongruity, as the Stooges mostly found themselves in the company of superiors. What better way to showcase their ignorance, their incompetence, and their status as social misfits than through their use of language?

A pun is defined as a humorous use of a word involving two interpretations of the meaning. Sometimes, different senses of the same word are involved, or sometimes it is similarity to different words. A malapropism is defined as a humorous misuse of a word. While there appears to be some overlap of these terms, in this chapter the pun will mostly refer to how it is used with homonyms, double entendres, and intentional interchanges of sounds. Malapropisms occur in Stooges films mostly by accident, resulting more from the Stooges' ignorance in their characters rather than cleverly and intentionally making humor out of word mistakes.

In contrast to the more accepted definitions of a malapropism, Helitzer

(1987, p. 55) uncharitably refers to the malapropism as "twisted language innocently spoken by a dolt." The malapropism has been used for centuries as a comic device to reflect negatively on a character, dating back at least to the writings of William Shakespeare. According to the *Oxford English Dictionary* ("malapropism" 1971, p. 1704), the derivation of the term originated in Richard Sheridan's 1775 novel *The Rivals*, in which he portrays the character Mrs. Malaprop always mangling the English language by using expressions such as "Make no delusions to the past." Her name is believed to have come from the French expression *mal à propos*, meaning "inappropriate."

Wordplay is a technique in which the nature of the words used becomes part of the subject of the work. Puns are one example of wordplay, as are "obscure words and meanings, clever rhetorical excursions, oddly formed sentences, and telling character names" ("Word play" 2005).

Curly Howard used many malapropisms that have become memorable parts of the Stooges films, such as "Are you casting asparagus on my cookin'?" (from *In the Sweet Pie and Pie*), "a chimineypanzee" (from *Dizzy Detectives*), and "It's a geezer ... an oil geezer" (from *Oily to Bed, Oily to Rise*).

Plays on words in general have been used as comic devices within several comedy forms. Comedian Steve Allen quotes David Freedman, who wrote most of Eddie Cantor's book materials, magazine articles, and radio scripts, as identifying puns as number one on a list of seven elements forming the basic pattern of humor (Allen and Wollman 1987, p. 27). Jane Snyder (1980) contends that while wordplay in general attempts to play with language, it also seeks to mirror reality.

The use of the pun can be traced back many centuries. The Roman philosopher Cicero was a noted punster of his day, using it effectively, for example, to attack the notorious Verres.[1] The Latin writer Lucretius also used this particular form of humor in his works (Snyder 1980). According to Skeat (2005), the best guess as to the etymology of "pun" is the English verb *pun*: "to pound words, beat them into new senses."

Walter Redfern maintains that the pun exists for two reasons: playfulness and dissatisfaction. He argues that all manner of wordplay have been preserved in cultures throughout history. He also maintains there is an inherent urge on the part of humans "to overlay, to add to, the given; to rewrite the script of linguistic existence" (Redfern 1984, p. 13).

Puns have traditionally been considered one of the lowest forms of humor. Paulhan argues that puns are "inferior, accidental, and need to be apologized for" (qtd. in Redfern 1984, p. 12). Perret (1982, p. 65) echoes these sentiments, adding that this is especially true when puns don't utilize visual imagery.

Puns do have their defenders, however. Perret (1982, p. 65) himself argues that when a pun does use visual imagery, it can be inspired. Shakespeare made liberal use of the pun (though not necessarily in a humorous context), well before his prose became the basis for dramatic structure and standards adopted by writers of visual comedy and drama. Edgar Allan Poe defended the pun when he exclaimed, "Of puns it has been said that those who most dislike them are those least able to utter them." Oscar Levant (1968, p. 100) updated Poe's assessment of the pun when he wrote, "A pun is the lowest form of wit — if you didn't happen to think of them first."

The pun in talking pictures began almost at the outset of this twentieth-century art form. Perhaps the earliest and most enthusiastic users of the pun were Groucho and Chico Marx. In tandem the two Marx Brothers weaved a tapestry of wordplay throughout their first feature films: *Animal Crackers* (1930), *Monkey Business* (1931), *Horse Feathers* (1932), and *Duck Soup* (1933). Other Hollywood comics of the thirties regularly practiced comic wordplay, including Eddie Cantor, Bert Wheeler, Robert Woolsey, and Andy Clyde. Clyde, who filmed at Columbia from 1934 to 1956, also worked with such Three Stooges standbys as director Jules White and writers Clyde Bruckman, Jack White, and Felix Adler. This association accounts for the parallel use of the pun in both Stooges and Clyde films.[2]

The Three Stooges' use of the pun and other wordplay can be traced back to two features they made with Ted Healy, before signing with Columbia Studios: *Soup to Nuts* (1930) and *Meet the Baron* (1933). Wordplays were not nearly as numerous or pronounced in the films the Stooges made with Healy at MGM as they were once the Stooges began their run at Columbia. Whereas Healy used wordplay as an occasional comic device, the Stooges were to make it one of their stocks-in-trade. In the Columbia films, wordplay was as commonplace as the face slap — and much more so than the infrequent but memorable pie fights. While the Stooges are not as notorious for their wordplay as they are for these physical sight gags, it was their use of language that was the thread holding their comedies together.

Although many of the Stooges' critics have decried the violent nature of the Stooges films directed by Jules White (see, for example, Maltin 1972, p. 130), this point of view rarely seems to translate to an appreciation for the dialogue of the less violent Curly films, many of which featured a large dosage of puns, malapropisms, and other wordplay. In both the violent and less violent films made by the Stooges, fans and critics alike prefer to concentrate on the physical nature of the Stooges' comedy over any other considerations. The clever wordplay and comic punning tend to get buried under the sight gags so important to slapstick comedy.

The use of puns, malapropisms, and other wordplay in the Three Stooges films at Columbia even extended to the titles of the films, nearly every one of which was a pun or other use of wordplay. For the viewer of these films in the theater or on television, these titles would foretell the excessive punning that awaited. This practice continued even in the feature films the Stooges made after leaving Columbia, with titles such as *Snow White and the Three Stooges, The Three Stooges Go around the World in a Daze,* and *Have Rocket—Will Travel.*

This chapter explores the incidences of puns, malapropisms, and plays on words in the Stooges' Columbia films. Humorous wordplay was as omnipresent in Stooges films as the physical sight gags for which they are better known. Indeed, these uses of language were not simply commonplace; they took place in every single Columbia film made by the Three Stooges.

Forms

Wordplay in the Stooges films is evident in dialogue, recitations, and signs. Dialogue was the most common form. Predictably, it was the third Stooge — Curly, Shemp, or Joe — who was most likely to bungle language and deliver the comic line, as he was always the simplest of the simpletons in any plot. Often, Moe or Larry also used wordplay; in rare cases, a supporting actor would deliver the line.

Recitation occurred infrequently in Stooges comedies, but it was used occasionally and proved a worthy device for wordplay. Moe Howard as Moe Hailstone in *You Nazty Spy!* and *I'll Never Heil Again* made speeches that allowed punning. In *I'll Never Heil Again,* for instance, the dictator says that he wants to "knock the stuffing out of Turkey." Both of these World War II parodies of the Axis powers feature fast-paced dialogue and a steady stream of puns aimed at mocking the enemy.

More common was the well-placed sign or graphic in the Stooges films. These took the form of opening titles and graphics, signs on buildings, desk nameplates, newspaper headlines, and just about anywhere else the written word could be displayed. These were convenient devices for wordplay, and it was rare indeed when the visually written word in Stooges comedies did not feature wordplay.

Again, even the titles of the films themselves were frequently written as puns or other wordplay. Some referenced current popular culture works, such as song, movie, or book titles, including *Men in Black; Pop Goes the Easel; Whoops, I'm an Indian; Termites of 1938; Tassels in the Air; Flat Foot Stooges; Violent is the Word for Curly; Yes, We Have No Bonanza; So Long, Mr. Chumps; I'll Never Heil Again; Some More of Samoa; Sock-a-Bye Baby; Beer Barrel Polecats; Sing a Song of Six Pants; Hold That Lion!; Crime on Their Hands;* and *Quiz Whizz.* Other times these titles made puns or parodied popular sayings or bromides, while reflecting some element of the story, including *Mutts to You; Saved by the Belle; Calling All Curs; Oily to Bed, Oily to Rise; No Census, No Feeling; All the World's a Stooge; In the Sweet Pie and Pie; Loco Boy Makes Good; Cactus Makes Perfect; They Stooge to Conga; The Yoke's on Me; A Bird in the Head; Love at First Bite; Three Hams on Rye; For Crimin' Out Loud;* and *Oil's Well That*

Ends Well. And some of the titles played on simple words or phrases, including *Restless Knights, Ants in the Pantry, Disorder in the Court, Goofs and Saddles, We Want Our Mummy, A Plumbing We Will Go, Matri-Phony, Micro-Phonies, Fright Night,* and *Fuelin' Around*.[3]

What follows is a synopsis of wordplay in each Stooges era (i.e., Curly, Shemp, and Joe), with an example from each film of its use.

The Curly Years (1934 to 1947)

The very first Stooges film for Columbia was *Woman Haters* in 1934, and the dialogue was entirely in recitative (Bruskin 1984, p. 256). While not abundant with puns, *Woman Haters* foreshadowed the wordplay that was to prevail in Stooges films for the next 25 years. Contrasted with the Shemp comedies, the Curly shorts tended to place more emphasis on storylines and, in the earlier films, greater contributions from the supporting actors. As a result, wordplay was not as prevalent in the earlier comedies as it became later. As the Stooges gained confidence and popularity, they began dominating their films to a greater extent. As their dialogue increased, so did the wordplay.

1934

Woman Haters—"Three gentlemen wait without" ( ). "Without what?" (BJ).[4]
Punch Drunks—I'm in a dilemma" (DG). "Yeah, I don't care much for these foreign cars, either" (M). "You don't understand. I'm stuck [in the mud]" (DG). "On me?" (M).
Men in Black—"What's your name?" (M). "Anna Conda" (PC). "On a counta what?" (M).
Three Little Pigskins—"What are you taking up at college?" (PC). "Oh, a dime here, a dime there" (M).

1935

Horses' Collars—"Anytime he sees a mouse he goes crazy" (L). "Why?" (DK). "Because his father was a rat" (M).
Restless Knights—"Rightfully, you are the Duke of Durham. You are the Count of Fife" (WB). "And I the Count of Ten?" (C). "No, you are Baron of Grey Matter" (WB).
Pop Goes the Easel—"I am an artist" (LW). "I am an artist, too!" (L). "Oh a pair of drawers" (C).
Uncivil Warriors—"You know, I quit my job at the bakery" (C). "Why?" (PC). "Oh, I got sick of the dough and thought I'd go on the loaf" (C).
Pardon My Scotch—"Are you laddies by any chance from Loch Lomond?" ( ). "No, we're from Loch Jaw" (C).

Hoi Polloi—"Professor Nichols" (RG). "Brother, can you spare a nickel?" (L).
Three Little Beers—"Are you gentlemen with the press?" (LB). "I used to be. But I didn't do any pressing. I went through the pockets, a sort of a dry cleaning" (C).

1936

Ants in the Pantry—"Where did you go to school?" (M). "Oxford" (C). "You better go back to high shoes" (M).
Movie Maniacs—"Hey fellas. Ain't I getting to look more and more like Barrymore?" (C).
Half-Shot Shooters—"Will you fight for this great republic and..." (EL). "Republican? Nah, I'm a Democrat" (M). "Not me. I'm a pedestrian" (C).
Disorder in the Court—"He's asking if you swear..." (EL). (Interrupts) "No, but I know all the words" (C).
A Pain in the Pullman—"What's that?" (M). "Fillet of sole and heel" (C).
False Alarms—"I grow on people" (JG). "So do warts" (C).
Whoops, I'm an Indian!—"You keep my wigwam?" (BJ). "You keep your own wig warm" (C).
Slippery Silks—"The idea's been in my head since I was ten years old" (M). "Oh, sort of aged in the wood" (C).

1937

Grips, Grunts and Groans—"Pin him down" (M). "But I ain't got no pins" (C).
Dizzy Doctors—"A man wants to know what to do about inflammation" (C). "Why call us, tell him to dial inflammation" (M).
Three Dumb Clucks—"Hey warden, can you plug my razor in, I wanna take a shave" (M). "I guess it's all right" (FA). "Sure, best razor I ever had" (M).
Back to the Woods—"I just love corned beef and savage" (C).
Goofs and Saddles—(Trying to tip off each other during a card game) "I just got four kinks in my back" (L). "You know, when I get kinks in the back, I generally go to the oasis. O-aces... O-aces..." (M). "That's nothin.' I been to the oasis twice" (C).
Cash and Carry—"Have you got any visible means of support?" (VD). "Sure, I got suspenders" (L).
Playing the Ponies—(as an alarm clock flies out of a suitcase) "How time flies" (L).
The Sitter Downers—"But I got two strikes" (bowling) (C). "Well, here's the third one" (slap) (M).

1938

Termites of 1938—"If a pie-eyed piper can call 'em out, I guess I can sober" (C).

Wee Wee Monsieur—"You, Foreign Legion, we, American Legion. Brother Legionnaires" (M).
Tassels in the Air—"It's a rare antique" (JM). "What, that old thing?" (M).
Flat Foot Stooges—"This is my brainchild" (M). "You're not even married" (C).
Healthy, Wealthy and Dumb—"This bed goes back to Henry the Eighth" (JM). "That's nothin', we had a bed that goes back to Sears Roebuck the Third" (C).
Violent is the Word for Curly—"Tonight we return to Hamburg and the Clipper ( ). "I never heard of such a thing. He's gonna get a hamburger with a zipper" (C).
Three Missing Links—"I wonder where that safari is" (MC). "Maybe they're safari away we'll never catch 'em" (C).
Mutts to You—"You remind me of a Colleen I once knew in the County Cary" (BJ). "And you remind me of a cop I once knew in the county jail" (C).

1939

Three Little Sew and Sews—"The admiral spins a fast needle" (M). "He's an old sew-and-sew" (L).
We Want Our Mummy—"I'd rather go to Tunis, then we could have tunis sandwiches for lunch" (C).
A-Ducking They Did Go—"Canvasback? That's what they used to call me when I was a boxer" (C).
Yes, We Have No Bonanza—"I whistle for the dog, and my wife comes out" (C).
Saved by the Belle—"Don't you hurt a feather on his bed... I mean, head" (C).
Calling All Curs—"He's suffering from acute alcoholism" (L). "Ain't he a cutie? He's a lap dog. He lapped up two cases of beer" (C).
Oily to Bed, Oily to Rise—"How can there be a bear down there?" (M). "It's barely possible" (C).
Three Sappy People—"Two two two? Whadda ya think you're doin', playin' trains?" (M).

1940

You Nazty Spy!—"A vicious cycle. We must kill it. Remind me to kill a cycle" (C).
Rockin' Through the Rockies—(Sign) NELL'S BELLES.
A Plumbing We Will Go—"Barrie-cuddie, and what a cutie" (C).
Nutty But Nice—"The dumbwaiter" (NG). "Hey, I resent that" (C).
How High Is Up?—"Looks like a V-8" (L). "Did you ever hear of a V-5?" (M). "What's that, a new car?" (L). "No, it's an old sock" (M).
From Nurse to Worse—"It's my favorite dollar... I raised it from a cent" (C).

No Census, No Feeling—"A three-litter man, eh?" (M).
Cuckoo Cavaliers—"Do you have a haddock?" (BP). "No, but I get a little attack down there every time I eat too much" (C).
Boobs in Arms—"Greetings little shut-in, do not weep or sigh, if you're not out by Christmas, you'll be out by Fourth of July" (C).

The use of puns was prevalent in the Stooges films, including the famous "Tunis sandwiches" remark by Curly in *We Want Our Mummy* (1939).

1941

So Long, Mr. Chumps—"Can we have some money on account?" (M). "Yeah, on account of we're broke" (C).
Dutiful but Dumb—(magazine cover) WHACK MAGAZINE. IF IT'S A GOOD PICTURE, IT'S OUT OF WHACK.
All the World's a Stooge—"Oh, pretty good, but I still don't smell so good" (C). "I'll say you don't" ( ).
I'll Never Heil Again—"Our first move is to knock the stuffing out of Turkey" (M). "I want a piece of Turkey" (C).
An Ache in Every Stake—"My father died dancing ... at the end of a rope" (C).
In the Sweet Pie and Pie—"Is this a musical saw?" (M). "Soiteny! It plays "I Hear a *Ripsody*" (C).
Some More of Samoa—"What's that?" (M). "Just a little thing to make big trees out of little saps" (C).

1942

Loco Boy Makes Good—"She was bred in old Kentucky, but she's just a crumb up here" (M).
Cactus Makes Perfect—"It's in his left pocket" (M). "Right" (C).
What's the Matador?—"Ah, Mexico. The warmth of your chili brings zest to my breast" (C).
Matri-Phony—(sign) MOHICUS, LARRYCUS, AND CURLYCUE ... THE BIGGEST CHISELERS IN TOWN.
Three Smart Saps—"Do you rhumba?" (BS). "Only when I take bicarbonate" (C).
Even as IOU—"Gimme Ripley. Yeah, believe it or not" (M).
Sock-a-Bye Baby—"Now you're getting your vitamins. Starches, vegetables, hypochondriacs" (M).

1943

They Stooge to Conga—"Why can't a chicken lay a loaf of bread?" (M). "She ain't got the crust" (C).
Dizzy Detectives—"That Dill sure has the chief in a pickle" (L).
Spook Louder—(in reference to a cat on a piano) "Kitten on the keys" (C).
Back from the Front—"We forgot our duffels ... bags" (bag is slang for woman) (C).
Three Little Twirps—"I get a bang out of a circus." (C) "Well, have your bang now" (M).
Higher Than a Kite—"I told them a navigator crawls in a swamp until it becomes a suitcase" (C).
"I Can Hardly Wait"—"A bonanza!" (M). "Oh boy, I just love bonanzas and cream" (C).

Dizzy Pilots—"You saw the garage" (M). "I see the garage, but I don't saw the garage. You are speaking incorrectly. You are *moidering* the King's English. Etcetera" (C).
Phony Express—"Get back there and mix some up while I do some spieling" (M). "I think you spieled enough already" (C).
A Gem of a Jam—(sign) DRS. HART, BURNS, AND BELCHER.

1944

Crash Goes the Hash—"I want to see if he intends to press his suit" (VD). "He should. A man can't get married in baggy pants" (C).
Busy Buddies—"Are you casting asparagus on my cookin'?" (C).
The Yoke's on Me—"That's no pelican, that's a gander" (M). "Mahatma Gander?" (C).
Idle Roomers—"I want my tip" (C). "I'll give you one, get out of here" (M).
Gents Without Cents—(sign) NOAZARK SHIPBUILDING COMPANY.
No Dough Boys—"You must be Wacki" (VD). "Ah, yes, very, very wacky" (C).

1945

Three Pests in a Mess—(sign) I. CHEATHAM, PRES.
Booby Dupes—(reading a song title) "Don't Chop the Wood, Ma, Pa's Coming Home With a Load" (C).
Idiots Deluxe—"Were you ever indicted?" (VD). "Not since I was a baby, your honor" (M).
If a Body Meets a Body—"You must be the Missing Link" (FK). "No, I'm the found Link" (C).
Micro-Phonies "A microphony" (M). "And a phony at the mic" (C).

1946

Beer Barrel Polecats—"Is this a musical saw?" (M). "Soiteny. It plays "I Hear a Ripsody" (C).
A Bird in the Head—"Well, gentlemen, here are your quarters" (VD). "Oh boy, two bits apiece" (C).
Uncivil War Birds—"As a matter of fact, General, we're caught with our tents down" (JT).
Three Troubledoers—"Who told you you need glasses?" (M). "An obstetrician" (C).
Monkey Businessmen—"That Mallard's nothing but a quack" (L). "That means duck" (M).
Three Loan Wolves—(sign) HERE TODAY, PAWN TOMORROW.
G.I. Wanna Go Home—"C'mon, give me a gander at that goose" (M).

Rhythm and Weep—"If you're gonna bump yourself off, what's the idea of the pie?" (M). "So I can digest right" (C).
Three Little Pirates—"I have many pigeon-blood rubies, but never have I been given the raspberry" (VD).

1947

Half-Wits Holiday—"That's neither hair nor there" (M).

The Shemp Years (1947 to 1956)

Shemp Howard became the third Stooge following Curly's retirement. Also, Jules White took over most of the directing chores during these years. The films with Shemp not only featured an increase in the levels of violence but also had faster-paced dialogue and more puns. These films placed less emphasis on storyline but a greater emphasis on dialogue than did the films with Curly.

1947

Fright Night—"Taps?" (M). "Yeah, taps (dancing)" (L).
Out West—How long do you wear a shirt like that?" (M). "Oh, about down to here" (S).
Hold That Lion!—"I smell something awful" (L). "You're telling me. Why don't you use cologne?" (M).
Brideless Groom—"Your little dreamboat is sailing" (S).
Sing a Song of Six Pants—"Where did you get this mess?" (S). "I bought it here" (VD). "Oh, what a beautiful *messterpiece*" (S).
All Gummed Up—"The mortar the merrier" (L).

1948

Shivering Sherlocks—"This joint gives me the creeps" (S). "Well, start creeping" (M).
Pardon My Clutch—"C'mon, let's get loaded" (M). "Wait a minute, you know I don't drink" (L).
Squareheads of the Roundtable—"The King demands your presence" (JP). "We ain't got any presents, the stores were all closed" (S).
Fiddlers Three—"Notify the FBI" (VD). "FBI?" (JP). "Yes, Flannagan, Brannigan, and Iskowicz, Detectives" (VD).
The Hot Scots—"Clean as a whistle. Let's blow" (M).
Heavenly Daze—Lawyer Vernon Dent is named I. Fleecam.

I'm a Monkey's Uncle—(opening title) MONKEYS HANG FROM THEIR TREES BY THEIR TAILS ... AND THEREBY HANGS OUR TALE.

Mummy's Dummies—"Suppose he has another toothache?" (L). "We'll cross that bridge when we come to it" (S).

Crime on Their Hands—(referring to getting head smashed with bookends) "Stop the presses" (S).

1949

The Ghost Talks—"That shutter. That confounded shutter" (PA). "I shudder to think of it" (S).

Who Done It?—"Oh, yes, Mr. Goodrich, I'm sorry, we were tied up" (L).

Hokus Pokus—"Listen, halibut, I'll filet you" (M).

Fuelin' Around—"It's our duty to posterior" (L).

Malice in the Palace—"A hundred karats? He sure knew his onions" (S).

Vagabond Loafers—"He only died in poverty, now I'll have to live in it" (ES).

Dunked in the Deep—"We're known as the Fish Market Duet" (L). "The Fish Market Duet?" (M). "Yeah, we sing for the halibut" (S).

1950

Punchy Cowpunchers—"I'm hittin' the trail" (JO). "Sounds like the trail hit him" (M).

Hugs and Mugs—"I'll bet you're a real lady killer" (NB). "Oh sure, the ladies take one look at him and drop dead" (M).

Dopey Dicks—(sign) SAM SHOVEL DETECTIVE.

Love at First Bite—"It was love at first bite. I was sittin' in a little restaurant eating bread and hot dogs, and waiting to be mustered out" (L).

Self-Made Maids—"What are those things?" (M). "Eyes, boat of 'em" (S).

Three Hams on Rye—"A rose by any other name would smell..." (M). "...And so do you" (L).

Studio Stoops—"I'm Brown from *The Sun*" (SP). "Aw, that's too bad, are you peelin'?" (S).

Slaphappy Sleuths—(sign) FULLER GRIME.

A Snitch in Time—(sign) ANTIQUES MADE WHILE-U-WAIT.

1951

Three Arabian Nuts—"The genius of the lamp?" (S).

Baby Sitters Jitters—"We work as a unit" (L). "Yeah, we're Unitarians" (S).

Don't Throw That Knife—"Wyckoff" (JW). "Because he don't brush his teeth, lady" (L).

Scrambled Brains—(sign) DOCTORS HART, BURNS, AND BELCHER.

Merry Mavericks—"What's vagrancy?" (S). "Boy, are you stupid. You take a flower, and it smells nice, that's vagrancy" (L).
The Tooth Will Out—"See that tooth? That's funny, I can't" (L).
Hula-La-La—"You see the point?" (M). "No, but I feel it" (L).
Pest Man Wins—"Don't let the guests know what you're doing" (ML). "You're a cinch, lady, we don't know what we're doing ourselves" (L).

1952

A Missed Fortune—(sign) HOTEL COSTA PLENTE.
Listen, Judge—"They have visible means of support" (VD). "Does he mean our suspenders?" (L).
Corny Casanovas—"They went in, maybe they're income tacks" (S).
He Cooked His Goose—"Belle? How did you know her name was Belle?" (M). "Wait a minute, all women are belles, like belle of the ball?" (L).
Gents in a Jam—"Meet chrome dome" (M). How do you do, Mr. Chromedome?" (ES).
Three Dark Horses—"You will be Secretary of the Fence, you, Secretary of the Inferior, and I'll be Toastmaster General" (M).
Cuckoo on a Choo Choo—"He's filthy with money" (PW). "Ah, he's filthy without it" (L).

1953

Up in Daisy's Penthouse—"I'm his best man, this is his worst" (M).
Booty and the Beast—"Why don't you try the choke?" (L). "Thanks, I will" (choking Larry) (M).
Loose Loot—"Rome wasn't built in a day, neither was Syracuse" (S).
Tricky Dicks—"You know, my sister was engaged to a guy with a wooden leg" (L). "Yeah, what happened?" (M). "She broke it off" (L).
Spooks!—"Dr. Jeckyl? We must hide" (S).
Pardon My Backfire—"How do you feel?" (S). "Like a baked potato" (M). "That's a hot one" (S).
Rip, Sew and Stitch—"I once had a granny who searched every nook and cranny" (S). "I did too, you know what she found? This" (slaps Shemp) (M).
Bubble Trouble—"What do you call this cake?" (L). "Marshmallow Jumbo" (CM). "Tastes more like marshmallow gumbo" (L).
Goof on the Roof—"I smell smoke; are you chewin' tobacco?" (L).

1954

Income Tax Sappy—"Makin' out the income tax is nothin'" (L). "Whatta you mean, nothin'?" (M). "When I get done, the income tax collector gets nothin'" (L).

Musty Musketeers—"We pray permission to wed our brides forthwith" (M). "If not forthwither" (S).
Pals and Gals—"You know, I could do things with a vein like that" (NW). "You mean operate?" (S). "That's right, and no small time stuff, either.... We'll use 20 men with pick and shovel" (NW).
Knutzy Knights—"We'll have her splitting her sides" (L). "East side, west side, front side" (S).
Shot in the Frontier—(sign) DIGGS, GRAVES, AND BERRY — UNDERTAKERS.
Scotched in Scotland—"'Tis Lorna Doone" (CM). "Hi Lorna, how you doon'?" (S).

1955

Fling in the Ring—"What does your watch say?" (M). "Tick, tick, tick, tick" (S).
Of Cash and Hash—"What's that on the stool?" (M). "Must be a stool pigeon" (S).
Gypped in the Penthouse—(whiskey label) ROTGUT, KY.
Bedlam in Paradise—(desk sign) I. FLEECAM, ATTORNEY.
Stone Age Romeos—(sign) B. BOPPER, CURATOR.
Wham-Bam-Slam!—(doctor's business card) CLAUDE A. QUACKER N.U.T.Z.
Hot Ice—"What does your watch say?" (M). "Tick, tick, tick, tick, tick" (S).
Blunder Boys—"A jerk with a quirk may do the work, or, a turk with a dirk may stick a clerk" (S).

1956

Husbands Beware—"Wait a minute, I'll get a styptic pencil" (L). "Well, watch your Styptic" (M).
Creeps—"It was 50 feet from head to tail, 50 feet from tail to head. It was a dandy lion" (L).
Flagpole Jitters—(poster) SVENGARLIC — HE'LL STEAL YOUR BREATH AWAY.
For Crimin' Out Loud—"What does your watch say?" (M). "It don't say nothin'; you gotta look at it" (S).
Rumpus in the Harem—"I'm Hassan Ben Sober" (VD). "I've had a few too many myself" (S).
Hot Stuff—(sign) DEPARTMENT OF INFERIOR.
Scheming Schemers—"Who do you think I am? Anyhow?" (L). "Oh, Anyhow?" (M).
Commotion on the Ocean—"That's a dish of fish. You can take my word for it, when it comes to fish, I'm a common sewer" (L).

The Joe Besser Years (1957 to 1959)

As most Stooge analysts will agree, the Stooges shorts took a dramatic turn for the worse when the final 16 two-reelers were filmed with Joe Besser replacing Shemp as the third Stooge. The storylines were mostly weak and sometimes used virtually the same script filmed earlier with Curly or Shemp. New scripts usually involved fantastic or impossible plots.

When the script mirrored an earlier short, the Joe Besser versions were similarly replete with puns. The difference, however, was that Besser's delivery was not as believable as Curly's. One example is *Oil's Well That Ends Well*, a remake of the earlier film, *Oily to Bed, Oily to Rise*. Besser repeats Curly's "It's barely possible" pun but grins broadly after he delivers the line, almost as if to say, "I'm not that stupid." Curly's line was delivered as though he really believed it, and it made for a funnier moment.

1957

Hoofs and Goofs—"Horsefeathers" (J).
Muscle Up a Little Closer—"An involved case of musical cardiac, rock and roll type. Lot of fat around the heart and plenty around the brain" (M).
A Merry Mix-Up—"We'll have a shingled roof... It's on the house" (L).
Space Ship Sappy—"We have landed on Sunev" (BR). "And the sunev we leave, the better" (J).
Guns A-Poppin'!—"You mean you have something to say in extenuation?" (VD). "No, no, not that. You see, I had a good reason" (M).
Horsing Around—"We gotta quit out horsin' around" (M).
Rusty Romeos—"These tacks'll never attack you again" (J).
Outer Space Jitters—(opening title) SUNEV.

1958

Quiz Whizz—"Oh boy, we'll be Montgomery's wards" (J).
Fifi Blows Her Top—(sign) HOWARD FINE AND BESSER STARS OF STAGE, SCREEN, AND RADAR.
Pies and Guys—"Oh see the little deer. Has the deer a little doe?" (J). "Yeah, two bucks" (L).
Sweet and Hot—"Giraffe" (M). "Great Neck" (ML). "Nein" (M). "Ten" (ML). "Eleven" (M).
Flying Saucer Daffy—"Give me the facts about that Candid Camera Contest" (M). "Wait'll I look over the figures" (L).
Oil's Well That Ends Well—"Eureka!" (M). "That's no good, we're looking for uranium, not eureka" (L).

1959

Triple Crossed—"Take a letter, to Mr. R. Mi. Dear Mi" (L).
Sappy Bullfighters—"I will kill you to pieces" (GL).

Passing the Muster on Puns, Wordplays, and Malapropisms

The use of puns, wordplays, and malapropisms was quite extensive in the Curly films of the thirties, abated somewhat in the Curly films of the forties, and was revived extensively in the Shemp films. As Jules White took more control over the direction of the Stooges films, the wordplay increased, since White's view of slapstick was to exaggerate—not just in the aspects of violence, but also in the use of language.

While creative use of language was consistent throughout the 190 Stooges films, the writers and producers made much greater use of puns and wordplay in situational films that found the Stooges in bizarre and unusual circumstances that differed from the norm. These "fish-out-of-water" scenarios, taking place in medieval times, colonial America, Nazi Germany, and outer space, apparently offered fresh opportunities for the creators to indulge their fancies and milk these situations for all they were worth.

Clever wordplay was liberally employed in the short films made by the Three Stooges and others at Columbia Pictures. Many of the Stooges films, such as *You Nazty Spy!*, *Some More of Samoa*, and *Fiddlers Three*, feature several examples of wordplay, taking prominence over the physical nature of the comedy. Given the preponderance of such creative use of language throughout their films, one may wonder why so many people know the Stooges only for the eye gouge, the face slap, or the thrown pie. While some of the experts in humor cited in this chapter have pointed to the use of puns, wordplays, and even malapropisms as low humor, such devices span millennia and have been used by some of the great dramatic writers in history. Perhaps it is not surprising, then, that the legion of Stooges critics and detractors would do well to pay attention to this aspect of their work.

Notes

1. Verres is the Roman word for "boar" or "swine." According to Plutarch (p. 230), Cicero was said to have used many "witty sayings" during the trial of Verres.
2. For example, see two of Clyde's films, *Andy Clyde Gets Spring Chicken* (1939) and *A Maid Made Mad* (1943). In the former, in reference to Clyde's trademark bushy moustache, Dorothy Appleby quips, "With all that spinach? I'd have to trim the hedges every time I

wanted to kiss you." In the latter, a store sign reads, "DRESSES HALF OFF ... UNDERWEAR REDUCED." For more similarities between the work of Andy Clyde and the Three Stooges, see Chapter 5.

3. Titles like these were common to films made by all Columbia short subjects artists.

4. Key:

(C) Curly Howard	(EL) Edward LeSaint	(ML) Marge Liszt
(J) Joe Besser	(ES) Emil Sitka	(ML) Muriel Landers
(L) Larry Fine	(FA) Frank Austin	(NB) Nanette Bordeaux
(M) Moe Howard	(FK) Fred Kelsey	(NG) Ned Glass
(S) Shemp Howard	(GL) George Lewis	(NW) Norman Willes
	(JG) Jane Gittelson	(PA) Phil Arnold
(BJ) Bud Jamison	(JM) James Morton	(PC) Phyllis Crane
(BP) Blanche Payson	(JO) Jacques O'Mahoney	(PW) Patricia White
(BR) Benny Rubin	(JP) Joe Palma	(RG) Robert Graves
(BS) Barbara Slater	(JT) John Tyrell	(SP) Stanley Price
(CM) Christine McIntyre	(JW) Jean Willes	(VD) Vernon Dent
(DG) Dorothy Granger	(LB) Lynton Brent	(WB) Walter Brennan
(DK) Dorothy Kent	(LW) Leo White	

Works Cited

Allen, Steve, and Jane Wollman. *How to Be Funny*. New York: McGraw-Hill, 1987.
Bruskin, David N., ed. *The White Brothers: Jack, Jules, and Sam White*. Metuchen, N.J.: Directors Guild of America, 1990.
Helitzer, Melvin. *Comedy Writing Secrets*. Cincinnati: Writer's Digest Books, 1987.
Levant, Oscar. *The Unimportance of Being Oscar*. New York: G. P. Putnam's Sons, 1968.
"Malapropism." *The Compact Edition of the Oxford English Dictionary*. Oxford: Oxford University Press, 1971.
Maltin, Leonard. *The Great Movie Shorts*. New York: Crown, 1972.
Perret, Gene. *How to Write and Sell Your Sense of Humor*. Cincinnati: Writer's Digest Books, 1982.
Plutarch. *Plutarch's Lives: Cicero*. Trans. Dryden; corrected and rev. Arthur Hugh Clough. Harvard Classics, Vol. 12. New York: P. F. Collier & Sons, 1909.
Redfern, Walter. *Puns*. New York: Basil Blackwell, 1984.
Skeat, Walter W. *Concise Etymological Dictionary of the English Language*. New York: Cosimo Classics, 2005.
Snyder, Jane. *Puns and Poetry in Lucretius' De Rerum Natura*. Amsterdam: John Benjamin, 1980.
"Word play." 7 Dec. 2005. <en.wikipedia.org/wiki/Word_play>.

2

Surrealistic Stooges: The Supernatural and the Extraordinary in Slapstick Comedy

Peter Seely

Surrealism, in the arts and literature, has received much examination from scholars and historians. While it has many ties to comedy, particularly in the realm of surrealistic literature, a direct correlation to comedy remains tentative at best. In general, this is unexplored territory.

This chapter examines surrealism and paranormal activity in the 190 Three Stooges short films. One might claim that the entire body of work produced by the Stooges is somewhat surrealistic. Seldom was there any situational continuity between Three Stooges episodes. The Stooges remained the same, but their occupations and environments rarely did. More to the point, the Stooges traveled easily through time and space: in the Stone Age, in ancient Rome, during the Middle Ages, in colonial times and frontier America, during the Civil War, World War I, the Great Depression, World War II, and the 1950s. They fought in Europe; took a taxi to Egypt; lived in the Orient, Scotland, and Mexico; and twice visited the mythical planet of Sunev. Shemp even found himself in heaven and on earth as an angel, perhaps the most surrealistic event of all.

For the most part, though, each Three Stooges episode had its own self-contained reality. Because of this ability to easily slip in and out of reality, our focus here is primarily on surrealistic events and imagery as they relate to the episode, not to the larger body of work.

A Study in Surrealism

The term "surrealism" was coined by the French poet Guillaume Apollinaire, in reference to his play *Les Mamelles de Tiresias*. But the individual largely credited with starting the surrealist movement was the French poet Andre Breton. In his *First Manifesto of Surrealism* (1924), Breton defined surrealism as "pure psychic automatism by which it is intended to express either verbally or in writing the true function of thought. Thought dictated in the absence of all control exerted by reason, and outside all aesthetic or moral preoccupations." In painting, the concept of surrealism is associated with the French Dadaists, with Pablo Picasso, and especially with Salvador Dali (Phaidon Dictionary 1973, p. 373). Surrealism has survived in American consciousness due largely to the enduring popularity not of the French Dadaists but of Spanish painters Pablo Picasso, who dabbled briefly in surrealism, and especially Salvador Dali, whose iconoclastic personality and hallucinogenic renderings found favor with new audiences in the 1960s and 1970s experimenting with psychedelic drugs.

The surrealist movement in art and literature owes its origins also to the groundbreaking research conducted by Sigmund Freud, establishing the existence of a subconscious mind and motives. This influence is reflected in the definition in the *Encyclopedia of Philosophy* as "based on the belief ... in the omnipotence of the dream, and in the disinterested play of thought" (*Phaidon Dictionary* 1973, p. 373). Similarly, the *Oxford Pocket American Dictionary of Current English* defines surrealism as "a twentieth century movement in art and literature aiming at expressing the subconscious mind, for example, by the irrational juxtaposition of images" (Abate 2002, p. 818).

Surrealism has political antecedents as well. Its earliest practitioners were often much more interested in surrealism as simply a change in the way paintings or writings were conceived. But at its core was political protest, especially in relation to French politics, and its characteristics were often applied to political philosophy as well.

Perhaps just as important as what surrealism is, is what it is not. According to Anna Balakian (1970), author of *Surrealism: The Road to the Absolute*, surrealism "is not mystical, metaphysical, or spiritually transcendent. Surrealism is not abstraction (it's juxtaposition). It may not even be esthetic. Surrealism is not expressionism — it's objective. Surrealism is not literary or allegorical (it's poetic imagery)."

Surrealism and Comedy

Surrealism had a place in comedy years before the Three Stooges. One of the founders of the surreal movement, Philippe Soupault, has been called a "comic surrealist" (Olson 2001, jacket cover). Chaplin's *The Little Tramp* includes a famous scene where Chaplin boils his shoe and eats it as if it were a piece of meat. The scene is both touching in its pathos and challenging in its surrealism. Chaplin treats the article of clothing as if it were a meal that could provide him with sustenance. This gag is one that was repeated on numerous occasions by the Stooges and other Chaplin successors, with a different object replacing the shoe.

Philosophically, comedy and surrealism have much in common. In particular, they share a penchant for antiestablishment values and an opposition to prosaic thinking. Kirby Olson (2001, p. 12), in his book *Comedy after Postmodernism*, states, "Humor [is] ... the intoxicating relativity of human things; the strange pleasure that comes from the certainty that there is no certainty."

But the issue here is not whether comedy is surreal but whether the Stooge comedies are surreal and to what extent the writers and creators of the Three Stooges comedies were inspired by surrealism.

Surrealistic Stooges

We earlier suggested that the entire body of work of the Three Stooges could be considered surrealistic. The Stooges drifted through time and space throughout the series, with little or no continuity between the episodes. Their occupations were rarely repeated; and despite having a poor work record (to put it charitably), they were usually working, however incompetently. Though not exactly surreal, there was the overwhelming sense of *déjà vu* through stock footage, particularly with pie fights and difficult slapstick maneuvers (e.g., being twice thrown from a train, only to land on broncing bulls). One of the most surreal aspects of the Stooges' larger body of work is that they were able to create four additional episodes with Shemp as the third Stooge after his death in 1956.[1]

Surrealism describes events that cannot be explained through any logical or semi-logical means. The Three Stooges films had numerous examples of characters jumping to conclusions about seemingly surrealistic events that, in fact, could be explained logically. For example, episodes like *Scotched in Scotland*, *Spook Louder*, and *The Hot Scots* feature "ghosts" and "monsters" that were really men in costume. *If a Body Meets a Body* features a flying skeleton head, and *Back from the Front* has a cooked turkey walking across a supper table; both of those incidents turn out to be the result of a bird entering the inanimate object and causing it to do seemingly surrealistic actions. Similar to these are occurrences in *The Ghost Talks* and *Creeps*. Shemp's hat appears to hop up and down on his head, but the events can be logically explained by the presence of a frog.

This chapter is not the first occasion when the Stooges have been thought surreal. In 1972, film critic Leonard Maltin (1972, p. 126) referred to Curly as "slightly surreal, (whose) little quirks were never questioned." Curly, who tended to exist in his own parallel universe anyway, might be considered the ultimate surrealist.

We focus here on ten categories of surrealism in the Stooges' work: ghosts and paranormal phenomena, traveling the heavens and beyond, inhuman beings, manimals, improbable and impossible circumstances, time/space issues, defying the laws of physics, inanimate objects coming to life, surrealistic design, and hallucinations. The first two categories are not ordinarily considered under the rubric of surrealism but fit our broader definition of surrealism in comedy. The remaining categories generally reflect subconscious thought (e.g., hallucinations) and thus constitute the larger concerns of surrealism.

Ghosts and Paranormal Phenomena

Ghosts make frequent appearances in the Stooges comedies, either in fact or through inference or mistaken identity. For example, in *The Ghost Talks* and *Creeps* (the latter remade with stock footage), the Stooges meet up with a real ghost when they are instructed to remove a suit of armor from an old house and find the suit is haunted. They also encounter a skeleton named Red. In two other films, *The Hot Scots* and *Scotched in Scotland* (the latter remade with stock footage), ghosts are suspected but don't actually appear until the very end. As the Stooges open a liquor cabinet, a skeleton playing bagpipes is revealed (in *Scotched in Scotland,* even paraphrasing a popular advertising slogan from a razor blade commercial as he is revealed).

Additionally, other paranormal events occur, such as reincarnation, a philosophy that falls squarely outside the realm of surrealism but is included here because it provided a bizarre alternative to more ordinary or routine environments. The Stooges exploit this theme in two short films, *Hoofs and Goofs* and *Horsing Around.* Both episodes deal with the aftermath of the death of the Stooges' beloved sister Birdie, who is reincarnated as a horse. This farce is carried to an illogical extreme. In the first film, it is revealed that Joe has dreamt the whole unlikely scenario after reading a book on reincarnation; his sister is, in fact, still alive. Yet in the second film, Birdie is still a horse. Strangely, the solitary time when there is continuity between Stooges films comes from one of the most improbable storylines imaginable.

Traveling the Heavens and Beyond

In several films, one or all of the Stooges exit the Earth's orbit for outer space, another planet, or heaven. In some cases, the relocation is involuntary. For example, in *Idle Roomers,* a wild "non-beast" in control of an elevator launches the Stooges into the stratosphere. Similarly, in *Three Little Sew and Sews*, a mistake by Curly in causing a bomb to explode turns the Stooges into flying angels. The angels motif occurs in a more seriocomic fashion in the two films *Heavenly Daze* and *Bedlam in Paradise*. Shemp dreams he has been in heaven and has to come back to Earth as an invisible being to reform Moe and Larry. At other times, the Stooges' travels are more voluntary. For example, in both *Space Ship Sappy* and *Outer Space Jitters*, the Stooges travel to the mythical planet of Sunev. Another mythical planet, Zircon, is featured in *Flying Saucer Daffy*. In this short film, Joe meets aliens from the planet Zircon and sees their flying saucer.

Inhuman Beings

Humans in the Stooges films occasionally take on characteristics that are unrealistic for their gender and their species. In one brief scene in *Sing a Song of Six Pants* (and the remake *Rip, Sew, and Stitch*), Shemp is working on his pants while he appears to be sitting on a table. He abruptly walks away from his legs, which are actually a dummy's legs, providing a logical explanation; but the occurrence is so bizarre that it falls naturally into this "inhuman beings" category. In two films, it is voice rather than body that is surreal. In *For Crimin' Out Loud*, a woman speaks with a deep, man's voice; and in *He Cooked His Goose* (and the remake *Triple Crossed*), Moe eats birdseed and begins chirping like a bird. Another "body parts" surrealistic scene is in *Dopey Dicks*, where the Stooges encounter a headless man.

Manimals

The "manimals" category goes one step beyond merely sounding strange. In this category are films in which animals, in some way, take on human characteristics. At times, the occasions are hostile, reflecting the ancient struggle of man versus nature. For instance, in *Dutiful But Dumb*, Curly struggles with a bowl of oyster stew and loses the battle. He finally capitulates, pulls out a pistol, and shoots the bowl of stew. At other times, the "manimal" joins forces with its human counterpart. In *Crime on Their Hands*, a gorilla has annihilated the Stooges' adversaries, who are hoarding a stolen diamond. At the end of the film, as Shemp boasts of his conquest, the gorilla says, "I helped!" Perhaps most surreal are those episodes in which the "manimal" seems to replace the human. In *Spooks!*, a bat flies toward the Stooges, possessing Shemp's head and making his verbal noises. And in *Guns A-Poppin'!*, Moe sees a bear driving his car, even putting its arm out to make a left turn.

Improbable and Impossible Circumstances

Situations that are impossible or extremely improbable are frequent fare in the Stooges films. This category considers the storyline more than any individual sight gag, line, or incident that would have been impossible. For example, two similar films, *Oily to Bed, Oily to Rise* and *Oil's Well That Ends Well*, use an amazing set of what may or may not be coincidences to enable Curly and Joe to get absolutely everything they wish for. Wishes also become an instant reality in *In the Sweet Pie and Pie*. The Stooges are in jail, wishing they could break out. Moe says wistfully, "If we only had a saw," to which Curly retorts, incredibly, "Hey, what about these?" as he raises his prison shirt to reveal an array of saws. A highly improbable gag is also exploited in *A Merry Mixup*, in which the Stooges are one of three sets of identical triplets. From the improbable to the impossible is but a short skip in comedy and slapstick. In *Cuckoo on a Choo Choo*, Larry and Shemp seemingly do the impossible: steal a train car. And in *Slaphappy Sleuths*, another form of transportation does the impossible. After having their gas station robbed, the Stooges trail the thieves' car directly into an office building.

Time/Space Issues

In the best traditions of surrealism, the Stooges defy the boundaries of space and time. Such accomplishments may occur through impossible physical feats, but more often the Stooges introduce aspects of modern-day Americana into other countries and in other eras. In this category falls *Back to the Woods*, one of the more surrealistic films the Stooges made, especially in terms of importing modern popular culture from future America. The film is set in colonial times. The Stooges are on trial and must carry their balls and chains into the courtroom. As they approach the bench, one after another they drop the three balls, which sound like the famous NBC chimes. Curly refers to Bologna watch time (a reference to Bulova watch time, which followed the chimes in radio's early years). A reference is made to horse racing in a 1930s context. Later in the film, as the Stooges are with their sweethearts, a music box is played. It begins to play a minuet but soon switches to swing tempo, and the Stooges and their ladies begin dancing in a swing style.

Time is ignored extensively in two comedies with medieval settings, *Squareheads of the Roundtable* and *Fiddlers Three*. In *Squareheads*, the Stooges are troubadours and need music to perform a dance. Moe instructs Larry to turn on the radio. Larry responds, "Are you kidding? This is ancient times." Moe's reply is apt: "This is an ancient radio." During a song-and-dance routine, the radio plays "Swanee River." Further references are made to trade-ins, *The Jolson Story*, and penicillin. In *Fiddlers Three*, a contemporary reference to being "given the gate" is mentioned, and the Stooges produce the "shave and a haircut, two bits" rhythm sound. Also, a bellows makes the sound "B.O.," alluding to a famous radio commercial for Dial soap.

Distortions of space are also featured in the Stooges' work. One example

The Stooges were not bound by natural laws in their films and traveled easily through time and space, as seen in this still for *Fiddlers Three* (1948).

is in *Yes, We Have No Bonanza*, set in the old West. In one scene, Curly is seen arriving at a saloon to begin his job. Filmed in a medium shot in the beginning of the scene, he appears to be riding a horse. As the camera pulls out, however, it reveals that Curly is actually riding a bicycle.

Defying the Laws of Physics

Related to the preceding category are films that defy the laws of physics. In this category are included animate or inanimate objects taking on properties that go beyond the point of plausibility. Light, for example, is the source of humor in three short films: *Dutiful But Dumb*, *They Stooge to Conga*, and *Nutty But Nice*. In *Dutiful But Dumb*, to disguise himself in the presence of military officers in Vulgaria, Moe pretends to be a lamp by putting a lamp and shade on his head. When the military men enter the room, one man pulls on Moe's tie, causing the lamp to light. In *They Stooge to Conga*, Curly, full of high-voltage electricity, lights up a bulb stuck in his ear. And in *Nutty But*

Nice, Curly removes a light bulb from a socket, and the bulb remains lit while Curly walks with it.

Radios and TV sets appear in implausible situations in four films: *Punch Drunks, Horses' Collars, Dutiful But Dumb*, and *Don't Throw That Knife*. In *Punch Drunks*, Larry races down the street with a radio playing *Pop Goes the Weasel* in pretransistor days. In both *Horses' Collars* and *Dutiful But Dumb*, Curly commandeers the inside of a radio and appears for a brief instance to be having a two-way conversation with a nemesis. These instances did have a logical explanation, but they are surreal experiences for the antagonists until they discover Curly inside the radio. In *Don't Throw That Knife*, in a scene similar to the two previous films, Larry removes a picture tube from a television set to fool a knife thrower who is a jealous husband trying to kill the Stooges. Larry reaches out from the television screen to grab the knife and stab the thrower in the buttocks.

Lamps and electrical appliances reappear in *A Plumbing We Will Go*. Here the Stooges' incompetence as plumbers causes water to travel through electrical wires and come out of the appliances. (The footage was later used in *Scheming Schemers* and *Vagabond Loafers*). Similar incompetence is shown in a surrealistic scene in *Who Done It?* (and the remake *For Crimin' Out Loud*). Shemp prepares his forensic camera, and when he presses the syringe, water sprays out of the camera lens.

In the world of the Three Stooges, objects take on improbable properties. In *Out West*, Shemp dares a cowboy to "shoot you for the drinks." The cowboy throws a coin in the air, and it freezes in midair until the bumbling Shemp can remove the gun from his holster to shoot it. The coin even makes change after being hit by the bullet. Later in the film, a cavalry commander instructs his forces to "go back." They respond by riding backwards. Even invisible objects take on texture and sound. In *Half-Wits Holiday* (and the remake *Pies and Guys*), the Stooges are eating make-believe food to learn table manners, yet they are able to achieve the same noise as their meal would make if they had real food.

Inanimate Objects Coming to Life

Inanimate objects commonly took on animate or even human qualities in many of the Stooges films, including *They Stooge to Conga, Three Little Pirates, Heavenly Daze, Bedlam in Paradise, The Hot Scots, Scotched in Scotland*, and *Loose Loot*. One of the favorite sight gags of Stooge film writers was to have a picture come to life. Sometimes this would have a logical explanation, as in *The Hot Scots* (and the remake *Scotched in Scotland*), when a thief removes a picture from a frame so he can disguise himself as the Arab in the picture in order to steal treasures from the house. In *They Stooge to Conga*, Moe removes a large photograph of Adolf Hitler, takes Hitler's place, and comes to life as Axis power representatives arrive in the room. In *Three Little Pirates*, Moe enters the picture frame so that he may hit a group of pirates over the head with a clock pendulum. He is able to do this only after Curly hurls a knife toward the picture of a woman holding a vase. As she sees the knife barely miss striking her, she screams in terror, drops the vase, and runs away. In *Heavenly Daze* (and the remake *Bedlam in Paradise*), Shemp causes a picture of a cowboy holding two six-shooters to fire the weapons to haunt Moe and Larry.

Perhaps the most surreal of all examples of pictures coming to life is in *Loose Loot*. In the movie's final scene, a group of women are trying to keep a briefcase full of money from the Stooges. They toss it around the room until one of them tosses it too high and it lands in the arms of Napoleon, who is in a picture on the wall. He turns and slowly walks away with the briefcase. He is then struck unconscious as Moe hurls a brick at his head. The Stooges proceed to enter the nineteenth-century painting and dance with glee, all the action taking place inside the picture frame.

Similar to having pictures come to life was the technique of having statues, wall mountings, household items, and even food take on animated qualities. In *Hula-La-La*, for example, a six-armed idol attacks Moe and Larry; and in *You Nazty Spy!* a statue offers to shake Curly's hand. Featured in *The Ghost Talks* and *Creeps*, in addition to other supernatural happenings, a creature's head (a wild dog, perhaps) comes to life and begins growling and barking viciously. And in *Malice in the Palace* (and the remake *Rumpus in the Harem*), Shemp is about to reluctantly eat a hot dog, thinking it has been made from a real dog. As he struggles to eat it, a dog-like tongue comes from the end of the hot dog to lick his face.

Equipment also seems to take on an independent life in the Stooges films. In one of the most famous Stooges scenes ever, from *Men in Black*, a hospital intercom keeps calling for "Dr. Howard, Dr. Fine, Dr. Howard." As the Stooges try to destroy the intercom, they still hear the voice calling them. Finally, they shoot the device, which exclaims, "Ohhhh. They got me!" In *Knutzy Knights*, Shemp holds a helmet that barks like a dog. And in *Pardon My Backfire*, a wire from a car horn dances and takes on a life of its own. Perhaps in the same subcategory is dental "equipment." In *The Tooth Will Out*, a set of teeth, made by dental student Stooges, comes to life and then attacks, sings, and talks.

Surrealistic Design

Surrealism is usually applied to the visual arts, typified by the paintings of Salvador Dali. But Dali's influence transcended the world of painting, as he made his mark in motion pictures (such as the silent film *Un Chien Andalou*) and in the world of fashion. He even assisted avant-garde designer Elsa Schiaparelli, designing buttons for her that looked like flies on chocolate, dice, and typewriter keys (Lucie-Smith 1985, p. 132).

Two films typify what is commonly understood as surrealistic design. The first is *Slippery Silks*. The Stooges are cabinetmakers who inherit a dress shop and are asked to make their own dress designs. What they come up with looks distinctly like dressers and vanities, made into ladies' dresses. *The Sitter Downers* takes the Stooges' designing incompetence to extremes as they are forced to build their own home. What results is a home with sideways doors, a bathtub on the wall, and stairs that start in the middle of the wall and lead nowhere (Larry explains that they are "shelves").

Hallucinations

The last category, hallucinations, is essential to understanding surrealism. Hallucinations have been with man since the dawn of time, and they have always affected his perceptions of reality, whether it be an oasis in the desert, the appearance of a spirit, or the hallucinations that are artificially induced by mental instability or psychedelic drugs. No matter how the hallucinations are achieved, they come about because of the workings of the subconscious mind.

This was perhaps dangerous turf for the Three Stooges to tread; in the times in which their films were made, drug consumption — especially of cocaine and marijuana — was not uncommon, particularly in the arts. The mental instability that was treated in such a light-hearted manner in the Stooges comedies would not likely pass muster with the current, politically correct Standards and Practices Departments of television networks.

Three films fall into this category. In *Mummies Dummies*, Curly imagines he sees an oasis as the Stooges are stranded in the desert. In *Cuckoo on a Choo Choo*, a drunken Shemp sees a giant canary. Most interesting is *Scrambled Brains*, in which Shemp is suffering from mental anxiety. Whether it is the condition he is in or his medication (Moe literally pours a bottle of pills down Shemp's throat), Shemp is hallucinating, and he believes his homely nurse is a beautiful blonde. In one scene, Shemp is practicing the piano. As he struggles with simple scales, an extra pair of hands emerges to play a boogie-woogie beat. He abruptly slams the keyboard lid down to obliterate the extra hands, but he succeeds only in damaging his own fingers. Moaning in pain, he watches as ten disconnected fingers play the scale he had been playing. This is truly one of the most surreal moments and episodes in the Stooges' film career.

At Odds with the Elements

Several studies have established that comedy has many inherently surreal aspects. Our contribution has been to show that slapstick comedy, and the

Three Stooges films in particular, contained many surreal moments. Whether the surrealism was intentional, accidental, or incidental, it was present in a significant number of episodes. This quality was present as early as their second film, *Punch Drunks* (1934), and as late as film 177, *A Merry Mixup* (1957). Indeed, one might argue that every Stooge episode, given the improbable nature of their surroundings, their circumstances, and indeed the very existence of the characters themselves, strains levels of credulity.

The Three Stooges may well be the most surreal group of comics ever assembled. Whether one truly believed their characters or not, they were consistently placed in the most bizarre and incongruous of circumstances, with the most unlikely results. Similar to almost every comedian or comic team in history, the efforts of the Stooges to deal with straight society were incongruous. The qualities that separated the Stooges from their counterparts, however, were the impressive total of such surrealistic scenes.

The Stooges were regularly placed in situations involving the supernatural and the mostly impossible. They battled wits with animals as smart and as perceptive as they were. They did not merely travel through time; they reached into the future and made it the present, whether the present was the Dark Ages or colonial times. The level of violence in some episodes was often so extreme as to defy the laws of physics. And these very stupid men were clever enough to embrace surrealism to fool their nemeses, in films such as *Dutiful But Dumb* and *Don't Throw That Knife*. They stole a train car in *Cuckoo on a Choo Choo*. But perhaps the best representations of how surrealistic the Stooges were can be seen in *Slippery Silks* and *The Sitter Downers*, where the Stooges' very sense of design reflected their surrealistic sensibilities.

Future studies in surrealism theory might do well to include a thorough examination of its elements in comedy. Ample evidence exists that a sense of humor was essential to the surrealist writers. And even those not familiar with elements of surrealism in art find humor in its very odd juxtapositions and incongruities.

Notes

1. When Shemp passed away suddenly in 1956, Columbia Pictures patched together four episodes: *Rumpus in the Harum, Hot Stuff, Scheming Schemers,* and *Commotion on the Ocean*. These films were remakes of earlier films made by rewriting portions of the script and reshooting them with Moe, Larry, and Joe Palma as a stand-in for Shemp. Palma was always filmed from the back or side to give the illusion that it was Shemp.

Works Cited

Abate, Frank R., ed. "Surrealism." *Oxford Pocket American Dictionary of Current English.* Oxford: Oxford University Press, 2002.
Balakian, Anna. *Surrealism: The Road to the Absolute.* New York: E.P. Dutton, 1970.
Lucie-Smith, Edward. *Art of the 1930s: The Age of Anxiety.* New York: Rizzoli, 1985.
Maltin, Leonard. *The Great Movie Shorts.* New York: Crown, 1972.
Olson, Kirby. *Comedy after Postmodernism.* Lubbock: Texas Tech University Press, 2001.
"Surrealism." *Phaidon Dictionary of Twentieth-Century Art.* New York: Phaidon, 1973.

3

Discovered Treasures: The Three Stooges' Missing Scenes

Brent Seguine

The Three Stooges have had difficulty earning respect from Hollywood's critical community. Regardless of those opinions, seventy-five years of enduring popularity reflects their due honor. One way in which the Three Stooges comedies are no different from other films in Hollywood history is the production process. Budgeting, casting, directing, and so forth are the same basic processes from film to film, studio to studio. And every film needs a script.

A final, filmed script is an amalgam of an idea, an outline, first draft, revisions, final draft, and the Hollywood executive decisions that may fall in between, and the Three Stooges short subjects scripts were no different. The family of Columbia Studios' producer Jules White donated his personal files to the Academy of Motion Pictures Arts and Sciences' Margaret Herrick Library, and these files contain all the final scripts of his Short Subjects Department. Studying many of these files is not only a great way for a Three Stooges fan to spend some time, but it provides insight into the creation of a motion picture.

A most interesting discovery, for example, was the fact that a Three Stooges script in White's files may be labeled "Final" but sometimes is quite different from the film we know. Unfortunately, White's files do not always document the revisions made between "Final" and the theatrical screen. That situation leaves a lot of unanswered questions and educated guesswork. Columbia was a budget-minded studio, its Short Subjects Department even more so, and it is reasonable to assume fiscal decisions were behind many unscripted revisions. Running times, film editing, and subsequent creative decisions certainly came into the equation as well. Moreover, distinct to the Three Stooges, their individual screen personalities created change, and tragedy in their personal lives altered films by necessity.

Nothing Goes to Waste

Columbia was among a group of studios known as "poverty row" in Hollywood because of its predominantly low-budget fare in the 1920s, 1930s, and 1940s and because it had no owned-and-operated theater chain, such as MGM's Loews chain, to distribute its output. More so than the major studios like Warner Brothers and MGM, Columbia watched every penny and rarely allowed usable film footage go to waste.

Gents Without Cents (1944) is an example. Though the film is best remembered for the Stooges' rendition of the classic burlesque sketch "Niagara Falls," that scene cannot be found in the *Gents* script. In its scripted place is an army induction sketch, which does not appear in the movie.

Moe, Larry, and Curly actually performed "Niagara Falls" one year earlier, for the feature film *Right Guy,* which was eventually released as *Good Luck, Mr. Yates* (1943). A low-budget musical comedy directed by Ray Enright, its main characters perform a revue show for the employees of a wartime naval shipyard. The Stooges appeared in this sequence under Jules White's guest direction, but the "Niagara" bit was cut before *Yates* was released. White wisely saved the edited footage for a Three Stooges short comedy and found it a home in *Gents Without Cents* one year later.

And what about the army induction segment? It was filmed two years later for *Rhythm and Weep* (1946).

One script had enough material that producer Hugh McCollum and director/screenwriter Edward Bernds decided to adapt it into two back-to-back productions, *Merry Mavericks* (1951) and *The Tooth Will Out* (1951). The version of *Merry Mavericks* in Jules White's file would run approximately twenty minutes. The original first half of *Merry Mavericks* was transplanted to become the second half of *The Tooth Will Out.*

Further reading reveals that the lifted scenes were altered by the time they were actually filmed for *Tooth.* Following is the original dentistry sequence for *Merry Mavericks.* Script deviations begin with shot #12, as they finish drilling Slim Gaut's ("Tortured Patient") tooth.

Merry Mavericks. Story and Screenplay by Edward Bernds. Directed by Edward Bernds. Produced by Hugh McCollum. Columbia No. 4161. Final Draft May 24, 1950.

12. Shemp: Let's see ... what's next...?
    While the boys' backs are turned, the cowboy pulls himself together and scuttles out of the door, holding his jaw.

Shemp: (turning) Oh, can't take it, huh?
(To Shemp and Larry)
Moe: *That's* why I got the dough first!

13. CLOSE SHOT AT DOORWAY
A man peeps timidly into the room. He is a grizzled little desert rat with a tremendous, bushy beard. He enters quietly.

14. MEDIUM SHOT
Shemp has discovered an interesting fact in the book.
Shemp: What d'ya know! After you drill a tooth you're supposed to fill it!
He turns, sees the desert rat and does a big take.
Shemp: Moe! Did you ever see a bush walking?
Moe and Larry recover from their surprise and hurry to the desert rat.
Larry: Step right in, sir ... you're next ... Doctor Howard will see you immediately.
Moe: Two dollars, please.

15. CLOSE SHOT SHEMP AND PATIENT
The little man hands over the money and climbs into the chair.
Shemp: Would you open your mouth please?
Desert Rat: It is open.
Shemp: (With an apologetic laugh) Oh, pardon me.
Shemp tries to find his mouth. He starts casually; Shemp tries again; then gets worried after a few seconds of unsuccessful looking. He takes his glasses off, can't find it and puts them on again.
Shemp: It must be around here somewhere!
There are inarticulate sounds from the desert rat.

16. MEDIUM SHOT
Moe gets impatient with Shemp's lack of progress.
Moe: Hey, quit beatin' around the bush! You've got to be systematic, that's all!
He pushes Shemp aside and begins very meticulously to part the hair. Soon he too loses patience. Larry laughs at his efforts.

17. CLOSE SHOT LARRY AND MOE
Moe, in the foreground, burns as Larry laughs. Without looking, he strikes backward with his fist and hits Larry on the head. He then pulls him forward.
Moe: All right, wise guy ... you try it!
Before Larry can make the attempt, Shemp stops him, the camera pulling back as he does so.
Shemp: Wait ... wait ... I'll get it! (to the patient) Would you kindly put your hand here, please!
He places the man's hand on the instrument tray. Then suddenly he picks up a dentist's hammer (prop) and hits it. The desert rat screams with pain, exposing his mouth. Before he can close it, Shemp sticks a small flag like a golf-marker in it.

18. MEDIUM SHOT
The boys congratulate one another.
Larry: Success!
They shake hands all around.

19. CLOSE SHOT DESERT RAT
He wrinkles his nose as he has to sneeze ... finally he lets go, sending the flag flying across the room.

20. MEDIUM SHOT
  The boys are downcast.
  Shemp: Oh, no!
  Larry: Do we have to go through all that again?

21. CLOSE SHOT PANNING
  The door crashes open as a big man enters. This is Pitts, the town marshal.

Merry Mavericks' original scenes with the marshal do not include the film's sight gags involving tooth-filling, varnish, sandpaper, and the like. Apparently, these were added at the expense of the desert rat character. The dental sequence ends at shot #27.

27. Pitts: You got the wrong tooth!
  He goes for his gun. Larry picks up a can of varnish and dashes it into Pitt's face. The marshal starts firing blindly and the Stooges run out, as we
  DISSOLVE TO:

28. The Red Dog Saloon ...

The *Merry Mavericks* script follows the film closely from this point to the end.

Running Times and Other Editing Room Losses

Columbia short subjects had running times that varied between sixteen and eighteen minutes for releases through the mid-1940s; by the late 1940s, fifteen minutes was the general rule. Maintaining that limitation, and a film's narrative structure, often meant that some scripted material was never filmed.

One of their earliest shorts, *Pardon My Scotch* (1935), opens on the day before the Prohibition repeal, with the Stooges as inept carpenters installing a new door in a drugstore owned by Mr. Jones (Al Thompson). Mr. Jones leaves the Stooges in charge of the drugstore, and the film then cuts to liquor salesman Mr. Martin's (Nat Carr) entrance. The original script reveals a few segments that precede Martin's entrance. Were these scenes filmed and lost in the editing room, or does their contribution to the Stooges' history exist only in print? In any event, these scenes do not contribute to the basic storyline of the Stooges' inventing an amazing new "scotch," and presumably they were dropped for both running time and narrative purposes. Beginning with shot #17, here are the missing scenes from *Pardon My Scotch*.[1]

Pardon My Scotch. Story and Screenplay by Andrew Bennison. Produced by Jules White. Directed by Del Lord. Columbia No. 206.

17. INT DRUG STORE — FULL SHOT
  The three boys are now clad in white coats and white overseas caps. There is a meek looking customer seated on one of the stools.

18. CLOSE SHOT — MOE AND CUSTOMER
Customer: I'd like a raspberry flip!
Moe: Flip a razz!
Curly: Flip a razz!

19. CLOSE SHOT — LARRY (at ice cream counter)
Larry: (reaching for a container) Flip a razz!
He reaches in, takes a scoop of ice cream, slings it and lets it fly out of scene.

20. and 21. CLOSE SHOT — MOE AND CURLY
Curly has the metal container with which he deftly catches the flying ice cream. He hands it quickly to Moe, who turns to the soda spigots, places the container beneath the spout and turns it on full force. The force of the charged water dislodges the ice cream ... it flies from the container into the air.

22. MEDIUM SHOT
Taking in Curly, Moe and the customer. Their heads are turned up looking into the air watching the ice cream. The customer has his mouth wide open ... the ice cream drops into his mouth. He closes it, a pleased smile comes to his face, he munches, then swallows the ice cream.

23. CLOSE SHOT — CUSTOMER
As he finishes the ice cream, he whines in plaintive tones....
Customer: I wanted raspberry with my ice cream!

24. CLOSE SHOT — MOE AND CURLY
Moe: The gentleman wanted raspberry!
At this Curly starts to give him a very violent raspberry and as he sticks out his tongue, Moe reaches over quickly and stretches it out of his mouth and lets it go ... it flips back with a plop.

25. CLOSE SHOT — CUSTOMER
He is laughing loudly at Curly's discomfiture.

26. CLOSE SHOT — CURLY
He takes a soda spoon, dips it into a crushed fruit bowl, draws it out and flips the syrup toward the customer.
Curly: There's your raspberry!

27. CLOSE SHOT — CUSTOMER
The syrup splatters in his eyes. He takes it with a yell, jumps from the stool and exits.

28. CLOSE SHOT — LARRY WITH ANOTHER CUSTOMER, at counter
Customer: I'd like a ham sandwich to take out.
Larry: A ham to go!

29. CLOSE SHOT — MOE
Moe: A ham to go!

30. CLOSE SHOT — CURLY
Curly: A ham to go!
Curly looks about and sees that he has to complete the order and proceeds to do so.

31. MED SHOT
Curly behind the counter. He seizes a large ham, turns quickly about and putting

it in a device, which is screwed to the worktable, he places the ham in its jaws and tightens it securely. Then out of the toolbox he pulls a knife or spoke-shaver. He takes out a gauge and sets it for about two inches and throws it deftly across the ham. He then takes the spoke-shaver, lays it behind the ham and with one heave cuts off a terrific two-inch slice.

He has difficulty in cutting slices of bread and picks up a hammer and large spike. He nails the loaf of bread to the worktable. He then saws off one large slab of bread. He saws the second slab where it's nailed and as he starts picking it up he discovers it is nailed down. He takes a prying iron, and with a couple of heaves pries the bread loose. He pulls the spike out and puts a large slab of ham on the bread; it covers it entirely and hangs out over the edges. He then puts another piece of bread on it. He takes his tri-square, then places a level on it; it is not quite to his satisfaction, so he takes a block plane and planes off a few shavings. When he is perfectly satisfied, the customer's voice is heard.

Customer's voice: Plenty of mustard!

Curly then lifts up the top piece of bread, reaches into his tool chest, draws out a pointed trowel which he dips into the mustard pot, and draws forth a large gob of mustard and plops it on the ham, then places the top of slice of bread on the ham. The mustard oozes out and Curly points the mustard up in brick-layer fashion.

Curly: A ham to go!

32. MED SHOT

Curly and customer at counter. Curly places the sandwich in front of the customer. It stands about six inches in height. The customer looks at it in amazement.

Curly: A ham to go!

The customer looks at Curly in disgust.

Customer: That's not going with me! Crate it and ship it....

The customer whips around on the stool and exits, Curly looking after him dumbly.

Curly: A victim of circumstance!

33. CLOSE SHOT

... of male customer at drug counter. He is tapping upon the counter with a piece of money.

Customer: Can I be waited on?

34. CLOSE SHOT — MOE

Moe: Comin' right up.

Moe rushes out toward the customer.

35. MED SHOT

At drug counter. Moe enters to meet the male customer.

Moe: What'll it be?

Customer: Can you recommend anything for removing corns?

Moe: Can I!

He reaches back on a shelf and takes a jar, which he shows to the customer, he nods his head offstage and Larry enters.

Moe: Gentleman wants a corn remover. Give him a little recommendation.

Larry: I used some of it last night and it took my corns away like that!

He snaps his fingers at the end of the speech. The customer is well pleased.

Customer: I'll take it.

As he reaches into his pocket for money, Larry reaches for another jar, which he holds toward the customer.

Larry: You better take this too.
Customer: What's that for?
Larry: To bring back the toes!

The customer walks out indignantly. Moe turns and glares at Larry and then stamps heavily upon Larry's foot. Larry screams.

Larry: Oh, my corn!

36. CLOSE SHOT — CURLY AND ANOTHER CUSTOMER

This customer is a frail sort of man. Very meek looking and is the type that might be a teacher of botany.

Customer: I'd like a bowl of soup.
Curly: A bowl!
Moe's voice: A bowl!
Larry's voice: A bowl!

37. CLOSEUP — CURLY

Curly: A bowl!
Curly looks around; there is no one to fill the order.
Curly: That's a coincidence.

He picks up a large bowl and tries to insert it into the soup container. The plate is too big. He jerks out the container and places it upon the little work-shelf beneath the counter. He is a bit nonplussed but gets an idea. He sees a tool chest at the end of the counter where he is working, opens it and draws forth a brace and bit. He bores a hole in the container. The soup flies out. He fills the bowl and puts the container back into the steam table. (Soup is still pouring out of the container.) Curly places the bowl of soup on the counter.

Curly: A bowl!
He gives the bowl a flip and starts it on down the counter.

38. CLOSE SHOT OF CUSTOMER

Sitting at counter in foreground. The bowl flies in and comes to a sudden stop in front of the customer who is much surprised. He picks up a spoon, tastes it, and screws up his face in agony. It is evident that it is not to his liking and he pushes it aside.

39. MED SHOT

Customer and Larry. Larry has his nose almost in the customer's face, watching him eat. As the customer pushes the bowl aside, Larry drops back.

Larry: What's the matter with the soup?
Customer: I don't like it.
Larry: (looks at him) Oh, you don't like our soup, eh?
Customer: No, I don't!

40. MED SHOT

Moe enters on the outside of the counter and leans over looking at the customer.

Moe: What did you say?
Customer: I said I don't like your soup and furthermore I'm not going to eat it.
Moe: (with narrowed eyes) Let me get this straight. You ordered a bowl of soup and you're not going to eat it.
Customer: That's correct!
Moe: You came into this store. We didn't send for you. You sat yourself down on our stool, and you pick soup! Is that right?
Customer: Quite!

Moe: Then you're going to eat soup!
Customer: Definitely not!

41. MED SHOT
Moe and customer. Moe enters on outside of counter, and sits on a stool opposite side of the customer. He realizes that his tactics are getting him nowhere. He changes and becomes quite sweet.

Moe: You know, we can't have dissatisfied customers here....

Moe reaches over and lifts the customer off the stool and places him on his knees. The customer looks wild-eyed.

Curly: If you want to be a big man and have muscles like me (he pats his stomach) ... You've got to eat your soup!

The customer is becoming more wild-eyed.

Moe: Now, once upon a time, there were four bears....

42. CLOSE SHOT — LARRY
Larry: Three bears!

43. MED SHOT
Moe with the customer in his lap, he glares at Larry, takes a spoon of soup and flips it on Larry.

44. CLOSE SHOT — LARRY
The soup hits him in the eyes and he staggers back.

45. MED SHOT — MOE, CUSTOMER AND CURLY
Moe: There were four bears, and one of them died!

The customer is looking at him wide-eyed and open-mouthed. Moe seizes his chance and tosses a spoonful of soup into the customer's mouth. It is immediately closed. His face screws up as....

Moe: There was a little girl with golden locks, and she met a big bad wolf in the forest, and she said, "What big eyes you have...." And the wolf said, "All the better to eat your soup with, my dear...." You know the big bad wolf was a sucker for soup.

During Moe's story the customer's eyes have been getting heavier and he has gradually gone to sleep. At the finish, he is sound asleep and Moe starts to sneak up on him with a spoon of soup, he is amazed.

Moe: Why the guy's asleep!

46. CLOSEUP — LARRY
Larry: What'll we do with him?

Moe: We'll put him in the back room. When he wakes up we'll give him the rest of the soup.

Although scripted scenes may not appear in a film, existing production stills offer evidence that such scenes may have been filmed and then cut in editing.

A production still from *So Long, Mr. Chumps* (1941), reproduced many times on licensed merchandise, pictures Moe and Larry with Curly, whose head is bound in a large carpenter's clamp. This bit is not in the film, but it is in the script, and the existence of the photograph implies it was filmed and cut. The film we know is basically accounted for throughout the script, so possibly this scene (and a few other small cuts) was cut for purposes of running time.

So Long, Mr. Chumps. Story and Screenplay by Felix Adler and Clyde Bruckman. Produced and Directed by Jules White. Columbia No. 484. Final Continuity July 18, 1940.

18. EXT SIDEWALK — TRAVELING SHOT
   The Three Stooges dressed in high hats and overcoats with fur collars, carrying canes, are strolling along.
   Curly: (excitedly) Look!
   They stop, look up, then rush out.

19. MED SHOT — AT CURB
   The Stooges rush to the curb where we see a hobo about to pick up a cigar butt. The Stooges make a dive and scramble for the butt.

20. MED SHOT — STOOGES
   Scrambling for the butt, Moe finally comes up with the lighted cigar butt in his hand, places it in a cigar holder, which he extracts from his pocket, then starts to puff lustily. Curly and Larry are disappointed as the tramp looks on flabbergasted, unable to believe his eyes. Moe puffs on cigar butt with ecstatic bliss.
   Moe: Mmm! A La Skunkadora!
   Curly looks at Moe then reaches in his pocket, comes out with a giant calabash pipe, steals the butt from Moe's holder, puts it in the pipe, snaps the lid of the pipe, locks it with a little padlock and starts puffing blissfully, blowing a cloud of smoke into Moe's face. Moe burns, looks off and exits.

21. MED SHOT — OF A TRAILER COUPLED TO A CAR
   On the trailer are all sorts of tools, paraphernalia, lumber, etc., and a sign reading: "Acme Construction." Moe enters the trailer, picks up something, which we do not see clearly, and hurriedly exits.

22. MED SHOT — CURLY AND LARRY
   Curly is still puffing on the pipe blowing smoke in Larry's face. Larry inhales it with relish as Moe hurries in to the scene. Moe approaches Curly and now we see that he has a carpenter's clamp. Quickly he puts the clamp over the top of Curly's head and under Curly's chin, then he screws it tight, imprisoning the pipe in Curly's mouth.
   Moe: Come on, we gotta find an honest man.
   He gets Larry by the hair, grabs the pipe which Curly can't let go, and drags them both out of the scene.

Rhythm and Weep (1946) has an interesting omission. Production stills indicate the scene was filmed, and two of the Stooges' costars, Nita Beiber and Gloria Patrice, recollect filming the scene.

Rhythm and Weep. Screenplay by Felix Adler. Produced and directed by Jules White. Columbia No. 4057. Final Draft April 16, 1946

   Moe, Larry, Curly, and their dancer girlfriends are in rehearsals for a Broadway show. In a sequence that does appear in the film, the Stooges appear on stage, in drag as ballerinas, to introduce the girls' ballet number.

   We're dressed as ballerinas.
   Of course, you know we're not.
   And what you're going to see now folks,
   Is something we ain't got!

3. Discovered Treasures (Seguine)

Brent Seguine discovered many missing and unfilmed scenes in the films of the Stooges, including this scene from *So Long, Mr. Chumps* (1941).

The Stooges attempt a ballet maneuver, bump into each other, and march off.

The missing scene, shot #78, is a companion to the preceding one:

78. LONG SHOT (piano music)
Curtain opens (in one) revealing the Three Stooges with their backs to the camera. Camera trucks forward. The Three Stooges turn around disclosing the three girls dressed as the Stooges. They start to recite:
Three girls (patter):
We hope that we've deceived you,
And now we're going to show,
What happens when your Draft Board says,
"You're in the Army, Joe!"
(end music)
First girl: Spread out!
She jabs one of the girls in the Stooges manner. Girl that is jabbed reacts like Curly. She turns and slaps the third girl in Stooge manner. They march off.

Rhythm and Weep's shot #78 also explains a minor continuity issue at the end of the film. Why are the girls seen backstage, wearing men's suits?

It is because we are missing that scene where they impersonated the Three Stooges.

Unfortunately, this scene was omitted from the final release. Not only is it a nice bookend to the earlier ballerina scene with Moe, Larry, and Curly, but it could have provided a good laugh in a short that is generally considered one of the Stooges' lesser efforts.

As discussed earlier, *The Tooth Will Out* (1951) was produced with the benefit of overrun of material from another short subject. Its final script reveals an example of an omitted scene. After the boys have paid their tuition at dental school, we segue to a slapstick scene in the classic Three Stooges style.

The Tooth Will Out. Story and Screenplay by Edward Bernds. Directed by Edward Bernds. Produced by Hugh McCollum. Columbia No. 4162. Temporary title "A Yank at the Dentist". Final Draft November 10, 1950

13. INTERIOR CLASSROOM (DAY) MEDIUM SHOT

The Stooges, wearing smocks, are working with plaster of paris, moulds, and sample dentures. Shemp addresses a "patient," a plaster skull.

Shemp: This won't hurt a bit, madam.

He then tries to pull out one of the skull's teeth. Miss Beebe comes along, and evidently smitten with Shemp, pats his cheek and giggles coyly. As she leaves Shemp, he puts the skull down.

14. CLOSE SHOT

The skull knocks over a bunsen burner so that the flame scorches Moe's back.

15. MEDIUM SHOT

Moe yells as the flame burns him, then reacts and hits Shemp. Miss Beebe turns angrily and hits Moe in exactly the same way he hit Shemp.

Miss Beebe: You let him alone, you big bully! Now get at those dentures! You all have your moulds?

Moe: Yes, teacher.

16. CLOSE SHOT STOOGES

Miss Beebe exits, and they begin to work with the plaster of paris.

17. CLOSEUP SHEMP

Making a mould, he flips a small glob of plaster off screen.

18. CLOSEUP LARRY

The gob plasters itself on his nose. He glares at it, his eyes crossing, then picks up a bigger gob and flips it at Shemp.

19. CLOSE SHOT MOE AND SHEMP

Shemp bends down to pick something up just in time for Moe to get the plaster. Moe burns, then reaches into Shemp's carefully made mould for a handful of plaster, which he tosses at Larry.

20. CLOSEUP LARRY

He ducks and the plaster flies over his head.

Larry: Nya-a-hh! Missed me!

He gets a big gob right between the eyes. He grabs a handful and retaliates.

21. CLOSE SHOT SHEMP AND MOE
   Shemp gets the gob in the back of the neck.
   Shemp: (to Larry) Hey, cut it out! (to Moe) What's the big idea!
   Moe: Shaddup!
   He takes another big handful of plaster and holds it under his nose.
   Moe: See this?
   Shemp: Yeah.
   He shoves it into Shemp's face.

22. CLOSE SHOT MISS BEEBE
   She enters a doorway, reacts and starts out of scene.

23. CLOSE SHOT LARRY
   He winds up and throws a big handful.

24. CLOSE SHOT SHEMP, MOE AND MISS BEEBE
   As Miss Beebe enters the scene and grabs Moe, the handful of plaster catches her. Angrily she scrapes it off and throws it back at Larry.

25. MEDIUM SHOT
   A free-for-all fight with plaster develops.

26. CLOSE SHOT AT DOOR
   Doc Keefer runs in, aghast.
   Doc: Stop it! Stop it, I say!
   He gets hit with a mass of plaster.
   Shot #27 then picks up the film's continuity with the denture-making scene.

Screen Personalities

By 1935, Curly Howard had emerged as the comic star of the trio. The Three Stooges films of 1935–1945 typically gave him the bulk of the comedy material. Many times Larry seems shortchanged in screen time, in comparison to Moe and Curly.

Matri-Phony (1942) was another showcase for Curly, a physical tour de farce. But, the final script for *Matri-Phony* presents Larry in the star role and Curly in the role played by Larry in the film. There is no evidence or notation in White's file to explain the switch, certainly a significant casting change to make between a final draft and actual filming. Lacking a documented explanation, we assume that either the producer Hugh McCollum or director Harry Edwards felt that Curly could do a better job with the scenes. Another unexplained change is the role of director: the final draft lists Del Lord in that job; the switch to Harry Edwards was also apparently a last-minute change.

What follows happens after the Stooges have incapacitated two Roman guards and stolen their uniforms. Contrary to the filmed version of *Matri-Phony*, Moe and Curly fill in as the guards, and Larry disguises himself as

Diana. We pick up with shot #64 and the scenes that highlight Octopus Grabus' (Vernon Dent) romance of "Diana" Fine.

Matri-Phony. Story and Screenplay by Elwood Ullman and Monty Collins. Produced by Hugh McCollum and Del Lord. Directed by Del Lord (?). Columbia No. 527. Final Draft Continuity January 12, 1942.

64. EXT DOOR — MED SHOT
   Smiling in anticipation, Octopus comes up to the door and raps on it.
   Octopus: Yoo-hoo, Diana. It's your own little Octopus ... come to take you in his arms!
   Larry's voice (off-screen falsetto): Just a minute, Ocky!
   Octopus: (coyly) Well, make it a short minute, my little kelp-fish!
   He turns his back to the door and leans against it. Humming, he opens a vanity case and starts primping.

65. INT ROOM — MED SHOT AT DOOR
   Moe looks off-screen and satisfies himself that everything is in readiness. He then yanks the door open and Octopus topples in yelling and lands smack on his back on the floor. Moe jerks him to his feet and dusts him off. Octopus looks off-screen and chuckles delightedly.
   Octopus: My little sanddab, you're positively ravishing!

66. MED SHOT AT TABLE
   Larry, in Diana's costume and with the shawl covering the lower part of his face, is seated at the table, rolling his eyes coquettishly at the Emperor. He sprays himself with a perfume atomizer and puts some behind his ears.
   Octopus: (entering) How about a little kiss, my little sardine!
   Larry: (shrinking away) Not now, you big squid ... you'll spoil my makeup! Sit down and eat everything before everything gets cold!
   Octopus laughingly chucks Larry under the chin, then picks up a bottle of wine.
   Octopus: (beaming) At least I can toast your beauty with sparkling wine!

Note shots #76–77. In *Matri-Phony*, Octopus makes reference to marrying Diana. When or where did the ceremony take place? The following unknown scene with the Minister (Monty Collins) explains everything.

76. MED FULL SHOT
   The Prime Minister pushes the door open and strides briskly over to the table. Moe and Larry look at each other wonderingly.

77. MED SHOT AT TABLE
   The Prime Minister extends his hand in a salute, then turns to Larry and the Emperor as he intones an incantation in double talk. During this the Emperor beams rapturously and Larry looks on in amazement. Moe and Curly come up from background and also look on dumbfounded.
   Prime Minister: (to Larry) Francey gamma would you fraddle scram?
   Larry: Yeah, man!
   Prime Minister: (to Emperor) Francey gamma do you udder fft?
   The Prime Minister extends his hand in another salute, turns on his heel and exits.

78. CLOSE GROUP SHOT

Octopus leans forward to embrace Larry, then stops short as he realizes Moe and Curly are still in the room.
Octopus: (looking up) Leave us! We want to be alone!
Moe and Curly look at each other.
Moe: Now wait a minute, Empy! You can't stay here alone with him ... her!
Octopus: But she's my wife! We were just married!

79. TWO SHOT — CURLY AND MOE
They react.
Curly: (smilingly) Oh! That makes it all right then! (to Moe) Come on, we're intruding!
He grabs Moe's arm and takes him to the door.

80. INT HALL — MED CLOSE SHOT AT DOOR
Moe and Curly step through the door, then suddenly pull up short as both take big reactions. They look at each other, then with one accord wheel and fling themselves against the door, as over scene we hear a key turn in the lock.

81. INT ROOM — MED CLOSE SHOT AT DOOR
Octopus, having locked the door, turns around. He tosses the key up in the air, catches it, and tucks it into the neckband of his blouse. Chuckling, he starts across the room.

82. CLOSEUP — LARRY
Reacting in panic.
Larry: Wait a minute, Empy! ... You got me all wrong!

83. MED FULL SHOT
Larry retreats around the table and the Emperor stalks him, Larry falteringly, as he indicates table.
Larry: L-let's eat, Empy! ... Everything's getting cold!
Emperor: Food, bah! It's love I want!
Larry giggles, grabs up the ladle, gives the Emperor a playful rap over the head with it as we hear a CLUNK. Larry then coyly dances out of scene.

84. CLOSEUP — OCTOPUS
He shakes his head dazedly for a moment, then laughs and runs after Larry.

85. INT HALL — CLOSE SHOT AT DOOR
Curly, looking through the keyhole, turns away and faces Moe in consternation.
Curly: Larry's leading by a length!
As Curly turns to again look through the keyhole, Moe gives him two-in-the eyes, and shoves him aside. Moe takes a quick look through the keyhole, then turns away in panic.
Moe: We've got to get him out of there! Gimme a hairpin!
Curly reaches for his head, then checks himself, whips out his sword and hands it to Moe. The latter starts working on the lock with the point of the sword.

86. INT ROOM — MED FULL SHOT
Octopus is still pursuing Larry, who hurls himself against the door and frantically rattles the doorknob trying to get out. He turns away in a fright, but as the Emperor charges over to him, Larry starts laughing coyly. Octopus, also laughing, grabs Larry in his arms. Larry shoves his hand down the front of the Emperor's blouse and tries to

find the key. The Emperor starts giggling uncontrollably and gives Larry a playful push. Larry gives the Emperor a harder shove, which sends him reeling back against the door.

87. CLOSE SHOT AT DOOR
   The blade of the sword comes through between the door and the jamb, sticking the Emperor in the seat. He lets out a loud yell.

88. INT HALL — MED CLOSE SHOT AT DOOR
   Moe, working the sword, lets out a yell of triumph.
   Moe: Touche!!
   Curly: Gesundheit!

89. INT ROOM — MED FULL SHOT
   Trying to distract the Emperor, Larry playfully goes into two or three rapid dance steps. This amuses Octopus, who gets into the spirit of the thing and tries to imitate Larry with awkward leaps and bounds. Larry finally skips over to an archway, and leaps onto a heavy silk cord and starts swinging on it.

90. MED SHOT AT ARCHWAY
   As Octopus playfully romps into scene, Larry comes back, on the back swing and kicks the Emperor in the face, knocking him flat.

91. CLOSE SHOT — EMPEROR
   As he lands in a sprawling heap on the floor, the key drops out of his blouse.

92. MEDIUM SHOT
   As Octopus sits up dazedly, Larry leaps down alongside of him and makes a grab for the key. The two of them struggle desperately for it; Octopus finally getting the key. He holds it up, chuckling triumphantly.
   Octopus: Now, my little clam, let's have a kiss!
   He tears the veil from Larry's face and reacts thunderstruck as he sees who it is.
   Octopus: Treason!!

93. MED FULL SHOT
   As the Emperor jumps up yelling for the guards, Larry with a sudden movement, grabs the key and gives the Emperor two-in-the-eyes. As the Emperor staggers back, Larry quickly pulls the cloak over his head. As the Emperor threshes around trying to free himself and muttering muffled yells for the guards, Larry sprints over to the door.

94. CLOSE SHOT AT DOOR
   Larry quickly unlocks the door as Moe and Curly sprawl headlong into the room. The three of them scramble to their feet and tear out of the room.

95. INT HALL LONG SHOT
   The Stooges, in background, start down the hall as a file of guards rush past camera. The Stooges wheel in their tracks and turn back to the door of the room.

96. INT ROOM MED SHOT AT DOOR
   Octopus rushes to the door as it swings open, smacking him in the head with a loud BONG and knocking him flat. The Stooges, with Curly "woo-wooing," rush over to his body and over toward a window. As the Emperor gets to his feet, the soldiers tear into the room and knock him flat again.

97. MED SHOT AT WINDOW

The Stooges turn, look around behind them, react with yells of fright, then turn and dive headlong out through the window.

One can safely conclude, in comparing *Matri-Phony*'s original script to the final filmed version, that Larry Fine was left at the altar.

Necessity and Tragedy

Curly Howard's health began to fail in the mid–1940s, as he suffered a series of minor strokes that led to an incapacitating incident in 1946 on the set of *Half-Wit's Holiday* (1947). His decline is noticeable in the films released in late 1945, and particularly in almost all of the 1946 releases.

Where *Matri-Phony* (1942) assigned Larry's scripted role to Curly, evidence indicates that the opposite occurred in the production of *Three Loan Wolves* (1946). Curly's failing health resulted in a role written for him to be assumed by Larry.

On its face, there is no file evidence of the Larry/Curly switch. But timeline notations on the script cover page show a lapse of one month between the "final draft" (January 15, 1946) and the "final revised" version (February 15, 1946). Also noteworthy, throughout Jules' files, scripts were typed on white paper and page and scene revisions on yellow paper. *Three Loan Wolves* is typed entirely on yellow paper and is the only script in this condition. In one month, the entire script was revised. Without a copy of the first, final script, one cannot specifically identify a reason. But the assumption is that Curly's and Larry's roles were switched to accommodate an ailing Curly.

Curly was forced to retire in 1947 after his attack on the set of *Half-Wit's Holiday*. Although this film's pie fight is widely considered one of the Stooges' funniest gags, Curly's absence in these scenes is conspicuous (he suffered the stroke shortly before they were filmed). Moe and Larry and supporting actors Emil Sitka and Symona Boniface do a fine job of taking on the comedic burden. But the question arises of what happened to Curly's scripted scenes. Below is the original, scripted pie fight for *Half-Wit's Holiday*, picking up with Symona Boniface's classic "Sword of Damocles" scene, featuring the scenes intended for Curly Howard.

Half Wit's Holiday. Screenplay by Zion Myers. Produced and Directed by Jules White. Columbia No. 4056. Released January 9, 1947. Final Draft April 15, 1946. "No Gents— No Cents." Shot May 2, 1946 — May 6, 1946

93. She looks up and the pie hits her in the face with a PLOP. She reacts, wipes the goo from her face. Her hands filled with meringue, she inadvertently throws the stuff away.

94. CLOSE SHOT MOE AND LULU
They are conversing as the meringue smacks Lulu right in the face. Both react. Moe looks off, sees something, angrily exits. (Intercut with the following scene.)

95. CLOSE SHOT CURLY AT REFRESHMENT TABLE

He has another pie in his hand and is avidly eating it. His hand adheres to the meringue and he shakes it, trying to dislodge the stuff onto the floor. Moe enters.

Moe: You feather-brained imbecile, you still trying to ruin us?

He slaps the pie out of Curly's hand.

96. CLOSEUP MRS. SHPRITZVASSER AND MR. TOMS

They are conversing as the pie flies in and hits Mrs. Shpritzvasser in the face. Mr. Toms resentfully exits toward the Stooges.

97. CLOSE SHOT MOE AND CURLY

They are still arguing as Mr. Toms enters, deliberately picks up a pie, taps Curly on the shoulder, and as Curly turns around, he plops the pie into Curly's face and indignantly exits. Curly resentfully reaches for a piece of pastry, as Mrs. Gotrocks enters behind him. Curly whirls to throw the pastry at Mr. Toms before Moe can stop him and on the back swing plops the cream puff into Mrs. Gotrocks face.

98. CLOSEUP MRS. GOTROCKS

Her face all gooey.

99. MEDIUM CLOSE SHOT CURLY AND MRS. GOTROCKS

Curly is about to make apologies, when Mrs. Gotrocks angrily picks up a cream puff.

Mrs. Gotrocks: You disreputable vagabond.

She throws the cream puff; Curly ducks.

100. CLOSEUP MOE

The cream puff lands between his eyes.

101. MEDIUM CLOSE SHOT CURLY, MOE AND MRS. GOTROCKS

Moe wipes the goo from his face, as Curly starts to laugh.

Curly (laughing): You forgot to duck.

He laughs uproariously again. Moe plops the goo into Curly's face.

Moe: So did you.

Mrs. Gotrocks is laughing heartily.

Mrs. Gotrocks: This is more fun than people.

Moe: What are you laughing at, you big baboon!

He plops a cream puff into her face. She indignantly throws a pie at Moe. Moe ducks.

102. CLOSE SHOT LARRY AND A GIRL

He is talking to a pretty girl. The girl looks up, frightened, and Larry whirls to see what she is concerned about, as the pie flies in and hits him in the face. Larry angrily exits.

103. MEDIUM SHOT MOE, CURLY AND MRS. GOTROCKS

They are all throwing cream puffs at each other and are all ducking them, as Larry steps into the fray.

104. CLOSE SHOT THE STOOGES

Moe and Curly each have a cream puff in their hand as Larry steps up and stops them.

Larry: Listen, you wise guys....

Without any ado, Moe and Curly splatter their cream puffs into Larry's face, then all start throwing.

105. CLOSE SHOT TWO WOMEN
They are talking as a pie and a cream puff fly in and hit each of them.

106. CLOSE SHOT A MAN AND A WOMAN
The man's back is TOWARD THE CAMERA. A cream puff hits him on the back of the neck; he turns to see what hit him and a pie hits him in the face. The woman looks on terrified, looks up to see where they came from, gets hit in the face with a pie.

107. CLOSE SHOT SEDLETZ AND QUACKENBUSH
They are in a secluded corner by the desk. Sedletz hands Quackenbush a check.
Sedletz: Well, my dear fellow, here's your thousand. Guess I lost.
As he hands him the check, he looks up. Suddenly they both react as they look off.

108. CLOSEUP CURLY
He is about to throw a pie. In back of him in the distance Moe and Larry are seen throwing pastry in all directions. Curly raises his hand to throw the pie, but is splattered with a pie himself. He raises his hand to throw the pie again and again gets hit. He reacts, again raises his hand and a third pastry splatters his face. Angrily he plops himself in the face with his own pie, then sticks his tongue out, just in time to get another pie in the kisser.

109. CLOSE SHOT QUACKENBUSH AND SEDLETZ
They are horrified. Sedletz grabs the check from Quackenbush, then laughs at him tauntingly.
Sedletz: Looks like I win after all ... start writing.
Now he laughs harder and a pie plops him in his face. Quackenbush pulls out a wad of money from his pocket, disgruntingly hands the bills to Sedletz, who meanwhile has been wiping the goo from his face.
Quackenbush: Here's your money and believe me I've learned that you can't make a silk purse out of a sow's ear.
Sedletz: Thank you ... and I've learned something too.
Quackenbush: What's that?
Sedletz: This!
He plops the gooey remains of the pie, which are in his hands, square into Quackenbush's face.

FADE OUT

THE END

Jules White arranged for Curly to have a cameo role in *Hold That Lion!* (1947), which starred Moe, Larry, and Shemp. Two years later, the same was done for *Malice in the Palace* (1949), giving Curly a short speaking role as the restaurant cook. Reportedly, his health problems so affected his performance that Jules White was unable to use the scene. If Curly had appeared in *Malice*, here is the scene that was written for him as discovered in the final draft.

Setting up Curly's unused scene, Larry has taken the lunch order for Hassan Ben Sober and Ghinna Rumma.

Malice in the Palace. Screenplay by Felix Adler. Produced and Directed by Jules White. Columbia No. 4119. Released September 1, 1949. Final Draft April 14, 1948. "Here We Go Shmow"

18. INTERIOR CAFÉ KITCHEN MEDIUM SHOT (DAY)
  Larry enters. The chef is putting on his fez and has removed his apron.
  Larry (yells): One rabbit and one hot dog!
  Chef: Fix it yourself ... I'm going to lunch.
  Larry: Lunch?
  Chef: Certainly ... you don't think I'd eat in this dump.
  He exits.

This is an extremely short segment, hardly noteworthy within the scope of a full script, but it is unfortunate that Curly's health did not allow him to provide us with this one final laugh.

A Complete Rewrite!

The film *Movie Maniacs* (1936) bears little resemblance to the script.

In the filmed version, Moe, Larry, and Curly stow away on a freight train to Hollywood, eager to make their fortune in movies. After they sneak onto the Carnation Pictures lot, a case of mistaken identity puts them in charge of production. Mishaps and slapstick ensue; the Stooges are found out and are chased from the studio.

In the original, scripted version, Carnation Pictures' latest project by Director Swinehardt is behind schedule and without an ending. Staff screenwriters Howard, Fine, and Howard are called to the rescue. Fired after a series of ridiculous script proposals, Moe forges Fuller Rath's name on an authorization to take control of the picture. Insanity and inferno ensue.

Inferno is the correct word, not an exaggeration. The original script called for the Stooges to burn down the soundstage! It describes sequences that one cannot realistically imagine being safely produced, at least not within the budget limitations of a Columbia short subject. It is interesting to note that White's file contains one production still that shows the Stooges dazed and covered in soot, standing among the ruins of a burnt soundstage. Probably, this was the result of creative set designing; it is doubtful that any of the fire segments were actually filmed.

Especially interesting are the script revisions (the freight train, sneaking onto the studio, and meeting Mr. Rath for the first time) that establish the Stooges as outside freeloaders in the actual film. The revisions are included in White's file as addendums, and the original script concept remains intact and labeled as "Final."[2]

What more fitting way could there be to close this discussion and analysis of Three Stooges scripts than to read how Moe, Larry, and Curly burn down a movie studio!

Movie Maniacs. Story by Felix Adler. Directed by Del Lord. Produced by Jules White.

3. Discovered Treasures (Seguine)

Columbia No. 213. Final script draft 10/22/35. Call sheet dated 11/27/35. Release date 2/20/36.

FADE IN on:
INSERT: Sign, reading: "CARNATION PICTURES, From Contented Actors"
DISSOLVE THROUGH TO:
INSERT: Sign on door: "FULLER RATH, President"
DISSOLVE TO:

1. Interior Private Office
This is the office of Mr. Rath, chief executive of the studio. The office is well furnished, but in an old-fashioned way; such as, at one side we see a letter press, and there is a roll-top desk, beside the flat desk which Mr. Rath uses for his business. At this desk there is a dictograph for inter-office communication, which will eliminate any necessity for a secretary. Mr. Rath's name is befitting his character, as he is usually in an irate mood. A "yes man" stands beside the desk, and Mr. Rath sits looking over a scenario and puffing vigorously on his cigar.

2. MED SHOT
Rath: Director Swinehardt is twelve days behind schedule on our super-special picture, and it is costing us thousands of dollars!
Yes Man: Yes, sir ... but he didn't have time to finish his scenario.
Rath: Didn't have time? Why he's worked on it for two years.
YM: Yes sir ... but, now he's stuck.
Rath: (impatiently) He's had every one of our authors on it!
Rath holds up script and shakes it angrily.
YM: (still very meek) Yes, sir ... everyone but Messrs. Howard, Fine and Howard.
Rath: Who are they?
YM: Yes sir. They're our best writers.
Rath: How long have they been working here?
YM: Yes sir. Three years.

3. CLOSE-UP
Rath takes this, then,
Rath: What have they ever done?
YM: Yes, sir. They wrote the snuff scene for "The Captain Hates the Sneeze."

4. CLOSE-UP
Rath thinks for an instant, then says
Rath: Oh, they're the ones who wrote that, eh?

5. WIDER ANGLE
YM: Yes sir.
Rath presses the button of the dictograph, as YM exits.
Rath: (into dictograph) Send in Howard, Fine and Howard.
He no sooner says this than we hear a knock, presumably from the door. Rath turns toward the door.
Rath: Come in.
From behind him through a window come the Stooges.

6. CLOSE SHOT at window
Through the window, right in back of Rath, come the THREE STOOGES. Larry carries an old battered violin case under his arm. Rath sees them and reacts, surprised.

Moe: (to Rath) Excuse us, boss. We were writing a burglar story, so we came through the window. We always act out our ideas.

7. MED SHOT — RATH'S OFFICE
Rath: (dubiously) I see. Sit down.
With this invitation, Larry pulls up a chair, sits in it, cocks his feet up on Rath's desk, reaches in the humidor for a cigar, puts six in his pocket, lights one, and settles back comfortably, while Curly goes over to a couch, plunks himself down on it, gives a yawn, and turns on his side, ready to go to sleep.

8. MED — Moe and Larry
Moe walks up to where Larry is sitting, hits him in the face, knocks his feet off Rath's desk, takes the cigar away from him and starts smoking it himself. He then turns around, looking toward the couch and Curly goes toward them.

9. WIDER ANGLE — Moe and Curly
Moe proceeds to give Curly a good bawling out.
Moe: Get up ... what's the idea of trying to go to sleep in the presence of your boss? Ain't you got no disrespect?
With that, he gives Curly a good smack. Curly counters with an indignant, reproachful stare as if he might return the smack ... but changes his mind upon looking into the pan of Moe, bending down close over him.
Moe: Get up!
Curly gets up and walks away. Whereupon, Moe plants himself in exactly the same position Curly was previously in.

10. MED SHOT — RATH'S OFFICE
Moe turns around comfortably on the couch and gets ready for a good snooze. Rath takes this.
Rath: (ironically) If you three are geniuses, this is all right ... but if you're not....
And as Rath scowls, the Three Stooges simultaneously get to their feet.
Three Stooges: What?
Rath: You'll find out. (picks up script) Now, listen ... this script needs a few changes. Our hero, a G-Man, is confronting Two-Face Maloney, Public Enemy No. 2.
Curly: (butting in) Oh! A face for each guy!
Moe gives Curly a look and he freezes up.
Rath: I won't go into detail, but what we need is a smashing finish!
MLC: Yes ... yes ... yes ... yes ... yes ... yes ... yes ... yes ... yes....
Moe: NO! (they freeze up) What is the finish?
Rath jumps to his feet and explodes.
Rath: How should I know? That's why I sent for you! (thoroughly exasperated) *Think of something*!!

11. CLOSE SHOT — Stooges
Moe assumes an attitude of deep thinking, looks at Curly who has a blank expression on his face. Larry sneaks out.
Moe: (to Curly) Come on ... use your head.
As he gives him a terrific kick in the pants, Curly lets out a yell.

12. CLOSE-UP — Curly
He goes into an attitude of deep thinking, and we hear a SOUNDTRACK of springs and gears unwinding. Over this soundtrack, Curly is heaving up and down from the terrific effort of thinking.

13. TWO SHOT – Moe and Curly
Moe, patting Curly on the back, says.
Moe: Atta boy ... think harder. Lemme have it now ... give it to me!
We hear the gear noise stop, and Curly stops his panting, turning to Moe.
Curly: I can't think of a thing.
Moe: Think about this!
He gives him a poke. He looks off, sees Larry on couch and goes over. Larry is snoring. Moe kicks his feet and Larry wakes up.
Moe: What're you doing?
Larry: I'm thinking.
Moe lifts him from couch by the hair.

14. CLOSE SHOT – Rath
He is working himself up into a frenzy, shaking in his anger something like Curly did in his thinking scene.

15. CLOSE SHOT – Moe and Curly
Curly points at Rath.
Curly: Look! He's *thinking*!

16. FULL SHOT – Stooges
Moe turns to Larry and says,
Moe: Start playing!
Larry, who has taken his violin from the case, starts playing "Old Folks at Home."

17. CLOSE SHOT – Larry
As he plays, we see his pants start slipping lower and lower, with each sweep of the bow. When they drop almost to his knees, he reaches down and pulls them up. (Note: He wears extra long shirttails, which cover his long underwear.)

18. FULL SHOT
Moe is pacing up and down, doing a Felix the Cat walk, trying to think. Curly follows him. Then Moe stops suddenly.
Moe: I've got it: the scene opens on a stormy night and the wind is howling.
Larry howls in Moe's ear. He socks Larry.
Moe: There's a dame up on the balcony ... she's covered with rings and jewelry. They call her Julio ... but we'll call her Jewelryette, for short. A guy at the foot of the ladder is roamin' around with a banjo ... we'll call him Romeo. He's hummin' a tune to her while roamin.' (dramatically) Friends, Romans and countrymen, lend me your ears. And he needed 'em, cause her Uncle Tom was comin' 'round the corner, he was.
Curly at this, breaks in with a shuffle, saying,
Curly: Hallelujah! Hey, hey! Hallelujah!
Larry: Halley Selassio! Hey, hey! Halley Selassio!
As he points across in front of Moe, Moe gives him a look, then taking his hat off, he hands it over to Larry who is standing on the other side of him.
Moe: Hold this.
He turns and gives Curly a sock. Taking his hat from Larry, he puts it on again and starts all over.
Moe: Friends, Romans, countrymen ... lend me your ears....
At this point Larry breaks in with,
Larry: Hallelujah! Hey, hey!

Whereupon Moe gives him a look, takes off his hat and hands it to Curly, turns and gives Larry a belt. He puts on the hat again and starts once more.

Moe: Friends, Romans and countrymen....

At this point, both Larry and Curly, from opposite directions, join in.

Larry & Curly: Hallelujah! Hey, hey!

Moe, now thoroughly burned, takes off his hat once more, gives a glance at each of them ... then realizing he wants to hit them both, quickly hands the hat over to the boss, sitting across the desk from them. As Moe turns to give the boys a belt, the boss, now thoroughly burned and holding Moe's hat, yells,

Rath: Hey! Hey!

Intending to stop this nonsense; but before he can continue, the Three Stooges do a running dive over the desk at him. He goes backwards over his chair, and the four of them land in a heap on the floor. Moe sits on his chest, and continues the story....

Moe: Friends, Romans and countrymen, lend me your ears. Two-Face Maloney cuts off his ears, hands them to him and says, "I'll not only lend 'em to you ... you can keep 'em." Boy, is that a story, or is it?

19. CLOSE SHOT — Rath

As he comes from behind the desk, furious, confronting the boys.

Rath: No wonder I haven't seen you. I remember now ... I left orders to fire you three years ago!

Curly: Hmmm! How time flies!

Rath: If you three are not out of here when I get back, I'll have you thrown out! You're fired!

He exits, jamming Moe's hat onto his head.

20. CLOSE SHOT — Stooges at desk

Curly: Now what're we gonna do?

Moe: We gotta do something colossal ... something anemic ... big, mediocre stuff! ... To get in good with the boss.

As Moe says this, he unconsciously picks up a rubber stamp from the desk.

Curly: Huh! You took the words right out of my mouth.

Moe: Then take them back.

He gives Curly a belt on the forehead with the rubber stamp he is holding in his hand. As Curly lets out a yell and turns, we see on his forehead is stamped "Fuller Rath" (hand written, like a signature). Moe takes this, looking from Curly's head to the rubber stamp, then brightens.

Moe: I got it!

Curly: Got what?

Moe: An idea. With this stamp, we'll run the studio ... we'll do things ... big things. We're on our way to fame and misfortune.

He starts to write a letter on stationery on Rath's desk; stamps it and all exit, Curly stepping in the wastebasket but marching on without heeding it.

Shots #21 through 43 continue essentially as filmed, with Swinehardt and the actors on the soundstage. The letter that Moe hands to Swinehardt is actually the forged letter from shot #20. The often-edited-for-TV kissing scene is not scripted but appears as a margin note without direction. Otherwise, the script continues as filmed, up to the point when the leading lady quits.

44. Interior Rath's office
Director and Yes Man are in the scene.
Swinehardt: When will Mr. Rath return?
YM: I told you it will be quite some time.
With this he exits, as the director yells after him,
Swinehardt: I'll not leave here until I've had this out with him!

Back to the Stooges, and script shots #45–51 again continue as filmed, with Curly in drag filling in for the leading lady. Curly and Larry's "love scene" plays out. Moe comes in, congratulates everyone, and slaps Curly on the back. His wig flies off, and Curly catches it.

52. Moe: (dramatically) Here's where Two-Face Maloney comes in, but there's no one to play the part. What will I do?
He walks some more, thinking. The script girls enters, gives him a look and says sarcastically,
Script Girl: Why don't you play it yourself?
Moe: Why don't you mind your own business? (then, thinking once more, says suddenly) I've got it! I'll play it myself! (turning to cameraman) Ready! Camera!

53. MED LONG SHOT
Script Girl: Now this is where Two-Face Maloney comes in.
Larry: Two-Face Maloney? What's he got two faces for?
Curly: I know ... double feature. One face for each picture.
Moe: (gives Curly a slap) Come on ... get going!
He and script girl exit from the scene.

54. CLOSE SHOT at camera
Moe enters the scene.
Moe: (to cameraman) All ready?
The cameraman nods.
Moe: Camera! Action!
And then Moe runs out of the scene.

55. FULL SHOT — Interior on set
Curly has just finished lighting a candle that is standing on a table.
Curly: (to Larry) Don't leave me, Sir Porcupine ... I'm afraid of myself in the dark.
Larry, who has been pacing up and down, comes to a stop in front of the window.
Larry: Don't be afraid, little gal. Porky will protect you.

56. CLOSER SHOT — Curly and Larry
(standing near window) As Larry finishes his lines, we see a face appear in profile at the window ... with a grotesque mask on it. Curly, seeing this, lets out a yell pointing toward it.
Curly: Look! Who's that?
Larry wheels around and looks.

57. CLOSE-UP — Face at window
The head of the mask turns around, and we see that it is cut in half at the nose, the other side disclosing Moe's face.
Moe: (as he turns) It's me! Two-Face Maloney!

He starts crawling through the window. Pan as he comes up to Curly. Curly shrinks back in fear.

58. MED CLOSE SHOT — The Stooges
    Curly: (in fear) What do you want?
    Moe: (menacingly) I want your husband!
    Curly: He's not home. He's gone fishing.
    Moe: Has he got worms?
    Curly: Yeah, but he's gone anyway.
    Moe: Well, I'll stick around a while!
   Walking over to a table, he sees a quart bottle half full of liquor and picks it up, presumably to read the label.
    Moe: Ah! Old Homicide Rye! Nine years old. (turning to Larry and Curly with a scowl) Excuse me while I flirt with the child.
   Removing the cork from the bottle, he puts the whiskey to his lips and drinks lustily.

59. CLOSE-UP — Moe
   He brings the bottle down, makes a very wry face and turns as if to spit.

60. MED LONG SHOT — group
   Moe, still making a wry face, turns and spits on the floor next to the curtain. There is an explosion as the liquor lands, and the curtain ignites starting a blaze.

INSERT: Of curtain, as it starts to blaze.

BACK TO SCENE:
    Moe: (to Curly and Larry) Keep acting! Make it real! Yell for help!

61. FULL SHOT — Interior on set
   Both curtains are now ablaze, as Moe, directing and acting at the same time, says,
    Moe: Keep acting!
   Curly lets out a fake scream, throwing himself onto the couch.
    Curly: Firemen! HELP! Oh, woe is me! Oh woe, woe!
   He rushes to Larry and sobs on his shoulder. He turns, comes up and starts to sob on Larry again, but Larry steps aside and Curly goes on his face. He gets up and acts all over the place.
    Curly: We are lost....
    Larry: (breaking in) ... the Captain shouted as he staggered down the stairs!
   Moe bumps their heads together.
    Moe: Keep acting, you fools!! Keep acting! (then continues) This will be the big punch of the picture! Our jobs depend on this! (turning off scene, he hollers to the prop man) Get that empty gunpowder can ... quick!

62. MED SHOT — Cameraman and crew
   The prop man in the foreground hollers,
    Prop Man: Yes sir!
   And dashes out of the scene.

63. CLOSE SHOT — Interior at side of set
   Another prop man is on with a couple of cans of powder, prop box, etc. On the wall hangs buckets, labeled: FOR FIRE ONLY. They are numbered. First prop man comes into the scene.
    1st Prop Man: Quick! Give me something to empty this powder into!
   He turns and starts to take the lid from the top of the powder can, as the second

3. *Discovered Treasures* (Seguine)

prop man looks around ... spots the fire buckets, takes one down and empties the sand out of it. He sets it down, and the first prop man pours the powder into it. We read # 13 on the bucket.
1st Prop Man: You should've had this all ready....
And as he finishes emptying the powder, he runs out of the scene with the empty powder can, followed by the second prop man.

64. MED SHOT — from Cameraman's angle
The set is blazing quite furiously.
Cameraman: (becoming uneasy, shouts to Moe) That fire is getting a little dangerous! Hadn't you better put it out?

65. MED SHOT — the Stooges
Moe stops his acting for a second to answer,
Moe: What? We're just starting to get some good stuff! Keep the camera going! (turns to Larry and Curly) Too bad the boss isn't here to see this beautiful scene!
They continue ad lib acting.

66. MED SHOT — Cameraman and crew
Shooting toward the set, which has increased blazing and is now burning dangerously.
Cameraman: Come on! These guys are nuts; let's get out of here before we roast.
As they tear from the scene, Rath, the boss, comes walking in. He is almost knocked down by the stampeding crew and cameraman, as they tear out. Madly, he rushes in to the Three Stooges.

67. MED CLOSE SHOT
Rath approaches the three boys furiously.
Rath: What is the meaning of this? I thought you were fired.
Moe: Right! This is the fire scene! ... where Two-Face Maloney sets the house on fire.
Rath: (yells) Put OUT that fire!!
Moe: (undaunted, continues) He tries to make love to the heroine, but she kicks him in the solar plexus, and that's where she sets the place on fire!

68. CLOSE-UP — Rath
He is exploding with indignation. With a voice like a cannon roar he screams,
Rath: PUT OUT THIS FIRE!!!

69. CLOSE-UP — the Stooges
They react.
MLC: Fire? What fire?
They look around and realize that the whole stage is ablaze.

70. LONG SHOT
(gunning down from the height) As the boys look around, they see that they are encircled by a ring of flame.

71. CLOSE-UP — The Stooges and Rath
They react and begin to get busy, running in all directions, trying to put out the fire.

72. MED CLOSE SHOT — a water cooler
A water cooler is in evidence. Curly rushes in, takes a lily cup, fills it with water, then drinks but does not swallow it; refills the lily cup with water and dashes to the nearest flame, spits the water on the flame, then pours the contents of the cup on it.

73. MEDIUM SHOT
Larry rushes to box containing axe and saw. On glass is inscribed: "In case of fire break glass." He smashes glass and runs out, leaving the tools inside.

74. CLOSE-UP — Moe and Rath
Moe: Quick! Give me your coat!
Rath complies, and Moe rushes to the nearest blaze, begins to beat it with the coat; suddenly finds the coat is blazing, and drops it, leaving it to burn.

75. CLOSE-UP — Rath
Rath: (excitedly) My wallet, with a thousand dollars in it, you fool!

76. MED SHOT AT FIRE
The set is blazing as Larry rushes in with a big fire extinguisher in his hands. He tries to squirt it on the fire, but it doesn't work. Quickly he reads the label: "TO OPERATE, TURN UPSIDE DOWN." Larry scratches his head for a second, then putting the extinguisher down, he uses it to lean against as he stands on his head. Just then, Moe rushes in.
Moe: (excitedly) What are you doing?
Larry points to the inscription on the fire extinguisher. Moe grabs him and pulls him up, then smacks him.
Moe: Get out of here, or I'll turn you inside out! Go on ... grab those fire buckets!
Moe picks up the extinguisher, turns it upside down and squirts himself in the face as Larry dashes in with a bucket of sand, which he aims at the fire. The weight of the bucket swings him around and he throws the sand right in Moe's face.

77. MED SHOT — Moe
As he sputters and spits out a mouthful of sand, fuming with irritation. Curly comes dashing into the scene, holding a fire hose in one hand, while in the other, he has a double-nozzle-Y-shaped. As he stops, Moe looks at it questioningly.
Moe: What's the idea of two of those things?
Curly: I'm in a hurry.
Slaps Curly on the back of the head.
Moe: Then get going! Fasten that to the water tank!
Curly: I tank I go now.
He runs out before Moe can hit him again.

78. FULL SHOT — Exterior at side of stage
Shot of automobile parts, etc., getting over that this section might be the garage of the studio. There are three large tanks in evidence, marked "oil," "distillate," "gasoline." The biggest one says "gasoline." Next to the gasoline tank is a fire hydrant. As Curly runs toward it, a gust of smoke comes into the scene, blinding him. Coughing and sputtering, he gropes his way around and fastens the hose coupling to the gasoline tank by mistake. Quickly, he turns on the gasoline and rushes out of the scene.

79. MED LONG SHOT — Interior of set
The blaze has almost died down as Rath and Moe have played the extinguisher on it. Suddenly Curly bursts in, shoves them aside and with a very cocky manner, says,
Curly: Step aside and let a man put out a fire that knows how!
Without a word of warning, he turns the lever that controls the nozzles, and a double stream of gasoline sprays into the smoldering set, igniting the almost extinguished

fire anew, and causing a tremendous conflagration. Without realizing that he has reignited the fire, he turns to Rath.
Curly: You'll be crazy about our picture.
As he says this,

80. CLOSER SHOT
The streams in the hose become ignited, and now instead of streams of gasoline, they are streams of flame.

81. CLOSE-UP — Larry
behind Curly
Larry: (frantically) Shut it off!

82. MED LONG SHOT — group
As Curly turns to see what Larry is yelling about, he turns the blazing hose on Moe, who is busily bent over beating out a bit of fire and has not noticed what Curly has done. The flame hits Moe in the fanny. He lets out a scream and grabs Rath, who is beside him, using him as a shield. Rath now gets the full benefit of the blaze as it contacts his rear. Moe screams at Curly.
Moe: Shut if off!!
Curly turns to Moe, and as he does, the stream of fire hits Larry, who is on the opposite side.

83. CLOSE-UP — Larry
As the flames hit him, he screams.
MED LONG SHOT — Moe, Rath, Curly and Larry
They rush to Curly and start to upbraid him. Curly looks down, sees the burning hose, lots of "woo woo woos!" ... drops it, picks up an axe and chops nozzle off the hose, thinking that will stop the flame. He keeps chopping sections off but the flame continues unabated. Moe rushes to Larry.
Moe: Where did you get that bucket of sand? Come on ... we better get some more!
Together, they rush from the scene.

85. MED SHOT — Side of stage
It is filled with smoke. Moe and Larry dash in to a section where on the wall are hung sand filled fire buckets. Grabbing the last two, Larry dashes out. Moe sees the #13 bucket on the floor (which we previously established as the one containing the gunpowder). Picking it up, he rushes from the scene.

86. MED LONG SHOT
Rath and Curly have the blaze almost beaten out as Larry rushes in and throws sand on them. Moe comes dashing in and with one mighty heave, he throws the gunpowder into the flame, causing an EXPLOSION.

87. LONG SHOT
When the smoke clears, what is left of the set is devoid of people with the exception of Rath, who is hanging on the chandelier, his clothes smoldering and smoking.
As the camera pans to the roof, we see the cutouts of the Three Stooges, where they went through it.

88. MED CLOSE SHOT — imprints on roof
The three battered Stooges stick their heads through the holes.
Moe: (goofily) Cut! Print that one!

89. MED LONG SHOT
The Stooges fall back through the imprints, taking Rath and the chandelier with him, as they pass him. The four of them stretch out.

FADE OUT

Hidden Gems

The preceding discussion contains only a sampling of the unknown and hidden gems in Jules White's files. Even though the Three Stooges' main body of film work was done in the shorts area, and in spite of the limited budgets used to produce those films, it is fascinating to find so much written material — and the occasional edited sequence — that never made it to theater screens.

For film historians, the scripts in these files provide heretofore unseen glimpses of Hollywood lore, artifacts that show that the Three Stooges filmography was created from the same processes typical in film production, regardless of budget or critical acclaim. And for fans, these unfilmed scenes provide new gems, and fans can cherish these films even more than they already do.

Moe: Cut! Print that one!

FADE OUT

Notes

This chapter features material based on writings by Brent Seguine previously featured in the following: "The Three Stooges' Hidden Hollywood," *The Three Stooges Journal* 100 (Winter 2001), pp. 14–16, 22; "More Three Stooges' Hidden Hollywood," *The Three Stooges Journal* 105 (Spring 2003), pp. 6–7, 14; "More Three Stooges' Hidden Hollywood," *The Three Stooges Journal* 106 (Summer 2003), pp. 12–14; "Rhythm and Weep, The Sitter Downers, You Nazty Spy!, and More Three Stooges' Hidden Hollywood," *The Three Stooges Journal* 111 (Fall 2004), pp. 13–14; *The Three Stooges Journal* 116 (Winter 2005), pp. 12–14, and *The Three Stooges Journal* 118 (Summer 2006), pp. 12–14, and *The Three Stooges Journal* 119 (Fall 2006), pp. 12–13.

1. Other published filmographies list this film as Columbia production #168; White's script is labeled #206.
2. *The Three Stooges Scrapbook* (Lenburg et al. 1982) filmography reports *Movie Maniacs'* filming dates as 10/25/35–10/29/35. The film's cast and production call sheet, attached to the script, is dated 11/27/35.

Works Cited

Lenburg, Jeff, Joan Howard Maurer, and Greg Lenburg. *The Three Stooges Scrapbook.* Secaucus, N.J.: Citadel, 1982.

4

A Comedy of Errors: Mistakes and the Humorous Results in the Three Stooges Films

Peter Seely

The years that the Three Stooges made short films for Columbia, 1934–1959, were a period of tremendous change in the United States politically and economically, and the motion picture industry was not immune to these changes. While storylines often reflected the social and political changes of the period, the economic troubles facing motion picture studios were often reflected in the quality of the later films of the Stooges. As film costs continued to spiral, budgets for the Short Subjects Department at Columbia remained constant. According to Columbia Shorts director Edward Bernds, "On the average, the two-reelers were budgeted at around $35,000. It wasn't that budgets decreased over the years; rather, it was that costs rose sharply and the dollar simply didn't buy as much. So the budgets remained the same, but you weren't able to stretch them as far as they could in the 1930s" (Okuda and Watz 1986, p. 14).

While not the sole reason, the stretching of the budgets was primarily responsible for the decline in quality of the Stooges films. Jules White, as head of the Short Subjects Department, offered this: "We were always fighting the budget and the time. I had a month's pay on the line with every picture, so I had to pinch every penny. That's a hell of a burden to have on your shoulders. I wince when I see some of the comedies now—if only I didn't have to skimp on them" (Okuda and Watz 1986, p. 19). The result of such skimping was numerous errors in the films of the Three Stooges, especially in their later efforts.

This chapter spotlights the errors of several Stooges films, which offer evidence of the austere budgets at Columbia and which also led many times to unexpectedly humorous results. Our examination is mostly qualitative, as a completely accurate quantitative study would be nearly impossible. Errors that might be glaringly obvious to an editor, writer, producer, or actor who worked on a given film might go virtually unnoticed by a viewer who didn't have direct contact with the picture. Confirming these errors with those who did work on the films is now impossible, as nearly all these individuals are deceased.

Therefore, the purpose here is to highlight some of the more noteworthy and obvious instances of mistakes, those apparent to viewers who saw the films during their original run in theaters and those seen by viewers in multiple airings on television. The chapter also looks at some of those errors not immediately discernible but apparent upon repeated viewings. Any quantitative references should be viewed not as absolute measurements but rather as establishing the prominence of mistakes in a particular category. Of the short films, 86 were found to have mistakes, but there were probably many more.

We start with the premise that mistakes in motion pictures are inevitable. Just as there are mistakes in any craft or endeavor, so there are mistakes in film. Even blockbuster films with multimillion dollar budgets from recent years, such as *The Matrix, Harry Potter and the Philosopher's Stone, Titanic, Star Wars—Revenge of the Siths*, and *Jurassic Park* have become notorious for their continuity errors and mistakes.[1] It makes sense, then, that pictures with small budgets, a multitude of different actors, and hectic production schedules would also produce errors. Jules White described how mistakes were not merely a reality but an economic necessity:

> If [shooting pickups or sight gags] was absolutely imperative, I'd wait until the next picture and shoot it while all the equipment was out. We had very little of that. We couldn't afford much. You'd take the best you could get for the money ... If you can't afford a pie, eat a cookie [Bruskin 1984, pp. 245–246].

White's business relationship to Columbia Pictures was significant in the gradual decline of production quality usually acknowledged by Stooge scholars and critics. White's remarks even betray a certain pride in making lemonade from lemons, or a silk purse from a sow's ear. His remarks about the absence of dolly shots from most Columbia short subjects reveal much about the prevalent attitude of the studio: "I did as few moving shots as I had to. Anything that cost money was no good for me" (Bruskin 1984, p. 244).

For our analysis in this chapter, we divide the errors in the films of the Three Stooges into six categories: editing, continuity, dialogue, stunts and sight gags, sets and properties, and acting. Nevertheless, the examples often overlap categories and shouldn't be considered exclusively within a dimension. For instance, an error discussed under dialogue may have actually been the result of poor acting. A mistake in continuity may have been the result of poor editing. Each example is cited in a category according to its most prominent characteristics.

Editing

Virtually any mistake left in a film can be considered an editing mistake, but we limit ourselves here to the jump cut in order to concentrate on what might be called "deliberate mistakes," or edits that were intentionally made to establish continuity between two different shots. A jump cut is "an image that jumps slightly from one screen position to another during a cut" (Zettl 1976, p. 453). At least 17 films and 20 different examples of the jump cut have been identified in the Stooges films, though undoubtedly there were many other, less noticeable jump cuts.

Jump cuts in Stooges films generally were used to connect two different shots from a single sight gag that had been filmed. Rather than film a continuous succession of sight material, directors used the common single-camera method, one that required that they reset the camera when going from a one-shot to one featuring multiple subjects or when a flow of action was impossible to shoot in a continuous sequence.[2]

Columbia used the jump cut in two Stooges films where the intention was to show continuous action. In *They Stooge to Conga*, Moe hits Curly, then Larry, with a hammer, and a jump cut was apparently needed for the gag. Likely, director Del Lord tried to film it continuously and found it unusable. In *The Sitter Downers*, a male dog gives flowers to a female dog by transferring them from his mouth to hers. Lord was apparently unable to follow the subsequent retreat of the female into the doghouse, followed by the male.

Because of the danger involved in many of the stunts in Stooges films, directors needed to use the jump cut in order to give the illusion of executing the stunts. In *Hoi Polloi* and *In the Sweet Pie and Pie*, the Stooges follow a dance instructor, who leaps out a window and into an outdoor fountain. In a similar scene in *False Alarms*, Moe and Larry bust down a door and land on top of it. The door slides toward a fireman's pole, and they fall down the hole in the floor and into a fire truck. Both of these scenes would have been impossible to film without causing injury to the actors.

Though in some instances the jump cut was justified, at other times the cuts were clumsy and obvious. In *A Plumbing We Will Go*, there is a short scene in which Larry catches the end of a pickaxe in Moe's suspenders. A cut to a close-up of Moe preserves the continuity. When the film was remade as *Vagabond Loafers*, however, director Edward Bernds pieced together the old two-shot and a new one, causing an unconvincing jump cut. The error is magnified when Larry's retort of "All right" is used in both shots. A similarly clumsy cut happens in *Beer Barrel Polecats*, where an establishing shot shows Moe falling face first and landing on an ice cream cone. The subsequent cut jumps slightly in action, and a few frames later the ice cream has disappeared from Moe's face.

Continuity

Continuity is "the impression that events, scenes, and shots flow smoothly and naturally in proper sequence, without any inconsistent transitions" (Weiner 1990, p. 110). A total of 34 films and 41 different examples of continuity errors were discovered in the Stooges films.

Automatic Dialogue Replacement (ADR)

The most obvious examples of continuity errors occur through ADR. In some films, the voice doesn't match the motion of the mouth. In *Dunked in the Deep* and *Commotion on the Ocean*, for example, Shemp's snoring noises do not match the movement of his mouth. Other errors of this type occur with Moe in *Flagpole Jitters* and with Moe and Christine McIntyre in *Of Cash and Hash*.

In at least two films, editors used ADR to provide additional dialogue to scenes where the actors' mouths couldn't be seen. In *Dizzy Doctors*, for instance, Vernon Dent chases the Stooges through a hallway and exhorts doctors to help him in the chase. The voice is lower than Dent's and is clearly not his. *Rip, Sew, and Stitch*, a remake with stock footage of the earlier film *Sing a Song of Six Pants*, has one scene in which actor Phil Arnold returns to the Pip Boys Cleaners, asking the Stooges to make a pair of pants to match the jacket the Stooges had ruined with a razor blade. In the original film, the scene ends as the Stooges faint. In the second film, Moe assures him they will alter the pants, and the off-camera customer says, "Thanks, so long." The voice is clearly not Arnold's and probably belongs to Columbia contract player Monty Collins.

Storyline

Some Stooges films have scenes that appear to make no sense in the context in which they are seen. Probably, such errors were caused by scenes or shots being cut from the final film. Toward the end of *Micro-Phonies*, when actress Symona Boniface exclaims, "As for these imposters...," the Stooges inexplicably emerge in pain from under a table. In *A Bird in the Head*, the Stooges are frightened of mad scientist Vernon Dent, yet in the next scene they are laughing and joking with him. In *We Want Our Mummy*, one shot shows a mummified Curly covered in a single bandage, but in the next shot viewers see that his arms are taped separately from his body.

Brent Seguine's discovery of additional script material from some Stooges films, as described in Chapter 3, points out a continuity error in *Rhythm and Weep*. Seguine notes that an additional scene was filmed with three women dancers dressed as the Stooges. This explains how the ladies mysteriously end up dressed in men's clothing at the end of the film.

Vector Changes

A vector is "a perceivable force with a direction and magnitude" (Zettl 1976, p. 392). At times in the Stooges films inconsistency occurs from one shot to another in terms of direction or some other error in terms of movement. In *Calling All Curs*, Cy Schindell answers a door to find the Stooges looking for a kidnapped dog. Schindell closes the door but, realizing who the callers are, does a doubletake toward the door; yet in the next shot, as the door is suddenly busted down, Schindell is now facing away from the door and gets flattened by it.

A similar vector change happens in *Hokus Pokus*. In the film's climax, the Stooges are on a flagpole that is breaking. When it finally gives way, it hurls the Stooges through a window just below. They land on the floor in a heap, but as the camera cuts away, we see the Stooges spread out and separated, facing in the same direction.

Remade Films and Stock Footage

Though budgets got tighter at Columbia in Short Subjects, the pressure to put out product continued, and the department was forced to remake earlier films (Bruskin 1984, p. 265). Under this practice, the Stooges would film a small number of new scenes, which would be inserted into old films, creating only slight variations in the plot. This economic reality was responsible for a multitude of inevitable errors. When stock footage was used in Curly shorts, problems occasionally arose when editors needed to combine footage of Curly before and after his first stroke (in 1945). As even casual viewers of the Stooges are aware, Curly's physical performance and spoken dialogue showed how much he was affected by the stroke. Gone were many of his trademark acrobatic moves and childlike shrieks. This lack of continuity was most evident in *Beer Barrel Polecats*, which featured stock footage from the earlier film *So Long, Mr. Chumps*, with a noticeable difference in Curly's energy.

Even more absurd were the film remakes featuring Shemp Howard and Joe Besser. As Moe and Larry were aging, the studio had no qualms about mining classic slapstick footage from earlier years, no matter how old the footage.

Guns A-Poppin'! was a remake of the 1945 film *Idiots Deluxe*, with Besser replacing Curly in the newly filmed scenes. In a scene where Moe is on the witness stand, there is a cut between a two-shot with Vernon Dent from the earlier 1945 film to a one-shot of Moe in 1957, who is wearing a different jacket, sporting a different haircut, and acting with a much softer demeanor. This mellower Moe was also used in close-ups filmed for *Hot Stuff*, a remake of *Fuelin' Around*.

Two other remade Shemp films also contain continuity errors. In the 1955 film *Fling in the Ring* (a remake of the first Shemp film *Fright Night*), a gangster named Big Mike is trying to fix a fight against a boxer whom the Stooges are training. In *Fling in the Ring*, Big Mike is played by Frank Sully; in *Fright Night*, Big Mike is played by Harold Brauer. Big Mike's accomplices are also played by different actors. This deception works until we see stock footage of Big Mike and company chasing the Stooges around a warehouse, and the old Big Mike and gang magically appear. And in *Who Done It?* (remade as *For Crimin' Out Loud*), the Stooges are detectives hired by Councilman Goodrich (Emil Sitka) for protection. At the end of the film, the Stooges rescue Mr. Goodrich. It is the first time they have all met, and the councilman asks, "Are you the detectives?" But when the scene is reprised in *For Crimin' Out Loud*, the councilman's ignorance no longer makes sense because he is hiring the Stooges from past experience with them.

An incredible error of continuity occurs in *Triple Crossed*, a remake with Besser of the Shemp film *He Cooked His Goose*. During a scene where Moe chases Besser up a chimney, he shoots and apparently hits Besser, except the editors leave in Shemp's cry of pain. In *Rusty Romeos*, a remake with Besser of the Shemp film *Corny Casanovas*, Joe Besser is courting a young lady, and we clearly see a picture of himself he has given to her as a present. Then, during a cutaway shot we see that Shemp's photo has been substituted for Besser's.

Dialogue

We have identified at least 19 films and 14 instances of mistakes occurring in Stooges films because of lines fumbled by actors. Five of those instances actually ended up as stock footage for other films. Like most categories of mistakes, the numbers increased in the later years of the Stooges' short subjects career because of Jules White's aversion to filming pickup lines. Many films, therefore, ended up with stammering delivery, unintentionally changed words, and mispronunciations.

Shemp Howard was the primary culprit of the fumbled lines. In at least six films Shemp fumbled a line and the producer chose to leave it in. Aside from the policy on pickups, there may be at least one other explanation for this decision. White considered Shemp to be the funniest Stooge on his own (Bruskin 1984, p. 235), and he thus may have had more leeway or propensity than the others to ad lib or change lines. In a tight situation in *Dopey Dicks*, Shemp combines the names of Moe and Larry and screams, "Mary." In *Scrambled Brains*, a door hits Moe in the face and his teeth fall out. An obviously ad-libbing Shemp offers, "Oh, his gum came out. His gums, I think."

Other actors were also guilty of muffed lines, including two instances that made it into two separate films. In *Hold That Lion!* and *Booty and the Beast*, a lion is seen roaming through a train. As alarmed passengers comment on this phenomenon, one person can be heard to utter, "Duck under the lion." And in *All Gummed Up* and *Bubble Trouble*, an angry Emil Sitka yells, "You haven't heard of me the last of me yet."

Stunts and Sight Gags

Errors with stunts can happen for many different reasons, including poor production execution, the undisguised use of stunt doubles, and the use of gags in remade films.

Poor Production Execution

Sometimes sight gag errors or stunt errors occur because of poor production execution rather than through any fault of the actors. In the final scene of *Three Little Sew and Sews*, the Stooges are obviously being suspended in the air with piano wire (Forester 1982, p. 45). In *The Ghost Talks*, the back of Shemp's shirt is inexplicably protruding from his body as a frog falls down the collar. And in *Sappy Bullfighters*, a film that employs stock footage from the Curly film *What's the Matador?*, a cut from a wide shot of a stuntman on an out-of-control bull to a closer shot of Joe Besser reveals that the actor is panicking, yet his bull is hardly moving.

Stunt Doubles

Given the physical nature of slapstick comedy, actors in Stooges films were often required to have stunt doubles, especially in the more dangerous scenes. Indeed, for a few such scenes, dummies were used. In the later years of their career at Columbia, the Stooges in particular could not perform some of the stunts required in the scripts (Forester 1982, p. 45). In such cases the producers employed stunt men who approximated the physical appearance of the actors, and the director shot the scenes in a longer shot. But often these attempts to mask the deception were insufficient.

Again, most of these problems occurred during the relatively inexpensive

Shemp films, and Shemp himself often needed a body double for the more dangerous or acrobatic stunts. In *Who Done It?* and *For Crimin' Out Loud*, Shemp has been poisoned and becomes spasmodic. In this sequence of fast cuts, the viewer can actually see the face of Shemp's double. In *Blunder Boys*, Shemp is riding a mechanical horse. In the longer shots, the stunt double is considerably heavier than Shemp. And in *Goof on the Roof*, Shemp crashes through the ceiling and lands inside a television, but the body in the television is clearly a dummy.

Other double deceptions occur in *Fuelin' Around*, *Hot Stuff*, and *Self-Made Maids*. In the first two films, Larry Fine pours an acid-like concoction around himself in a circle on the floor. As the stunt double waits for the floor to come crashing down, the viewer plainly sees that the actor is a double, one who is much thinner than Larry. For *Self-Made Maids*, Moe Howard is called upon to play three different roles. In a scene where the Stooges are tormenting Moe as an older man, the viewer can see that the face of the younger Moe is not Moe, but a substitute.

Films Remade after Shemp's Death

Perhaps one of the most striking examples of Columbia Pictures' austerity, and Moe and Larry's desperation to keep their comedy team going, occurred after Shemp died of a heart attack in 1955. In 1956, Columbia released four films: *Rumpus in the Harem*, *Commotion on the Ocean*, *Hot Stuff*, and *Scheming Schemers*. These four films were remade and adapted from earlier films and made extensive use of stock footage. As had been the practice at Columbia for years, additional footage was shot. Some of these new scenes featured an encounter with just Moe and Larry, with Shemp occasionally referred to in the third person. Others had Moe, Larry, and a fake Shemp, played by his double Joe Palma. These scenes were filmed without actually showing Shemp's face, yet even a casual observer could tell the difference.

This deception is most obvious in *Hot Stuff*, and it is Palma's voice that betrays the deception. Palma utters his only word of these four films, a gruff "Right!" in response to a command from Moe. Twice in this film, Palma tries to imitate Shemp's trademark "bee-bee-bee-bee" noise, with unsatisfactory results.

Sets and Properties

Most motion pictures make extensive use of sets and properties to simulate environments. Today these environments are often achieved through sophisticated computer-generated effects created by highly paid special effects personnel. Even during the years of the Stooges films at Columbia, it was accepted practice to matte actors in a studio on top of a film, such as a scene that is supposed to take place in a moving car. Often this would require a suspension of reality, since the viewers understand what they see but accept it anyway. But sometimes these backdrops are so artificial that suspending reality is nearly impossible and instead they call attention to the artificial nature of the shot.

The same can also be said of certain properties. Animals, for example, can be impractical to use in slapstick films but have such inherent comic value that filmmakers use them anyway, substituting a stuffed or fake animal for the real thing. When that animal exhibits uncharacteristic behavior, it calls attention to its ersatz nature, producing (perhaps unintended) humorous results. In *Ants in the Pantry*, at a society party, Larry is chasing a mouse with a hammer. His attempts to beat the mouse senseless fail when the mouse appears to fly or leap off its human perches. In a similar fashion, a flying skunk is featured in *Cuckoo on a Choo Choo*, *I'm a Monkey's Uncle*, and *Stone Age Romeos*.

When inanimate properties take on animate characteristics, the results can also be awkward and unintentionally humorous. In *Knutzy Knights*, the Stooges are trying to prevent the celebratory blowing of trumpets by firing fruit into the bells of the horns. After getting lodged into the bell, the fruit inexplicably moves into the lead pipe. For *Heavenly Daze* and *Bedlam in Paradise*, the director tries to pass off a flat, painted board as a rain cloud, complete with two holes in the middle for the "rain" to come through. And Larry is surprised when he looks into a mirror and it breaks in *Gypped in the Penthouse*, but one can actually see a stick retreating and a hole in the wall behind the mirror after it breaks.

Actor Miscues

Several errors are the direct or indirect results of poor acting. In one of the most famous scenes in a Stooges film, for example, Curly is taking an oath in *Disorder in the Court* and consistently has problems remembering to raise his right hand. Later in the film, Curly is attempting to prove that a gun found at a murder scene was not loaded, but he winces in anticipation of the gun firing before he unintentionally proves the gun was, in fact, loaded.

In other examples, supporting actors had poor reactions in trying to execute a stunt. For instance, during a pie fight in *Pies and Guys*, an actress exhorts the pie throwers, "Now you stop that!" but closes her eyes in anticipation of a pie hitting her in the face. In *Malice in the Palace*, a guard sticks out his arms to break his fall after being knocked unconscious by a vase. And in *Goofs and Saddles*, during a card game, Curly asks for as many cards as he can get for a pair; actor Stanley Blystone apparently forgets that a pair is two and deals Curly three cards.

Two Stooges films feature obvious examples of poor acting by a supporting character, leading to an error. In *All the World's a Stooge,* an actor who should be disgusted smiles at Curly after delivering his line. And Tom Kennedy shows a delayed reaction of pain after hitting his hand on a pipe in *Loose Loot.*

To Err Is Human

Although we have presented mostly a qualitative study, some interesting — if unscientific — numbers emerge. Of the 97 films Curly made with the Stooges, we identified errors in 37 films, or 38 percent. Of Joe Besser's 16 films with the Stooges, 7 showed up with mistakes, or 44 percent. Moreover, of Shemp's 76 films, errors were identified in 42 pictures, or 55 percent.

While these numbers are unscientific, they correlate with the assertion made at the beginning: the longer the Stooges worked at Columbia, the more were the shortcuts taken with the production. When asked why the Columbia short subjects held up better than those of other studios, Jules White replied that "they were done a little bit better and cost a little bit less" (Bruskin 1984, p. 233).

White joined the Short Subjects Department in 1933, just a year before the Stooges began making films at Columbia. There is a correlation between the time White became more active in the directing of the Stooges films and the increasing number of errors. White's directorial debut with the Stooges came in the 1938 film *Three Missing Links,* number 34 of the 190 Stooges films at Columbia. Fourteen of the 33 films made by the Stooges before White's first film as director were identified with errors, or 42 percent. In films after White's directing debut, errors were identified in 70 out of 167 films, or 42 percent. But of the 101 films directed by White, 56 were identified with errors, or 55 percent. In contrast, of the 89 films that were directed by someone other than Jules White, 30 were identified with errors, or 34 percent.

The purpose here is not necessarily to blame White for the escalating number of errors in the Stooges comedies as their tenure wore on at Columbia. While White's comedies had a significantly higher percentage of errors than those by other directors, additional variables should be considered. For example, the large percentage of errors in films he directed is offset somewhat by the number of remakes and use of stock footage that resulted in certain mistakes being unavoidably repeated in later films. Though White took pride in his ability to produce low-budget, relatively high-quality short subjects, there is evidence that much of the impetus to do so came at the behest of Columbia Pictures (Bruskin 1984, pp. 260–261).

A more charitable way of viewing White's films with the Stooges, and of the Stooges' work at Columbia as a whole, may come in paying tribute to their ability to make consistently humorous, low-budget films while all motion picture studios, Columbia included, were concentrating most of their resources on higher-profile features. The fact that the Stooges survived the deaths of two crucial members of their comedy organization, amidst a climate of austerity and indifference within their own studio, was no mean feat. And for those who have watched these films over and over again on television, the error or mistake provides just one more layer and dimension of humor for their fans to cherish.

Notes

1. One of the most "Stooge-like" errors occurred in the 1987 motion picture *Three Men and a Baby*, where a cardboard person used in a crowd scene accidentally shows up in an inappropriate scene.
2. *Dizzy Doctors* is an example of one Stooges film where the jump cut was used to show an impossible action. Vernon Dent is chasing the Stooges through a hallway, and the Stooges alternately come out of doors on either side of the hall. This "nonerror" technique is repeated in several other films.

Works Cited

Bruskin, David N., ed. *Behind the Three Stooges: The White Brothers: Conversations with David N. Bruskin.* Metuchen, N.J.: Directors Guild of America, 1984.
Forester, Jeffrey. *The Stoogephile Trivia Book.* Chicago: Contemporary, 1982.
Okuda, Ted, and Edward Watz. *The Columbia Comedy Shorts: Two-Reel Hollywood Film Comedies, 1933–1958.* Jefferson, N.C.: McFarland, 1986.
Weiner, Richard. *Dictionary of Media and Communications.* New York: Webster's New World, 1990.
Zettl, Herbert. *Sight Sound Motion: Applied Media Aesthetics.* Belmont, Calif.: Wadsworth, 1976.

5

Hail Columbia! A Deconstruction of the Columbia Studios' Style in the Three Stooges and Other Comedy Shorts

Peter Seely

The terms "comedy short" and Columbia Studios are nearly synonymous in the minds of even the casual film observer, largely because of the long-lasting pervasiveness of the Three Stooges comedy films in American popular culture. When television arrived on the American scene in the late 1940s, it signaled a new era in mass entertainment, and no group was to be affected by this development more than the postwar "baby boomers." And by the late 1950s, as television was already firmly entrenched as an American pastime, it was the comedy shorts, particularly those of the Three Stooges, that seemed to find a ready-made audience.

Comedy shorts, or two-reel comedies, were short films produced by the major motion picture studios as filler to go along with triple feature presentations. Though they might be sold as a package by one studio along with other films, it wasn't mandatory that one studio's comedy shorts run with feature-length films produced by the same studio (Bruskin 1984, p. 239). It is safe to say that, at least in the case of the Three Stooges and Laurel and Hardy, the short subjects were more enduring and frequently of higher quality than the feature films they accompanied.

While Columbia shorts (almost exclusively because of the success of the Three Stooges) are more permanently ingrained in the minds of television viewers than are those produced by other studios, the short subjects were a staple of virtually all of the major studios, and several smaller ones as well. According to Leonard Maltin (1972, p. 3), the author of the definitive book on the subject of two-reel comedies, *The Great Movie Shorts*, each studio was able to create an identity even in its short subjects, one that was largely based on actors, writers, executives, the facilities, budgets, and whatever inherent identity the studio was already emoting.

This chapter describes the identity that existed at Columbia Studios during the years they produced short films (1934 to 1959). Many of the characteristics of the Three Stooges films, for example, can be referenced immediately by millions of American television viewers and moviegoers. This situation is due in large part to the comic genius of the Stooges, but it can also be traced through hundreds of shorts produced by Columbia, of which the Stooges were merely a part (though undeniably the biggest and most important part). The Stooges have been credited, and rightly so, with virtually defining a style and a genre (slapstick). But a close examination of the style of Columbia shorts not made by the Three Stooges reveals several commonalities and characteristics heretofore credited almost exclusively to the Three Stooges by casual viewers or those unfamiliar with Columbia's output.

The Hollywood Studio System and Short Films

Nearly every major film studio in Hollywood had a short films department: Warner Brothers, MGM, Paramount, RKO, Universal, and, of course, Columbia. Minor studios or entrepreneurs also were engaged in these activities, for example, the Hal Roach Studios, Mack Sennett, and Educational Pictures. According to Maltin (1972, pp. 3–27), the short films produced by the major studios were easily identifiable with that organization's style. MGM's short films, much like their features, were the "class" of the industry. RKO, the studio that brought viewers *Citizen Kane*, had the most elaborate sets and backgrounds. Warner Brothers shorts were perhaps the most eclectic, covering everything from comedies to musicals to newsreels to patriotic shorts. Those produced by Educational, and even a "major" such as Paramount, were almost always cheaply made, even more so than those made by Columbia.

Columbia Studios had a reputation far and wide as being a "lesser" studio than the other majors, associated more with "B" pictures than with high-quality major productions. That reputation began to change somewhat with the 1934 film *It Happened One Night*. They were, nonetheless, to carve out the most significant and most lasting piece of movie shorts history in the work of the Three Stooges: longer lasting than newsreels, *Our Gang,* and even Laurel and Hardy.

The "Columbia difference" will be discussed at greater length and with more specificity later in this chapter. But a good starting point is to examine some of the major people associated with shorts at Columbia. The head of that department was Jules White, the individual who was perhaps more responsible than anyone else for the style and humor of the Three Stooges. Further, it was White who hired an impressive array of talented individuals, people who could work in the same element, with mostly the same actors, the same sets, and much of the same production techniques, and achieve some level of quality and uniformity in the end. These individuals included directors such as White himself, Del Lord, and Edward Bernds; producers such as White, his older brother Jack, and Hugh McCollum; and writers such as Ellwood Ullman, Felix Adler, and Clyde Bruckman. These were the creative, "above-the-line" people who were largely responsible for the look that was adopted by Columbia. Music and sound effects were similarly to prove invaluable in establishing the Columbia shorts' identity.

To understand the essence of Columbia Studios' style, one must examine large numbers of comedy shorts in addition to those by the Three Stooges. The largest number examined here was made by comedian Andy Clyde (who made 78 short films for Columbia; see Maltin 1972, pp. 91–102). Also considered in this chapter are the short films by Buster Keaton, El Brendel, Charley Chase, Harry Langdon, Hugh Herbert, Monty Collins/Tom Kennedy, Joe Besser, Joe DeRita, Wally Vernon/Eddie Quillan, Gus Schilling/Richard Lane, and Walter Catlett.

The films of the Three Stooges were the most famous and most enduring of those produced by Columbia Studios, or any other studio. They have endured mostly because of the extraordinary talents possessed by each of the Stooges individually and the tremendous synergy they possessed as a comedy team. However, what they accomplished was not strictly of their own making. The numerous facets of Three Stooges comedies, many of which are described in this book, have become known to generations of film and television viewers, and their films contain some of the most recognizable and beloved moments in comedy history. But these films were often the product of an amazing team of producers, directors, writers, supporting actors, sound effects teams, acting extras, and stunt men, whose talents became most associated with the Three Stooges. Further, in some instances, other comics from the Columbia Studios stable with the same resources were able to equal the Stooges for comic effect. In other instances, the material may have been tried out on other comedy teams but rarely with the results produced by the Three Stooges.

A Brief History of Short Subjects at Columbia

Jules White was hired in 1934 to head the Columbia Short Subjects Department. In addition to Lord, White, Bruckman, Adler, McCollum, and

Bernds, White had hired his brother, Jack White, who was referred to most of the time as "Preston Black," apparently to avoid the garnishing of his wages by his first wife (Bruskin 1984, p. 148). Jack White had previously worked for the great slapstick director Mack Sennett and had built up a greater reputation to that point than had his brother Jules. In the estimation of Leonard Maltin (1972, pp. 6–7), the studio was at its peak in the late thirties and early forties: "There was an abundant use of location shooting, the gags were ingenious, the performers fresh, and the pace unexcelled."

According to actress Ann Doran, most filming took place in three to five days, and the "hours were backbreaking — twelve to sixteen hours a day" (Maltin 1972, p. 7). Filming time took even less when the budgets began to decrease during World War II, averaging between $14,000 and $20,000 for a film (Bruskin 1984, p. 221). Ellwood Ullman confirmed that the budgets were larger in the thirties, and more of Columbia's facilities were available for those films (Maltin 1972, p. 7). Columbia's Short Subjects Department closed in 1958.

The most famous and prolific of Columbia's group of short subjects comedians was the Three Stooges, who made 190 shorts. The Stooges' career spanned from Columbia's most heralded days to the times when films were made very quickly with small budgets. However, other comedians of note also made short film series with Columbia during that time.

Andy Clyde

This Scottish-born comedian made a total of 149 short films between 1929 and 1956 (Maltin 1972, pp. 94–102), 79 of those filmed for Columbia, starting in 1934 (the first 68 films were made for Educational Pictures, and two others were made in the 1950s for RKO). Clyde's film career nearly perfectly paralleled that of the Stooges at Columbia. The same group of writers, producers, and directors was used for these films, and to a great extent so was the group of supporting actors. Clyde's output had much in common with the Stooges. While he didn't travel through time and space nearly as much as the Three Stooges did, the same sorts of storylines were often used, and the evolution from stronger stories to greater use of slapstick that characterized the films of the Stooges was also present in the films of Clyde.

Clyde's identity in the Columbia shorts was that of an eccentric old man. With his trademark bushy moustache, wire-rimmed glasses, and ill-fitting three-piece suit and hat, Clyde looked like an old man even before he started at Columbia (he was born in 1892 and was 37 years old when he made his first short comedy at Educational). Clyde was second only to the Three Stooges in popularity during his time with Columbia ("Andy Clyde Biography").

Unlike the Stooges, Clyde had a successful feature film career apart from the Columbia shorts, appearing mostly in the Westerns of Hopalong Cassidy and Whip Wilson, and he went on to play supporting characters in television series such as *Lassie* and *The Real McCoys* in the fifties. Clyde was also featured in a number of bit parts in television series such as *Love That Bob* and *The Andy Griffith Show*. He died in 1967.

Buster Keaton

Nearly as famous and enduring as the Three Stooges was Buster Keaton. During the early part of the Stooges' career, Keaton's reputation had far exceeded that of the comedy trio, due mostly to his brilliant work in silent feature films. Keaton's reputation was much less sparkling in the short films he made. Keaton's decline as a comic acrobat and even his inability to learn lines have often been attributed to alcoholism, which was apparently at its destructive peak during most of his shorts career, which spanned from 1934 to 1941.

Keaton made 16 shorts at Educational and only 10 with Columbia. While he was far from Columbia's most prolific star during his time at the studio (1939 to 1941), his films are among the most memorable and among the best of the studio's output, in spite of their many detractors.

Charley Chase

The film career of Charley Chase spanned from 1929 to 1940. His short comedy output totaled 79 films, including 60 at MGM and only 19 at Columbia, the latter having been filmed from 1937 to 1940 (Maltin 1972, pp. 62–68). Chase's short film reputation was made primarily at MGM, but his career at Columbia was notable as well. In addition to his own shorts, Chase had worked as a writer, producer, and director on other short films at Columbia, including five by the Stooges. Of all the comedies examined for this chapter, the films of Chase were the most atypical. *The Heckler*, for example, focused on an obnoxious heckler at a baseball game. Chase is in virtually the entire movie and is at his comic best. The film broke the mold of the predictable comedies for which Columbia was becoming known. The basic script for *The Heckler* was also recycled for Shemp Howard in the 1946 Columbia film *Mr. Noisy*.

Harry Langdon

Like that of Keaton, Harry Langdon's comedy reputation was mostly made in silent feature films. According to Leonard Maltin (1972, p. 68), by the time sound films came about, Langdon was already on a pattern of self-destructing behavior leading to a deterioration of his reputation and career. Not the least of these factors, according to Maltin, was Langdon's decision to direct his own films. His comedy shorts career was fairly brief and undistinguished: 43 films between 1929 and 1945, including 8 for MGM, 8 for Educational, 5 for Paramount, 1 for RKO, and 21 for Columbia (Maltin 1972, pp. 72–74). Probably more than anyone else, Langdon and Keaton typified Maltin's characterization of Columbia as a studio for "comedy veterans who ... had seen better days" (Maltin 1972, p. 8). and as a stopover for comedians on the downside of their careers.

Other comedians who made comedy shorts for Columbia included Stooges Shemp Howard, Joe Besser, and Joe DeRita, plus Hugh Herbert, El Brendel, Wally Vernon and Eddie Quillan, Gus Schilling and Richard Lane, Walter Catlett, Monty Collins and Tom Kennedy, Vera Vague, Leon Errol, Sterling Holloway, Harry Von Zell, and Max Rosenbloom and Max Baer (Okuda and Watz 1986).

By examining the films of these comedians, one can see that a great deal of the look, sound, and humor of the Three Stooges was a direct result not of the Stooges themselves but of what came largely from the Columbia Studios, a kind of uniform look and comic feel.

Producers and Directors

In the Columbia Short Subjects Department, the producers had the greatest responsibility for the end results of the film. At Columbia during most of the shorts period, there were only two producers: Jules White and Hugh McCollum. As head of the shorts department, White obviously wielded a great deal of power. Further evidence of the producer's control over the comic characters of the Three Stooges, and presumably of other actors as well, was offered by White: "We developed their characters. From the time they came to Columbia, there was nothing they did that I didn't approve. If I liked it, it stayed; if I didn't, it was gone" (Bruskin 1984, p. 214).

White's brother Sam offered this analysis of the "filtering process" that went through the films made at Columbia:

> The creative process for the making of a particular film occurs in the producer's office with the writer and director, step by step, sentence by sentence, rehearsing every single scene, sometimes with the actors present. So when the comedians performed, they interpreted many creative ideas that come from Jules via the writer and director. That's how he influenced the Stooges' development [Bruskin 1984, p. 215].

Nonetheless, the role of a director in these comedies should not be understated. The main directors at Columbia were Jules White, Del Lord, Hugh McCollum, Edward Bernds, Charles Lamont, Harry Edwards, and Preston Black (a.k.a. Jack White). The Three Stooges were a slapstick comedy team from the very beginning, as were most other Columbia comedians. But there are pronounced differences between the Stooges films directed by Lord and those directed by White, differences that can easily be seen in these films, and likewise with the films of other Columbia comedians. The films directed by Lord are invariably more humane, usually with better scripts, and contain much less slapstick violence.

The films directed by White, on the other hand, are invariably more violent. The reason may be in part the fact that White stepped up his directing duties as budgets were becoming tighter for the shorts, and he was assuming more of the overall duties on individual films himself. According to Maltin (1972, p. 130), because of the need to fill time in a film, White might call for the continuation of a sight gag, and that invariably meant extending the slapstick and the violence. One might also argue, however, that Jules White had a greater understanding of what was funny than did other Columbia directors.

White is credited as either producer or director in 340 of the short films made at Columbia (Bruskin 1984, pp. 442–451).

Writers and Scripts

The main writers for short comedies at Columbia were Jack White, Felix Adler, Clyde Bruckman, and Ellwood Ullman. These names are highly familiar to Stooge scholars, but the writers were quite active in the other films as well.

It is common knowledge that several Stooges shorts often were remade with stock footage, and Columbia even used footage that had originally been shot with Curly for films made by Shemp Howard or Joe Besser. Jules White acknowledged that a script might be made "as many as five or six times" (Bruskin 1984, pp. 442–451). Films were remade of certain Shemp shorts (with a body double) after his untimely death in 1956 just to have new Stooges product to show. Likewise, certain sketches that were originally made as films for other comedians were recycled for the Stooges, and vice versa. One of the Stooges' best known films was *A Plumbing We Will Go*, made in 1940. This was remade by the Stooges as *Vagabond Loafers* in 1949. But the story was also made into a film by El Brendel and Shemp Howard as *Pick a Peck of Plumbers* in 1944. And an earlier script featuring Brendel, *Plumbing for Gold*, had been made in 1934, and portions of that script made it into the Stooges' *Scheming Schemers* in 1956 (Bruskin 1984, pp. 442–451).

The Stooges' 1944 film *Crash Goes the Hash* features the Stooges as employees of a cleaners who are drafted into duty as reporters. Virtually the entire script had been done previously, in 1937, by Edgar Kennedy and Monty Collins, in *New News*. In the 1947 Three Stooges film *Out West*, the Stooges call in the cavalry to save a saloon (owned by a beautiful young singer portrayed by Christine McIntyre) from being taken over by outlaws. Similarly, this plot had already been done in the 1945 film by El Brendel and Harry Langdon called *Pistol Packin' Nitwits*, and even featured McIntyre in the same role. Further, the Brendel/Langdon short helped give birth to another Stooges short, *Three Troubledoers*, where Dick Curtis plays a dastardly villain trying to coerce McIntyre into marrying him. Another wholesale lifting of a script takes place in the 1946 Shemp Howard and Tom Kennedy film *Society Mugs*. The short is nearly a word-for-word replication of the Stooges' 1938 film *Termites of 1938*.

In the 1941 Buster Keaton short *General Nuisance* (his last for Columbia), there are two scenes that recur in Stooges shorts. Keaton is cleaning loving cups in one scene, which actually turns into a clever dance and acrobatic number with actress Elsie Ames. This loving cup scene had been used in the 1936 Stooges film *Half-Shot Shooters*. But in another scene, Keaton is asked by Monty Collins to take off his clothes, a gag later appropriated in the Stooges' 1946 film *Rhythm and Weep*. A Joe Besser short *Hook a Crook*, from 1955, borrows from a Stooges short from 1943, *Dizzy Detectives*. And, in Andy Clyde's 1942 film *All Work and No Pay*, after Clyde accidentally swallows a stolen diamond, a gorilla tries to get it out of him. This same plot was later used in the Stooges films *Crime on Their Hands* (1948) and *Hot Ice* (1955).

One plot that was used at least three times in Columbia films was having a scene take place on the train, where the protagonist can't help disturbing a whole sleeping car. This happened with the Three Stooges in the 1936 film *A Pain in the Pullman*. It also occurred in Andy Clyde's *The Watchman Takes a Wife* (1941) and with Buster Keaton in *Pardon My Berth Marks* (1940). In the former film, Clyde even ends up on a broncing bull after being thrown from the train, just like the Stooges.

More commonplace than wholesale borrowing of plots and scenes from other movies was adapting lines from script to script, including ones that were frequently used by the Stooges:

"Why don't you call your shots?" (Andy Clyde, *You Were Never Uglier*)

"I'm dying and you're asking riddles?" (Clyde, *Two Jills and a Jack*)

"There's a man who wants to kill me — you're the man!" (Andy Clyde, *Two Jills and a Jack*, and Buster Keaton in *Pardon My Berth Marks*)

"Quit lyin'" (pun on "lion") (Andy Clyde, *Pardon My Nightshirt*)

"I was talking to another idiot" (Vernon Dent, in Buster Keaton's *Pardon My Berth Marks*)

"Jeepers creepers, what a night" (a bird once again, in Buster Keaton's *Taming of the Snood*)

"Are you ready?" "Yeah, I'm ready" (Joe Besser, *Army Daze*, and Wally Vernon and Eddie Quillan in *He Took a Powder*)

"I'll tell him a two or thing" (Joe Besser, *Army Daze*)

"One of us is crazy and it can't be you" (Bud Jamison, in Buster Keaton's *Nothing But Pleasure*)

Actors

Many of the actors who appeared in the Columbia films are familiar to close observers of the Stooges. There is a great deal of overlap between those who appeared in Stooges shorts and those who appeared in the films of other comedians. Vernon Dent was a regular in the Andy Clyde comedies, most often playing a jealous husband or tormentor of Clyde, much as he did in the Stooges films. Bud Jamison also played the same sorts of roles for which he was known in the Three Stooges comedies, appearing frequently as a butler, policeman, and detective. He even reprised his role as the butler in *New News* for the derivative Stooges comedy *Crash Goes the Hash*.

Other actors who made frequent appearances in other Columbia films away from the Stooges included Christine McIntyre, Frank Lackteen, Dick Wessell, Shemp Howard (in his own films and those of others), Dudley Dickerson, Dorothy Appleby (a regular in the Keaton comedies), Monty Collins, Eddie Laughton, Tom Kennedy, Kenneth McDonald (though his non–Stooges appearances were rare), Emil Sitka (likewise), Stanley Blystone, Fred Kelsey, Cy Schindell, Matt McHugh, and Dick Curtis.

Some actors made a single appearance in a Stooges film but were regulars in other films. For example, Dick Wessell appeared in *Fright Night* and the remake *Fling in the Ring* but regularly played Andy Clyde's deadbeat brother-in-law. Matt McHugh appeared in *Pardon My Clutch* and the remake *Wham-Bam-Slam!* and was a regular in other films. Conversely, some regulars such as Emil Sitka and Jacques O'Mahoney were almost exclusive to the Stooges, Sitka rarely turning up elsewhere, and O'Mahoney not at all.

Sound Effects

Undeniably, a great deal of the memorable humor of the Three Stooges comedies was derived from the sound effects. Yet while generations of television viewers grew up associating certain sounds with the violence and slapstick of the Three Stooges, these same sound effects were used countless times in other comedies. The sound effects at Columbia Studios were derived conceptually from cartoons. They were seldom done live or recreated for a film. Columbia had a large library of sound effects that were used and reused in a variety of films (Bruskin 1984, pp. 248–249). These sound effects include the sound of a baseball bat on the head; the honking horns and bell-ringing that a person heard after drinking extremely strong liquor; the single clang of a bell when one is shot in the buttocks by a gun; the twanging sound made when an arrow hits the posterior region; the sound of someone drinking water; a lion howling; an indescribable, supposedly humanly emitted sound that resembled a train whistle; a punch in the stomach; a manual drill; and a male grunt when someone suddenly falls down or is hit by surprise (this last sound, which supposedly is emitted by a particular actor, can be found dozens of times in different Columbia films).

Gags

Brief sight gags or portions of scenes were repeated in other comedies besides those of the Three Stooges. The gags reprised by or from the Stooges include the following:

being outwitted by furniture — Shemp in *Hokus Pokus* and *Flagpole Jitters* (Andy Clyde in *You Were Never Uglier*)

a frightened African American in numerous comedies such as *Hold That Lion!*, *A Gem of a Jam*, and *Vagabond Loafers* (Dudley Dickerson in Andy Clyde's *Pardon My Nightshirt*, *Host to a Ghost*, and *Spook to Me* and Hugh Herbert's *Nervous Snakedown*)

a wall mounting of a doglike creature that comes to life and barks — *Spooks!* and *Creeps* (Hugh Herbert's *Nervous Snakedown* and Andy Clyde's *Spook to Me*)

gum stuck on telephone — *Fifi Blows Her Top* (Andy Clyde's *Two Jills and a Jack*)

climbing into the upper berth of a bunk bed — *I Can Hardly Wait* (Andy Clyde's *Pardon My Nightshirt*)

a hole in the floor, and people falling through it — *A Plumbing We Will Go* and *Vagabond Loafers* (Andy Clyde's *Pardon My Nightshirt*)

shaking hands with a hand in a fireplace — *Scrambled Brains* (Andy Clyde in *Mr. Clyde Goes to Broadway*)

being burned by a hot towel — *Cuckoo Cavaliers* (Andy Clyde in *He Was Only Feudin'*)

a soldier's walk leading to slapstick — *Wee Wee Monsieur* and *Boobs in Arms* (Dudley Dickerson in Andy Clyde's *Pardon My Nightshirt*) the NBC chimes when hit on the head — *I'm a Monkey's Uncle* (Andy Clyde in *Marinated Mariner*)

bumping head on upper berth of a sleeping car — *A Pain in the Pullman* (Buster Keaton's *Pardon My Berth Marks* and Bud Jamison in El Brendel's *I Spied for You*)

a talking bird — *Disorder in the Court* and *Crash Goes the Hash* (Buster Keaton's *Taming of the Snood* and Andy Clyde's *A Maid Made Mad*)

a glass door continuously breaking — *Men in Black* (Buster Keaton's *Pardon My Berth Marks*)

hanging out of a window holding on to a telephone — *Studio Stoops* (Buster Keaton in *So You Won't Squawk*)

hanging perilously on a flagpole — *Hokus Pokus* and *Flagpole Jitters* (Buster Keaton and Elsie Ames in *Taming of the Snood* and Andy Clyde in *A Maid Made Mad*)

soap bubbles emerging after eating — *Baby Sitters Jitters* (Andy Clyde in *Love Comes to Mooneyville*)

bringing crooks into another room to trick them — several, including *Scrambled Brains* (El Brendel in *Olaf Laughs Last*)

a powder puff mistaken for a pancake — *Uncivil Warriors* (Joe DeRita in *Jitter Bughouse*)

a frog's croak mistaken for an uncouth belch — *The Ghost Talks, Creeps!* (Andy Clyde and Shemp Howard in Clyde's *Money Squawks*)

the protagonists riding away on a bull at the end of the film — *A Pain in the Pullman* (Andy Clyde in *Boobs in the Woods*)

a man getting trapped in a wall — *Cash and Carry* (Andy Clyde in *Host to a Ghost*).

The Columbia Touch

By far, the most frequent elements that made the Columbia shorts alike were the sound effects and the supporting actors. They are perhaps the most identifiable of all elements of the Columbia short subjects. While that is significant, the most important commonalities between Three Stooges films and other comedies were the writing and the gags. Storylines, dialogue, sight gags, and scenes were freely appropriated, often creating a sense of *déjà vu* in the most extreme cases.

The production and directing of these short films were instrumental in giving them their identity as well. These aspects are inextricable from the writing, and they set a tone for all of the comedy teams and solo performers at Columbia.

The Three Stooges were far and away the most famous, the most successful, and probably the most talented actors to produce short films at Columbia. But many of the elements that gave the Stooges comedies their identity — dialogue, plots, sound effects, and sight gags — were freely incorporated into other films being produced at Columbia Studios. While the Stooges often receive the credit for the innovative humor in these comedies, it is clear that the Stooges' use of these elements often came years after they had already been incorporated into other Columbia films. Many of these elements, it could be argued, were used even more successfully in films other than those by the Stooges.

None of these facts and observations diminishes what the Stooges accomplished. If anything, they shine a new brilliance on what the Stooges did. In spite of the many comic actors at Columbia having access to the same exact resources as the Stooges had, it is the Three Stooges who endured and are remembered today. Sadly, the world of popular culture has largely forgotten and ignored the work at Columbia of comedy greats such as Andy Clyde, Buster Keaton, and Charley Chase, as well as the lesser lights that populated the studio's lot. These forgotten films would likely resonate with devoted fans of the Stooges films.

Works Cited

"Andy Clyde Biography." Yahoo!Movies. 14 Dec. 2005. http://movies.yahoo.com/shop?d=hc&id=1800028008&cf=biog&intl=us.
Bruskin, David N., ed. *Behind the Three Stooges: The White Brothers: Conversations with David N. Bruskin.* Metuchen, N.J.: Directors Guild of America, 1984.
Maltin, Leonard. *The Great Movie Shorts.* New York: Crown, 1972.
Okuda, Ted, and Edward Watz. *The Columbia Comedy Shorts.* Jefferson, N.C.: McFarland, 1986.

II. STOOGE PSYCHOLOGY AND RELIGION

Psychology has been a staple as a setup for comedy for years. The visage of a Freud-like character as the archetype for German psychologists has been used in comedy film in the talking era. Comedian Bob Newhart made a career mostly out of a gentle and funny approach to psychology. And as the Baby Boomers, Twenty Somethings, Gen-Xers, and Gen-Nexters age on television, psychology becomes a necessary component of our screen characters' lives.

Likewise, religion has been an important source of comic inspiration. While the Hayes Code of the 1930s, combined with a puritanical approach by the motion picture industry, made having fun with Judaism or Christianity *verboten* for many years, religions beyond the mainstream were often fair game in burlesques of other countries. These attitudes largely remained throughout the 1960s. Once groundbreaking television shows such as *All in the Family* and *Monty Python's Flying Circus* began challenging these taboos, however, jokes at the expense of mainstream organized religions also became commonplace.

Less obvious is how both psychology and religion *inform* comedy. In the case of psychology, this can be seen in the examples stated above; but beyond sketch comedy, the infiltration of humor by the field of psychology is more subtle, at least until we deconstruct the films. In this section, Chapter 6 makes the case for Freud's concept of id, ego, and superego applying to Moe, Larry, and Curly. Chapter 7 considers pathos. Chapter 8 tackles the violent side of human nature and discusses how it is often highly exaggerated. Chapter 9 looks at class and antiaristocracy themes, examining both the figurative and literal pies in the face of their mental and socioeconomic superiors.

And how has religion informed the ethos of film comedy? Television has more overtly acknowledged the religious influences throughout its existence, in shows such as *Leave It to Beaver, Father Knows Best, The Andy Griffith Show, All in the Family,* and even *The Simpsons,* but these influences are less obvious in film comedy. Chapter 10 examines the Stooges' Jewish roots and illustrates how the Jewish tradition of humor affected their comedy. Chapter 11 finds Christian and Buddhist applications and themes in the examination of trinities in Stooges films.

6

Deconstructing the Three Stooges: Freud's Concept of the Id, Ego, and Superego

Tim Snyder

The Three Stooges provide an opportunity to explore the three major components of personality introduced by Sigmund Freud: the id, ego, and superego. Specifically, Curly can be seen as the representation of the id, Moe the ego, and Larry the superego. In the Stooges films, these three components interact in a chaotic world that verges on self-destruction, yet somehow thrives.

From a review of the Three Stooges films, we suggest that another Freudian concept also emerges. The Stooges appear to be driven by the Thanatos, which is the so-called death instinct that is a powerful undercurrent within the personality. The Stooges consistently put themselves in positions that are not only stupid but also life threatening. The Thanatos in their characters appears to override the life instincts, which push for the preservation of the individual.

The Id

According to Freud, each individual at birth has a primitive component of the personality present, which he calls the id. The id is completely unconscious and is the psychic source of the powerful life and death instincts (Freud 1940). The id operates on the pleasure principle: its needs must be met immediately and completely, with little regard for rationality or logic. Thus, the id is hedonistic, self-centered, and impulsive. Because the id has no direct contact with reality, however, it cannot alone meet its needs. Curly is the embodiment of the id.

Instances of Curly's id-like behavior abound throughout the short films. According to Edelstein (2000), Curly has a "happy-go-lucky hedonism" easily recognized by his "quavery falsetto trill." Every time he is at the buffet table "stacking the deck," sneaking food from his friends, or becoming frustrated to the point of being childish, he is personifying the concept of the id. Curly's mode of operation in everyday life is impulsive, irrational, and illogical; seldom does he think before he acts. Curly is not without insight, however. Or perhaps the expression "out of the mouths of babes" is occasionally justifiable. As suggested by Pierce (2005), Curly is able to see the true nature of the dictator Hailstone in *You Nazty Spy!*: "Mmm, a parasite." Yet, his energy may drive the rest of the personality— Moe and Larry— for better or for worse (in their case, usually for the worse). But he hasn't much interest in controlling the others; he's generally content to follow the lead or even give in. Indeed, the famous "Curly Shuffle" typifies Curly's retreat from difficult situations where he cannot get what he wants. Clearly then, the personality cannot function with the id alone: the ego must evolve in order to satisfy the powerful id.

The Ego

According to Freud (1940), the second component of the personality to emerge is the ego. The ego emerges in order to satisfy the id's needs, but it operates on the reality principle. The ego is in contact with the real world; therefore, it must determine what are viable conditions in reality that will satisfy the id. The ego "acts as an intermediary between the id and the external world" (Freud 1933, p. 2). As such, it is in a constant struggle with the id. The ego essentially fights for the survival of the individual; while the id simply "wishes" for satisfaction, the ego must find satisfaction from reality. For example, when the id is pushing for sexual gratification, the ego must determine what course of action is appropriate for this urge. In normal personality development the ego becomes the dominant part of the personality, as it oversees both the id and the superego.

Moe's character seems to be the most like the ego. He is the ringleader, the boss, and the one who attempts to keep the others in line. He is usually the most rational and logical of the three (which isn't saying much), and he is the one who seems most in contact with the real world. Moe is the one who directs behavior, orders things to be done, monitors performance, and negotiates the demands of the external world. Unfortunately, Moe tends to keep his cohorts in line through violence. Writes Edelstein (2000): "Moe ... doesn't seem fully alive unless he's poised to strike one of his underlings ... Why does Moe hit? ... in retaliation to injury ... in response to injury ... as an answer to a bad pun." Perhaps this behavior is a reflection of his actual childhood: "I was constantly fighting," acknowledges Moe in his memoir *Moe Howard and the Three Stooges* (Howard 1977, p. 15). Or perhaps, it is a reflection of the almost untenable position of the ego who is "just as big a screw-up as Curly or Larry" but "lacks their ability to shrug failure off" (Edelstein 2000). Moe's position within the triad is that of the coordinator of the group — but he maintains this position by using physical violence. He cannot succeed without the others, but he sometimes succeeds in spite of them. However, the personality cannot fully function with just the id and the ego; the superego is needed to complete the psychological picture.

The Superego

Freud (1940) suggests that the superego is the last component of the personality to develop. The superego represents the internalized morals and rules from one's parents and from society as a whole. The superego is the conscience aspect of the personality, the part that tells us right from wrong. The superego pushes us to be perfect. It strives for self-control, delay of gratification, and resistance to "bad" impulses. It creates the sense of shame and guilt when its moral code is violated. It is essentially the counterbalance against the amoral id, and the ego has to balance both the id's and the superego's desires when making decisions.

Larry is the embodiment of the superego. He tries to keep Curly's and Moe's moral behavior in check. Although Larry stays in the background for most of the Stooge episodes, he still tends to influence the trio through his conscientious objections. Every time he says "Hey, you guys, knock it off" or "Hey you two, quit playing around," he demonstrates the conscience flexing its muscle. According to von Busack (1997, p. 4), "Larry is really the eye of the storm.... When Fine was agitated into a double take, you could feel aftershocks from it." Larry is the one who often attempts to guide the Stooges in the morally right direction. Unfortunately he is consistently disregarded and does not follow through. For instance, he takes a stance against Moe's orders, saying, "I'll do it when I'm good and ready." But when pressed by a threatening Moe, he quickly acquiesces: "I'm ready!" Like the superego, Larry often knows the "right" thing to do; it just doesn't happen.

Interaction of the Three Components

The Three Stooges show an interesting personality dynamic when performing in their films. Moe, the ego, was able to coordinate and supervise the other two, writes Spatt (1994), not because of self-interest, "but more an innate ability to control or lead others, or cause them to be submissive." Curly, the id, exerted a great deal of pressure on the other two and, as a result, tends to skew the personality as a whole to be hedonistic and impulsive. Larry, the (weak) superego, was not able to influence any of the other two to a great extent and is therefore often pushed into the psychological background. Whether the Stooges are "fixing" the plumbing in a house, infiltrating a Confederate army camp, or drilling for oil, this personality dynamic consistently emerges. From a psychodynamic approach, therefore, the Stooges' personality system was ruled by the instinctual needs of the id.

Thanatos

Freud suggested that the id also houses the Thanatos, or drives that seek the injury to or death of the organism. He introduced this concept in order to explain self-destructive behaviors, such as suicide, aggression, and war. Like the life instincts (e.g., libido), these death instincts push for expression and therefore can have a dramatic impact on the personality.

In the Three Stooges episodes, one can readily identify Thanatos operating. The Stooges are not just ignorant, stupid, or clumsy—they repeatedly put themselves into positions that could cause immediate death. When Moe lights a match to look into an oil well, or Curly looks down a gun barrel, it demonstrates the overriding urge to cause bodily damage to himself. Indeed, much of what they do involves a flirtation with death. Kluge (1999–2000) observes that such reckless behavior gives the id what it desires—violence. But he emphasizes that slapstick comedy generally weakens the consequences of violence through visual and auditory cues. For example, poking someone in both eyes simultaneously is a cruel, vicious act. Pairing that with a resounding aural DOINK, however, allows the viewer to find humor in an otherwise violent behavior. Interesting enough, only in four episodes do the Stooges actually die as a result of their behavior: *Half-Shot Shooters, You Nazty Spy!, I'll Never Heil Again,* and *Three Little Sew and Sews.* The Thanatos in their personality dynamic pushes itself to the limit, and as a result the trio engages in unnecessary reckless behavior—but they survive.

A Personality Disorder

The Three Stooges exemplify the three components of Freud's theory of personality—the id, ego, and superego. Although the Stooges' personality system was extremely dysfunctional, it worked well enough for them to exist in the "real" world most of the time. Several other aspects of Freud's theory come to mind when analyzing the Stooges, and further investigation might be fruitful. For example, the libido seems to be subtly introduced in many of their episodes and might drive some of their behavior. In addition, the Stooges frequently use defense mechanisms, which protect the ego from disturbing knowledge that might disrupt the functioning of the personality. For example, the Stooges rationalize all types of outrageous behavior; if they mess something up, it must be someone else's fault. The Three Stooges were the masters of comic genius, but perhaps they represented more than a simple Nyuk, Nyuk, Nyuk.

Works Cited

Edelstein, David. "Moe Better Blues: Are the Three Stooges Martyrs, Demons, or Anti-Role Models?" *Slate Magazine,* 21 April 2000. Accessed 8 Oct. 2005. http://slate.msn.com/id/80966.

Freud, Sigmund. *New Introductory Lectures on Psychoanalysis.* Trans. W. J. H. Sprout. New York: Norton, 1933.

_____. "An Outline of Psychoanalysis." *International Journal of Psycholanalysis* 21 (1940): 27–84.

Howard, Moe. *Moe Howard and the Three Stooges.* Secaucus, N.J.: Citadel, 1977.

Kluge, Daniel. "Psychoanalysis and Film." Dallas Society for Psychoanalytic Psychology Fairhill Scholarship Competition 1999–2000. Undergraduate Division. Accessed 26 Dec. 2005. http://www.dspp.com/papers/kluge.htm.

Pierce, Charles P. "Woise Guys." *The Boston Globe,* 27 Feb. 2005. http://www.boston.com/ae/movies/articles/2005/02/27/woiise_guys?pg=full.

Spatt, Dave. "Stoogology, or The Stooge in You." OSLA Arts & Law Home Page 1994. Accessed 26 Dec. 2005. http://www.artslaw.org/Stooge.htm.

von Busack, Richard. "The Moe, Larry, and Curly School of a Timeless Social Disorder." *Metro Santa Cruz,* 16–22 Jan. 1997. http://www.metroactive.com/papers/metro/01.16.97/cover/stooges1-9703.html.

7

You Gotta Have Heart: The Pathos of Slapstick and the Three Stooges

Peter Seely

The concept of *pathos* in humor is a staple that has been studied frequently over the years. From the writings of the Greek comic Aristophanes to the many bittersweet writings of Shakespeare, comedy and tragedy have been inextricably linked. This paradox is perhaps most famous in the twentieth century through the writings of George Bernard Shaw and the films of Sir Charles Chaplin. Apart from isolated studies and acknowledgments of this phenomenon, however, the union of comedy and tragedy in slapstick comedy is rarely mentioned, with the exception of the works of W.C. Fields and Laurel and Hardy, and almost exclusively with regard to the feature films of these artists. The use of such seriocomic elements in later slapstick comedy, including the more "lowbrow" comics like the Three Stooges and Abbott and Costello, and even the shorts of Buster Keaton, has remained relatively ignored.

This chapter examines the use of pathos in various comedy shorts of the Three Stooges. While the majority of this book highlights the many and various ways the Three Stooges made millions of viewers laugh, this chapter is devoted to those unusual times when the films of the Stooges were actually able to touch the hearts and souls of their fans.

Pathos: Its Origins and Adaptations in Film

Pathos is a concept defined by Aristotle as an attempt to explain the human emotional responses generated by communication. In the aftermath of Freud, this term has also come to describe a psychological response and today is considered one of the primary means of persuasion in human communication (Samover and Mills 1986, p. 222). The word is Greek in origin, and translated it means passion or suffering. It is defined in the *American Heritage Dictionary* (1976, p. 250) as "a quality in something or someone that arouses feelings of pity, sympathy, tenderness, or sorrow in another."

Another key point of reference here is the important work by Walter Kerr called *Tragedy and Comedy*. In his book, Kerr points out that tragedy and comedy have almost always co-existed, tragedy being traced to 535 B.C., and comedy recognized in 486 B.C. He likens the creation of comedy to "the royal twin that is born five minutes later, astonishing everyone and deeply threatening the orderly succession of the house. It is the mistake of nature" (Kerr 1967, p. 20).

A further consideration of Kerr's (1967, p. 19) theories sheds some light on why the polar opposites, tragedy and comedy, have somehow always been closely linked:

> Comedy, it seems, is never the gaiety of things; it is the groan made gay. Laughter is never man's first impulse. Comedy always comes second, late, after the fact and in spite of it or because of it. Comedy is really the underside of things, after the rock of our hearts has been lifted, with effort and only temporarily.... Man's primary concern is with the rock, with his heart, with tragedy.

According to Kerr (1967, p. 149), when motion picture films appeared around the turn of the twentieth century, comedy was given another palette from which to work, and it essentially was " a blank check ... Film had to find itself from scratch. It also had to find comedy — its comedy, all comedy — from scratch." It is from this backdrop — the beginning of motion picture comedy — that we proceed with this inquiry.

Most film scholars would likely trace the origins of pathos in celluloid comedies, at least in any significant way, to the work of Charlie Chaplin. The first film where Chaplin flirted with pathos was *The Bank*, where his character, the "Little Fellow," wakes up in a bank to find his beloved in the arms of a cashier. The pathos is evident in the extreme sadness the character feels upon witnessing this betrayal (Sobel and Francis 1977, p. 173). Prior to this film, Chaplin had not been thought of as a character associated with pathos.

It is generally not disputed that despite the physical, slapstick nature of Chaplin's comedy, he did in fact incorporate pathos into works of his more mature period, beginning with the aforementioned *The Bank* (1915). An argument could be made that Chaplin actually approached pathos in two slightly earlier films, *The Masquerader* (1914) and *A Woman* (1915). In *A Woman*, a cross-dressed Chaplin wins the affections of a married man and proves him to be an immoral, lascivious person. This film perhaps provided the moral foundation and a model of pathos for *Tootsie* over 60 years later.

Chaplin's work is arguably in a class by itself, apart even from the great Buster Keaton. According to Kerr, Chaplin's work as a comedian is "impure," especially compared to Keaton's. And yet, Kerr (1967, pp. 211–212) tells us, *no one* would question Chaplin's superiority to Keaton. This assertion is certainly debatable, for if we are to acknowledge that Keaton's humor was more "pure" than Chaplin's, it might also follow that Keaton's comedy is in some ways superior to, or at least funnier than, that of Chaplin.

Kerr's notion of pure versus impure comedy rests primarily on the use of pathos that, it has already been acknowledged, was sprinkled liberally through Chaplin's work. Kerr (1967, pp. 210–211) argues:

> There was no admixture of sentiment, no bid for pathos, no confusing of the tragic modes. Keaton was cool, detached, and very strictly funny, never suggesting for a moment that we need worry ourselves about what might happen to him.
>
> We were to see limitation functioning as humor without emotion, just as Keaton never displayed any emotion. Keaton, known as the man who never smiled ... never seemed to feel. He personified, as sparely and cleanly as a comedian could, that "absence of feeling" ... associated with the comic. Keaton's comedy was Euclidean.

In stark contrast to Kerr's analysis is that of one of Keaton's biographers, Tom Dardis (1979, p. 90):

> [Keaton's early films] were strongly personal films, and not to everyone's taste. Right from the beginning there were those who found Buster's comedies disturbing rather than funny ... this is the main reason why Buster never rose to the level of universal acceptance achieved by Chaplin and Lloyd. Today Buster's films are seen as paradigms of the human condition, as existential films that deal with Heidegger's *Dasein*.

Regardless of which point of view one subscribes to, it is fair to say that both Chaplin and Keaton blazed a trail in slapstick comedy for future comedians, especially those in short subjects like The Three Stooges and others. Further, both comic actors did so while incorporating a fair amount of pathos into their films, creating a blueprint for slapstick comedy that was probably best typified in later years on television by *The Honeymooners*.

Pathos and the Three Stooges

As has been noted elsewhere in this book, the humor in the comedy shorts produced by Columbia Studios, and the Stooges in particular, was broad and exaggerated on all levels — dialogue, gags, sound effects, and physical violence — leaving little room for heartfelt storylines. Nonetheless, there were instances throughout the Stooges' 190 short films when pathos was allowed to flower.

It is useful to subdivide the evaluation of the Stooges' work according to phases of their careers: the Curly years (1934 to 1947), the Shemp years (1947 to 1956), and the Joe Besser years (1957 to 1959). While these lines of demarcation might be arbitrary in some instances and purely chronological in other instances, they are entirely appropriate here. Aside from simply featuring a different third Stooge, the writing and directing of these films changed as the Stooge changed. The transition from Curly to Shemp produced a gradual change, despite the different talents of the two brothers. But with the transition from Shemp to Joe Besser, changes were more abrupt and immediately noticeable. Therefore, these subdivisions are most appropriate.

The Curly Years

The earliest Columbia shorts made by the Stooges were quite different from what followed in the years to come. While slapstick was always the predominant motif, the definition of characters was not as sharp as it later became, and the storylines were not nearly as predictable. These less-defined characteristics can be seen most prominently in the first four Stooges comedies produced in 1934. This situation changed fairly dramatically in the seven shorts produced in 1935. By 1936, the Stooges films had taken a much more formulaic approach. The titles and opening music, which had been unique to each film, were now consistent; and unlike some of the early films, the names Moe, Larry, and Curly were almost always used. While not all Stooges fans agree on their favorite third Stooge, one premise can generally be accepted — that the stories in the Curly years were better written and executed than their later counterparts. At the very least, they were more thoroughly developed, with more use of location shooting than the succeeding episodes. This greater attention to plot and detail seems to have produced more plots containing at least some degree of pathos.

The Shemp Years

The Shemp years are dominated by the presence of Jules White, who directed nearly three-fourths of these films. By contrast, the Curly episodes featured eleven different directors. White's strengths as a director included the ability to produce a film quickly and cheaply, with a generally faster pace and greater degree of violence than those of the other directors. While these factors don't necessarily preclude the inclusion of pathos, there was seldom any room for any meaningful human emotion. Therefore, the Shemp films produced the smallest number of episodes featuring pathos.

The Joe Besser Years

The sixteen short films made by the Three Stooges from 1957 to 1959 featuring Joe Besser as the third Stooge are widely criticized as the worst films they made. In terms of pathos, however, there was a sharp increase. Jules White directed all the Besser shorts, and at first glance they would appear to have his imprimatur all over them, including the tendency to recycle old plots and gags and make them into new films. Of the sixteen Besser shorts, seven were remakes, some using stock footage featuring shots of Moe and Larry aged 15 to 20 years younger than when the new films were made. However, differentiating the Besser shorts from the earlier films was the tendency to show more heart. Of the sixteen films, nearly all have some degree of pathos; some films feature much more than others. A typical Joe Besser film shows Joe feeling sad about some situation over which he has no control (e.g., *Hoofs and Goofs, Fifi Blows Her Top, Oil's Well That Ends Well,* and *Sappy Bullfighters*). There seemed to be a conscious effort to soften some of the storylines and give them more emotional appeal.[1]

Degrees of Pathos

For the purposes of this chapter, pathos is viewed on three levels:

- Third-Degree Pathos — The film includes a momentary or possibly recurring situation that involves some tragedy or sadness but that is played very broadly and may be accompanied by sight gags or jokes. As these situations are so fundamental to the very nature of comedy, this is the most prevalent category; therefore, only representative samples are cited.
- Second-Degree Pathos — The film definitely involves a situation eliciting some degree of pity or sympathy from the viewer. Most certainly, humor will be associated with it, but overall the sequence is treated sympathetically.
- First-Degree Pathos — A significant portion of the plot of the film is devoted to pathos.

Third-Degree Pathos

Because the nature of third-degree pathos is that it is a passing or brief moment of the film, many examples in the Stooges films are related to a wide variety of human problems. Unrequited love is one common thread within this category. In *False Alarms*, a chubby woman named Minnie (played by June Gittelson) is sad because she can't get a boyfriend. Lenore (played by Victoria Horne) is constantly crying because she can't get the attention of her love, a drunken and hallucinating Shemp, in *Cuckoo on a Choo Choo*. The Stooges themselves are deprived of their loves when a three-timing woman (played by Connie Cezan) trifles with their emotions in *Corny Casanovas* and in the remake *Rusty Romeos*. And in *Gents in a Jam*, Mrs. Magruder (played by Kitty McHugh) is reunited at the end of the film with her long-lost love, Phineas Bowman (played by Emil Sitka), who also happens to be Shemp's rich uncle.

Some of the Stooges films dealt with extremely sad circumstances, but they are played almost entirely for laughs. Suspicions of the Stooges as baby kidnappers make up the plots of *Mutts to You* and *Sock-a-Bye Baby*. Marital infidelity is the primary theme of *Three Dumb Clucks* and the remake *Up in Daisy's Penthouse*, where the Stooges' father divorces their mother so that he may marry a younger woman. Other films feature sad situations that are represented as such, including a lost wedding ring in *Muscle Up a Little Closer* and the delay in the Stooges being able to get married in *The Sitter Downers* and *Three Smart Saps*. Moe suffers a nervous breakdown in *Idiots Deluxe* and the remake *Guns A-Poppin'!*, Joe Besser mourns his departed sister in *Hoofs and Goofs*, and the Stooges suddenly and sadly lose their jobs in *Sappy Bullfighters*. A touching sentiment, an old fire chief not wanting to part with the horse and buggy for firefighters, is broached in *Flat Foot Stooges*.

Second-Degree Pathos

Unrequited or sought love contributes a significant portion of the plots in other Stooges films. In *Three Troubledoers*, Curly is out to prove his bravery to his newfound love Nell, so that he may marry her. In *Fifi Blows Her Top* (essentially a remake of *Love at First Bite*), Joe recalls how he lost his love, Fifi, in Paris and is crestfallen to find out she has married and moved in across the hall from the Stooges' apartment. *Rumpus in the Harem*, a remake of *Malice in the Palace* and one of the four "Shempless" Shemp shorts, changes the focus from the first film (the boys trying to recover a government diamond) to trying to get the diamond to raise money to prevent the "Sultan of Pishposh" from buying their sweethearts. In spite of the humorously melodramatic beginning, it is played with some heart.

Sweet and Hot, like *Idiots Deluxe* and *Guns A Poppin'!*, deals with a psychological problem. This time, a crippling stage fright prevents Tiny (played by Muriel Landers) from pursuing a promising musical career.

Nearly all of the remaining Stooges films that include some element of pathos have to do with the Stooges being "friends indeed," so to speak. These films depict the Stooges being drawn into a variety of situations where they encounter people needing help. These people in need always happen to be female. In one such film, *Loco Boy Makes Good*, the Stooges turn from being three men trying to pull off an insurance fraud into a three-man team trying to rescue a hotel for the elderly lady manager. In *Oily to Bed, Oily to Rise*, the Stooges find oil on an elderly widow's property and try to rescue the deed for her, after the widow has naively sold it to investment con men. And in *Oil's Well That Ends Well*, a partial remake of *Oily to Bed*, the Stooges are trying to raise money for their father's expensive operation and accidentally discover oil.

First-Degree Pathos

First-degree pathos in the Stooges shorts deals with the Stooges helping females in need in all but one film. In probably the best example of pathos in a Stooges comedy, *Cash and Carry*, the Stooges are gold prospectors living in a shack in a junkyard. They encounter a young woman and her crippled younger brother, who are too poor to pay for the boy's operation. A scheme to get money finds the boys unwittingly breaking into the U.S. Treasury. The Stooges, along with the boy and his sister, appear before President Roosevelt, who grants the Stooges executive clemency and promises to pay for the boy's operation. In a similar situation, the Stooges are inspired to help a mother (played by Ruth Skinner) and her daughter who have been dispossessed from their home in *Even as IOU*.

In *So Long, Mr. Chumps*, the Stooges are looking for an honest man. Dressed in Dickensian attire (perhaps to call attention to the pathos of the situation), they encounter a grief-stricken woman whose husband is in jail after being wrongly convicted of a crime. *Nutty But Nice* finds the Stooges as restaurant servers/entertainers who immediately leave their jobs to help search for the kidnapped father of a chronically depressed little girl. The ending has the Stooges rescuing the father and the Stooges performing at the restaurant for the girl and her father.

The one film of first-degree pathos that wasn't a variation of the "friend indeed" motif was one of their very last films, *Flying Saucer Daffy*. While the premise is somewhat absurd — Joe is trying to win a photo contest by capturing a picture of a flying saucer — it is literally a Cinderella story. Joe is living with his cousins Moe and Larry and their mother. Joe's aunt is the image of the evil stepmother: doting over Moe and Larry, abusing Joe, and drinking excessively. While on a camping trip with Moe and Larry, Joe snaps a picture of what he thinks is a flying saucer but is in fact two paper plates stuck together. The unwitting fraud ends up landing Moe and Larry in jail. When Joe returns to the campground, he sees a real spaceship, piloted by two beautiful English-speaking space women. In the end, Joe is rich and has a ticker tape parade in his honor, while the "ugly stepsisters" Moe and Larry wind up in straitjackets in a sanitarium. More than any other film, *Flying Saucer Daffy* strives for pathos with its lifting of the Cinderella story. But unlike films such as *Cash and Carry*, *So Long, Mr. Chumps*, or *Nutty But Nice*, which dealt with actual human tragedy and emotions, the fairy tale adaptation and ludicrous premise end up drowning the film in bathos.

The Heart of the Three Stooges

The short films of the Three Stooges were written, produced, and directed for laughs. However, the writers and producers, aware of the need to put together a good story as well as laughs, must have made a conscious decision on a few occasions to put pathos into the comic mix. The many accidental or incidental inclusions of the third-degree pathos may well have been the simple manifestation of comic theory and its inevitable meeting with tragedy. But many efforts seemed to be sincere attempts to inject the elements of heart and sympathy into what would have otherwise been standard comedy romps, raising content of the films to second- or first-degree pathos.

While much comedy may be inherently tragic, the Three Stooges, perhaps more than any other comedian or comedy team in history, represent a brand of humor associated with cheap sight gags, violence, and inane wisecracks. Certainly the average viewer or critic, even those who cheerfully accord the Stooges their due in the slapstick realm, would be reluctant to associate any kind of emotional depth to their films. Ironically, in addition to the aforementioned qualities commonly associated with the Stooges, the characters of Moe, Larry, Curly, Shemp, and Joe were frequently mean, sadistic, and dishonest. The discovery of any genuine human emotion and appeal is therefore surprising and makes the Three Stooges a fascinating subject for study.

Notes

1. Besser (1984, p. 172) himself recounted in his autobiography, *Not Just a Stooge,* that he had hoped to tone down the violence and have Moe and Larry clean up their images.

Works Cited

Besser, Joe. *Not Just a Stooge.* Houston: Excelsior, 1984.
Dardis, Tom. *Keaton: The Man Who Wouldn't Lie Down.* New York: Limelight, 1979.
Kerr, Walter. *Tragedy and Comedy.* New York: Simon and Schuster, 1967.
"Pathos." *American Heritage Dictionary* New York: Dell, 1976. p. 250.
Samover, Larry, and Jack Mills. *Oral Communication: Messages and Response.* Dubuque: Wm. C. Brown, 1986.
Sobel, Raoul, and David Francis. *Chaplin: Genesis of a Clown.* London: Quartet, 1977.

8

Much Ado About Nothing: Violence in the Three Stooges Comedies

Don Morlan

Evidence abounds in American popular culture that the popularity of the Three Stooges remains strong into the twenty-first century. The Three Stooges Fan Club, based near Philadelphia, is one of the best-organized and strongest fan clubs in the country. Gary Lassin, the publisher of *The Three Stooges Journal*, a quarterly publication of the fan club, opened the "Stoogeum" in 2004. The Stoogeum is a large, impressive museum devoted to rare and valuable artifacts from throughout the comedy team's history. The licensing of the Stooges' likenesses in pop culture is among the most profitable and tightly controlled one will find.

Ironically, even though the Stooges' popularity has been consistently high, the likelihood of seeing the boys in most television markets in the country continues to decline. Program directors in far too many localities cater to the whims of local and national media activist groups who vigilantly monitor and count violent acts on television.

When the Stooges are seen at all, they are usually aired in the wee hours of the morning or in other dayparts when children are not a primary consideration. This scheduling pattern represents a significant turnaround and non sequitur when one considers that the target audience for the Stooges on the big screen from 1934 to 1959 and on television and in full-length features in the sixties consisted primarily of children.

In this chapter, we challenge the concern with violence in the Three

Stooges comedies as "much ado about nothing." Our position is that to the many children who grew up with the Stooges, they were no more than cartoon characters, and becoming engrossed in a two-reeler was no more real to those children than their favorite cartoon characters. Hence, any evaluation of the Stooges as to violent content should be made by a comparison of the shorts to animated cartoons.

Here, we briefly review the literature relevant to the effects of violence in animated cartoons on children. We then analyze violent content in two of the most popular cartoon series, *Road Runner* and *Tom and Jerry*. Building on this background, we make a case supporting the premise that the violence in the Stooges comedies is no more real to children than is the violence befalling Tom in the classic Hanna and Barbera creation.

Effects of Cartoon Violence on Children

Concern about the effects of violence on children is voluminous and somewhat inconsistent. An effort to isolate research on the effects of *cartoon* violence on children, however, results in far fewer studies and a similar degree of inconsistency.

Walter G. Hapkiewicz (1979) conducted a literature review of children's reactions to cartoon violence and found, at the time, only 10 studies directed to the topic. The pioneer study by Bandura, Ross, and Ross (1963) involved the infamous Bobo doll being struck by a human dressed as a cat. The study found that, after viewing the film, children were more likely to strike the Bobo doll when given the opportunity. Later qualifications indicated, though, that children were not necessarily more likely to strike another human being after viewing the film — perhaps indicating that children are brighter than we might think and can distinguish a Bobo doll from a real person.

Hapkiewicz concluded that studies up to 1979 supported the premise that viewing cartoon violence tended to cause assaultive behavior in children; however, consistency in these findings occurred only when aggression toward inanimate objects was studied. Such effects were not found with the same consistency when interpersonal assaultiveness was the dependent measure.

Baker, Lange, and Ball-Rokeach (1969), in one of several national commissions on violence, were more critical of the effects of cartoons on children. Their report highlighted the tendency of network personnel to overemphasize violent content in programming targeted primarily for child audiences, namely, Saturday morning cartoon programming. They found that in 1967 and 1968, 93.5 percent of the programs with a cartoon format contained violence. During those two years children were likely to see an average of 22.5 violent incidents per hour.

Baker and his colleagues also concluded that no firm evidence exists that young children can differentiate between fantasy and reality in television programs and that no indications existed in 1969 that fantasy programs are less harmful to children than ones based in reality.

Some of the best-known research on television violence was conducted by George Gerbner of the Annenberg School of Communication at the University of Pennsylvania. Gerbner developed his theory of "cultivation" (Gerbner 1969), postulating that humans are socialized through the collective programming they watch over a period of years, leading to a cultivation of incorrect and negative views of many aspects of society. Gerbner, who is critical of cartoon violence and slapstick comedy, even offered his negative view of the Three Stooges in a 1997 article for *Atlantic Monthly:* "Pratfalls are dangerous. To make pain seem painless is sugarcoating power, sugarcoating the message of power. People don't understand that humor can be very violent and cruel."

Heller and Polsky (1976) conducted a series of studies measuring effects of television violence on large groups of the American population. One such study treated effects of cartoon violence on children lacking a family home environment. Two groups of children were studied — one consisting of emotionally vulnerable children and the other consisting of psychiatrically normal children from broken homes who lived in institutional settings.

Children in both experimental groups did demonstrate an increase in aggressive behavior in clinical settings immediately after viewing violence in cartoons. Careful content analysis of the increased aggressivity, though, indicated that it fell short of any increase in actual violence or interpersonal assaultiveness in the day-to-day lives of these children. Such behavior was contrasted with experimentally induced behaviors in which aggressivity under laboratory conditions may not be reflective of the child's behavior in real-life circumstances.

When the behavior of the psychiatrically normal children was isolated, results indicated significant changes in postcartoon viewing of verbal and attitudinal aggressivity. However, the results showed no significant changes in actual assaultiveness or interpersonal violence in these children's postviewing classroom, schoolyard, or evening institutional behavior.

Both groups of children readily identified with cartoon characters but seemed to distinguish the violent problem-solving antics of cartoons from practical behaviors that were available to them for solutions to real or actual situations in their own lives.

Hodge and Tripp (1986) in their semiotic approach to children and television reviewed a bounty of research that supported a relationship between television violence and aggressive behavior in children. They did, however, draw a distinction between what is real to children and what is fantasy:

Common sense would say that children will not be so strongly affected by what they do not believe in, though this common sense view has not found favour amongst the many industrious researchers who have counted up "violent incidents" on television without any account of whether the violence is realistic or not. As a result of these horrific figures, cartoon violence, in which characters like Tom and Jerry suffer violent death and deformity at an alarming rate per programme, has become a favourite target of lobbyists on children's television [Hodge and Tripp 1986, p. 102].

In very early research, Feshbach (1961) became a major proponent of the "catharsis" theory of media violence, namely, that watching media violence can reduce aggression rather than increase it. Cartoons then would be credited with providing an outlet for children to vent aggressive tendencies. The catharsis theory has roots in classical Greece. Aristotle talked of the effect of the horrific incidents in Greek tragedy as a catharsis, or a purification or purging of the emotions such as pity and fear.

More recently, concurrent studies of television violence provided somewhat contradictory results. The University of California-Santa Barbara conducted a comprehensive study of violence on television from 1994 to 1997. The researchers concluded, "Children under 7 are particularly at risk [of imitating cartoon violence] because of limited ability to distinguish fantasy from reality" (Smith et al. 1969, p. 14). In contrast is the study by Jeffrey Cole and the Center for Communications Policy at UCLA, which conducted the Network Television Monitoring Project, analyzing television content from 1995 to 1997. Their report dismissed the notion of most slapstick comedy and television violence having negative effects. The researchers even found a decline in the level of cartoon violence in contemporary children's fare. Cole did distinguish between traditional children's cartoons and programs such as *Beavis and Butthead* and the *Simpsons*, whose primary targets are adults, but noted that both programs ran early enough to be seen by children (Cole 1996).

This cursory review of literature results in no surprises. Several summary points can be made. First, the quantity of research restricting observation to effects of cartoon violence on children is small. Second, while ample evidence indicates that viewing violence in cartoons has increased aggressive behavior in children, such conclusions are not unchallenged. Perhaps the greatest qualification of such research is in attempts to expand efforts beyond the immediate laboratory setting to the everyday lives of children. Some evidence exists, too, that children can and do differentiate between violence in real and fantasy situations.

One fact is clear in the literature. Animated cartoons have been the entertainment of choice for children throughout the history of motion pictures and television. While criticism of cartoons and their effects continues to find outlets, the quantity of cartoon fare available to children on local television has never diminished.

Violence Boomerangs: Road Runner *Cartoons*

Unlike locating research dealing specifically with violence in cartoons, finding cartoons that feature violence is easy. Perhaps the most violent and lasting of cartoon series was launched in 1948 by Warner Brothers featuring a roadrunner and Wile E. Coyote. The plot of the series never varied: The coyote tried in vain to capture the roadrunner, and all his schemes backfired with violent and painful results.

Chuck Jones, creator of the series, soon found that eleven such violent gags were needed to fill each cartoon (Maltin 1980). Several rules were adhered to in all the *Road Runner* cartoons: they always took place in the same desert setting; the two characters never spoke; the roadrunner never left the road; the coyote's injuries were always self-inflicted; and, no matter what misfortune the coyote suffered, he always appeared intact after the fade-out, ready to try again.

Maltin argued that those who feel that *Road Runner* cartoons are senselessly violent miss a key point — namely, that the roadrunner never does harm to or physically hurts the coyote. Every pain Wile E. suffers is the result of his own boomeranged chicanery. The roadrunner, as he stops to survey the repeated injuries, even looks sympathetic as he gives out his "beep beep."

The fact that *Road Runner* cartoons never featured one living being doing harm to another renders them less than appropriate for measuring effects on behavior. That same fact also makes the cartoons inappropriate for comparison with the Three Stooges comedies. To deny Moe Howard the role of provider of most of Curly, Shemp, Larry, and Joe's pain is to deny sliced bread.

The Mouse Catches the Cat: Tom and Jerry *Cartoons*

One of the most successful and enduring cartoon series ever filmed was MGM's *Tom and Jerry*, initiated in 1940. The famous cat and mouse became the studio's leading cartoon stars, and their popularity has endured for nearly three-quarters of a century. *Tom and Jerry* eventually won seven Academy Awards for MGM as best cartoon. One such Oscar winner, "Quiet Please" in 1945, highlighted violence, as most entries in the series did. The number of violent acts befalling Tom in each episode paralleled that of the roadrunner.

Unlike the *Road Runner* cartoons, however, Jerry or his bulldog compatriot was either the direct or indirect cause of all of Tom's pain. Moreover, unlike the violence in *Road Runner* cartoons, the violent cat and mouse acts in the *Tom and Jerry* series occurred in the home, using means and weapons sometimes available to youngsters watching the cartoon. In "Quiet Please," for example, Tom chases Jerry with a skillet, a shotgun, and a hand axe; and Jerry retaliates with one of his favorite punishments — plugging Tom's tail into a live electrical outlet.

Although parent groups and media action groups have been vocal in criticism of the violence in these cartoons, television markets have not removed *Tom and Jerry* from the available fare for the nation's children. The cat and mouse act remains one of the most frequent cartoon offerings in the country.

In 1975 — a period of transition for the animated cartoon from the theaters to television — Joe Barbera and Bill Hanna, *Tom and Jerry* creators, proposed a new *Tom and Jerry* series for Saturday morning television. The new series completely recreated *Tom and Jerry* as pals walking on twos instead of fours. The new series was a colossal bomb with the new kiddie generation (Maltin 1980, p. 303). Within a very short period the traditional *Tom and Jerry* fare was back on Saturday morning television, and their visibility continues.

Indeed, Turner Broadcasting System aired a daily *Tom and Jerry* show for years. The Cartoon Channel has also relied heavily on this evergreen, and numerous videos are available in any video rental store in the children's department.

The Three Stooges: Cartoon or Reality

The Three Stooges comedies were actually like cartoons to the children who watched them on the silver screen in cinema's golden age. Television airing of the comedies in children's viewing time renders the same result with the new fan generation of the television age. In the 1940s, the Three Stooges were shown with other short subjects in context with the popular cartoons of the day. For years the Turner Broadcasting System aired the Three Stooges five mornings a week with cartoon shows. And, of course, the Stooges appeared in cartoon format on television in the sixties.

To the perceptive eye of a child, just as Tom never "really" got hurt by Jerry and always bounced back immediately from being squashed, mashed, singed, electrocuted, tattered, and torn, no one ever explicitly died in a Three Stooges comedy, and the Stooges — just like Tom — usually bounced back from their supposed pain in the next frame to be totally intact and normal.

Certainly the Stooges were masters at violent sight gags so popular in slapstick comedy of the era. In a few instances, the violence could be called excessive. Okuda and Watz (1986) cite two comedies that included gags "too sadistic in nature to induce laughter": *Pardon My Backfire* and *They Stooge to Conga*. In *Pardon My Backfire*, a probing wire enters Larry Fine's nostril and exits through his ear. *They Stooge to Conga* contained what many have labeled the single most violent act in Stooge history — a climbing spike worn by Curly Howard plunged into Moe Howard's eye.

There are other examples of what might be viewed as over-the-top violence in Stooges comedies. For instance, in *Scrambled Brains*, Moe places a light bulb in Vernon Dent's mouth and smashes it shut on the bulb. And in *Boobs in Arms,* a German soldier falls and lands on the long, sharp point on the top of a helmet. Even in those instances, however, the characters bounced back almost immediately to normalcy, similar to Tom's recovery from having his tail plugged into an electrical outlet. One should also remember that these very graphic instances represent only four of the 190 Columbia shorts.

Almost all of the Stooge comedies utilize the classic eye gouges, belly pokes, hair pulls, and face slaps as primary gag fare. In fact, one would be hard pressed to locate a Stooges short featuring Curly or Shemp without such activity (the Joe Besser films contained considerably fewer such gags). We contend that such antics do not constitute harmful violence for children for at least three reasons. First, such sight gags were a staple of most slapstick comedy of the time, including teams such as Abbott and Costello, Laurel and Hardy, and virtually every other star of comedy short subjects. Second, children then and now didn't and don't see the action as real and happening to real people. Third, contemporary cartoons, available on cable to children on the Cartoon Channel and other channels throughout much of the day, contain numerous incidences of graphic and sometimes more realistic violence that far exceeds what the Stooges, Jones, and Hanna-Barbera ever attempted, such as *Beavis*

The extreme violence featured in Stooges films reached new heights in some of the middle years of the films made with Shemp, including this scene featuring Stanley Blystone from *Slaphappy Sleuths* (1950).

and *Butthead, ImuYasha, Family Guy, American Dad,* and especially *South Park.*

Jules White, long-time director and head of Columbia Pictures Short Subjects division, perhaps summarized the point best:

> I patterned the characters — the Stooges in particular — as living caricatures. Analyze it and you'll find it's true. They weren't for real, so you couldn't take things seriously, like the eye-poking or hand slapping bits. So how can anyone pick on this stuff and call it violent? I see more genuine violence in a single night of television viewing than in all my years of making pictures.
>
> If we removed the knockabout aspect from these comedies, it would have taken away their appeal. Their flavor would be gone. Audiences love to see this kind of humor and we always aimed to please. It's like the westerns; take away the cowboy's six-shooter and there's no gunplay; without gunplay it's a lousy western. The same applies to slapstick comedy: no slapstick, no laughs [Okuda and Watz 1986, p. 25].

Is Violent the Word for Curly?

The main premise of this chapter is that children see Moe, Larry, Curly, Shemp, and Joe as cartoon characters much more than real people they might expect to meet on the street. The elements of comedy are so exaggerated that a firm sense of reality eludes even the most gullible viewer. The question then arises concerning the harm cartoon violence poses to children. A limited view of the literature reveals two conclusions. First, little research has been done on the effects of cartoon violence on children when compared to the overall research on real-life situations depicting violence. Second, the research that is available fails to be conclusive. Most doubtful, perhaps, is the belief that viewing cartoon violence in a laboratory setting transfers to real-life situations for children.

Parallels between one of the most violent cartoons in film history, *Tom and Jerry,* and the Three Stooges comedies suggest that the decision of program directors nationwide that the Three Stooges are not appropriate fare for time slots targeting children amounts to no less than discrimination against the Stooges. While program directors have capitulated to media action groups relative to the airing of the Stooges, cartoons with violent content have perpetuated and endured on the airwaves for over half a century. Further, the landscape of contemporary children's fare on television has taken violence to extreme new levels.

Finally, the Telecommunications Act of 1996 should make most of the arguments about violent television moot. That law included a provision that requires television set manufacturers to install the so-called V-chip in all televisions manufactured with a 13-inch or larger screen. This technology is used in conjunction with the television ratings system developed in the late 1990s. The ratings allow the V-chip to flag programs with undesirable content. While the ratings system is voluntary, all national broadcast networks have adopted it, and most cable networks and independent television stations have done the same. Spike TV, which at this writing is the only national network running the Stooges, rates their films as TV-PG. Disregarding for now the First Amendment implications of the V-chip's blocking the Stooges, the technology should put to rest the age-old arguments about the negative effects the Stooges have on children.

The Stooges' consistent and profound popularity in American popular culture is unsurpassed. It is time for their critics to cease making "much ado about nothing."

Works Cited

Baker, Robert K., David Lange, and Sandra Ball-Rokeach. "Mass Media and Violence: A Report to the National Commission on the Causes and Prevention of Violence." Vol. II. Washington, D.C.: U.S. Government Printing Office, 1969.
Bandura, Alfred, D. Ross, and S. A. Ross. "Imitation of Film Mediated Aggressive Models." *Journal of Abnormal Psychology* 66 (1963): 3–11.
Cole, Jeffrey, director. "The UCLA Television Violence Report 1996." Part III. Accessed 24 Jan. 2006. http://www.digitalcenter.org/webreport95/netfind.htm.
Feshbach, S. "The Stimulating versus Cathartic Effects of a Vicarious Aggressive Activity." *Journal of Abnormal Psychology* 63 (1961): 181–185.
Gerbner, George. "Toward 'Cultural Indicators': The Analysis of Mediated Message Systems." *AV Communication Review* 17, no. 2 (1969): 137–148.
Hapkiewicz, W. G. "Children's Reactions to Cartoon Violence." *Journal of Clinical Child Psychology* 8 (1979): 30–34.
Heller, Melvin S., and Samuel Polsky. *Studies in Violence and Television*. New York: American Broadcasting Co., 1976.
Hodge, Robert, and David Tripp. *Children and Television: A Semiotic Approach*. Stanford, Calif.: Stanford University Press, 1986.
Maltin, Leonard. *Of Mice and Magic: A History of American Animated Cartoons*. New York: McGraw-Hill, 1980.
Okuda, Ted, and Edward Watz. *The Columbia Comedy Shorts: Two-Reel Hollywood Film Comedies, 1933–1958*. Jefferson, N.C.: McFarland, 1986.
Smith, Stacy L., Barbara J. Wilson, Dale Kunkel, Daniel Linz, James Potter, Carolyn M. Colvin, Edward Donnerstein, Jay M. Berhardt, Jane Brown, Shelley Golden, Ellen Wartella, Charles Whitney, Dominic Lasorsa, Wayne Danielson, Adrianna Olivarez, Nancy Jennings, Rafael Lopez, Joanne Cantor, and Amy Nathanson. "National Television Violence Study." Volume 3. 21 Jan. 2006. http://www.ccsp.ucsb.edu/execsum.pdf.

9

A Pie in the Face: The Three Stooges' Antiaristocracy Theme in Depression-Era American Film

Don Morlan

If one were to ask the person in the street, "What is the most memorable comedy ploy of the Three Stooges?" the response most likely would be the pie fight. Results of research in the early 1990s relative to the Stooges' contribution to anti-Nazi propaganda in the late 1930s via *You Nazty Spy!* (1940) generated unexpected national media attention. The story appeared in hundreds of newspapers across the country. The most common headline or lead-in in some way referred to "a pie in Hitler's face." Not only does the American public relate the Stooges to pie fights, but apparently the press does, too.

This association raises three natural questions: How frequent were pie fights, who were the victims of the pies, and what (if any) social themes pervade these episodes? This chapter answers each of these questions, and the answers may surprise some readers. Most surprising may be the fact that the Three Stooges used their comic antics to contribute to the antiaristocracy/antiwealth theme so prevalent in Depression-era films. Just as the Stooges contributed to anti-Nazi sentiment in America in the late thirties and forties, they also made significant contributions to uplifting the morale of Americans during the economic crisis of the Great Depression.

Pie Fights in the Stooges Comedies

Surprising to many "Stoogemaniacs," bona fide pie fights occur in only five of the 190 Columbia comedies. The first such battle appears in the 1941 film *In the Sweet Pie and Pie*, which finds the boys marrying three society girls immediately prior to being hanged. When the boys are pardoned, the girls attempt to embarrass the boys at a high-society party. Perennial supporting actress Symona Boniface, who appeared in all the pie fight comedies, threw the very first pie in a Stooge short subject.

It was six years before another pie fight was filmed, in *Half-Wits Holiday*. That particular fight, which began with Symona Boniface's classic remark, "Why, young man, what's wrong? You act as if the sword of Damocles was hanging over your head," was included as stock footage in all the later pie fights: *Pest Man Wins* (1951), *Scheming Schemers* (1956), and *Pies and Guys* (1958).

Perhaps also surprising to many Stooge fans is that Curly appeared in only one pie fight — the first. *Half-Wits Holiday*, which introduced the classic

Despite the fact that there were only seven pie fights in Stooges films, the pie fight remains one of the Stooges' most famous signatures. Here is a still from the first and most famous pie fight, in *Half-Wits Holiday* (1947).

fight to be seen many more times, was Curly's final comedy with the team, and the concluding pie fight scene was shot without him — presumably following his stroke.

Even though only five comedies included actual pie fights, other comedies featured pies, as well as various and sundry other matter, in the face. Curly received the very first pie in a Stooges comedy — two pies, in fact — from atop a piano in the final scene of *Nutty But Nice* (1940). The mystery pies soared through the air in *Spook Louder* (1943), which prompted the final question, "Who threw those pies?" Clay was the first missile used for throwing, in *Pop Goes the Easel* (1935); and cream puffs were the weapons on two occasions: in *Slippery Silks* (1936) and *Three Sappy People* (1939).

The Victims

The victims of the pies, without exception, were the wealthy in "hoity-toity" social settings. As indicated earlier, Symona Boniface, one of the most popular supporting actresses in shorts of the time, was involved in all the pie fights. Even though she was an active participant, she was always the clear victim of the melees. Her society friends and party guests were also victimized with a pie in the face.

In all five comedies the Stooges portrayed characters on the polar extreme of the victims in terms of social standing. They appeared as condemned convicts about to be hanged who are suddenly pardoned, as exterminators who bring their own pests to a society party, as bumbling plumbers, and twice as low-life ruffians who try to become gentlemen.

Social Theme

The recurring social theme in all the pie-throwing comedies was that of antiaristocracy and antiwealth, a popular theme in Depression-era films. Plots were quite repetitive. Low-life ruffians were thrust into high-society meetings and quickly made a shambles of the elitist climate. The result in each case was the same — society matrons and patrons were relegated to the level of the ruffians and made to look foolish. Indeed, a deeper analysis of this recurring theme in the pie fight comedies shows that the Stooges — amid their slapstick nonsense — were making a meaningful and calculated contribution to the prevailing political climate of the time.

Film historians and critics have generally accorded the Stooges and other slapstick comedians of the day little or no attention for their contributions to uplifting public morale during the Depression. The overlooking of slapstick comedy has been quite similar to that relating to anti–Nazism prior to Pearl Harbor.

This chapter addresses what the Great Depression did to people in the

United States, the role of the motion picture in the era, and specific contributions of the Three Stooges to Depression-era morale building.

What the Depression Did to People

The year 1932 saw a strange occurrence in the United States: more than three times as many persons left the country as entered it. The United States no longer appeared to be the "Promised Land" (Ellis 1970). As the economic crisis worsened, the common people turned against the rich in society. The more destitute and hungry people became, the more they appeared to distrust and resent those of means. Social class structure in the United States shifted dramatically as the middle class all but disappeared and the country found itself more and more consisting of just two social classes — the rich socialites and virtually everyone else.

A few of the rich and powerful recognized the plight faced by most Americans. A rich man with a country estate near Governor Roosevelt's in New York was quoted as saying that the country was doomed unless it could free itself from the rich, who had shown "no realization that what you call free enterprise means anything but greed" (Ellis 1970).

Most wealthy Americans, though, did nothing to enhance the sagging morale of most citizens. Newspapers continued to report debutante banquets costing thousands of dollars, and President Hoover was insensitive enough to allow himself to be photographed on the White House lawn feeding his dog at a time when many Americans were unable to adequately feed themselves.

At the core of capitalism was the belief that God looked with favor on the rich. J. P. Morgan told a Senate committee, "If you destroy the leisure class you destroy civilization." When reporters pressed for a definition of the leisure class, Morgan said it included all who could afford a maid. In 1931, according to *Fortune* magazine, one million families still had servants. One wealthy family announced that it had solved its Depression problem by discharging 15 of its 20 servants — although the family members showed no curiosity or concern about the fate of the unemployed fifteen (Ellis 1970).

What the Depression did to many Americans was virtually destroy their morale and force them to question the very essence of the capitalistic system. When the masses are down in spirit and morale, they strike out at something — and the rich were quite convenient and appropriate for that purpose during the Depression. The values of the rich and aristocratic were also being called into question by Huey Long and his Share the Wealth program and by Father Charles Coughlin in his weekly radio broadcasts from Royal Oaks, Michigan.

The Motion Picture in Depression-Era America

The 1930s have been described as the period of the motion picture's greatest influence on American life (Jowett 1976). At the onset of the Depression in the early 1930s, movie attendance decreased somewhat; however, by 1934 more Americans were going to the movies on a regular basis than at any other time in history.

The motion picture was a family medium of entertainment. Movie bills changed often — sometimes as frequently as three times a week — and the well-established practice of block booking provided easy outlets for the hundreds of movies pouring out of Hollywood each year.

Robert McElvaine (1984) summarizes the central focus of the motion picture in American culture at the time:

> Although music, radio, books, magazines, comics, sports, and other forms of mass entertainment were all significant in the thirties, nothing else was as central to American popular culture in that decade as motion pictures. There are good reasons for concentrating attention on Hollywood. Movies were the preeminent form of popular culture in the 1930's. Almost everyone who could afford to (and millions who could not) went to the cinema frequently throughout the decade. During the depths of the Depression in the early thirties, an average of 60 to 75 million movie tickets were purchased each week.

Feature films of the era did not ridicule the wealthy as people; however, their values were assuredly called to task. The Hollywood vision of businessmen, greed, and the rich became more and more unfavorable as the thirties progressed.

Gold Diggers of 1933, a Warner Brothers musical about the Depression, made a clear indictment of the values of the rich as being wrong. The upper social classes were portrayed as prejudiced, foolish, and believing that money can solve all problems. In this musical Dick Powell attempts to overthrow his society blueblood background with a stage career. When the family attorney and his blueblood brother come to rescue him, they, too, end up falling in love with showgirls and shaking their aristocratic upbringing. The central theme of *Gold Diggers* consisted of upper-class values conflicting with those of the commoner and the commoner winning out in the end. The overall effect of such movies was to neutralize and equalize the classes in society — always to the lower level. The theme proved vastly popular to moviegoers throughout the thirties.

The unification of the classes on film was perhaps done best by Frank Capra in his screwball comedies from 1931 to 1941. Andrew Bergman (1971) describes the appeal of the screwball comedy to the moviegoer:

> The overwhelming attractiveness of the screwball comedies involved more than the wonderful personnel. It had to do with the effort they made at reconciling

the irreconcilable. They created an America of perfect unity: all classes as one, the rural-urban divide breached, love and decency and neighborliness ascendant. It was an American self-portrait that proved a bonanza in the mid-thirties.

Capra's first screwball comedy, *It Happened One Night* (1934), was also Columbia's first major success, winning an Academy Award for best picture. Claudette Colbert and Clark Gable — both on loan to Columbia — won best acting awards, and Frank Capra took the Oscar for best director of 1934. The anticlass theme is most apparent in the film. Peter (Gable), a common working man trying to get by in times of economic distress, and Ellen (Colbert), who has millions, are thrust together in an unlikely setting amid both their frustrations. In the end, however, the classes are neutralized, and the commoner wins the day — and Ellen.

Mr. Deeds Goes to Town (Columbia, 1936) pits the values of rural America against the city. As might be expected, values are again neutralized, with rural American values being the clear winner. Capra's other offerings of the era were *Lost Horizon* (Columbia, 1937), *You Can't Take It with You* (Columbia, 1938), *Mr. Smith Goes to Washington* (Columbia, 1939), and *Meet John Doe* (Warner Brothers, 1941).

The screwball comedy in the Depression era was not unique to Frank Capra. Universal's 1936 comedy *My Man Godfrey*, directed by Gregory LaCava and starring William Powell and Carol Lombard, delivered the theme of unification of the classes perhaps better than any other film of the era. The story centers on a wacky society family who visits a Depression era "hobo camp" to recruit the services of a butler. Powell, an aristocratic blueblood in disguise and on the run from a spoiled romance, takes the job. As might be expected, Powell, as butler Godfrey, manages to straighten out the family's maldirected values in the 93-minute run of the movie.

Cultural and film historians alike have clearly documented the role of the motion picture in attempting to uplift Americans' morale in the economic distress of the Great Depression. Yet those same historians apparently have overlooked or ignored the substantial contributions of slapstick comedy in the 1930s to the same cause.

Especially worthy of note are the comedies of the Marx Brothers. Groucho Marx played the role of a parasite on society during most of the Depression-era films. He regularly had some temporary foothold in society, a position reached by trickery or misunderstanding. His blueblood counterpart, Margaret Dumont, was the loser to Groucho, Harpo, and Chico's commonality in all seven films in which she appeared: *The Cocoanuts* (1929), *Animal Crackers* (1930), *Duck Soup* (1933), *A Night at the Opera* (1935), *A Day at the Races* (1937), *At the Circus* (1939), and *The Big Store* (1941) (Eyles 1992). While most of the Marx Brothers films were subtle in specific reference to class differences relating to the Depression, *Horse Feathers* was a striking exception. According to Eyles, "It was the first of the Marx films to truly satirize the period in which it was made. It gave college education a vigorous shaking, with comments on prohibition and the Depression thrown in."

The Three Stooges' Contributions to America's Morale in the Depression Era

Earlier research (Morlan 1991, 1992, 1993) developed a case for inclusion of the Three Stooges in the history of American thematic film. Moe Howard was undeniably the first screen comedian to portray and satirize Hitler, in *You Nazty Spy!* (1940). That comedy beat Charlie Chaplin's *The Great Dictator* to the screen by a full nine months. Yet film historians have summarily ignored the contributions of the Stooges, as well as other slapstick comedians of the time, to pre–World War II film propaganda.

An analysis of the Stooges films makes clear that in the years before the boys became involved with European political themes, they were major players in the drama of boosting Americans' morale during the depths of the Depression. The antisociety theme that prevailed in feature films of the period was also a mainstay of many Stooges comedies from 1935 on.

Indeed, long before Symona Boniface was sending and receiving cream pies, the Stooges had taken on society in a variety of arenas. The Three Stooges were natural and obvious candidates for taking on the values of high society and the aristocracy in the Depression era. Most of the roles they portrayed were somewhere below the common denominator in American society. They were unemployed or in jail or total bumblers in the performance of any job they might temporarily hold. Yet in all their comedies featuring a marked division of the social classes, the Stooges either emerged winners or were successful at bringing society matrons and patrons to their level.

Conflict between the upper and lower strata of society was the theme in a total of 34 of the 190 Stooges' Columbia shorts from 1934 to 1958. We have already analyzed the five comedies involving pie fights and several others featuring flying foodstuffs and other missiles. Let us turn now to the Stooges' earlier, and perhaps more significant, efforts at equalizing the social classes in Depression-era America.

The boys could and did bring havoc to a formal dinner party. Proper etiquette and refined eating habits were the object of the jokes in at least four comedies. In *Pardon My Scotch* the boys unwittingly become bootleggers, and the process destroys a dinner party. The dinner party theme was repeated in *Termites of 1938*, which finds the Stooges being mistaken for professional escorts and invited to a society party, and much later in *Income Tax Sappy* (1954), where the Stooges find themselves in the unusual position of themselves being the aristocrats, or *nouveaux riches*.

Probably the most classic Stooges dinner party occurs in *Three Sappy People*. The boys are mistaken for psychiatrists and hired by Don Beddoe to examine his wife at her birthday dinner party. Included among the courses of the dinner are Curly shaving at the table with an electric razor and all three boys attacking a "tamale in spring." The dinner ends with a cream puff-throwing fest equal in intensity to any of the later pie fights.

A takeoff on the Pygmalion theme of attempting to transform a flower girl into a lady was a common and recurrent plot structure for Stooges shorts ridiculing the social class. In *Hoi Polloi,* a professor bets a friend that he can turn the Stooges into gentlemen. While the original *Hoi Polloi* did not contain a pie fight, the theme was remade on two occasions with pies added: *Half-Wits Holiday* and *Pies and Guys*.

Playing golf was not a priority for most Americans during the Depression. In fact, golf was identified with the rich and greedy by those suffering most from the economic distress. It is only fitting, then, that the Stooges would do a parody on golf. In *Three Little Beers*, not only do the Stooges ridicule golfers and their mannerisms, but they also manage to virtually destroy the golf course with their novice playing.

The Stooges try to make a living as exterminators in *Ants in the Pantry*. They bring their own pests to release amidst a swanky socialite party, and of course the party results in bedlam. The comedy was redone as the *Pest Man Wins*, with flying pies added to the pests.

The "Hotel Costa Plente" is the scene for two antisociety comedies: *Healthy, Wealthy, and Dumb* (1938) and *A Missed Fortune* (1952). Curly (Shemp in the later version) wins a radio contest, and the boys move into the swanky hotel, where they are stalked by three gold-digging socialites.

One of the Stooges' most memorable comedies, which features "The Alphabet Song," is *Violent Is the Word for Curly* (1938). Moe, Larry, and Curly are mistaken for visiting professors at a swanky, private girls' school, and in just one classroom session they relegate the students and the administration to the Stooges' version of mainstream American society values.

The wealthy's attraction to and expenditures for their pets are the subject of mockery in *Mutts to You* and *Calling All Curs*. In the former, the boys operate a dog-washing service, and in the latter they run a dog hospital. Their credibility as vets is threatened when a prize poodle pointedly named "Garçon" disappears.

Many Stoogephiles consider Curly's performance in *A Plumbing We Will Go* as one of his best. The Stooges are called as plumbers to repair leaks in a society mansion during a party. Once again the party — as well as the plumbing in the mansion — is trashed. The comedy was remade with Shemp as *Vagabond Loafers* and *Scheming Schemers*.

In addition to dinner parties and cocktail parties, the boys also torpedoed a socialite bridge party in *No Census, No Feeling*. Posing as census takers, Moe, Larry, and Curly crash a bridge party and volunteer to cater refreshments. Their punch recipe ingredient — alum — turns the party into a hilarious, puckered-mouth affair.

Another of Curly's top performances finds him disguised as a star soprano in *Micro-Phonies*. When Symona Boniface mistakenly assumes a beautiful voice belongs to Curly, the boys are invited to her elite party to perform. The results are predictable.

The Stooges made ten additional and less notable comedies that all had a common denominator — they ridiculed the values of the rich and resulted in equalizing the classes. These films were *Tassels in the Air, Three Little Sew and Sews, All the World's a Stooge, An Ache in Every Stake, Three Smart Saps, Spook Louder, Crash Goes the Hash, Heavenly Daze, Bedlam in Paradise,* and *Listen Judge*.

Feature-length films in the 1930s that addressed Depression or financial class issues tended to ridicule the values of the rich rather than the people themselves. The Stooges did both. Their style of physical and visual comedy made laughing stocks of the people; however, underlying the slapstick was a definitive indictment of what the wealthy valued in their lives.

When the Stooges were gainfully employed in the Depression theme comedies, they represented the lower stratum of society. Twelve distinct occupations are evident in the 34 comedies: con artist, exterminator, plumber, brewery worker, interior decorator, bootlegger, dog washer, census taker, iceman, newspaper reporter, custodian, and short-order cook. In other comedies they were unemployed, in jail, or mistaken for higher-class roles in society. In all, though, they represented the values of mainstream America in opposition to high society and wealth.

Kathleen Chamberlain (2002) compares the comedy of the Stooges to the classic *commedia dell'arte*. Her analysis aptly explains the appeal of Moe, Larry, and Curly as spokesmen for the "common man" in Depression-era America:

> And all the Stooges qualify as "common men," ones who end up reducing the rich, the snobbish, the smart, and the arty to the lowest common denominator. Just as there are no atheists in foxholes, there are no snobs with a pie in the face ... However wacky, the Stooges, like the ZANNI of the COMMEDIA, represent the common man. When they find themselves in social situations that threaten to overwhelm the common man, they respond the only way they can and still survive — they give "society" a pie in the eye and a kick in the pants.

As American as Apple Pie

The motion picture played a significant role in attempting to equalize the social classes during the Depression. Hollywood was successful at challenging the values of the wealthy and equally adept at neutralizing the differences in the classes and allowing the common man to rule the day.

Unfortunately, the contributions of slapstick comedy to this effort have been largely ignored by film and twentieth-century popular-culture historians. Yet the Stooges ridiculed both the rich as people and their values in at least 35 of their 190 Columbia films. Moe, Larry, and Curly were major players in Hollywood's effort to uplift America's morale in the economic crisis of the Great Depression. In the 1930s, the Stooges frequently took on the upper class. And beginning in 1941 they added the famous pie fight scene.

While such pie fights occur surprisingly infrequently — in only five of the Stooges' 190 Columbia shorts — they have a consistent victim: the members of the elite social class. They also have a consistent outcome. The result of every pie fight is to convert members of society to the status of "commoner." The pie fights thus are among the final contributions the Stooges made to the battle of the classes.

Notes

This essay was originally published in *Popular Culture Review* 7, no. 2 (August 1996) pp. 99–100. Far West Popular and American Culture Associations, sponsored by the University of Nevada, Las Vegas. Dr. Felicia Campebell, ed.

Works Cited

Bergman, Andrew. *We're in the Money: Depression America and Its Films*. New York: Harper and Row, 1971.
Chamberlain, Kathleen. "The Three Stooges and the *Commedia dell'Arte*." In *The Film Comedy Reader*. Ed. Gregg Rickman. New York: Limelight, 2002.
Ellis, Edward Robb. *A Nation in Torment*. New York: Coward-McCann, 1970.
Eyles, Allen. *The Complete Films of the Marx Brothers*. Secaucus, N.J.: Citadel, 1992.
Jowett, Garth. *Film: The Democratic Art*. Boston: Little, Brown, 1976.
McElvaine, Robert S. *The Great Depression: America, 1929–1941*. New York: Times Books, 1984.
Morlan, Don B. "An Analysis of the Three Stooges' Contributions to World War II Propaganda: Dictator Moe Hailstone, et al." Paper presented at the conference of the Popular Culture Association, San Antonio, 1991.
_____. "Slapstick Comedy Contributions to Pre–WWII Film Propaganda: The Three Stooges and Abbott & Costello." Paper presented at the conference of the Popular Culture Association, New Orleans. 1993.
_____. "The Three Stooges' Contributions to WWII Propaganda: Moe Hailstone and Adenoid Hynkel's Race to the Screen." Paper presented at the conference of the Popular Culture Association, Louisville, 1992.

10

Slap-*shtik*: The Three Stooges in the Context of Jewish Humor and Vaudeville

Faye Ringel

Whack! The sacrificial club descends, striking death on the victim's skull and fear in our hearts. But wait! It's only a *slapstick*—see, the victim leaps up alive again, good as new.

Horror! The victim, like Oedipus, like Gloucester, is ritually blinded. But wait! His eyes aren't hurt a bit—they've been poked and gouged, and yet he sees.

It's funny. If tragedy is the genre that accepts and embraces death, that celebrates and elevates death, then comedy exists to defy and deny it. It teaches us not to fear the Reaper, for the grain springs up anew, and so do we. Comedy and tragedy both deal in death and mutilation, but some comedy also deals with sex, love, and marriage. Physical comedy, however, purely engages death and mutilation — it is in some sense pre-Oedipal — and the Three Stooges are its purest proponent, leaves of the most ancient tree, the roots.

But we will not speculate further on what preliterate, prehistoric comedy might have been like (although the Stooges did some great caveman routines, and we can imagine the havoc their painter routine could have wreaked on the Lascaux cave artists). Instead we will place their particular brand of physical comedy in the context of two traditions: the Jewish tradition of clowning and nonverbal humor and that of Jewish-American vaudeville and burlesque.

Like many comedians in early sound films, the Three Stooges came out of vaudeville and the Broadway stage. Unlike stars such as Eddie Cantor and the Marx Brothers, they did not achieve fame until they went to Hollywood. Like Cantor and the Marx Brothers, and like Sophie Tucker and Fannie Brice, however, the original Three Stooges were Jewish. Their *shtik*, "stooging," had a long history in live theater, brought to its apex in vaudeville by their original employer, Ted Healy. Even though the Stooges are rarely cited in the histories of variety entertainment, the early days of Moe and Shemp Howard's and Larry Fine's careers were spent in the small time and the big time of early twentieth-century vaudeville.

The Stooges' relation to the history of Jewish humor is more problematical—even embarrassing. They are part of a 2,000-year tradition of nonverbal, physical comedy, condemned and suppressed but resilient, surviving from ancient Rome to the *shtetl* to the vaudeville stage. The Three Stooges' role in this tradition has been denied or even erased. Rarely are they cited in histories of Jewish humor, which has always privileged verbal irony over slapstick comedy. Nevertheless, the Stooges' antecedents can be found in *purimshpils*, the ritual clowning of the *letz* and the *nar*, and the tradition of the schlemiel and schlimazel.

Slap-shtik

What is "shtik," and what is "slapstick"? Though they sound as if they should be related, and in this chapter they are merged into a portmanteau word, they are actually quite different in their etymology. Slapstick, as noted above, is the feigning of real violence. Literally, the word refers to an ancient implement—in use as early as Roman comedy—whose two flat pieces of light wood are joined to produce a loud slapping noise, and incidentally to sound as though it is inflicting ultra-violence on the victim when it is not. The *Oxford English Dictionary*'s first entry for the word, however, dates only from 1896, and characteristically it is a derogatory reference to "the slap-sticks, rough-and-tumble comedy couples abounding in the variety ranks" ("Slapstick" 1999). Yet what are undoubtedly slapsticks in action can be found in illustrations from the seventeenth century and on statues of Roman mimes.

"Shtik," on the other hand, has nothing to do with "sticks" but derives instead from Yiddish/German "Stück," meaning piece or play ("Shtik" 1999). Thus, originally, a *shtik* was verbal: stage dialogue or a gag. Eventually, however, the term came to incorporate the stage business—often physically violent—that accompanied the patter, until in 1971 Sig Altman, surveying *The Comic Image of the Jew*, could declare that "in American comedy, the word *shtik* (for comic bit) is used universally" (p. 185). For the Stooges, however, slapstick was their *shtik*.

The Jewish Comic Tradition

The Jewish tradition of physical comedy — and the opposition to that tradition — is at least as old as the Roman conquest of Israel. Jewish actors in the Roman theater often played the fool, and these fools took the brunt of rabbinic disapproval. The *letz* (fool) of Roman times became the *nar* of the European Middle Ages, which in Eastern Europe continued until the nineteenth century. Sandrow (1977, p. 10) calls them "simple silly gross clowns ... who hit each other over the head with bladders [more slapsticks] and took pratfalls." Because they were nonverbal and because they were positively embarrassing to the respectable, they are rarely found in anthologies of Jewish humor. We know about them mainly because they were periodically excommunicated! They exemplify the persistent power of physical comedy — a power exercised by the Stooges today.

The underground, carnivalesque tradition of slapstick comedy surfaced once a year — at the Feast of Purim, the Jewish equivalent of Mardi Gras. On this day, the world was turned upside down, and all that was normally forbidden — drunkenness, irreverence to teachers and elders, cross-dressing, theater — was encouraged. Records of Purim plays (the *Purimshpil*) and entire scripts exist from the fourteenth century on, and from these we can trace the history of the *lets* and *nar*. According to Sandrow (1977, p. 10), "The earliest, and for a long time the only, professional Yiddish theatrical performers were ... clowns." Besides general mayhem, Stooges-style, the Purim play repeated the mock battle, death, and resurrection pattern familiar from the English mummers' plays, and from Christian passion plays. *Purimshpils* were performed in the Bensonhurst, Brooklyn, streets of Moe, Shemp, and Curly's childhood, as they are performed today in Crown Heights and other Hasidic enclaves.

The Jewish tradition encompassed other types of clowns. The term "Payatz" was applied to the Pagliacci type of *commedia dell'arte* clown, who is crying inside (and sometimes outside) through his white makeup. In the older *Purimshpil* tradition, the Payatz acted as the Prologue to the play. "If the audience's attention seems to be waning," Sandrow (1977) writes, "he may stand on his head, or he may spin out puns based on Hebrew and Yiddish words that sound alike but mean different things" or even parody prayers. In the 1920s and 1930s, Yiddish theater star Herman Yablokoff became radio's "Phantom of the Air — Der Payatz," his identity a public relations secret, with his signature song "When your heart is torn to shreds with sorrow — laugh, laugh, Payatz" (Yablokoff 1995, p. 310). This style of tragicomedy was prized in both high and low Yiddish culture. King Lear and his Fool in the *Yiddish King Lear* were acclaimed as part of the Payatz tradition of "laughter through tears — emphasis on the tears."[1] This sort of verbal masochism, the ability "to joke and laugh in the face of misfortune and despair" (Saper 1993, p. 80) may not be so far removed from the sadomasochistic antics of the Stooges, who allow us to laugh at what we would normally fear—mutilation, destruction, humiliation.

The *badkhen* was a hyperverbal clown, who specialized as a wedding jester and as such survives in the Hasidic community to this day. He would give comic sermons, make the bride and the guests cry, then improvise commentary about the affair while entertaining in other ways. According to Sandrow (1977, p. 11), one nineteenth-century Russian *badkhen* "played the fiddle behind his back—with gloves on!" Before he became a Stooge, Larry Fine had a similar *shtik*: he would "do a Russian dance while playing the violin" (Lenburg et al. 1982, p. 27).

Besides recalling these professional comedians, the Three Stooges of the first era (Curly, Larry, and Moe) also enacted a classic trio from Yiddish folklore: the schlemiel, the schlimazel, and the bully or persecutor.[2] The first two figures are famous, but the third is necessary for there to be a drama—someone, after all, must torment or set up the fools; someone must be the presenter of their foolishness, to motivate the plot. The tormentor may be a Gentile—a Haman, a Cossack, a Hitler—or else an ignorant, cruel Jewish man: in either case, Moe fits the part to perfection. No wonder he could send up Hitler in *You Nazty Spy!* and *I'll Never Heil Again* better even than Charlie Chaplin himself.[3]

The schlemiel is a more familiar figure in Yiddish folklore, literature, and criticism. Like Curly, he is childish, stupid, inept, and clumsy at everything he tries. As Nathan Ausubel (1948, p. 344) observes in his *Treasury of Jewish Folklore*, schlemiels had to be pitiable as well as laughable: "In order to survive, they had to be eternally hopeful, untiringly enterprising, and yet ... pathetic flops." The schlimazel, on the other hand, may wind up in the same place as the schlemiel, but he is not so much idiotic as simply luckless (the name derives from the German and Hebrew words for "bad luck"). Like Larry, he receives the punishment and blows of fate that might originally have been destined for the schlemiel. He may be smarter than Curly, but he messes up just the same. In Yiddish folklore, schlemiel and schlimazel constantly had to shift occupations, and sometimes they seemed to live from the air alone, leading to the nickname *luftmensch*—air-man. Most Stooges short films have the boys try out a new occupation—painting, cooking, plumbing, teaching—and fail at it, with comic results.[4]

In literature, these folk figures have been used to inspire pathos and tragedy as well as comedy. Isaac Bashevis Singer's "Gimpel the Fool" is the archetypal schlemiel, elevated to the stature of Holy Fool and identified with the storyteller himself. Gimpel's tormentors, like Moe, engage in verbal and physical abuse: they devise tortures both physical and psychological; they cuckold Gimpel and force him to pay for their pleasures. In another example,

Bernard Malamud's short story "The Jewbird," a skinny black bird plays the role of schlemiel or schlimazel, perpetually running and flying from "Anti-Semeets" (Anti-Semites), while his Moe-like antagonist, beefy, Jewish Harry Cohen, torments him, sets a cat on him, and finally engages him in a burlesque battle — but this is tragedy, not comedy, and the Jewbird dies, plucked by crows. In the same way, Curly is perpetually tortured by Moe, while Larry often receives the punishment by mistake.

The Stooges are not unique in enacting these roles: Eddie Cantor and Georgie Jessel — and of course Harpo Marx — also presented the innocent schlemiel on stage and screen. In Cantor's earliest "as told to" autobiography, *My Life Is in Your Hands*, he describes an early blackface version of this vaudeville act as "sissy-bully team, he the boor and I the cultured pansy-like Negro with spectacles" (Cantor 1932, p. 122). While Moe and Shemp were touring in vaudeville, they shared the RKO circuit with Eddie Cantor performing his routine with Bert Williams, the African American blackface entertainer. Even when Cantor was not blacking up, he was playing the schlemiel. Cantor "had a mauling scene in almost every show ... thumped, thwacked, and twisted into a cruller on the stage" (Cantor 1932, p. 29), based on memories of a neighborhood bully who would mercilessly wake him in the morning by pummeling and knocking him onto the floor. Transformed into physical comedy, the dreadful memories were "a standard element in [Cantor's] repertory of fun" (Cantor 1932, p. 187).

Though many Yiddish-speaking artists and patrons made an easy transition to American vaudeville, the carnivalesque side of Yiddish tradition, not to be accommodated on the blue-nosed Keith circuit, on Second Avenue, or in the art theaters, found expression in unprintable dirty jokes,[5] obscene "blue" records, rowdy music-halls, and, eventually, the form of variety entertainment known as burlesque. Minsky's, the most famous burlesque house, originally shared space with a Yiddish theater; according to the memoir of Morton Minsky, the strip-shows included not only baggy-pants physical comedy but serious dramatic sketches: "There would be a slight story line that always wound up in tragedy and tears. It reminded me much of the pattern of the plays that were showing in the Yiddish theater downstairs in the same building" (Minsky and Machlin 1986, p. 6).

There is a book to be written on the missing or erased tradition of Yiddish burlesque and vaudeville. Moe and Shemp were undoubtedly connected to these "unrespectable" forms of entertainment, but other than some tantalizing hints, such forms remain undocumented. Moe did try his hand at the "legitimate" Yiddish theater; as late as 1927 he "worked intermittently at the Jewish Community House in Bensonhurst, producing and directing plays" (Lenburg et al. 1982, p. 21).

Despite these connections with Jewish tradition, for many years the Three

Stooges did not register as Jewish with most audiences. They had achieved that highest goal of their generation of entertainers: assimilation into the nonethnic American mainstream. Recently, Generation X comedian Adam Sandler "outed" the Stooges as Jewish on his recording "Chanukah."

Vaudeville

For scholars of popular culture, however, the news of the Stooges' ethnic origin is no surprise, nor is their desire for complete assimilation. Both have been detailed in Neal Gabler's *An Empire of Their Own: How the Jews Invented Hollywood* (1988) and Michael Rogin's *Blackface, White Noise: Jewish Immigrants in the Hollywood Melting Pot* (1996). Like the movie moguls who sought to get away from immigrant origins, and like vaudeville performers Al Jolson and Eddie Cantor, the Howard brothers and Larry Fine sought out comic material that would be 100 percent American. This material included, in their earlier days, blackface minstrel routines. As Rogin (1996, p. 27) notes, "Blackface, the performance of the white man's African American, opens the door to the meanings of whiteness in the United States." For whatever reason (and many theories exist), first the Irish and then the Jews found that their easiest entry into the American theater was through blacking their faces and affecting a Southern accent.

Some variety performers, like Moe and Shemp, varied their personas as their careers advanced. Weber and Fields, who were born Orthodox Jews, played for years in blackface, then achieved vaudeville stardom doing physical comedy stunts, and eventually became America's best-known comic Germans (*Vaudeville* 1997). According to Robert Snyder (1989, p. 138), "In 1912, the long-popular stars Weber and Fields enumerated their most effective routines. The list began with a poke in the eye." Photographs from this era show Weber and Fields sometimes in blackface and sometimes in what could be called Jewface (as stereotyped immigrants)[6]. Later, as vaudeville impresarios, they sought out and booked physical comedians such as the Stooges.

The memoirs of the Stooges found in the *Three Stooges Scrapbook* include the blackface origins of Moe and Shemp's career and a rare picture of the two of them, looking more Irish than black, but labeled as blackface minstrels. During and after World War I, Moe and Shemp played blackface vaudeville: "They played a blackface routine for RKO and a whiteface one for Loew's ... Shemp jokingly recalled the blackest [*sic*] moment of his life as the time he was working blackface in a minstrel show and the manager skipped with the payroll and the cold cream" (Lenburg et al. 1982, pp. 42–43). Unlike Jolson and Cantor, however, the brothers did not continue in blackface disguise, nor did they take that routine to Hollywood. Instead, they changed direction and took up a different vaudeville *shtik*: stooging for Ted Healy.

Stooging was not invented in 1922 by Healy or the Howards — or by the violinist Larry Fine who joined the act in 1925. The term was already in existence referring to the butt of vaudeville physical comedy, who received the punches of the headliner, just as the straight man set up the punchlines of verbal humor. Healy remarked in a newspaper interview: "A stooge always comes in handy when you feel like throwing something at somebody. Whenever I'm in doubt or feel mixed up, I always hit the nearest stooge" (qtd. in Lenburg et al. 1982, p. 13). During the twenties, Healy was the undisputed star of the group, one of the highest-paid vaudevillians of his day. He even transferred the act, nearly unchanged, to Broadway — sometimes with Moe, sometimes without — and then to Hollywood for the Stooges' first movie, *Soup to Nuts* (1930); apparently the anarchic, improvisational style of comedy traveled well. Then Healy and the boys split (the reason has been the subject of many speculations). Suddenly, the Stooges were on their own, floating signifiers, and stooging was transformed from mere vaudeville echo to Hollywood self-sufficiency.

Larry Fine (born Feinberg) followed a different route through vaudeville — that of the comic musician. He played for weddings, suffered through Amateur Nights, sang along with silent movies in the very small time up and down the East Coast, and finally achieved full-time employment in one of vaudeville impresario Gus Edwards' kid shows, "Newsboy Sextette, playing the violin, dancing, and telling jokes in a Jewish dialect" (Lenburg et al. 1982, p. 27). Healy recruited him as a Stooge provided he lost the violin.

Curly (Jerome Howard), younger than the others, did not come up through vaudeville or minstrelsy. Instead, he hung around theaters and watched his brothers perform; but it was not until 1932, during their Broadway phase, that Curly was added to the act. His success came solely from the movies; unlike the others, he seems to have been something of an introvert offscreen, without the manic energy needed to survive in the six-shows-a-day world of variety.

As Rogin (1996, p. 90) notes, later forms of entertainment may have killed earlier ones, but "each of these spectacles ... linked to its predecessor." Sound films killed both vaudeville and the silent films that had provided some employment for variety performers like Larry Fine. Film comedy of the 1930s carried over the *shtiks* and the vaudeville performers themselves and even, for a short while, the blackface of minstrelsy. The latter, subject of the first sound feature, *The Jazz Singer*, and one of the most popular early musicals, Eddie Cantor's *Whoopee!*, faded quickly from the scene, while the Stooges' anarchic, simple plot comedies, descendants of their vaudeville act, have had a much longer run.

For example, the Stooges' doctor routines, found in many of their movies and exemplified by the short film *Men in Black* (not a prescient title, but a take-off on the ultra-serious, Pulitzer Prize-winning Sidney Kingsley play *Men in White*), get to the heart of physical comedy's defiance of death. The mallet for anesthesia is a direct descendant of the ancient slapstick and of the doctor of the mummers' plays or the *commedia dell'arte*. The operating room scene, with its ritualized dialogue and mayhem, also reflects vaudeville's Dr. Kronkhite (Dr. Sickness) routine, first performed by comedians Smith and Dale at the turn of the century.

Transcending Vaudeville

Just as rabbis and scholars wished to erase the Jewish tradition of physical comedy, so American culture would like to forget some aspects of vaudeville, burlesque, and the minstrel show. Those who once patronized these popular art forms are dying, their memories growing less reliable. For the rest of us, how many know what we are missing? Bill Irwin, often cited as a "new vaudeville" entertainer, describes the "cultural, dream-like memory" of vaudeville, something that "inspires nostalgia for something we've never known" (*Vaudeville* 1997). Indeed, the popularity of the Stooges' film work, especially their classic short subjects, goes on and on, unchanged, enrapturing a new generation, who have no childhood memories of variety, of early films, or even of early television. Out of context, deracinated from vaudeville and Jewish tradition, the Stooges' comedy lives and triumphs once more over those old antagonists Time, Pain, and Death.

Notes

1. See also Goldberg (1983), Saper (1993), and Kaufman (1993) on this aspect of the Jewish comic tradition.
2. This is not the only way to read the trio's roles: Peter Brunette (1991, p. 184) in "The Three Stooges and the (Anti-)Narrative of Violence: De(con)structive Comedy" sees them as a little family, within which "they reenact the family struggle ... with Moe, "moi," as "the ego, the controlling figure, the father, the one who pretends to rationality and the Logos." See also Chapters 6 and 11, where the Stooges are described as fitting the roles of ego and superego.
3. Erens (1984, p. 154) in *The Jew in American Cinema* comments on Chaplin's version of Hitler, without mentioning Moe's. She compares many of Chaplin's characterizations to "the figure of the Shlemiel, well known in Jewish folklore" but never mentions the Stooges. Langman (1987) notes the typical roles of the Stooges but does not relate them to the Jewish folklore.
4. See Boyer (1993, pp. 3–12), who conflates the schlemiel and schlimazel into the "Schlemiezel" for another view of the tragic and black comic overtones of these folk figures.

5. See Telushkin (1992), who explains euphemistically why they are so unprintable. Also see Cohen (1986), "Yiddish Origins and American Transformations," who sees American vaudeville as the transition between Jewish popular tradition and the movies.

6. See Sobel (1961, p. 203), *A Pictorial History of Vaudeville*, for the pictures. Sobel notes "their well-known eye-jabbing business" but does not include a picture or a word about the Stooges.

Works Cited

Altman, Sig. *The Comic Image of the Jew: Explorations of a Pop Culture Phenomenon*. Rutherford, N.J.: Fairleigh Dickinson University Press, 1971.

Ausubel, Nathan. *A Treasury of Jewish Folklore*. New York: Crown, 1948.

Boyer, Jay. "The Schlemiezel: Black Humor and the Shtetl Tradition." *Semites and Stereotypes: Characteristics of Jewish Humor*. Ed. Avner Ziv and Anat Zadjman. Contributions in Ethnic Studies 31. Westport, Conn.: Greenwood, 1993.

Brunette, Peter. "The Three Stooges and the (Anti-)Narrative of Violence: De(con)structive Comedy" *Comedy/Cinema/Theory*. Ed. Andrew Horton. Berkeley: University of California Press, 1991.

Cantor, Eddie, as told to David Freedman. *My Life Is in Your Hands*. New York: Blue Ribbon, 1932.

Cohen, Sarah Blacher. "Yiddish Origins and Jewish-American Transformations." *From Hester Street to Hollywood: The Jewish-American Stage and Screen*. Ed. Sarah Blacher Cohen. Bloomington: Indiana University Press, 1986.

Erens, Patricia. *The Jew in American Cinema*. Bloomington: Indiana University Press, 1984.

Gabler, Neal. *An Empire of Their Own: How the Jews Invented Hollywood*. New York: Crown, 1988.

Goldberg, Judith. *Laughter through Tears: The Yiddish Cinema*. Rutherford, N.J.: Fairleigh Dickinson University Press, 1983.

Kaufman, Rhoda. "The Yiddish Theater in New York and the Immigrant Jewish Community: Theater as Secular Ritual." Diss. UC Berkeley 1986; UMI Diss. Information Service, printed 1993.

Langman, Larry. "Slapstick," "The Three Stooges," "Howard, Moe, Shemp, Curly." *Encyclopedia of American Film Comedy*. New York: Garland, 1987.

Lenburg, Jeff, Joan Howard Maurer, and Greg Lenburg. *The Three Stooges Scrapbook*. Secaucus, N.J.: Citadel, 1982.

Minsky, Morton, and Milt Machlin. *Minsky's Burlesque*. New York: Arbor House, 1986.

Rogin, Michael. *Blackface, White Noise: Jewish Immigrants in the Hollywood Melting Pot*. Berkeley: University of California Press, 1996.

Sandrow, Nahma. *Vagabond Stars: A World History of Yiddish Theater*. Jewish Publication Society of America. New York: Harper, 1977.

Saper, Bernard. "Since When Is Jewish Humor Not Anti-Semitic?" *Semites and Stereotypes: Characteristics of Jewish Humor*. Ed. Avner Ziv and Anat Zadjman. Contributions in Ethnic Studies 31. Westport: Greenwood, 1993.

"Shtik." *Oxford English Dictionary*. CD-ROM. New York: Oxford University Press, 1999.

"Slapstick." *Oxford English Dictionary*. CD-ROM. New York: Oxford University Press, 1999.

Snyder, Robert W. *The Voice of the City: Vaudeville and Popular Culture in New York*. New York: Oxford University Press, 1989.

Sobel, Bernard. *A Pictorial History of Vaudeville*. New York: Citadel Press, 1961.
Telushkin, Rabbi Joseph. *Jewish Humor: What the Best Jewish Jokes Say about the Jews*. New York: William Morrow, 1992.
Vaudeville. Video documentary, American Masters Series. WGBH-Boston. 26 Nov. 1997.
Yablokoff, Herman. *Der Payatz: Around the World with Yiddish Theater*. Trans. Bella Mysell. Silver Springs: Bartleby Press, 1995.

11

Larry — the Existential Stooge

Ted Levitt

The personalities and characters of the Three Stooges, as with any celebrities, resonate with cultural stereotypes, personal identity, and media conventions. Beyond a possible pickup line of "Who's your favorite Stooge?" their individual personae have roots in many cultural traditions and expressions. These character peculiarities were almost certainly not predetermined or intentional and may well have been overlooked by actors, writers, and directors. Still, after the fact, one can see the cultural and comedic standards the originators of the Stooges took for granted and incorporated into their characters. It is more interesting, perhaps, to look at the ways the Stooges broke from these stereotypes and reflected other, more diverse hierarchies.

Three is not a dominant number for comedy teams. Two-man teams more easily come to mind, such as Abbott and Costello, Laurel and Hardy, and Martin and Lewis (see, for example, Maltin 1985 and Burr 1979). It is still easier to recall comedians that worked as solo acts, either as stand-ups or in movies with a varying cast of foils, partners, and straight men. A three-person team was certainly not revolutionary, but it does suggest a different balance and, by necessity, a different hierarchy. It also reflects aspects of culture that a two-man actor single act obviously could not (see the discussion by Epstein 2004 of various comedy teams comprising two or three or even more people).

The essential characteristic of Western culture that the Stooges seem to contradict is its practically defining dualism. Good or bad, friend or foe, black or white: the stereotype allows for little middle ground or complexity. This oversimplification makes recognition, decisions, and understanding far less difficult. One of the most useful, if tragic, examples is the politician who sees the world as either with us or against us and Americans as either patriots or subversives. The two-person comedy team almost embodies this standard: straight man and foil, authority figure and follower, boss and worker. Uncomplicated by any middle man, Western dualism is easily maintained and easily applied. To suggest a dualism that is more comprehensive, as well as the basis and definition of much Western thinking, the two-man team embodies the mind/body split that characterizes so much of our cultural heritage. If Abbott is the mind, Costello is the body. The two are generally seen as separate and co-equal and, as an aggregate, the totality of reality.

The Stooges clearly contradict this simple construction. Moe and Curly are easily the counterparts of most comedy teams. Moe is mind; Curly is body. The addition of Larry to the formulation is what gives the Stooges a group dynamic that, if not unique, is certainly uncharacteristic of comedic tradition. Clearly, multitudes of examples of this apparently nondualistic structure occur in our heritage.[1] They tend to be more complicated and open to interpretation, but also more useful and flexible. In fact, they may be considered more representative of Eastern culture and philosophy. Perhaps Larry more usefully equates to the Buddhist middle way and a less rigid world view that allows for shading and crossover.[2]

Western Trinity

One Western hierarchy that is reflected in the structure of the Stooges is the Holy Trinity. Catholic theologians have tried repeatedly over the centuries to define the three elements, allowing characteristics to each that are not present in the others (for recent discussions of the Holy Trinity see, for example, Hedley 2004, Letham 2005). The difficulty of this effort reflects the very Zen idea of holistic thinking. The Trinity may be composed of three parts, but the components are ultimately inseparable and best defined as a whole. The Stooges are also a trinity. From dualistic cultural theories it is clear that Moe is the Father — the authority, the boss, the obvious leader. So Curly must be the Son — the underling, the spiritual made flesh, the more human and flawed, even childlike. Continuing this comparison to its conclusion, Larry is the Holy Spirit — the most difficult to grasp and the one with the least obvious human, religious, and cultural corollaries. His existential purpose is to unite the three, to support continuity and humanity without a clear role or purpose of his own.[3] That defines, as well as anything, Larry's purpose as a Stooge. In a theological context, he may be as close to the Holy Fool as the Holy Spirit.[4] His function is necessary but variable. It shifts from one paradigm to the next but is mostly ineffable and better defined by anecdote, better seen in context than are the characters of Moe and Curly.

Turning from theology to psychology, one can consider the psychological formulations of the id, ego, and superego (Freud 1962). Again, the three may be defined as individual entities, but the only reasonable way to understand them is as a whole, each overlapping components of a personality. Contrary to the findings of Tim Snyder (in Chapter 6), to us Moe is the superego, the imposed authority, the planner, the one most likely to be aware of the social structure and its constraints.[5] Curly is mostly pure, childish id. He is immediate and selfish, and he has little patience for convention and restraint. Without Moe's authority (and punishment), Curly would likely be entirely self-serving and spontaneous — like the impulsive child he represents, he is energy without reflection, desire without conscience.

But we again have the problem of Larry. By process of elimination, he is the ego, once again the middle that unites opposites, the connection between extremes (Fineburg 2001). He is a mixture of Moe and Curly, of id and superego. He can join Curly in a passionate, sometimes surreal flight of uninhibited reaction. He can equally assist Moe with punishment and restraint of Curly. If he weren't there, we would have significant trouble defining his absence, but the dynamic of the Stooge hierarchy would be inevitably altered and simplified. He is, like most of us, just trying to get by, a shifting package of characteristics and traits, often feeling constrained by all sides and unable to commit to a particular course or identity. As in *Waiting for Godot* (Beckett 1997; see also Graver 2004), if Curly and Estagon are body, Vladimir and Moe the intellect, then they are waiting for Larry in order to be complete, to have a sense of their own existence.

Other Western trinities lend themselves to a similar analysis but are perhaps less compelling. Karl Marx (1975) defined the struggle between capital and production, between boss and worker. In this context, Larry must represent the amorphous middle class, the bourgeoisie, the societal element that fears losing status yet lusts for admittance to the elite. Once again, the middle class is more than a placeholder between boss and worker, but it has no clear boundaries with them and may largely be subject to self-definition. In other words, the middle class makes class struggle between lower and upper classes problematic, not only because of its presence as a buffer, but because of its bleeding into the other two and blurring all distinctions. Analogously, Larry mitigates the impending warfare between Moe and Curly. If fear and greed are the elemental forces in society, Larry probably experienced measures of both in regard to his counterparts. Still, he clearly shares characteristics with both Moe and Curly, while doing his best to remain distinctive (for further insight, see Larry Fine's own book *A Stroke of Luck* 1973).

Like reality itself, and especially that of the nondualistic and the Eastern, the trinity of the Stooges is far from neat. In the beginning of the act, Ted Healy functioned as the straight man, and "his Stooges" functioned as a unit, offering the opportunity for Healy's famous "triple slap." The distinctions between the

Stooges were far less distinct than those between all three on the one hand and Healy on the other. It was Abbott with three Costellos. It may have been more opportunity than intention that the Stooges developed from this cohesion after they split from Healy and went out on their own. The individual personae certainly evolved, however, and became three perspectives of one gestalt.

Since it usually is unwise to ignore history when proposing any theory, the question of Shemp must be addressed. Shemp has more definition than Curly, is less pure id and more adult. He suffers Moe's authority as Curly did, but he seems to be more sympathetic. In other words, the suspension of judgment when Moe slapped Curly was easier because Curly appeared as more of a force of nature and less an individual personality. Shemp is less elemental and a more complicated personality. He is, therefore, better able to evoke sympathy when subject to insult, pain, and regret. Perhaps Shemp, as a less childlike version of Curly, represents the biblical fall from grace and its attendant loss of innocence. Having more maturity, he is a more credible threat to the Father (Moe), and the balance is forever altered. But if Curly had original innocence, then Shemp must have original sin.[6] His character was born destined to unfavorable comparison to Curly. While not his fault, his own comedic qualities are often not appreciated nor recognized, and he is judged guilty of his lack of Curly-ness. Larry's function in this new hierarchy was, unremarkably, little changed. As a character, he achieved no additional clarity or purpose. The comparison to the indistinct, nonindividualized Larry is pointless — there are not enough distinctions to compare. Larry remains Larry: the intermediary and middleman between opposing forces.

While it may be tempting to ignore the two latter-day Curlys, their existence as pretenders offers, if anything, additional support for the role of Larry as Holy Fool, Holy Ghost, bourgeoisie ego. Joe Besser and Curly Joe DeRita offered their services when the act was in decline and the characters of the Stooges were losing identity, distinction, and complexity. In the *Wizard of Oz*, the man behind the curtain is presented as an intermediary between Dorothy and Oz himself but is, in fact, an imposter (Baum 2000). Larry's role as intermediary also became mostly illusion, and the last two Curlys were essentially imposters. With the characters of all Three Stooges simplified, childlike, and nonthreatening, Larry's role lost its purpose and therefore its necessity. He became a placeholder, with little subtlety or context.

The Unholy Trinity

The Stooges, as they say, belong to the ages. Explication need not mitigate enjoyment, but it is hardly required for appreciation either. The humor of the Stooges is the intellectual equivalent of a pie to the face. It is immediate, visceral, and emotional. As a gestalt, it is simply funny (or not). Analysis of the trinity is like squaring the circle. It is interesting as an exercise, but ultimately it gets one nowhere.

Still, theologians, psychologists, economists, and writers of articles will always believe that understanding requires analysis, analysis requires hierarchies, and hierarchies require differentiation. Fortunately, it is not necessary to then try to reassemble the pieces, because the sum of the parts is no further than a DVD player.

Slapstick may well be the least cerebral of comedic forms, and the Stooges were certainly not academics. It is, in fact, the essential purity of their humor that renders analysis harmless. Scholarship is to the Stooges as poetry is to love. One has no requirement for the other, but it is human nature to intellectualize. Deconstruction is the way we try to understand reality. Humor and love are among ways we actually experience it.

We are certainly closer to Larry than we are to Moe or Curly. We try to maneuver between extremes of opinion and authority, between mind and body, between intellect and emotion. We often identify with these but are rarely defined by them. We are, like Larry, mostly harmless and uncertain. We will do our best, but we will never clearly understand. We are, we hope, necessary, and we are, we believe, unique. But we mostly resemble Larry, the existential Stooge.

Notes

1. Galian's book *Beyond Duality* (1995) confronts familiar concepts of duality such as male-female and up-down. His book purports to present ways to help readers bring balance and harmony to their lives by transcending such duality.
2. See Burtt (1955) for a comprehensive primer on the basic doctrines of Buddhism.
3. For an introduction to existentialism and its roots in various literary works (not the Stooges comedies!), see Kaufmann (1988).
4. Richard James (2005) agrees, noting that in the famous threesomes of the Marx Brothers and the Stooges, "Larry and Harpo most often play the Fool." James states that what distinguishes the Fool from the buffoon is that the "Fool does not try to influence the outcome of events. He may be content to simply be, or may be so ignorant of what is going on, that he is simply swept along by the tide of events."
5. Richard von Busack (1997) also disagrees. In his article "Pure Slap Shtick," he sees Moe as the "egotistical" force that keeps the group in order, while he sees Larry as the "emotive super-ego."
6. Tatha Wiley (2002) presents an interesting discussion of the evolving concept of original sin. Compare the work of Blocher (1999), who focuses on a rigorous interpretation of Genesis and Romans.

Works Cited

Baum, L. Frank. *The Wonderful Wizard of Oz: 100th Anniversary Edition*. New York: HarperCollins, 2000.

Beckett, Samuel. *Waiting for Godot: A Tragicomedy in Two Acts.* New York: Grove, 1997.
Blocher, Henri. *Original Sin: Illuminating the Riddle.* Grand Rapids, Mich.: Eerdmans, 1999.
Burr, Lonnie. *Two for the Show: Great 20th Century Comedy Teams.* New York: Messner, 1979.
Burtt, E. A. *Teachings of the Compassionate Buddha.* New York: Signet, 1955.
Carone, James (as told by Larry Fine). *A Stroke of Luck* Hollywood: Siena, 1973.
Epstein, Lawrence J. *Mixed Nuts: America's Love Affair with Comedy Teams from Burns and Allen to Belushi and Aykroyd.* New York: Public Affairs, 2004.
Fineburg, Morris. *Larry, the Stooge in the Middle.* San Francisco: Last Gasp, 2001.
Freud, Sigmund. *The Ego and the Id: The Standard Edition of the Complete Psychological Works of Sigmund Freud.* New York: Norton: 1962.
Galian, Laurence. *Beyond Duality: The Art of Transcendence.* Scottsdale, Ariz.: New Falcon, 1995.
Graver, Lawrence. *Beckett: Waiting for Godot.* Cambridge: Cambridge University Press, 2004.
Hedley, George Percy. *The Holy Trinity: Experience and Interpretation.* Minneapolis: Fortress, 2004.
James, Richard. "The Holy Fool." 28 Dec. 2005. http://www.haze.ca/fez/fool.html.
Kaufmann, Walter. *Existentialism: From Dostoevsky to Sartre.* New York: Plume, 1988.
Letham, Robert. *The Holy Trinity: In Scripture, History, Theology and Worship.* Phillipsburg, N.J.: P&R, 2005.
Maltin, Leonard. *Movie Comedy Teams.* New York: New American Library, 1985.
Marx, Karl. *Karl Marx: Economy, Class and Social Revolution.* New York: Scribner, 1975.
von Busack, Richard. "Pure Slap Shtick." *Metro Santa Cruz.* 16–22 Jan. 1997. Accessed 26 Dec. 2005. http://www.ratical.com/ratville/3stooges75yrs.html.
Wiley, Tatha. *Original Sin: Origins, Developments, Contemporary Meanings.* Mahwah, N.J.: Paulist, 2002.

III. THE STOOGES GO TO WAR

Of all the jobs ever attempted by the Stooges, featured most frequently were their stints in the military. Indeed, of their 190 films, 23 contained military themes as a significant part of the plot: *Uncivil Warriors, Half Shot Shooters, Wee Wee Monsieur, Three Little Sew and Sews, Saved by the Belle, You Nazty Spy!, Boobs in Arms, Dutiful But Dumb, I'll Never Heil Again, They Stooge to Conga, Back from the Front, Higher Than a Kite, Dizzy Pilots, The Yoke's on Me, No Dough Boys, Uncivil War Birds, G.I. Wanna Go Home, Fuelin' Around, Dunked in the Deep, Love at First Bite, Hot Stuff, Commotion on the Ocean,* and *Fifi Blows Her Top.* In several of these films, the Stooges used their trademark brand of incompetence to advance the military concerns of their side or foil those of their opponents.

The films of the Three Stooges spanned three wars with American involvement: World War II, the Korean War, and the early stages of American action in Vietnam. World War II is the only one of these conflicts in which they became directly involved. They also managed to fight in the Civil War and World War I. Most of the time a war was used as just another situation and backdrop for the Stooges' mayhem. Of course, the consequences were much higher in a war than they were in other situations, and while the boys somehow managed to muddle through to help the side of righteousness, they occasionally pushed their superiors too far, as in their court-martial shooting in *Half-Shot Shooters.* Of greater interest to this study is the portrayal of the militaries of the three major Axis powers — Germany, Italy, and Japan — in the films of the Three Stooges. These portrayals were fairly uncommon for comedies of the period, and thus make for a fascinating study within slapstick comedy.

This section focuses on the role of the Three Stooges during World War II. While the Stooges are not well known for political commentary, the films examined here feature an unusual amount of wartime propaganda. Chapter 12 reveals how Moe Howard preceded Charlie Chaplin by nine months in portraying Adolf Hitler and in lampooning the Führer and the Axis powers at a time when President Franklin D. Roosevelt was struggling with an isolationist Congress and an American public opposed to interventionism in the European theater. Chapter 13 provides a more in-depth examination of the portrayals of Hitler, and also looks at these portrayals within the context of the Stooges' Jewish heritage, which may well have played a role in these bold and striking films that attacked the Nazis with gusto, sometimes well before such a sentiment was accepted nationwide. Chapter 14 examines the somewhat shameful portrayals of the Japanese during the World War II films, analyzing the Stooges' use of war propaganda to attack an entire race of people.

12

The Three Stooges' Contribution to World War II Propaganda: Moe Hailstone and Adenoid Hynkel's Race to the Screen

Don Morlan

    The great Charles Chaplin has been credited with creating the first satirical screen portrayal of Hitler in his first talking production, *The Great Dictator*. Given the isolationist climate in the country in 1939 and 1940 preceding Pearl Harbor, such historic designation is a significant event for the student of World War II propaganda. The primary purpose of this chapter is to challenge that long-accepted belief by demonstrating that the first comedian to create a satirical portrayal of Hitler on screen was, in fact, Moses Harry Horwitz, alias Moe Howard of the Three Stooges, in the 1940 Columbia two-reel comedy *You Nazty Spy!*

    The purpose here is not to detract from the great Charles Chaplin or his creation of Adenoid Hynkel in *The Great Dictator*. The movie was, is, and forever will be a true classic contribution to American film comedy. Rather, the intent here is to give credit where it is due to another classic element in American film — the slapstick genius of the Three Stooges — particularly the comic ability of Moe Howard.

    Another purpose of this chapter is to demonstrate that the Stooges were apparently unnoticed or ignored in their Nazi-bashing by the strong isolationist sentiment in the country, unlike all the rest of Hollywood, including Chaplin. *The Great Dictator* appears to be the only comedy cited as objectionable by those openly attacking film propaganda.

Isolationists' War against Hollywood

The year 1936 marked a turning point, when Hollywood's attention began focusing on political developments in Europe as potentially salable screenplay. Studio heads were constantly on the lookout for plays, novels, articles, or anything else in print that could be quickly developed into a film story. By 1936 such material relating to foreign developments was becoming plentiful, and European conditions were attracting greater public attention and concern from the American public.

Newsreels were among the first films to attract criticism from the outspoken element in the country. Ironically, attacks on newsreels came from both sides of the war issue. On the one hand they were criticized for not treating developments seriously enough — catering to parades, festivals, and beauty contests over hardbreaking news. When newsreels did attempt to portray events as they were unraveling in Europe, however, they endured the wrath of isolationists. *The March of Time* was once accused of being pro–Fascist and a propaganda tool for the J. P. Morgan interests (Jowett 1976). Just four years later nine episodes of the RKO series were cited by a Senate subcommittee as inciting America to war (Culbert 1990).

With the exception of *The Great Dictator* in 1940, criticism was evidently confined to serious, dramatic screen offerings. While many films were eventually branded as propaganda tools from 1936 to Pearl Harbor, five titles have been singled out by film historians as being the most offensive to America-first critics.

Spain in Flames (1936) was a documentary film dealing with the Spanish Civil War. The film was banned in many American markets, including the entire state of Pennsylvania, because of its references to "Fascist," "Nazi," and "German" (Jowett 1976).

Blockade (1938) provided a fictional treatment of the Spanish Civil War. In addition to the anticipated opposition from the isolationists, the film was criticized from within the film industry as threatening the loss of foreign markets for American films. *Blockade* was boycotted and picketed by Catholic organizations throughout the United States and earned the label "leftist propaganda" from the Knights of Columbus (Jowett 1976).

The first purely anti–Nazi Hollywood release was the Warner Brothers 1939 production of *Confessions of a Nazi Spy*. The film was made at the urging of J. Edgar Hoover and portrayed the actual, documented exposure of a German spy ring in New York City in 1938. The patriotic theme throughout the movie was unmistakable: "Nazi Germany is an enemy of the United States" (Jowett 1976).

Adolf Hitler was named and portrayed in a fictional film for the first time in the 1940 release *The Mortal Storm*. The film made clear that all Germans were not Nazi sympathizers; however, the Nazi threat to Germans and the world was graphically portrayed (Jowett 1976).

Man Hunt was released in 1941. Joseph Breen, the head of Hollywood's self-regulating Production Code Administration, called *Man Hunt* a "hate the Hun film" (Koppes and Black 1987). The movie was a well-produced thriller featuring big game hunter Walter Pidgeon aspiring to stalk Adolf Hitler for sport. Breen charged that the film characterized all Nazis as brutal and inhuman while all Englishmen were sympathetic characters.

Three sources of opposition to Hollywood efforts to treat political themes from the late 1930s up to Pearl Harbor can be identified. Two — the studio heads themselves and the self-regulating agencies — operated from within the industry. The third existed in the isolationist, America-first movement that found its core in the U.S. Congress.

Studio Heads

Less politically inclined and more conservative studio heads objected to some early efforts at politicizing motion pictures because of the threat of losing Europe for American film products. Germany and Italy alone provided U.S. film studios about 30 percent of their foreign profits — an estimated $2.5 million annually (Jowett 1976). Warner Brothers has been credited with leading the way in war film propagandizing. Film producer Joseph Mankiewicz recalled, "Warner Brothers had guts. They hated the Nazis more than they cared for the German grosses" (Friedrich 1986). Jack Warner often noted that he received consistent criticism from other studio owners for putting foreign markets in jeopardy for the entire industry.

Once German and Italian markets were lost for American films, this source of opposition vanished. Koppes and Black (1987) summarize the development and its effects:

> On August 17, 1940, Germany banned American films from areas under its control, a move that was not unexpected but still shocking. Italy naturally followed suit. Not only did American studios have incentives to cooperate with their President, but now the last major restraint — market pressure — had been removed. Hollywood took its gloves off.

Industry Self-Censors

In 1922, then Postmaster General Will B. Hays accepted the position of president of the newly created Motion Picture Producers and Distributors of America (MPPDA) (Jowett 1976). For eleven years the MPPDA, which came to be known as the "Hays Office," existed as a self-regulating agency created principally to ward off external attempts at censoring motion pictures. Hays had fostered an interest in motion pictures since the presidency of Woodrow Wilson, and his role as "sentinel" of the celluloid was intended to be in the best interests of the industry.

By 1934 the studio heads had become more and more daring in what they would show on film. Sex and violence became a favorite target of conservative opposition to screen content, mainly led by the Roman Catholic hierarchy. Intense pressure and threatened boycotts from organized religious groups prompted Hays to upgrade the enforcement mechanism in his office, the Production Code Administration (PCA), and place Joseph I. Breen, a conservative Catholic journalist, at its head. Breen's anti–Semitic and anti–Communist leanings, coupled with a renewed authority of the PCA, presented major obstacles to political film themes in the late 1930s and early 1940s.

Congressional Isolationists

The most persistent and vicious attacks on the motion picture industry, though, came from the isolationists and America-firsters — particularly those in the U.S. Senate. Perhaps having grown frustrated with the increasing failure of their attempts to curb interventionist sentiment in the Roosevelt administration, the American press, and the public at large, the isolationists made the motion picture industry a focal target in 1941.

Senators Gerald P. Nye of North Dakota, Burton K. Wheeler of Montana, and Bennett Clark of Missouri were leaders in a congressional attack on the movie industry. On August 1, 1941, Nye and Clark called on the Senate's Committee on Interstate Commerce to investigate the "sordid story of war propaganda in the film" (Nye 1941). Later the same evening Nye delivered a nationally aired radio address in which he characterized the motion picture industry as "one of the most, if not the most powerful instruments of propaganda." He accused the industry of operating as a war propaganda machine with the same efficiency as if it were directed from a single bureau. He continued:

> But when you go to the movies, you go there to be entertained. You are not figuring on listening to a debate about the war. You settle yourself in your seat with your mind wide open. And then the picture starts — goes to work on you, all done by trained actors, full of drama, cunningly devised, and soft, passionate music underscoring it. Before you know where you are you have actually listened to a speech designed to make you believe that Hitler is going to get you if you don't watch out. And of course, it's a very much better speech than just an ordinary speech at a mass meeting. And you pay for it. The truth is that in 20,000 theaters in the United States tonight they are holding war mass meetings and the people lay down the money at the box office before they get in.

The efforts of Senators Nye and Clark were successful in creating a specially impaneled subcommittee of the Senate Interstate Commerce Committee to investigate "war propaganda disseminated by the motion picture industry and of any monopoly in the production, distribution, or exhibition of motion pictures." Senator Nye was the chief spokesperson for the isolationist cause and the leadoff witness. Heads of the major studios were called to appear to defend the charges against the industry. The Senate Committee had listed several films as "suspect" pertaining to war propaganda, including films produced by Warner Brothers, RKO, Columbia, 20th Century–Fox, Paramount, and British Pictures, as well as several episodes of *The March of Time*. None of the movies listed by the subcommittee were comedies; however, *The Great Dictator* was on an additional list of offensive movies cited in Senator Nye's testimony and his August 1, 1941, address.

Even though the subcommittee hearings succeeded in giving Senate isolationists a national forum, three elements appear to have combined that seriously diluted any hoped-for impact on the motion picture industry by the investigators. First, by September 1941, public opinion in the United States was moving swiftly to support the internationalist leanings of the Roosevelt administration. Second, perusal of the hearing record indicates that the arguments forwarded by the isolationist legislators leading the attack did not fare well with the rebuttals from studio heads. Most of the cited films had not even been viewed by the opposition legislators. At one point in the hearings, Senator Nye admitted to having seen only one picture in the past six years. Third, the special counsel to the studio heads, Wendell Willkie, proved to be a formidable spokesperson for the industry.

After just 17 days in session, subcommittee chair Senator D. Worth Clark, Idaho, announced an adjournment. The hearings were officially abandoned on Monday, December 8, 1941—the morning after the Japanese attack on Pearl Harbor. The subcommittee never issued a report of its hearings.

Hailstone-Hynkel: Race to the Screen

With two obvious exceptions, Hollywood's efforts to comment on world political events leading to World War II were confined to pictures of a serious or dramatic nature. On January 14, 1940, Columbia Pictures released the forty-fourth in a series of 190 Three Stooges comedies, *You Nazty Spy!* With that release Moe Howard became the first screen personality to satirize Adolf Hitler and Nazi Germany in a comedy vehicle. Hitler's aides Goering and Goebbels were aptly portrayed by Curly Howard and Larry Fine, respectively. Comparison of production schedules and release dates of *You Nazty Spy!* and *The Great Dictator* leaves no doubt that Moe Howard's portrayal of Dictator Hailstone beat Chaplin's Adenoid Hynkel to the screen by nearly nine months.

The Great Dictator

The first recorded indication of the idea of Chaplin doing a Hitler mistaken identity picture is recorded in 1937 by Chaplin himself as having been suggested by Alexander Korda (Chaplin 1964). The first record of Chaplin talking to others about the concept of a Hitler film occurred in the summer of 1938 (Robinson 1985).

Part of the mastery of Chaplin films can be attributed to the fact that most were the total creations of one man — Charles Chaplin. As Theodore (1951) notes, "Chaplin's films are indeed one man jobs — producing, writing, directing, acting, editing, and later, musical arrangements." He even served as hairdresser for Paulette Goddard in *The Great Dictator*. It is no surprise, then, that Chaplin pictures were a long time in the making. No major studio controlled *The Great Dictator*; Chaplin set his own schedule and worked until he was satisfied the picture was ready for release. Even though his Hitler movie may have incubated for some time, the actual production schedule follows:

Production Started: January 1, 1939
First Shot: September 9, 1939
Final Shot: October 2, 1940
Premiere: October 15, 1940

Unlike the Stooges' *You Nazty Spy!*, Chaplin's satirization of Hitler did not escape the critics of propaganda — both inside and outside the industry. Reacting to the Hollywood grapevine, the German consul in Los Angeles objected to the proposed picture to Joseph Breen as early as October 1938. Later, though, after a private screening on September 6, 1940, Breen applauded the picture as "superb entertainment [that] marks Mr. Chaplin, I think, as our greatest artist" (Koppes and Black 1987). In March 1939, the British Board of Film Censors doubted the suitability of Chaplin's project for exposition in England because of the board's rule that no living personage could be represented on the screen without his or her written consent (Koppes and Black 1987).

Chaplin reported that during the production of *The Great Dictator*, he began receiving crank letters that increased after the film was completed. The pro–Fascist sentiment in the United States seemed so strong to Chaplin that, at one point, he seriously discussed with Harry Bridges of the Longshoreman's Union the possibility of having some of his men at the opening in case of pro–Nazi demonstrations (Chaplin 1964).

Even President Roosevelt, whom most expected to applaud the message of the picture, received the impact of *The Great Dictator* coolly. The president had requested a copy of the film for private screening and later called Chaplin to the White House. His only comment, according to Chaplin, was, "Your picture is giving us a lot of trouble in the Argentine" (Chaplin 1964).

You Nazty Spy!

In his opening statement before the Senate subcommittee investigating propaganda in motion pictures, Senator Nye made the following statement (Culbert 1990):

> The truth is that there are only between 200 and 225 of what are called "quality" pictures produced by American producers annually. A so-called "quality" picture is one, I am told by the trade, costing $250,000 or more to produce. It is in that field of production that any percentage of propaganda ought to be estimated. Not in that field made bulky by reason of the "shorts" and the so-called western pictures or comedy or slapstick productions.

Perhaps it can be attributed to that elitist attitude of Senator Nye that none of the watchdogs of the American borders seemed to ever take note of the following chain of events, as described by Erwin Dumbrille (1991), noted Hollywood film editor and life-long student of short subjects.

Jules White, head of the Columbia Pictures Short Subjects Department and long-time producer/director of Stooges comedies, walked into his brother Sam's office in mid–1939 and said that he was planning a comedy about Hitler. Moe would be Hitler, Curly would be fatso Goering, and Larry would be Dr. Goebbels. Sam replied to his brother that it was a rather grim situation in Europe, and wondered whether he could make it funny. Jules' reply was, "I'll make it funny" (Dumbrille 1991).

Not only did White fulfill his promise to make the two-reel comedy funny, but he also included direct and unmistakable references to Hitler's Germany. The comedy opens with three government cabinet members of the kingdom of Moronika plotting to find someone stupid enough to be dictator. Three wallpaper hangers working in the next room are selected to fill the roles of dictator and two ministers. Popular belief at the time was that Hitler had, at one time, been a paperhanger. The birth of Dictator Moe Hailstone is complete with an accidental origination of the Hitler moustache. References are made throughout the comedy to the "beer hall putsch," "storm troopers," "Mata-Herring," and "concentrated camps," and the comedy features a well-portrayed oratorical display by Dictator Hailstone delivered to the masses from a balcony.

The comedy was shot quickly. Shooting began on December 5, 1939, and finished seven days later on December 12. Cutting was finished on December 26, and the short was released to theaters on January 19, 1940. Production cost was approximately $18,500 (Dumbrille 1991).

You Nazty Spy! was a rush job from shooting to release. Most of the Stooge comedies involved longer shooting schedules and were released from six months to a year after final cutting. The accelerated production schedule did not, however, deter from the quality of the short by industry standards: *You Nazty Spy!*

received the honor of "Short of the Week" from trade publications. Considering the number of short subjects flowing from all production studios in 1940 Hollywood, the honor is not to be taken lightly. Dumbrille (1991) also reported that the comedy played many first-run movie houses that did not regularly exhibit two-reel comedy material.

In spite of Moe's Hitler being the first, Chaplin's interpretation is easily the more famous of the two. Indeed, in their later film *I'll Never Heil Again*, the Stooges themselves paid homage to Chaplin's achievement. Parodying the famous scene where Chaplin as Hitler plays with a large, helium-filled balloon that represents the world, the Stooges do virtually the same thing, making the world into a ball and therefore another plaything for the dictator.

The irony present in Jules White's creation of Moe Howard's portrayal of Dictator Moe Hailstone is that it escaped not only the criticism of the isolationists but apparently even their attention. Two reasons for such neglect are possible.

The first rests with Columbia Pictures. Of all the film-producing studios in Hollywood during the prewar era, Columbia did not appear to be a major target of the isolationists. While some Columbia films were listed by the subcommittee, Columbia chief Harry Cohn's lack of political involvement in events leading to World War II could well have been the reason for apparent leniency from Senate isolationists. In 1933 Columbia released a documentary called *Mussolini Speaks*. Mussolini was so impressed that he proposed decorating Cohn who traveled to Rome for the ceremony. Cohn was so taken with Mussolini that he kept an autographed picture of the dictator on his wall upon his return to Hollywood, and he restructured his office to match that of Mussolini (Friedrich 1986).

Even though Cohn was Jewish, he maintained no public loyalties to international causes. Louis B. Mayer had to spend an hour on the phone with Cohn to solicit a contribution to Jewish relief. After Cohn made the donation, he complained to an aide, "Relief for the Jews! Somebody should start a fund for relief FROM the Jews. All the trouble in the world has been caused by Jews and Irishmen" (Thomas 1967).

The same reason for the lack of criticism from the isolationists rests with the elitist attitude toward slapstick comedy, especially short subjects: Senator Nye's opinion of short subjects, Westerns, and slapstick comedy was apparently common among film critics of the time. As previously noted, *The Great Dictator* was the only comedy film listed by the Senate investigating committee as being suspect for its propagandistic content. In addition to the Three Stooges, another slapstick comedy team was going all out for the "war preparedness" effort throughout 1941. Abbott and Costello made three films that year—*Buck Privates, In the Navy*, and *Keep 'Em Flying*—extolling the virtues of life in the army, navy, and air force. All three were overwhelming box office successes; however, none received even the slightest notice from the America-firsters.

A Propaganda First

It is undeniable that Moe Howard was the first screen personality to satirize Adolf Hitler and the Nazi ideology. The vehicle portraying Hitler and Nazism, *You Nazty Spy!*, was being seen in theaters across the country nine months prior to the premiere of *The Great Dictator*. That fact holds special significance to the student of World War II era comedy propaganda. It should also be a significant revelation for all film historians.

It is also probable that more Americans were exposed to Moe Howard's creation of Hitler than Chaplin's. The popularity of the Three Stooges and other short subjects has been documented countless times. Koppes and Black have confirmed that 80 million Americans — two-thirds of the total population at the time — went to movies every week in 1939 and 1940. The number of short subjects seen by those 80 million people certainly exceeded the number of feature films seen, given the method of distributing short subjects. Moreover, the quality of *You Nazty Spy!* resulted in its showing in first-run movie houses that did not normally show short subjects. It is reasonable to conclude that the comedy received maximum exposure when compared to other short subjects of the time.

These facts should be a wakeup call to film historians. It is time to give proper historic credit to Jules White and the Three Stooges — particularly Moe Howard — for making a significant contribution to World War II film propaganda.

Works Cited

Chaplin, Charles. *My Autobiography*. New York: Simon and Schuster, 1964.
Culbert, David E. *Film and Propaganda in America: A Documentary History*. Vol. II. New York: Greenwood, 1990.
Dumbrille, Erwin. Personal correspondence, 5 July and 27 July 1991.
Friedrich, Otto. *City of Nets: A Portrait of Hollywood in the 1940s*. New York: Harper and Row, 1986.
Huff, Theodore. *Charlie Chaplin*. New York: Henry Schuman, 1951.
Jowett, Garth. *Film: The Democratic Art*. Boston: Little, Brown, 1976.
Koppes, Clayton R., and Gregory D. Black. *Hollywood Goes to War*. Berkeley: University of California Press, 1987.
Nye, Gerald P. "Our Madness Increases as Our Emergency Shrinks." *Vital Speeches*, Vol. 7 (15 Sept. 1941), pp. 720–723.
Robinson, David. *Chaplin: His Life and Art*. New York: McGraw-Hill, 1985.
Thomas, Bob. *King Cohn: The Life and Times of Harry Cohn*. London: Barrie and Rockliff, 1967.

13

"Hang Hitler!" — The Three Stooges Take Potshots at Nazis

Lynn Rapaport

The American film industry is a combination of art and business. In the early twentieth century, in an attempt to control the film industry, many cities and states established censorship boards to delete scenes that might offend conservative ideas of morality or might threaten public order. The most important censorship that Hollywood undertook occurred in 1934, spearheaded by William Harrison Hays, who headed the Motion Picture Producers and Distributors of America, also known as the Hays Office. Hays and some alarmed movie executives feared that unless Hollywood avoided social and political issues and produced only films considered "wholesome" and "pure entertainment," the federal government would censor the movies or break up the industry. The solution was to abide by a production code (PCA) that imposed sharp restrictions on how movies treated a wide range of subjects. Article X of the Production Code stated: "The history, institution, prominent people and citizenry of all nations shall be presented fairly. No picture shall be produced that tends to incite bigotry or hatred among peoples of differing races, religions or national origins" (Avisar 1988, p. 92). This code was designed to secure the universal appeal of Hollywood movies and their financial success throughout the world.

Industry policy was especially sensitive to films dealing with foreign countries. Until the late 1930s the American movie industry was economically dependent on a world market for the success of its products. In Europe more than 35,000 theaters showed American movies regularly. Movies that dealt realistically with Adolf Hitler and Nazi Germany, Mussolini and his Roman empire, or the Spanish Civil War were likely to be banned overseas and opposed by American isolationists at home. While other media debated social and political issues freely, the PCA code cracked down on movies with political messages, and many films made in the early 1930s were locked up and not shown again until the 1960s.

The United States, in the throes of the Great Depression, followed an isolationist foreign policy to keep out of the war. Most Americans were unwilling to be drawn into European power struggles or to take sides between Hitler and his intended victims. When World War II erupted in 1939, a Gallop poll showed that 96 percent of Americans opposed entering the war (Robinson 1994, p. 506). Besides the isolationist attitude, there was also suspicion of propaganda in favor of both isolationists and those wanting America to enter the war — interventionists. Indeed, North Dakota Senator Gerald P. Nye, an isolationist, charged Hollywood with making feature films that were propaganda vehicles to mobilize the American public for war.[1]

During the 1930s Hollywood faced a dilemma regarding how to depict the Nazis and their Allies. The Jewish studio heads worried that any mention of Nazi anti–Semitism might be construed as covert propaganda designed to edge American into the war to save their fellow Jews. These moguls also feared that humorous treatments of Nazis, more than drama, would reveal an anti–Nazi tilt. Thus, Hollywood discreetly avoided making overtly anti–Nazi films, as they were reticent to fan the flames of domestic anti–Semitism or exacerbate problems for Jews in Germany (Lipman 1991, pp. 236–237). This attitude remained unchanged until the Japanese attack on Pearl Harbor in December 1941.

Portrayals of Hitler

Although Adolf Hitler loved movies, he resisted seeing himself portrayed on screen. Under Nazi control, the German film industry forbade characterizations of Hitler or episodes of his life to be used as subject matter for film. Hitler was to appear only in newsreels and documentaries and wanted no artificial Hitlers as rivals. In 1937 when Larry Blake, a Brooklyn-born actor, was cast as Hitler in *The Road Back,* an adaptation of Erich Maria Remarque's sequel to his novel *All Quiet on the Western Front,* the Nazis launched an all-out campaign against Universal Studios to abandon the production. The screenplay was strongly anti–Nazi and told the story of the conditions faced by defeated German soldiers of World War I upon returning home. Although the Nazis had a strong but clandestine influence in Hollywood, Carl Laemmle Jr., Universal's studio head, resisted the pressure. After Laemmle lost managerial control over Universal, however, the new regime under Charles R. Rogers yielded to many of the Nazis' demands. *The Road Back* was gutted: all Hitler scenes were removed or destroyed, and extensive cuts were made to the anti–Nazi tone of the picture. Larry Blake's performance as Hitler was never seen, except by a limited number of personnel at Universal Studios.[2]

The Three Stooges

In 1934, The Three Stooges signed with Columbia Studios to make eight two-reel comedies, or "shorts," as they are familiarly called, each year. There was no written contract; they merely shook hands with studio president Harry Cohn. "As long as I am head of this studio, you boys will always have a job here at Columbia," Cohn said (Carone 1973, p. 105). Every year for the next 24 years the Stooges shook hands with Harry Cohn in his office to renew their contract. The Stooges filmed their comedies quickly, and the films were released eight times a year, to enable the Stooges to make personal appearances at theaters and night clubs. In exchange, the studio paid the trio $60,000 per year, which was divided evenly: each Stooge earned $2,500 per short, for an annual salary of $20,000.[3]

Two-reelers were in great demand by movie theaters across the country. Long before the advent of "coming attractions," shorts were considered "curtain raisers," to be shown before the full-length feature movie. Film historians estimate that by the late 1930s, about 88 million Americans — two-thirds of the country's population — frequented neighborhood movie houses weekly. There were approximately 17,500 theaters in the country then. In these theaters, attendees were entertained by two-reel comedy shorts, newsreels, and sometimes cartoons before each full-length feature. Prior to television, newsreels provided the only moving pictures of the rest of the world. Cartoons and shorts filled the need for light entertainment.

Of the Stooges' 190 Columbia shorts, eight dealt directly with World War II. They had nationalistic and patriotic themes, with Moe parodying Hitler. Five were anti–Nazi, and three were anti–Japanese. Again, given this isolationist climate, with heavy censorship, it is surprising that two of their anti–Nazi shorts were released before America entered the war. Indeed, *You Nazty Spy!* was released in January 1940, and its sequel, *I'll Never Heil Again,* was released in 1941. The Stooges released three additional anti–Nazi films in 1943 after the United States entered the war: *Back from the Front, They Stooge to Conga,* and *Higher Than a Kite.* Their anti–Japanese shorts *The Yoke's on Me* and *No Dough Boys* came out in 1944. The eighth short, *Gents Without Cents,* also released in 1944, dealt with World War II on the home front.

You Nazty Spy! and *I'll Never Heil Again*

"Any resemblance between the characters in this picture and any persons, living or dead, is a miracle," reads the opening titlecard of *You Nazty Spy!* The camera pans across the library of Charles Ixnay's lavish home, showing ornate and heavy furniture. The camera stops on a medium shot of Mr. Ixnay and two other distinguished-looking men, Mr. Onay and Mr. Amscray, gathered in conference. They are the wealthiest and most powerful men in the kingdom of Moronika. They are discussing the economic problems facing their country. Moronika's munitions business is failing, and their king is for peace, so they decide to bring in a dictator to start a war. They settle on Moe Hailstone, a paperhanger. As Moe plots the takeover of various countries, his colleagues Pebble and Gallstone meet increasing opposition. Eventually they lock themselves into the lions' den. In the original script, the first lion says (in a German accent), "Ach! Dot guy tasted awful!" "Yah! I got indigestion," says the second lion. "Me too! Phooey!" remarks the third lion. This scene was changed to a shot of a burping lion wearing the Reichsführer's hat — still a sharp political cartoon indicating that Hailstone and his aides were eaten by the lions!

Even though Moe Hailstone, Gallstone, and Pebble are eaten by lions in *You Nazty Spy!*, they are back in the sequel, *I'll Never Heil Again*, which was released on July 4, 1941. This second Jules White-directed short lacerating the Third Reich opens with the titlecard "The Characters in this Film are all Fictitious. Anyone Resembling Them is Better off Dead." Amscray, Ixnay, and Umpchay, who last time unseated the king of Moronica, Herman the 6-7/8s, now want to unseat the dictator, Moe Hailstone.[4] Yet Hailstone is bent on world dominance. The king's daughter, Gilda, who is in cahoots with the cabinet ministers, is disguised as an astrologer and tells Moe that the other members of the Axis nations are plotting against him. Moe meets with his Axis partners — Chizzilini (an obvious parody of Mussolini), the Minister of Rum (nicknamed the Bay of Rummy), Stalin, and a Japanese crony. They fight over who will control the world. Curly throws a billiard ball rigged with explosives at Moe. The camera pans to a side wall, on which we see several stuffed animal heads. Closely interspersed in the center are the three heads of the Stooges. The king of Moronica is reinstated.

In *You Nazty Spy!* and *I'll Never Heil Again*, Hailstone is portrayed as a common man thrust into the position of dictator by Moronika's business class. For instance, when Mr. Ixnay, Onay, and Amscray discuss ousting the king and replacing him with a dictator, they look specifically for someone "stupid enough to do what we tell him!" They find Moe Hailstone, who with his two helpers (Larry and Curly) is papering Mr. Onay's dining room.

As was mentioned in the previous chapter, popular belief at that time was that Hitler had once been a paperhanger and interior decorator. Indeed, this

The Stooges consistently lampooned the Nazis, and Moe created a wonderful comic parody of Hitler, preceding Chaplin's Hitler in release by nine months. Here the Nazi Stooges battle Napoleon (Johnny Kascier) in *I'll Never Heil Again* (1941).

paperhanger motif reappears in Mel Brooks' *The Producers,* in Hitler's solo, "Heil Myself," when Hitler sings, "I was just a paperhanger, no one more obscurer, got a phone call from the Reichstag, told me I was Führer." Slapstick paperhanging was also a favorite routine of the Stooges.

In the Stooges' World War II shorts, Hitler is characterized not as an Aryan superman but as a comic buffoon whose actions have tragic consequences. For instance, in *You Nazty Spy!* Mr. Ixnay offers Moe the "greatest opportunity of his life"— to become a dictator. When Moe asks what a dictator does, he's told, "Makes love to beautiful women, drinks champagne, and never works. He makes speeches, promising the people plenty, then gives them nothing — and takes everything! That's a dictator!" Convinced that the role seems profitable, Moe agrees to be dictator and makes his cronies officers, Curly as Field Marshall Gallstone and Larry as Pebble, the Minister of Propaganda. Moe then asks Mr. Ixnay what he needs to do to become dictator, and Mr. Ixnay tells Moe to start a beer putsch.

Nazi Germany's expansionist policies are also ridiculed. For example, in a balcony scene Moe makes a speech to a large crowd. Wearing a trench coat, with Curly in a fancy uniform and Larry in formal afternoon attire, Moe parodies Hitler's oratory style, menacing facial features, and Nazi expansionist policies:

> We will throw off the yoke of Monarchy to make our country safe for Hypocracy. Our slogan will be: Moronika for Morons ... Moronika must expand. We will extend our neighbors a helping hand — yes, sir — we'll extend them two helping hands, and help ourselves to our neighbors.

As Moe reaches the second line of this speech, the script calls for him to talk "faster and faster, his lips flying and his words coming with great speed and with those funny high sounds made by letting the sound track slow down. As Moe's lips and words reach great speed, the cheers keep tempo."

There are also references to the Nazi book burning, Hitler's treatise *Mein Kampf*, and concentration camps. For instance, in *You Nazty Spy!* Moe questions Curly about the value of books. At one point, the script was to have been more critical, as the following lines were penciled into the script, yet eliminated in the final production:

> MOE: What are you reading?
> CURLY: My Kampfire!
> MOE: What Moron wrote that? How dare you read a book! Suppose you learn something. Loyal Moronicans shouldn't read. Take your troops and have them burn up all the books in Moronica.

Instead, the short goes as follows:

> LARRY: But why burn up all the books?
> MOE: Because there are too many bookmakers ... The bookies are overrunning the country.

Moe also orders an innocent man (accused of treason) to be sent to a "concentrated camp," and then changes his mind to send him to the lions.

The Nazi storm troopers are also ridiculed. For instance, in *You Nazty Spy!* when Moe sends for the Storm Troopers, four men rush in wearing rain gear — rain slickers, sou'wester hats, and rubber boots. Over their shoulders, instead of muskets, they carry closed umbrellas.

Other Stooges World War II Shorts

Hollywood, especially after America's entry into World War II in 1941, began producing films with Nazis in sinister roles. These films were entertaining, profitable, and effective propaganda for the Allied cause. While most of the productions were dramas, a good number incorporated humor. The same was true for war songs — most, in the tradition of songs from World War I, were serious or maudlin; but some, typified by Spike Jones's *Der Führer's Face,* mocked the Axis.[5]

Between 1943 and 1945, the Three Stooges released five additional shorts that satirized Hitler and the Japanese. Some shorts showed the Stooges as American soldiers who joined, or attempted to join, American troops overseas. For instance, in *Back from the Front* (1943)[6] the Stooges are American sailors — Inky, Winky, and Dinky — who survive an enemy torpedo. Adrift on a raft, they come upon a German battleship. They disguise themselves as Nazi sailors and capture the entire naval ship.

In *Higher Than a Kite,* the Stooges want to join Britain's Royal Air Force to fight the Nazis, but fail the entrance exams. They end up in what they think is a sewer pipe but is actually a blockbuster bomb headed for Nazi Germany. After crashing through Nazi headquarters, the Stooges find German aviation uniforms, put them on, and fight the Nazis. In *They Stooge to Conga,* released in 1943, although not soldiers, the Stooges are repairmen who stumble upon a Nazi nest while looking for work. In all these shorts the Three Stooges outwit the Nazis, and the shorts end with the demise of Hitler, the Nazis, and the Axis powers.

By 1944 the Stooges' World War II shorts became less focused on Hitler and more anti–Japanese. Two shorts in particular, *No Dough Boys* and *The Yoke's on Me,* portray the Japanese in stereotypical fashion. For example, in *No Dough Boys* (originally titled *The New World Odor*), the Stooges, dressed up as Japanese soldiers for a magazine advertisement, are mistaken for real Japanese soldiers by a group of Nazi spies. In *The Yoke's on Me,* the Stooges, who were given 4F status when they tried to volunteer for the army, decide to help their country by becoming farmers. They come across three Japanese soldiers who have escaped from an internment camp. While both shorts deal with the war at home and the Japanese as enemies, they include many Nazi references. Indeed, in *No Dough Boys,* Moe, while disguised as a Japanese soldier, has a mustache, making him look like a Japanese version of Hitler.

The Role of Humor

Anthropologist Mary Douglas (1991, p. 305) describes the role of the joker as a privileged person who can say certain things in certain ways with immunity. Safe within the permitted range of attack, the joker lightens for everyone the oppressiveness of social reality, demonstrates its arbitrariness, and expresses creative possibilities of the situation.

In *You Nazty Spy!* and *I'll Never Heil Again,* confrontations between the Allies and Axis, who are struggling to control the world, are treated as games — golf and basketball. For instance, in *You Nazty Spy!* Moe organizes the famous

Peace Conference of Oomphola — obviously parodying the Munich Peace Conference of September 1938, where the Munich agreement was signed to give Germany the Sudetenland. Four distinguished-looking delegates in formal afternoon attire are seated around a conference table when Moe orders the conquest of the country Starvania. The delegates are not so sure about these plans. "Yeah! A peace of this and a piece of that country," chimes in Vance Rippemup — a take-off on the German Foreign Minister Joachim von Ribbentrop. "Gentlemen! You must understand I'm trying to form a powerful axle — and you know what it takes to make an axle go!" Moe declares, parodying the creation of the Axis partners.

He argues for a corridor through the country, Double Crossia, to give Moronika an outlet to the Look Sea. The delegates jump up and yell, and they get into a fight using golf clubs and balls. The Stooges prevail and knock out the delegates. "Oh boy, that's what I call a peace conference!" Moe declares.

In *I'll Never Heil Again,* Moe calls to order a meeting of Axis parties. Moe hits the Bay of Rum on the head with a gavel, saying, "Gentlemen of the Axis. Your blitz is on the fritz. I am the only winner, so I should rule the world!" When the delegates object, Moe reaches forward and grabs the globe from its holder, declaring, "The world belongs to me!" Chizzilini, a take-off on Mussolini, jumps to his feet and grabs at the globe. They fight over who will control the world and get into a basketball game, using the globe as a ball. The Stooges race around the conference table, and Moe, Curly, and Larry toss the globe to each other. The Three Stooges huddle.

"Put that ball down or I'll take away your medals," Moe says to Curly.

"You can't. I bought them in a pawn store," Curly replies. (The original script was more blatantly anti-Nazi; as penciled into the margins, Curly was to reply, "Say, who do you think you are, Hitler?")

As Chizzilini strangles Moe, Moe offers, "Hey Chizzilini. Wait a minute. Why should you and I fight? Let them kill each other, and you and I will share the world." (This is a take-off on the Pact of Steel that the governments of Italy and Germany signed.). As Moe extends his hand to shake Chizzilini's, he throws his fellow dictator to the ground. He now declares that the world is his own. Curly protests and takes the globe for himself. After Moe threatens Curly, Curly breaks the globe over Moe's head. "You shattered my world! You shattered my world!" Moe screams, as he chases Curly.

In *You Nazty Spy!* and *I'll Never Heil Again,* Hitler and the Nazis pose a threat to the social order, and this physical and ideological conflict is resolved by their abolition, as the films reach narrative resolution with the demise of Hitler, the Nazis, and the Axis powers.

In addition to game playing, the Three Stooges use many puns and wordplays in their shorts to mock the Nazis and the Axis powers. These occur often in opening titles, graphics, signs on building and walls, desk nameplates, newspaper headlines, maps, and wherever the written word could be displayed. For example, the word "Nazty" in the film's title *You Nazty Spy!* is an obvious malapropism by combining Nazi with nasty. The names of Moronika's three cabinet ministers — Mr. Amscray, Mr. Ixnay, and Mr. Onay — are Pig Latin for Mr. Scram, Mr. Nix, and Mr. No. Mattie Herring — an obvious parody of the World War II spy Mata Hari — is a spy disguised as an astrologer in *You Nazty Spy!* When Moe discovers she is really there to poison him, he orders, "Get the confessions of this nasty spy, then shoot her!" — a take-off of the 1939 film *Confessions of a Nasty Spy*.

Behind every world power is a trademark patriotic slogan, a motto that inspires fervent loyalty among the masses, and Moronika is no exception. In *You Nazty Spy!* the motto is "Moronika for Morons." Moronika is an obviously play on the word "moron" and is misspelled with a "c" rather than a "k" in the sequel *I'll Never Heil Again*, the result of a typographical error. The name "Hailstone" could be thought of as hailing a stone at Hitler. Plays on the word "heil" appear as "heal," and in later shorts, rather than saluting "Heil Hitler," the Stooges salute, "Hang Hitler." Hailstone's speeches are gutteral gibberish akin to a barking dog.

In *You Nazty Spy!* Moe Hailstone declares that any military general worth his stripes knows that if one masters the geography of South Starvania, one has taken the first step toward ruling the world. He studies a map showing South Starvania countries and waterways. The countries include Asperin, Hang Gover, Bath, Gin Rickia, Bolonia, Nux Vomika, Double Crossia, Moronika, Mikey Finlen, Shonzi, Chin Chin, Hotcha, Kotcchke, and Oomphola. The waters are shown as Razzle Lake, Dazzle Lake, Look Sea, See Sea, Bay of Window, Sea of Biscuit, and Bay of Rum. In *I'll Never Heil Again,* the continent has already fallen to the sword of the ruthless dictator Moe Hailstone. Hailstone proves himself an expert of geography and terrain by nimbly reviewing the maze of Starvanian countries and waterways shown on a sketchy relief map. The following countries are displayed on the map: Great Mitten, Cast Toria, Hot Foot, I Ran, He Ran, She Ran, They Ran, Also Ran, Slap Happia, Pushover, Bulge-area, Atisket, Atasket, Staywayoff, Jerkola, Jug O' Salvia, Yom Kippers, Truck on Down, Big Zipper, Toot Sweet, Isle of Cork, Rubid-Din, and Woo-Woo. Waterways include Hot Sea, Tot Sea, Corkscrew Straights, Vulgar River, Straights of Rye, and Cant Sea.

Other Nazi references pop up as wordplay in the remaining six Stooges' World War II films. For example, in the 1943 short *Back from the Front,* the Stooges are on board a Nazi warship called the *S.S. Schickelgruber.* Larry, disguised as Goebbels, carries a briefcase that reads, "Minister of Propaganda — Specialist in Lies and Bunk"; Larry's parody of Goebbels even includes his nasty limp. Moe also uses the term Schickelgruber to refer to a well-known German dictator in the shorts *They Stooge to Conga* and *Higher Than a Kite.* In these Stooge shorts, Marshall Gallstone and General Boring refer to Göring, General Bommel refers to Rommel, and Rippemup refers to Ribbentrop.

Visual symbols also play significant roles in denigrating Hitler and the Nazis. For instance, the Three Stooges use "the mustache" to symbolically represent Hitler in the World War II shorts. In *You Nazty Spy!* Moe is transformed into Hitler when a piece of wallpaper gets stuck below his nose, as he scratches it while pondering whether he should become the dictator of Moronica. And, in *No Dough Boys* and *The Yoke's on Me,* while impersonating Japanese, Moe becomes a Japanese version of Hitler, symbolized by buck-teeth, a Japanese accent, and a Hitler-style mustache. In *I'll Never Heil Again,* as a major insult to Hitler, Curly grabs Moe's mustache and deftly rips it off as though it were a piece of cloth Velcroed to Moe's upper lip. "Give me back my personality," Moe demands as he snatches his mustache from Curly.

The Stooges also mock the swastika, Nazis, the goosestep, and the Gestapo. For instance, in *You Nazty Spy!* and *I'll Never Heil Again,* the banners decorating the walls show two snakes crisscrossing to form a swastika, an obvious association of Nazism being snakelike. In *Back from the Front* and *They Stooge to Congo,* the Stooges refer to Nazis as "ratzis." At the end of *They Stooge to Conga,* when the Stooges uncover a nest of Nazi spies, the Nazi Hugo tells his Japanese crony to grab the Stooges "in the name of the new world odor." The Stooges tear off Hugo's clothing, revealing his swastika-print long underwear.

"So you Rat-zis want the world! Well TAKE it!" Larry says as he crashes a globe over Hugo's head.

Besides being snakelike and rats, Nazis are also portrayed as dimwitted. For example, in *Back from the Front,* the Stooges, disguised as Nazis, sneak into a meeting where Nazi officers are discussing the American spies who have stowed away aboard the ship.

"What would the Führer say if he heard about this — three Americans making fools of a shipload of Germans," screams the ship's captain to his staff.

Mimicking Hitler, Moe barks German gibberish. "You failed to catch three spies! Blow out your brains!" Moe orders.

"But my Führer, we are Nazis. We have no brains!" replies the captain.

The Stooges make fun of the goosestep, by exaggerating the foot movements when they are impersonating Nazis, or leaving their legs extended in the air. The Gestapo is also ridiculed. For instance, while on a farm in *The Yoke's on Me,* the Stooges come across some geese on a farm.

"Oh, I read about them," Curly says; "they come from Germany. The goose-stapo!"

"Kill that gander so we can have roast goose for supper!" Moe orders.

"Oh, we'll have propaganda for dinner," replies Curly.

Jewish Humor — Making the Enemy Small

According to a tale in the Talmud, the prophet Elijah said that there will be a reward in the next world for those who bring laughter to others in this one (Morreall 1990–2000). Using comic form, the Three Stooges sought to shatter the image of Hitler and the Nazis. The notion of Moe, who is Jewish, impersonating Hitler is a boundary crossing that serves several purposes. Within the precincts of Jewish humor, the masquerade is derived from the spirit of Purim, in which, for one day each year, saints and villains become interchangeable through an exchange of clothing and other theatrical gestures. It also demonstrates an awareness of Jewish powerlessness in the fight against Hitler and is thus a strategy for exposing conventional norms and empowering society's outcasts and helpless victims. Obviously, none of the Stooges' World War II shorts portray Jews as subhuman or racially inferior or portray Aryans as superior. On the contrary, through masquerade and impersonation Hitler is turned into a schlemiel! The schlemiel is the characteristically comic character — the Jewish version of the fool. The *Universal Jewish Encyclopedia* defines the schlemiel as one who "handles a situation in the worst possible manner, or is dogged by an ill luck that is more or less due to his own ineptness" (Revel 1943, p. 115). In Jewish literature, the schlemiel is often caught up in situations that reflect the historical problems of the Jewish people. The Stooges' impersonation of Nazis and in many scenes "passing" as Nazis flies in the face of Nazi racial segregation and notions of purity and pollution, given the Nuremberg Laws, including laws against miscegenation, and the Nazi ideology of racial purity.

In the United States, assimilation was a major theme in films throughout the late silent era and into the 1930s and 1940s. Films of that time often portrayed entrepreneurial zeal, upward mobility, show-business fame, and similar apotheoses of the remade self (Rosenberg 1996, p. 18). Even though most of the major studios' heads were Jewish themselves, Jewish characters practically disappeared from their films. For instance, when director Richard Quine wanted to use a specific actor for a certain part in his film, Harry Cohn, the cofounder and president of Columbia Pictures, refused. "He looks too Jewish," Cohn replied, adding, "Around this studio the only Jews we put into pictures play Indians" (Friedman 1987, p. 35). Jewish character actors found little if any work during this period, and many changed their names to deemphasize their heritage. Even Hollywood adaptations of original works featuring Jewish characters eliminated or de-Semiticized their ethnicity.

Nonetheless, the Three Stooges displayed subversive approaches to Jewishness in film at a time when it was a highly sensitive matter.[7] Indeed, the Stooges wore their Jewishness unselfconsciously. They were antiheroes who flaunted their Jewishness at a time when assimilation and ethnic self-denial were integral to the American film industry. For instance, in many of the Stooge films there are Jewish characterizations and snippets of Yiddish or Jewish cues sprinkled in. For example, in the short *Mummy's Dummies,* 489 Shekels was the fair-sounding price for one of the Stooges' factory rebuilt chariots. In *G.I. Wanna Go Home,* 418 Meshugena Avenue is the mailing address of the Stooges' fiancées. In the short *Space Ship Sappy,* "Oy Gevalt," the Yiddish declaration meaning "Oh, my God" or "what in the world," is Moe's impassioned cry for help as his spaceship goes out of control. In the short *Mutts to You,* fugitive Larry must convince an angry policeman that he really is Chinese. Larry nearly pulls it off, telling the cop, "Huck mir nischt a chynich, and I don't mean efsher." Had the cop spoken Yiddish, he might have known that Larry had told him, "Don't bother me, get off my back, and I don't mean maybe." In the short *Half-Shot Shooters,* the Stooges, upon discovering that World War I has ended, declare "Mazel Tov" and "L'Chaim." Curly also wishes Moe "Mazel Tov!" in the short *Calling All Curs* after the Stooges discover their prized dog Garçon has given birth. And, in the first clip of *You Nazty Spy!* the Stooges respond to the cabinet ministers with "Shalom Molechem" a wordplay on Shalom Aleichem, telling the audience that they are Jewish. In *I'll Never Heil Again,* Yom Kippers is a country on the map of Starvania.

Moe, Curly, and Shemp's parents, Jennie and Solomon Gorovitz, fled anti–Semitic persecution in late nineteenth-century Europe. They were second cousins from Lithuania. Solomon Gorovitz studied at a rabbinical seminary in Vilna, and before he was to graduate, gangs of Russian soldiers roamed through Lithuania forcing young men to join the Russian army. Being conscripted meant years of hard service, and Jews in the military were forced to convert to Christianity. The family realized that Solomon was in danger, and heard stories of riches and religious tolerance in the United States. They decided to send Solomon to America and quickly arranged a marriage between him and his cousin Jennie (a common practice at the time.) The couple wed and hastily moved to America. Moe, Curly, and Shemp Howard were born Moses (1897), Jerome (1903), and Samuel (1895) Horwitz. For many years, they were considered the three least accomplished sons of their parents. Their older brothers, Irving and Benjamin, sold insurance and had a "real job."

Larry was born Louis Feinberg on Philadelphia's south side, the oldest of four children of watch repair/jewelry shop owner Joseph Feinberg and his wife Fanny Lieberman. He went into vaudeville, playing violin, dancing, and doing Jewish dialect. He met Moe Howard in 1925 and joined the Three Stooges with Moe's brother Shemp. When Shemp left and Moe's younger brother Jerome joined the act as Curly in 1934, the Three Stooges began making two-reel shorts for Columbia Pictures.

Rooted in vaudeville, the Stooges allegorized and universalized the newcomer, making him or her applicable to the experience of many immigrant groups. As mentioned above, they displayed their Jewishness overtly, particularly at a time when assimilation was the main trend. Yet the Three Stooges were also as American as apple pie. Their zany, anarchic energy, their subversive wordplay, and their dizzying nonsequiturs suggest a kind of Melting Pot meltdown, a carnivalesque transformation of the American landscape that was to have important reverberations in American comedy and satire far beyond the Stooges' era.

The Stooges' humor often stemmed from their natural lack of intellect combined with a sense of irony and incongruity. They are both schlemiels (the comic fool) and schlimazels — the unlucky or inept person who fails at everything.[8] For instance, the Stooges always claim to have expert knowledge on things, which they never have.[9] There is also a narrative of violence — slapping, poking, and pinching — that occurs rhythmically, at regular intervals, acting like punctuation, a system of commas, periods, paragraph breaks, for the larger narrative (Brunette 1991, p. 176). Eye gouging, hair pulling, pie and cake-throwing scenes, slaps, slugs, bonks, nyuk-nyuks, and woo-woos are frequent examples of the Stooges' mayhem.

War Films and the Three Stooges

Film historian Garth Jowett calls movies the "democratic art" because the early industry came from waves of immigrants flooding America in the late 1800s and early 1900s. Early films appealed to nonaffluent patrons by borrowing melodramatic plots, slapstick, and broad humor from vaudeville (Koppes and Black 1987, p. 3). Prior to television, the Hollywood film, along with newspapers, magazines, paperbacks, and radio, shaped public perception and set the public agenda on important and trivial issues.

Films register the feeling and attitudes of the periods in which they were made. In the 1940s the major studios were controlled by many of the original Jewish immigrants who had founded the motion picture business earlier in the century. While they publicly did their best to assimilate into American culture and appeal to mainstream tastes, one suspects they relished the chance to malign the man who was exterminating their people back in Europe. And their weapon was humor.

Films about war can serve many functions, from portraying historical evidence to reflecting national preoccupations. Films often portrays war as idealistic, courageous, heroic, and glorious. Thus, they can provide a powerful medium for mobilizing aggressive nationalistic feelings against other peoples — "the enemy." In the process, films can serve as an essential instrument in furthering national policy, and as a potential weapon of propaganda. Propaganda itself has multiple uses — from posters, films, and comic strips exposing the home front to images of the enemy, to the psychological warfare intended to directly influence action of enemy troops and civilians (Margolin 1976, p. vii).

War films can also serve as escapist entertainment. Humor, in fact, serves several functions — it is a vehicle for critical thinking, it promotes group solidarity, and it helps people survive in a hostile environment. "By making our enemy small, inferior, despicable or comic, we achieve in a roundabout way the enjoyment of overcoming him — to which the third person, who has made no efforts, bears witness by his laughter," says Sigmund Freud (1960). Mary Douglas (1991) argues that joking allows for purification as the experience of laughter is cathartic. Moreover, joking consists of challenging the relevance of the dominant structure, as the joker performs with immunity the act that wipes out the venial offense (Margolin 1976, p. vii).

Some films make history, while some try to rewrite it. Others invent it from scratch. Films set out to entertain, enlighten, educate, and at times change minds. Humor can be a venue for change, lending comedians, as well as the audience, a forum to discuss important social and political issues safely. *You Nazty Spy!* and *I'll Never Heil Again* were the Stooges' first propaganda shorts. These shorts embodied a resistance to the rise of Nazism by satirizing the idiosyncrasies of Hitler and National Socialism at a time when strong censorship codes restricted this and parodies of Hitler did not constitute prominent forms of entertainment.

These Stooges shorts have a distinctive capacity to communicate — in image, plot, characterization, music, and style — an interpretation of the people and the times that made them. These shorts use humor, and especially Jewish humor, to convey their messages. In *You Nazty Spy!* and *I'll Never Heil Again* role reversals stem from the actions of a paperhanger who uses his dictatorial powers to dominate. Social and economic hierarchies are inverted, and, if only for a short time, the values of the oppressed reign supreme. They carry both the theme of "Jewish power" and the feeling of Carnival onto a broader canvas. Realism is hardly the aim; their success involves social, cultural, and personal politics and values, in that they provide a vision of the past through comical relief. The films parody Hitler and the Nazis, while consoling the victims through comedy. They work as propaganda films, war movies, and entertaining comedies. They told their story at a time when cinema was the dominant form of mass entertainment and enlightenment both at home and abroad.

Through slapstick and anarchic themes and energy, the Stooges undermined the Nazi power hierarchy. In spite of the public's fear of becoming involved in foreign nationals' conflicts, and their adversity to references to political events overseas, the Stooges shorts were successful, making money for Columbia.[10] Their work also helped bring the Nazi threat to the forefront of moviegoers' attention. Lorna Gray, who plays Mattie Herring in *You Nazty*

Spy!, recalled the shorts creating quite a stir when they were released in theaters. "None of the studios had done that kind of thing at the time," she said (Fleming 1999, p. 72).

Moe's political speeches in *You Nazty Spy!* and *I'll Never Heil Again* featured more wordplays than did most other Stooge shorts. This was probably due to the writers' irresistible urge to lampoon the names of the Fascist dictators (see Chapter 1). And these shorts also impacted Hitler. Elwood Ullmann, the screenwriter for many Stooge shorts, remembered the Stooges shorts' director, Del Lord, telling him that the anti–Nazi parodies landed the Three Stooges on Hitler's so-called death list.

Notes

This chapter was adapted from *American Judaism in Popular Culture,* Leonard Greenspoon et al., eds., Vol. 17 in *Studies in Jewish Civilization* (Omaha: Creighton University Press, 2006; distributed by University of Nebraska Press).

1. Because of Nye's charges, on September 9, 1941, a special subcommittee of the Committee on Interstate Commerce began an investigation of "war propaganda disseminated by the motion picture industry and of any monopoly in the production, distribution, or exhibition of motion pictures" (Koppes and Black 1987, p. 17).

2. As quoted by Gorden Stulberg, a vice president of Columbia Pictures Corp., in Mitchell (2000, pp. 6–8).

3. For comparison, note that Claudette Colbert was the highest-paid film personality in 1937, grossing $301,994 (*Motion Picture Herald* 1940, p. 44).

4. In *I'll Never Heil Again* the name of one of the cabinet members is different from that in *You Nazty Spy!* In *I'll Never Heil Again*, Mr. Amscray is replaced by Mr. Umpchay (Pig Latin for Chump).

5. The tune was written by composer Oliver Wallace and recorded by musician Jones. It became an instant hit. Capitalizing on the recordings popularity, Walt Disney changed the name of his studio's unreleased cartoon, tentatively titled *Donald Duck in Nutzilant*, to *Der Führer's Face*.

6. *Back from the Front*, originally titled "A Sailor's Mess" (Stooge Production #522), was written on August 6, 1941, five months before Pearl Harbor. In its original version it had no Nazi themes; on the contrary, it centered on the Stooges on a Navy ship. Sam Briskin, second in command to Harry Cohn, the Hollywood-based vice president in charge of production, rejected the script on grounds that it ridiculed the Navy. The script was later rewritten and changed completely to include a pro–United States/anti–Nazi slant. The revised script was approved by Briskin on May 26, 1942.

7. Blacks, Asians, and non–Anglo foreigners (Slavs, Hungarians, Turks, Arabs, and Gypsies) were continually stereotyped in American film of the 1930s. See Chapters 15–17 for more detail on these groups and how they were portrayed in Stooges films.

8. Compare Ringel in Chapter 10, where she discusses the schlemiel and the schlimazel and then adds a third element, the "bully," who she argues is essential for the drama, to set up the foolishness.

9. For example, in *They Stooge to Conga*, they claim to be telephone repairmen. This theme comes up again as they try to cook a fancy meal in *An Ache in Every Stake*, make rocket fuel in *Fuelin' Around* and the remake *Hot Stuff*, and make scotch in *Pardon My Scotch*.

10. The Three Stooges films have also succeeded in preserving mass-market appeal over

time, reappearing in Three Stooges festivals nationwide. Indeed, in late 1958 Columbia pictures released the 190 Three Stooges shorts to television via its television subsidiary, Screen Gems, which syndicated the series. They became so popular that in 1959 Columbia contracted with them for a new series of feature films. Their short-subject series was one of the longest-running and most durable, with a new lease on life via television. By 1960 their pre-1948 Columbia shorts were airing in 156 cities, were the best moneymakers in their category, and won them the coveted Laurel Award for two consecutive years. In a 1996 survey of 1,200 adults, 55 percent of Americans could not name one Supreme Court justice, yet 59 percent could name all the original Three Stooges.

Works Cited

Avisar, Ivan. *Screening the Holocaust.* Bloomington: Indiana University Press, 1988.
Brunette, Peter. "The Three Stooges and the (Anti-)Narrative of Violence: De(con)structive Comedy." *Comedy, Cinema, Theory.* Ed. Andrew Horton. Berkeley: University of California Press, 1991.
Carone, James (as told by Larry Fine). *Stroke of Luck.* Hollywood: Siena, 1973.
Douglas, Mary. "Jokes." *Rethinking Popular Culture.* Ed. Chandra Mukerji and Michael Schudson. Berkeley: University of California Press, 1991.
Fleming, Michael. *The Three Stooges: An Illustrated History.* New York: Random House, 1999.
Freud, Sigmund. *Jokes and Their Relation to the Unconscious.* Trans. James Strachey. New York: Norton, 1960.
Friedman, Lester D. *The Jewish Image in American Film.* Secaucus, N.J.: Citadel, 1987.
Koppes, Clayton R., and Gregory D. Black. *Hollywood Goes to War.* Berkeley: University of California Press, 1987.
Lipman, Steve. *Laughter in Hell: The Use of Humor during the Holocaust.* Northvale, N.J.: Jason Aronson, 1991.
Margolin, Victor. "Foreword." *Propaganda: The Art and Persuasion of World War II.* Ed. Anthony Rhodes. New York: Chelsea, 1976.
Mitchell, Charles P. *The Hitler Filmography: Worldwide Feature Film and Television Miniseries Portrayals, 1940 through 2000.* Jefferson, N.C.: McFarland, 2000.
Morreall, John. "Humor in the Holocaust: Its Critical, Cohesive, and Coping Functions." *Scholar's Conference Papers 1990–2000* (from the Annual Scholars' Conference on the Holocaust and the Churches). Ed. Marcia Sachs Littell. CD-ROM, Vista-Intermedia.
Motion Picture Herald, 27 Jan. 1940.
Revel, Herschel. "Schlemiel." *Universal Jewish Encyclopedia.* New York: Ktav, 1943.
Robinson, David. *Chaplin: His Life and Art.* New York: McGraw-Hill, 1985.
Rosenberg, Joel. "Jewish Experience on Film: An American Overview." *American Jewish Yearbook 1996.* New York: American Jewish Committee, 1996.

14

Slapstick Satire: The Three Stooges' Portrayals of the Japanese in World War II Comedies

Don Morlan

Chapters 12 and 13 detail the portrayals of Nazis in the Three Stooges short films of the World War II era. This chapter provides a similar examination of the Stooges' film images of another of America's enemies in the 1940s — the Japanese.

Never has there been a more vicious and derogatory example of stereotyping an entire race than the Hollywood portrayals of the Japanese during World War II. Clayton Koppes and Gregory Black (1987) in *Hollywood Goes to War* and Bernard Dick (1985) in *The Star Spangled Screen* vividly differentiate the portrayals of the Germans and the Japanese on the American screen. The Germans were Europeans and white and looked like Americans. Race was never a factor in portrayals of Germans, unlike the yellow, buck-toothed caricatures of the "monkey-like" Japs. Since most portrayals of the Japanese came after the bombing of Pearl Harbor, it is doubtful that Hollywood created the racial stereotyping of the Japanese; rather, filmmakers most likely were reinforcing the already well-entrenched bigotry in Americans' minds.

Much of the hatred for the Japanese was probably well earned. The brutal treatment of American and British prisoners of war captured by the Japanese was well known. Only 4 percent of Allied prisoners died at the hands of the Germans during the war, whereas 27 percent died while in Japanese captivity (Koppes and Black 1987).

Even though most Americans found Nazism abhorrent, they still made distinctions between Nazis and "good" Germans. Germans were more like us. Americans listened to Beethoven and Brahms on Sunday afternoon; they respected Goethe, Schiller, and Thomas Mann; and they lauded German science. It was difficult for Americans to balance the fact that the same nation that gave us Beethoven and Brahms also gave us Adolf Hitler and Josef Goebbels. Hollywood filmmakers regularly distinguished Nazis and Germans; however, Japs were always Japs.

War correspondent Ernie Pyle was quoted as saying, "In Europe we felt that our enemies, horrible and deadly as they were, were still people. But out here [the Pacific] I soon gathered that the Japanese were looked upon as something subhuman or repulsive; the way some people felt about cockroaches or mice" (Koppes and Black 1987).

Bernard Dick stated that the distinction Hollywood made between the way the Germans and Japanese raped women was based on the distinction it made between the Germans and Japanese in general: Germans were inhuman; Japanese were subhuman. In addition to being duplicitous, the Japanese were viewed as barbaric. Hollywood made a careful distinction between Nazi sadism and Japanese savagery. The Nazis branded, lashed, crucified, and performed mass executions. The Japanese would bind and cut out tongues for sport; they tossed Chinese babies into the air and bayoneted them. In contrast to the "good German" and the occasional good Nazi, good Japanese were almost unheard of (Dick 1985).

Hollywood wasted no time in implementing America's "Slap the Jap" policy. By the spring of 1942, the racial epithets were flying fast; "monkey" was the most common, along with its variants "monkey people" and "ringtails." When "rat" was used, it was prefixed by "yellow" or "slant-eyed."

No attempt was made to show a Japanese soldier trapped by circumstances beyond his control, or a family man who longed for home, or an officer who despised the militarists even if he supported the military campaign. This absence stood in sharp contrast to the portrayal of the German soldiers, who were shown as decent human beings distinct from the Nazis.

Koppes and Black (1987) cite two war action films as being particularly vivid and cruel in portraying the Japanese. In *Back to Bataan*, the Japanese are faceless, treacherous hordes. They kill civilians, torture wounded men, and use the jungle to their advantage. They send a message to the Americans saying if they surrender they will be "treated fairly, but the Japanese then kill the first person who stands up." The Office of War Information found these depictions of Japanese tactics to be accurate. The film made no attempt to explain Japanese behavior or develop a Japanese character.

Guadalcanal Diary is littered with references to "Japs" and "monkeys who live in trees." The enemies are described as apes and monkeys who hide in trees and use unfair tactics to lure unsuspecting Americans to their death. When the character Nolan is asked how he feels about killing people, he replies, "Well, it's kill or be killed — besides, they ain't people" (Koppes and Black 1987).

When asked about the words they most associated with Germans during the war, Americans picked two — "hard working," a highly positive trait, and "warlike," a negative term but one uttered not without an undercurrent of admiration. On the other hand, the words associated with the Japanese — treacherous, sly, and cruel — were unambiguously condemnatory.

Richard A. Oehling (1980), then academic dean at Assumption College in Massachusetts, summarized two primary themes in Hollywood's portrayals of the Japanese that reinforces the arguments of Koppes and Black and of Dick. The most persistent theme in American wartime accounts of the Japanese was their cruelty and brutality in the conduct of war, followed closely by portrayals of Japanese duplicity and treachery.

In short, the Japanese could not be trusted. When the Japanese were not engaged in barbaric and cruel acts, they were portrayed to look distrustful — mustached, thick glasses, squinty-eyed, with absurdly wide grins dominating their faces.

In summary, film portrayals of the Japanese during World War II were starkly different from those of the Germans and other enemies. Vicious and cruel stereotyping of an entire nation is a mild descriptive. While distinctions were made in film between "good guys" and "bad guys" among our white, European enemies, the mere fact of being Japanese rendered one the scum of the earth.

Three Stooges' Portrayals of the Japanese

When examining the portrayals of the Japanese in Three Stooges comedies, two observations can be made. First, Stooge portrayals of the Japanese are very much in line with those taken by all Hollywood films at the time, in terms of negatively stereotyping an entire race. The racial characteristics described earlier are evident in the Stooges comedies when the Japanese are portrayed. "Japs" are toothy, bespectacled with black wire-rim glasses, and squinty-eyed. Rather than being portrayed in a slapstick comedy as savage and cruel, the Japanese were portrayed as being unbelievably stupid and incompetent.

A second observation is that, compared to the portrayals of the Nazis, the Stooges didn't film as much footage about the Japanese. References to the Japanese do occur briefly in several shorts, often with overriding Nazi themes. And both Nazis and Japanese are portrayed in two ways in Stooge comedies. A favorite ploy of the Stooges is to disguise themselves as Nazis and Japs and, in doing so, emphasize the stupidity of both. When actual Nazis and Japs are portrayed by supporting actors, their stupidity and incompetence are reinforced.

Two Stooge comedies—*I'll Never Heil Again* and *They Stooge to Conga*—have funny, albeit very brief, references to the Japanese. *I'll Never Heil Again* is more noted for its satire of Hitler and the Nazis; however, a clever commentary on the Japanese can be found in the concluding footage of the film. Ministers representing members of the Axis meet to discuss the war effort and in so doing engage in a "battle for the world." After a rhumba dance line in preparation for the battle for the globe, the fighting breaks loose in earnest, and the Japanese minister constantly stops the action, whips out his camera, and states, "Picture, please." The association of the technology with the race is not lost on the audience. Nevertheless, the Japanese character is not as stereotypical as later portrayals, perhaps because this short was released in July 1941, five months prior to the Pearl Harbor provocation for America's entry into the war. That the Stooges included any reference to the Japanese at all at this point is significant.

In *They Stooge to Conga*, like *I'll Never Heil Again*, most of the war theme material in this comedy is in reference to the Nazis. Brief appearances by a Japanese officer reinforce the stupidity stereotype, and Moe and Larry briefly disguise themselves as Hitler and Tojo.

Only two Stooges comedies stand out as making extensive use of the Japanese as a theme: *The Yoke's on Me* and *No Dough Boys*. In *The Yoke's on Me*, the Stooges become farmers as a last resort when every branch of the armed service turns them down. They buy a dilapidated farmhouse but discover that no livestock are there except for an ostrich. Later the Stooges encounter three Japanese men who have escaped from a local relocation center. Their flight is cut short, however, when the Stooges' ostrich consumes gunpowder, laying an explosive egg.

There is little logical connection between the two parts of the plot of this comedy. The three Japanese soldiers enter the scene late in the comedy for no apparent reason. The racial stereotype, though, is explicit. The Japanese men wander about aimlessly at times, with protruding teeth, and are generally inept at most things they attempt to do. It is interesting to note that this Stooge comedy was blacklisted by some television stations because of its racial content (Lenburg et al. 1982).

In *No Dough Boys*, the Stooges are dressed as Japanese soldiers for the entire film. They are modeling as Japanese soldiers for a photographer. When their boss is called away, the trio goes for lunch at a diner, still in costume. The waiter mistakes them for three escaped Japanese soldiers and calls the police. Before the police can arrest them, however, the Stooges get away and take refuge in a room full of Nazi spies awaiting the arrival of three ju jitsu experts. The Stooges pose as the ju jitsu men and speak in broken English with phony accents. Ironically, the real ju jitsu men do not speak at all in the film. The roles are apparently played by actual Japanese men, though there is only

The Japanese were portrayed as dim-witted and hapless during several World War II shorts. Here they tangle with three (uncredited) Japanese acrobats they just impersonated in *No Dough Boys* (1944).

one closeup in the film as a basis to make this judgment. Another irony is that the Stooges are not given some of the stereotyped Japanese costuming, whereas one of the real Japanese men appears to be wearing fake teeth.

Joan Howard Maurer, Moe's daughter, has related a humorous family story concerning the production of this comedy. One of the days spent shooting the film ran very late, and Moe hurried home without taking off his Japanese costume and make-up. He was playing ball with his son, Paul, in the front yard, and neighbors called the police to report a Japanese soldier in the Howard's yard bothering Paul (Lenburg et al. 1982).

We Have Met the Enemy

In terms of quantity, the Stooges' portrayals of the Japanese during World War II era comedies fall far short of their treatment of the Nazis during the same time period. Comedies featuring Japanese portrayals were, however, among some of the best made by the Stooges.

The propagandistic content of the Japanese comedies also pales when compared to the Nazi films. The Stooges were trailblazers in bringing the Nazi message to the American screen. Moe Howard was the first screen personality to portray Hitler, and the Stooges heaped satire on European politics long before doing so was accepted by mainstream American public opinion. Beginning with the brief "camera/picture please" gag in *I'll Never Heil Again*, the Stooges featured portrayals of the Japanese until 1943 — long after Pearl Harbor and at a time when the Japanese were "fair game" on the silver screen.

Neither were the Stooge' portrayals of the Japanese unique in any respect when compared to the treatment given them by all Hollywood filmmakers during the war. Identical racial stereotypes appeared in the Stooges comedies that appeared in other Hollywood portrayals of the Japanese. "Japs" were bucktoothed, bespectacled, squinty-eyed people with silly grins on their faces. Only the barbaric cruelty of the Japanese so prevalent in war action films was replaced with excessive incompetence and stupidity in the Stooges shorts.

Notes

This chapter was published in its original form in *Studies in Popular Culture* 17, no. 1 (October 1994), pp. 29–43. Popular Culture Association American Culture Association in the South. Dr. Michael Dunne and Dr. Sara Dunne, eds.

Works Cited

Dick, Bernard F. *The Star Spangled Screen*. Lexington: University Press of Kentucky, 1985.
Koppes, Clayton R., and Gregory D. Black. *Hollywood Goes to War*. Berkeley: University of California Press, 1987.
Lenburg, Jeff, Joan Howard Maurer, and Greg Lenburg. *The Three Stooges Scrapbook*. Secaucus, N.J.: Citadel, 1982.
Oehling, Richard A. "The Yellow Menace: Asian Images in American Film." *The Kaleidoscopic Lens: How Hollywood Views Ethnic Groups*. Ed. Randall M. Miller. Englewood, N.J.: Jerome S. Ozer, 1980.

IV. Race, Ethnicity, and Gender in Stooge Films

Widespread concerns with racial stereotypes in film can be confirmed as early as 1915 with the release of *Birth of a Nation*, D. W. Griffith's epochal glorification of the Ku Klux Klan. Groups such as the NAACP staged protests, decrying the fact that Griffith was fomenting racism in a period when the Klan had all but died. Not long after the advent of aural mass communication, further concerns arose about the portrayals of racial and ethnic minorities. After radio debuted on a regular basis in late 1920, and after voice dialogue was introduced in films in 1927, the two-dimensional portrayals of various minority groups were given a voice, one that often added a nastier stereotypical element to already questionable portrayals. Gosden and Correll's radio version of *Amos 'n' Andy* became an almost instant target from some segments of the African American community for its reliance on fractured English dialogue and advancement of negative stereotypes of the black race. When the television version debuted in 1951, it was met almost immediately with opposition and was cancelled in 1953; by 1966, it was off TV for good.

Other groups were not nearly as mobilized as African Americans to protest what might be considered stereotypical and unfair portrayals of race or ethnicity. Latin stereotypes, long a staple of television and film, were critically examined in the supposedly enlightened 1960s, perhaps best characterized by the protests against the "Frito Bandito," Frito-Lay's cartoon, Pancho Villa–like Mexican whose charge was selling Frito's corn chips. By the 1970s, the so-called women's movement, which had gained momentum in the 1960s, reached full flower, and the differences could be duly noted in the increase of more positive and stronger portrayals of women in motion pictures and television. Likewise, the American Indian evolved from a lowly savage to a noble and spiritual presence by the 1970s. Images of other stereotyped groups, such as Arabs and Europeans, were mostly accepted or ignored.

The films of the Three Stooges were fairly typical in the way the racial and ethnic groups were portrayed. An African American mostly fit the menial but amiable character that had become so commonplace in American cinema. An Indian was a savage to be feared, though not incapable of providing plenty of slapstick laughs when necessary. A Latino was usually a bandido, a temptress, or a hothead, and sometimes all three. The Arab was a wealthy sultan, a murderous cutthroat, or a voluptuous maiden, but always an undesirable character. Europeans from England, Scotland, Ireland, France, Italy, or Russia were simply props, adopting whatever one-dimensional qualities advanced the Stooges' causes.

Females, on the other hand, were a different proposition altogether. While women were not a minority in the literal sense, screen portrayals nevertheless relegated them to the back burner, especially where most comedies were concerned (at least during the era of the Stooges). This was often the norm in the Stooges films; but unlike the racial and ethnic groups, women were occasionally front and center and proved to be the Stooges' equals (if such is possible). Often, not only were they the Stooges' mental superiors (as most people were), but they also bested the Stooges physically.

This section examines all of these groups: the Negro (Chapter 15), the American Indian, the Latino, and the Arab (all Chapter 16), and the many Europeans (Chapter 17) that dotted the Stooges films. Chapter 18 gives perspective on the portrayals of females in the Stooges comedies, weighing them against literary, sociological, and feminist views. Chapter 19 offers an overview of the multitude of women's roles in the films.

15

The Image of the Negro in the Three Stooges Shorts

Peter Seely

"The dramatic possibilities of Negro life, which is so rich and varied, and the potentialities of the Negro actor, already demonstrated in even the poor media accessible to him now, will reveal themselves when this social vision arrives."
— Harrison, *The Negro and the American Cinema*

Given the saturation of the short films of the Three Stooges in our society, it is a fairly easy leap to assume that the portrayals of African Americans in these films could well have had an influence on how the race is perceived by a non-black population. For generations of viewers, their main exposure to the race's members has come through cinematic and television portrayals, particularly at the time the films were made and their subsequent airing on early television. This chapter evaluates the portrayal of the Negro (a term consistent with the polite term at the time these films were made) in the Stooges films, within the context of contemporary films during the Stooges era and of research concerning racial portrayals.

The role of the Negro in film history has been analyzed extensively, from early silent features, through the racist overtones of D.W. Griffith's *Birth of a Nation*, through the excessive stereotyping of the Negro in the first decades of silent and talking pictures, and all of the subsequent developments in both Negro-produced and predominately white films.

On its release, *Birth of a Nation* met with strong opposition from Negroes nationwide. Despite its long-term success at the box office, the film alienated Negroes for its blatant representation of Negroes as sly, underhanded, lazy people. The film also attempted to elevate the status of the Ku Klux Klan. The strong negative reaction to *Birth of a Nation* had two important consequences. First, it seemed to genuinely surprise Griffith, who later tried to counter the public perception of the director as a racist, by offering writings and films that celebrated the rights of man (Bogle 1989, p. 16). Second, for decades, it altered the ability of film directors to portray the Negro race in a villainous or evil context.

The use of the Negro in subsequent films for many years to come was far from uplifting, however. Bogle (1989, p. 4) noted, for example, that Negroes began to play roles that whites had formerly played in blackface in movies and on vaudeville. Such portrayals, according to Thorp (1939), were mostly scrapped so that the appearance of a Negro on screen was always an "amusing and agreeable experience." Bogle also defines the main types that were used to portray Negroes in the early years of film: the coon, the mammy, the buck, the Tom, and the mulatto.[1] Further, Reddick (1975, p. 4) developed 19 subcategories that were frequently used for Negro portrayals in the early years of film, four of which are focused on in this chapter: the savage African, the devoted servant, the natural-born cook, and the mental inferior.

Here, we apply the findings of Reddick to the Stooges comedies. While devised in 1944, Reddick's theories dovetail with the important years of the Stooges' work. Out of 100 so-called important films up to this time, Reddick (1975, p. 4) identifies 75 as anti–Negro, 13 as neutral, and 12 as pro–Negro. Pro-Negro portrayals include representations beyond stereotypes to roles of heroism, courage, and dignity. Neutral refers to films featuring an equal balance between pro- and anti–Negro sentiments. The anti–Negro category includes representations indicative of the aforementioned prevailing racial stereotypes.

The Negro in Film

The last years of the silent era in the twenties helped to develop and perpetuate these stereotypes. The *Our Gang* comedy shorts (a close relative of the Stooges shorts), which spanned the silent to the talking era, particularly made for better celluloid representations of race relations (Reddick 1975, p. 9). The cast, which included the Negro characters Stymie, Farina, and Buckwheat, was much more democratic. Perhaps because these characters were children, they were able to show a broader spectrum of race relations and more respectful portrayals of the Negro in relation to their white counterparts than did most films of their day.

With the advent of talking pictures in 1927, something of a "golden era" arrived for the Negro in film (Bogle 1989, pp. 36–37). Ironically, this began with Al Jolson's minstrel portrayal in the first major talking picture, *The Jazz*

Singer. By the thirties, Negroes were assuming many on-screen roles. While nearly always conforming to Hollywood stereotypes, many of these actors were just happy to be working during such severely depressed economic times. Since whites were in all of the positions of power in the mostly white cinema, it was up to the creative input of Negro actors and actresses to create memorable screen characters (Bogle 1989, pp. 36–37), a feat for which these individuals deserve an enormous amount of credit.

In the thirties, actors such as Stepin Fetchit, Willie Best, and Mantan Moreland, along with actresses such as Hattie McDaniel, Louise Beavers, and Josephine Baker, began to chisel out the characterizations of the Negro on-screen. These actors and actresses have subsequently received both praise and derision for their portrayals, which helped to perpetuate the rampant Hollywood stereotypes but which also made for memorable, enjoyable, and likable characters for white audiences. Out of this climate came the Three Stooges' comedy, including the contributions from the Negro supporting actors.

The era during and just after World War II, given the racism and hatred the United States was fighting in Nazi Germany, forced the film industry to re-examine somewhat the role of Negroes in films; and the subsequent development of television caused Negroes to hope for broader, more accurate representations on the small screen (McDonald 1992, p. 5). Unfortunately, what developed during the decade of the fifties was largely a continuation of the stereotyped roles for Negroes that had been carried over from the film and radio industries (McDonald 1992, pp. 28–29), including *Amos 'n' Andy* and *Beulah*.[2] When Negroes were not being portrayed in the fashion of the major characters of these programs, they were not being used at all.

The ensuing decades postdate the Stooges era of film contributions and thus are not of concern in this chapter except from a historical perspective. The 1960s and beyond were years filled with slow but gradual progress toward the broadening of representations of the African American experience in American society. While there were many ups and downs in television portrayals, from *I Spy, Good Times,* and *Cosby*, to present-day examples, African Americans undeniably were appearing in television and film in much greater numbers. However, the breadth of roles of blacks on television progressed much more rapidly than the glacial pace of democracy and equal rights portrayed in silent films and the first three decades of talking pictures.

Analyzing the Negro in Stooges Films

While this chapter focuses primarily on the portrayal of the American Negro, it also includes three other ancillary groups: Black Africans (portrayed by American Negroes), Nubians (portrayed by dark-skinned Negroes), and

South Seas Natives. Other people of color and other nonwhite minorities are examined in Chapter 16.

For this chapter, the various portrayals are further subdivided into two categories: Actual, using representatives of the group (or what is offered as one by the producers), and Stooge portrayals, including the Stooges disguised as Negroes in minstrel contexts and random dialogue relating to the portrayals of these groups.

Of the 190 Stooges shorts for Columbia, 25 contained a representation or reference to the American Negro, Black African, Nubian, and South Seas Native. The breakdown of these representations is as follows:

	Actual	Stooges
American Negro	17	6
Black African	2	0
Nubian	4	0
South Seas Native	2	0

American Negroes

The very first Stooges film for Columbia, *Woman Haters* (1934), featured an actor named Fred Toones, whose screen name was "Snowflake." He had appeared previously as a "knucklehead valet" in the feature film *Go into Your Dance*, starring Al Jolson; he also appeared in the feature films *Lady by Choice* and *The Biscuit Eater* (Bogle 1989, p. 38). In *Woman Haters*, Snowflake portrays a train porter, appearing on screen twice for a total of approximately one minute, speaking three lines. The role of the porter was a common one for Negro actors and was one of the few roles available to male Negroes in the white cinema for some time. Snowflake plays the happy worker who, despite the Stooges' mayhem, manages to retain his happy-go-lucky demeanor. He was never to appear again in a Stooges short; however, there is a brief reference to him years later in *Some More of Samoa* (1941), when the Stooges encounter an island native and call him "Snowflake."

Uncivil Warriors is the only Stooges film for Columbia that featured a Negro in a nonstereotypical role: a baby. Moe had rounded up a baby to support a lie the Stooges were attempting to put over on a group of Confederate officers during the Civil War. The wrapped baby is supposed to be the offspring of Curly (appearing in drag), who tells the officers, "He looks just like the captain." As the captain pulls away the blanket, he reveals the deception and the Negro baby. He angrily retorts, "Looks like me, does he?" whereupon the Stooges abandon the Negro child, leaving him with the exasperated captain. One can only speculate whether the writers would have allowed such callous behavior to occur with a white baby.[3]

Uncivil Warriors also began a practice that was repeated in several subsequent Stooges shorts, where a line of dialogue would cause one or more of the Stooges to slip into a "darkie" routine. This usually followed a line about the South and was accompanied by shuffling and pronouncements of "hallelujah" and "yowza." The circumstances for this routine were much more incongruous in these subsequent films than in *Uncivil Warriors*, where it had an appropriate context.

A Pain in the Pullman once again features a Negro as a porter. The role is played by Ray Turner, who appears on camera for less than a minute and speaks one line: "Take your bags, boss?" This line foists upon the actor the ultimate humiliation: having to refer to the ragamuffin Stooges as "boss." When a small monkey leaps out of the Stooges' train berth and into Turner's arms, the shocked porter lurches backward, stumbles, falls, and runs away in a slapstick routine that was repeated occasionally in other films.

For Negro women, the role of a maid was the most common one in motion pictures during the period of the Stooges shorts, and Columbia wrote and cast this role in three of the Stooges films. In the first of these, *Termites of 1938* (1938), an unidentified actress plays a simple-minded maid for a society lady, Mrs. Van Twichett, played by Bess Flowers. Flowers asks Mandy, the maid, to find the phone number of the Acme Escort Service, so that she can find an escort for a society dinner. As Mandy checks the many listings for companies named Acme, Flowers muses to herself that she hopes they're "discriminating." The maid, in her best broken English, queries, "'scriminatin'?" She then finds the closest word to that under Acme, which is "exterminating."

The role of the maid was reprised in *Calling All Curs* (1938), featuring Willa Pearl Curtis as the maid. The Stooges are veterinarians who are returning a prize dog to the wealthy Mrs. Bedford. Unfortunately, Mrs. Bedford's dog, Garçon, has been kidnapped, and the Stooges have taken another dog and glued mattress stuffing to him to disguise him. When the Stooges arrive with the dog, they are greeted by the maid, who instructs the boys, "Keep him away from me; I don't like dogs." The maid returns to her housecleaning and while vacuuming, in an attempt to keep the dog at bay, holds the nozzle close to him and proceeds to suck some of the fake fur off the dog. Astonished, she tries it once again, only to get the same result. Staring at the dog in disbelief, eyes bulging, she exclaims, "You is scalped! I'm getting' outta heah." While not as overtly stupid as the maid in *Termites of 1938*, the portrayal is gratuitous nonetheless in its use of behavioral stereotypes.

The third and final appearance by a maid, or a Negro in general, occurred 13 years later in *Income Tax Sappy* (1954). Unfortunately, this final appearance, which was made in the television era, could not break the stereotypical mold of previous Stooges films or of the prevailing stereotypes that were still enduring in the visual media. Nonetheless, this portrayal is noteworthy. In this film, the Stooges have cheated on their income tax returns and have become wealthy in the process. They have unwittingly invited an undercover IRS agent (played by Benny Rubin) over for dinner. Their maid, Frances, is once again played by an uncredited Negro actress. The role is, of course, stereotypical. What is interesting, however, is the manner in which the actress carries herself and the way she is treated by the other actors. After she fills his plate with mashed potatoes and gravy, Shemp says, "Thank you, thank you very much." While this is a small courtesy, the line is significant because it is only the second time a Negro is offered *any* courtesy in the Stooges films.[4]

Dudley Dickerson

The Negro actor who made the most appearances in Stooges films — and the only Negro actor to make multiple appearances in Stooges' shorts — was Dudley Dickerson (1906–1968), who appeared in a total of eight shorts between 1940 and 1956. His trademarks were his bulging eyes, coon English, and predictable occupations. Dickerson was, however, one of the most prolific Negro actors of the day, appearing mostly as a Columbia contract player in 84 films between 1935 and 1966 ("Supporting Cast" 2005). Unfortunately, he did little to change the stereotypes for Negroes that were so common during this period. Like most Negro actors at the time, Dickerson was restricted to the usual male roles: bellboys, janitors, waiters, and such.

Dickerson's first appearance in a Stooges short was in *A Plumbing We Will Go* (1940). A favorite of critics and fans alike, the film features Dickerson in a slapstick routine that has become one of the better-known scenes from the thousands featured in Stooges films. So strong was the episode that it was later remade with Shemp and titled *Vagabond Loafers* and *Scheming Schemers*, both of which used stock footage from the original film.

In *A Plumbing We Will Go*, the Stooges are hired as plumbers in a large house where they manage to destroy both the plumbing and the electrical system. With the exception of Curly's famous scene where he is trapped within a maze of pipes in a bathtub (remade with Shemp for the later films), Dickerson, who is on the screen for several minutes, manages to otherwise steal the show. In this film, Dickerson plays the role of a cook, complete with the all-white uniform and high white hat associated with the "Rastus" style cooks of this period. While the Stooges are working on the plumbing, they end up rerouting the water into the electrical system and therefore (in the world of the Stooges) through various electrical appliances including a television, stove, and light fixture. Dickerson is first confronted with a spinning sink faucet, then with a clock whose hands are spinning out of control. The clock falls off the wall into a bowl of batter, which splashes on the face of the incredulous but obviously helpless cook. An electric light bulb in the ceiling light fixture fills with water and explodes. Finally, the stove begins shooting water out of every orifice. The drenched kitchen provides an opportunity to have the befuddled Dickerson fall all over himself in a scene of hilarious, memorable slapstick. Dickerson races out of the kitchen and returns shortly wearing a rain slicker and hat in his final attempt to battle the stove. While Dickerson's appearance is clearly an unsophisticated comic device, this memorable performance is but one example of a Negro actor during this period who created a screen image that became an inseparable part of the plot.

Dickerson reprises his role in *They Stooge to Conga*. Incredibly, he plays a domestic (identified in the script as "Wilbur the Cook") for a group of Axis power officers living in an American home. This time the Stooges are repairmen working on a broken doorbell. Moe orders Dickerson away from the work area so he can concentrate on the doorbell. He then climbs on top of a kitchen table and, following a tug of war with Larry and Curly, loses his footing, causing the table to topple and to spring the batter into the air and onto Dickerson's head. Later, an exploding telephone startles Dickerson, who backs into a waffle iron that grips his behind like a vicious animal, causing Dickerson to scream and race out of the kitchen.

A Plumbing We Will Go was remade twice with Shemp in *Vagabond Loafers* (1949) and *Scheming Schemers* (1956). Stock footage of Dickerson's original screen appearance was incorporated, and two short scenes featuring Dickerson were shot especially for *Vagabond Loafers* (and later used as stock footage for *Scheming Schemers*). One featured the slicker-wearing Dickerson entering the living room during the party, brandishing a meat cleaver and informing the guests, "Sorry, folks, dinner called on account of rain." Later he encounters the villainous Kenneth McDonald and Christine McIntyre. Startled to see the Negro cook with a cleaver, they inform Dickerson that they are looking for a drink of water. Dickerson advises, "Turn on anything, you'll get it!" These brief scenes were the last ones Dickerson filmed with the Three Stooges.

As was the case with scenes featuring the Stooges themselves, the original kitchen scene and the scenes with the meat cleaver were filmed nine years apart. What is noteworthy about the later-filmed sequence is that, although brief (both scenes total around 15 seconds of screen time), the scenes include none of the stereotype identifiers so apparent in the original filming. Apparently, the Stooges writers and producers finally were able to use Negroes simply to advance the storyline, and not to cheapen their appearance by advancing racial stereotypes. However, this should not be interpreted as any attempt to give additional employment to Negro actors or to right any wrongs, but rather as a way to match the original script and film for consistency and continuity.

Dickerson made a very brief appearance as a frightened nurse in *From Nurse to Worse* (1940). His next appearance was as a guard in *A Gem of a Jam* (1943). While the Stooges are being chased by crooks in a hospital, Dickerson is stopped by the police who want him to try to grab a trio of killers. This request prompts Dickerson to exclaim, "What? Who's gonna grab who?!" As Dickerson creeps around fearfully, he backs into a mannequin, causing him to panic and run away, screaming. Trying to escape, he plays tug of war with a doorknob with the Stooges, who are on the opposite side of the door trying to get to the other side. He later encounters Curly, who has fallen into a trough of what appears to be wallpaper paste, which gives him a ghostly, inhuman appearance. Thinking Curly is another mannequin, the startled Dickerson offers, "You sho' is ugly!" The ghostly Curly waddles behind Dickerson, who turns around again in surprise, as Curly says, "Now you follow me." A shocked Dickerson screams and flees. Moments later, Curly sits down in front of Dickerson, who is lying on the floor, hiding behind Curly's seat. What follows is a humorous sequence where Curly and Dickerson clasp hands and engage in a variety of hand and finger games. Neither actor knows whose hand he is holding. It is noteworthy that the grasping of a white hand by a Negro hand itself was a highly unusual occurrence. When Dickerson discovers that the hand he

The image of the frightened black man was a staple in many Columbia short films, including this scene featuring Dudley Dickerson from *A Gem of a Jam* (1943).

is holding is Curly's, he runs away screaming. Despite Moe's warning, Dickerson smashes through a locked door, followed by a frightened Moe and Larry, who are just as afraid of the ghostly, pursuing Curly.

Next for Dickerson was *Hold That Lion!* (1947), which was only the third short for the new third Stooge, Shemp. Dickerson plays a train porter, who is shining his shoes in his cabin room. A lion, let loose earlier by the Stooges, has entered the room. Unaware of the situation, Dickerson hums to himself and continues shining. At one point, he grabs the lion's tail, thinking that it's a rag, and wipes his shoes. When the lion roars in discomfort, Dickerson looks up with his bulging eyes, screams, and tries to leap out the window of the train. When the opening proves too small, half of Dickerson's portly body remains in the train. The lion takes a swipe with his paw at the porter's rear end, ripping the seat of his trousers, and the panicking Dickerson screams, "Hep, hep, I'm losin' mah mind." While the scene is vintage Dickerson, it is probably the most demeaning act he performs in all of his years with the Stooges. The short was remade with Dickerson's stock footage as *Booty and the Beast* (1953).

Dickerson's final film with the Stooges that did not feature stock footage was *Who Done It?* (1949). This film finds the Stooges' writers and producers firmly gripping prevalent stereotypes. Dickerson made a brief appearance as a janitor in an office building where the Stooges have a detective agency. Near the beginning of the film, a closeup shows Dickerson warily entering their office, with a zoom out to reveal the sleuthing Stooges bound and gagged. It is Dickerson to the rescue as he asks the Stooges, "Whassa matta, boys?" As the Stooges try to regain their composure, Dickerson stares, eyes wide open and mouth agape in amazement. This role is notable because of Dickerson's discovery. While he is still exhibiting stereotypical behavior, it is the only episode in which a Negro is a cast as a "hero," since it is he who rescues the Stooges.

Other Stooges films tried to emulate the comic success of those featuring Dickerson's Negro stereotype with other Negro actors, producing mixed results. In *Heavenly Daze*, Shemp has died. With their small inheritance, Moe and Larry have rented an expensive apartment and clothes, along with a butler, in order to impress a rich investor into underwriting a bogus invention. Moe and Larry call for the butler, Spiffingham, who answers off-camera in a British accent. When he enters the picture, we see that he is a Negro butler, played by Sam McDaniel. McDaniel initially has a cool, genteel demeanor, but the façade is quickly dropped as Shemp knocks on the door and enters the apartment. While the omniscient camera sees Shemp, the butler cannot. He sees a hat and coat handed to him and asks Moe and Larry whether the clothes belong to them. The two Stooges, initially frightened by the presence of Shemp's ghost, are now calm and matter-of-fact about it, in contrast to the frightened Spiffingham.

Bogle (1989, p. 52) noted that Willie Best, in a tight situation in the film

The Littlest Rebel, replied that his mind wasn't worried but his "body don't believe it." McDaniel's performance is reminiscent of Best's. In *Heavenly Daze*, while Spiffingham is shaking, the doorbell rings. Moe and Larry encourage him to answer the door, but McDaniel declines, thinking it is once again Shemp's ghost. Larry calmly frightens the butler further by informing him that Shemp's ghost is already in the room with them. McDaniel looks down and asks, "Feet, why don't you get goin'?" Later, the invisible Shemp dons the hat and coat and moves about the room. The frightened Spiffingham makes his final exit by running out of the room.[5]

Negro Stooges

In six films, the Stooges themselves offered stereotyped interpretations of the American Negro. No real evidence indicates that the Stooges themselves held any personal prejudices or were otherwise predisposed to mocking Negroes. Moe Howard relates an interesting story about his first encounter with racism in the South. It happened in Jacksonville, Florida, in 1931, before the Columbia shorts were filmed and while the Stooges were primarily a traveling stage show. After taking a walk outside the theater where the comedy team was appearing, Moe encountered an elderly Negro man. On seeing Moe, the gentleman leaped off the sidewalk and into the gutter. Thinking the man had seen a snake, Moe likewise jumped into the gutter, whereupon the man jumped back onto the sidewalk. Moe jumped back up, and so on. Moe asked the man what was going on, and the gentleman informed him that a black man could not walk on the same side of the street as a white man. According to Moe's account, he replied, "Mister, this is not my city, but it's my country and I can walk with any man I choose to." He proceeded to put his arm around the man, who soon became frightened and walked away. Upon re-entering the theater, Moe discovered that the stagehands weren't speaking to him and that the show was closed. Apparently the theater employees and conductor had seen Moe's gesture and told him, "We don't want any nigger lovers in our theater or our city, so get movin'."[6]

While this anecdote was offered as a somewhat noble gesture on Moe Howard's part, the Stooges' on-screen behavior doesn't necessarily jibe with this liberal attitude. It was noted earlier that in *Uncivil Warriors*, the Stooges performed a recurring routine of mocking Negro men. Since so many parts of the Stooges' act were honed in their vaudeville days, this was likely a touch developed by the Stooges themselves.

Larry Fine in particular seemed to favor this routine. In *Uncivil Warriors* Curly joins Larry, but Larry does the routine solo in *You Nazty Spy!* and *I'll Never Heil Again* and is accompanied by Shemp in *Hula-La-La*. The routine featured references to the South, shuffling of feet, and "hallelujahs."[7]

Two Stooges films show a return to the minstrel days. In *Three Pests in a Mess*, Moe gets his face covered in ink and then bumps into Larry. A disgusted Larry asks, "What's the idea, porter?" When he realizes that it is Moe, he gets down on his knee like Al Jolson and says, "Mammy." Moe slaps Larry and admonishes him for calling him "porter." It is unclear whether Moe was upset with being confused with a Negro or whether it was just his usual impatience with a fellow Stooge.

The second film hearkening back to minstrelsy is *Uncivil War Birds*, featuring a Civil War theme. In this film the Stooges are trying to get a map from a group of Union officers. To distract them, the Stooges enter in their minstrel wear and begin singing a Brooklyn-ized version of "Dixie." At one point the Stooges break into a dance, and Curly rubs the makeup away from his eyes. The Union officers react quickly and chase the Stooges out the door.

This film is significant for several reasons. The Stooges were on the side of the Southern Confederates. Given the liberal agenda of some of the Stooges shorts, this stance was somewhat out of character.[8] This film was routinely dropped from the syndication cycles of some stations when the Stooges films reached television, presumably because of the questionable racial content. *Uncivil War Birds* features the only appearance by the Stooges in blackface and wearing what may be described as Uncle Tom garb. It seems improbable that anyone would seriously think that the Stooges in blackface were real Negroes, though such a suspension of reality was not uncommon in Stooges films. Moreover, the film features what is arguably the strangest and most perverse line uttered in any of the Stooges films. As the blackfaced Stooges are plotting to get the map, Moe retorts, "Brother, you-all ejaculated a mouthful."

While the portrayals of American Negroes were defiantly stereotypical, both by members of their own race and the Stooges themselves, such representations were relatively mild when compared with the portrayals of their Black African, Nubian, and South Seas Native counterparts. With a small number of exceptions, the writers saved the most extreme stereotyping for the latter three groups.

Black Africans

In *Three Little Twirps* (1943), Caucasian actor Duke York plays the Sultan of Abadaba, a spear-throwing circus performer. Of greater relevance is *Three Missing Links* (1938), which says it takes place in "Darkest Africa." This film contains some of the most degrading representations from among any of the Stooges shorts. The Stooges arrive at the hut of Dr. Ba Loni Salomi, a witch doctor wearing a top hat, ring in his nose, grass skirt, and skin paint.

Some of the representations in this film show the stereotyped representations of Africans rather than American Negroes. For example, the witch doctor is planning to eat the Stooges. The specter of cannibalism was a recurring one in films with African themes during this period and correlates with the savage representation identified by Reddick in his 1944 study (Reddick 1975, p. 4). But the connection is made to the American Negro in a scene where Curly is tied to a table. Curly, as the heaviest Stooges, is the most desirable to eat. The witch doctor, now sporting a chef's hat, takes a cleaver and motions over Curly's chest and stomach, musing, "short ribs ... soup bone." The comparison with American soul food is an obvious one. After the Stooges make a daring escape, they push one of the "cooks" into a boiling pot, causing him to scream in the all-too-familiar manner of the American Negro in Hollywood cinema.

Nubians

The Nubian plays a more substantial role in Stooges films than the roles for the Black Africans in *Three Little Twirps* and *Three Missing Links*. In general, however, the dark-skinned Nubians played subordinate roles to the lighter-skinned Arabs, around whom much of those films revolve. Specifically, the Nubian, in contrast to his lighter-skinned counterparts (see Chapter 16), typically played a faithful servant, usually in the form of a palace guard. This is seen in *Wee Wee Monsieur*, *Malice in the Palace*, *Rumpus in the Harem*, and *Three Arabian Nuts*.

In *Wee Wee Monsieur*, the Stooges are attempting to rescue their captain from Arab captors, led by Caucasian Vernon Dent. Guarding the captain is John Lester Johnson, who plays a tall, muscular Nubian guard. After the Stooges knock out Dent, the guard leans over him, mourning, "oh, massa, massa," whereupon he, too, is knocked out.

Malice in the Palace and *Rumpus in the Harem* (featuring stock footage from the earlier film) again show a Negro actor as a Nubian guard. One difference between the Nubian and the American Negro is that unlike the latter, the Nubian is to be feared; he is usually brandishing a scimitar. In one scene, Moe removes the turban from the guard's head and hands it to him to wipe his sweaty brow. The guard, played by an American Negro, thanks him, without a trace of stereotypical dialect. He is rewarded by being hit on the head with a metal vase.[9]

It should be noted, however, that the original script for *Malice in the Palace* called for a denigrating, stereotyped scene for the Nubian guard (played by Everett Brown, in an uncredited appearance). The guard is actually named "Sambo" to further his denigration. Pages 18 and 19 of the original copy show a scene just before the Stooges encounter the Emir:

79. MEDIUM SHOT NUBIAN AND EMIR
  The Emir is lighting his hookah which rests on a small table.

NUBIAN: (Southern Negro accent): Beg yo' pahdon, Yo' Highness, have you all seen three loafing leapfrogers around heah?
EMIR: Drinking again, eh Sambo?
NUBIAN: No Sah, Yo' Highness — no Sah!
With that, he backs out, bowing and looking around.

80. CLOSEUP EMIR
Forgoing action

81. MEDIUM LONG SHOT
Nubian backs into pond.
NUBIAN: Ah faw down.

Fortunately, someone had the good sense to cut this scene. Nevertheless, the film still features a scene with the Stooges pelting the Nubian in the face with fruit, including a banana that winds up in his mouth. Throughout, though, the Nubian does not exhibit any of the stereotypical shuffling Negro behavior so common in other shorts.

Three Arabian Nuts features Wesley Bly in the role of a genie, who comes to the Stooges by way of a magic lamp. He is tall and muscular and wears a turban and the baggy pants worn by Arabs in American films of the period. This episode is unusual, not only for its farcical premise, but also for its use of the Negro actor. There are several stereotype indicators: the genie is there to "serve" the Stooges, granting their every wish, the very reason they are being pursued by a group of cutthroat Arabs. Also, Shemp insists on calling the large, powerful genie "Amos," an obvious reference to the popular character from the radio and television program *Amos 'n' Andy*. Shemp twice refers to the genie as "Big Boy," a variation on the derogatory term for Negroes, "boy."

But what is different about this film's portrayal is that the Nubian is both powerful and intelligent. Despite Shemp's attempts to bring him down in status, the genie is strong and cool. Bly is also the hero of this episode, the only time a Negro performed in this manner except for Dickerson's saving the Stooges in *Who Done It?* However, heroism is not the lasting impression. After Bly has vanquished the cutthroats, Shemp summons "Amos" to fulfill his earlier wish for a million dollars. In his last moment of total servitude, the genie genially offers, "Coming, master," entering the room with a wheelbarrow full of money.

South Seas Natives

Two Stooges films — *Some More of Samoa* and *Hula-La-La* — dealt with adventures in the South Seas. *Hula-La-La* features mostly darkened white actors, plus a handful of Negroes in "native" attire, and the "Southern" routine. *Some More of Samoa* offers an encounter with an island native. When Moe refers to him as "Snowflake," the man responds, "No Snowflake. Kingfisher." Moe and Larry slip into their predictable *Amos 'n' Andy* routine:

LARRY: Hiya, Amos.
MOE: Hiya, Andy.
LARRY: Where's Lightnin'?
MOE: I don't know, but I think it's gonna strike any minute.

The exchange is concluded with the obligatory "hallelujah" before the Stooges are finally captured.

Black and White — In Black and White

The picture painted of the American Negro in the films of the Three Stooges is essentially a negative one. Applying Reddick's scale to the 25 representations of Negroes, including American Negroes, Black Africans, Nubians, and South Sea Natives, one finds found a total of seven neutral portrayals, 18 negative portrayals, and not a single instance that could reasonably be called a positive portrayal. Clearly, the films of the Three Stooges, for the most part, were following the contemporary Hollywood conventions when portraying Negroes. Arguably the results may have been different had the Stooges been actively engaged in feature-length films featuring Negroes during the period of their greatest popularity. Indeed, given the Stooges' overall track record, the portrayals would likely have been even more negative. The nature of short subjects was such that while stereotypes abounded, the full depths of the Negro stereotype had not been mined, at least as those personified by Mantan Moreland and Willie Best.

The neutral representations, however, do deserve some attention. The only such representation during the early years of the Stooges (or the Curly shorts) is the Negro baby in *Uncivil Warriors*. The remainder of the "neutral" shorts were filmed with Shemp, and any tendency for these portrayals to lean to the positive side of the ledger (for example, Dickerson in *Who Done It?*, Sly's genie, or the maid in *Income Tax Sappy*) was more than offset by the stereotypical roles and attempts to degrade the Negro through dialect or status that existed in their other films.

The Stooges shorts were not without their social merits, however. When compared with Stepin Fetchit, Mantan Moreland, or Willie Best, the male Negro portrayals were not nearly as humiliating. Never in a Stooges film was a Negro portrayed as unemployed, lazy, or crooked. While some attempts were made to portray the Negro male as uneducated, the characters were seldom defeated when it came to plot twists.

Negro women did not appear as often or fare as well as Negro men. Negro women appear only three times in the Stooges films, and all are maids. Only the maid in *Income Tax Sappy* can charitably be described as neutral, while the maids in *Calling All Curs* and *Termites of 1938* are subliterate and clearly inferior to the white characters.

15. The Image of the Negro in the Three Stooges Shorts (Seely)   195

It was noted earlier that the only repeat appearances made by a Negro actor in Stooges shorts were made by Dudley Dickerson. Given the changes that occurred within the personnel of the Three Stooges, had the producers been open to the idea, Dickerson might have made for an inspired choice for a third Stooge. He was acrobatic, with an expressive face and an innate sense of comic timing. He was a willing fall guy (a necessary requisite of being a third Stooge) and possessed the same sense of cowardice and stupidity as the Stooges themselves.

Dickerson had been a semi-regular in the Columbia short films of Andy Clyde. The Scottish-born Clyde, while a very comical actor, was not nearly as dominating a screen presence as the Three Stooges. However, the films of Clyde were stylistically similar to those of the Stooges (see Chapter 5). Dickerson's appearances in the Clyde films allowed producers to exploit the Negro stereotypes to an even greater extent than in the films of the Stooges. At the same time, giving Dickerson more space in these films showcased him as Clyde's equal or near-equal in the storylines. And while there was humor to be found in Dickerson's bulging eyes and screaming rants, his greatest moments in all of these films came when he engaged in pure slapstick, the source of most of the Stooges' humor as well.

If a defense of sorts were to be offered of the Stooges comedies, one might point out that no racial or ethnic group came out particularly well in Stooge comedies. Examinations of other racial and ethnic groups and nationalities in other chapters turn up portrayals of Arabs as cutthroats and thieves, the Japanese as dentally deformed Fascists, and Latinos as alternately lazy or revolutionary.

To some extent, even whites took it on the chin from the Stooges. In Chapter 9, Don Morlan comments on the antiaristocratic nature of some Stooges' films, in which the boys show their ability to tweak the noses of the powerful and successful, even instituting anarchy when it suited them. And despite the Stooges' lack of breeding and education, more often than not the Three Stooges, purposefully or unwittingly, got the upper hand on these groups.

The portrayals of American Negroes, Black Africans, Nubians, and South Seas Natives in the Three Stooges' films were alternately excessive, comic, sympathetic, stereotypical, and ultimately revealing about the prevalent portrayals of Negroes in motion pictures made in Hollywood. For better or for worse, the American Negro and the ancillary groups were the most conspicuous of all racial and ethnic portrayals in these films. Yet one should note that the Stooges themselves often embodied some of the prevalent Negro stereotype indicators of the times.

While the Three Stooges occasionally treated the Negroes (and other minorities) in their films as inferior — for example, calling Wesley Bly "Amos" in *Three Arabian Nuts* and ordering Dickerson around in *They Stooge to*

Conga—the Stooges were not typically portrayed as superior to them. Indeed, of all types portrayed in these films, the Stooges are themselves shown as the most uneducated, dimwitted, lazy, and destructive characters. No matter what the situation, the Stooges were up to the task of being the most idiotic participants.

Notes

1. Bogle's title, *Toms, Coons, Mulattoes, Mammies, and Bucks,* is blatant evidence of these categories.
2. This point, however, is highly debatable. While the main characters of *Amos 'n' Andy* were simply black actors portraying the stereotypical characters written by creators Freeman Gosden and Charles Correll, they were all enormously creative talents. Further, the supporting cast consisted mainly of professionals, including portrayals of lawyers, doctors, and judges, roles that were denied to blacks in the white cinema and that were not seen again on television until the late 1960s. Television producer Hal Kanter maintains that Louise Beavers' *Beulah* was popular with white audiences, not because of its perpetuation of racial stereotypes, but because her character seemed solid, nurturing, and in control and because she was an ideal ruler of the household (*Altered Images,* Marlon T. Riggs, director, 1991).
3. The shot of the Negro baby was edited out of the film in some television markets.
4. The only other time a courtesy is extended to a Negro is by Moe to Dudley Dickerson in *A Gem of a Jam.* At the end of the episode, a terrified Dickerson is charging toward the door, and Moe has the decency to tell him that it's locked. This was not so much a courtesy as a life-or-death warning to a crazed man out of control.
5. *Heavenly Daze* was remade as *Bedlam in Paradise* (1955), almost entirely with stock footage. Contrary to information given in Lenburg, Maurer, and Lenburg's otherwise fine book, *The Three Stooges Scrapbook* (1982, p. 162), McDaniel's appearance in *Heavenly Daze* did not make the final cut of *Bedlam in Paradise.*
6. Howard (1977, pp. 53–54) further relates that 40 years later, outside a supermarket in West Hollywood, he ran into one of the stagehands from that appearance that wouldn't hang their scenery. He begged for Howard's forgiveness, explaining that he went along with the others in order to keep his job. Such circumstances were probably fairly typical, where otherwise nonprejudiced whites were compliant with the majority as a means of keeping employment.
7. *Hallelujah* was the name of a popular movie from 1929 that featured an all-Negro cast.
8. As stated in previous chapters, during the Curly years Stooges films regularly dealt with anti-Nazi and anti-Axis themes, pro-New Deal stances, and activism in World War II.
9. *Rumpus in the Harem* featured another Negro guard, who was sleeping in the hallway, also getting knocked on the head with a vase. His only line is a stunned "Hello!" Whether this was intended as another stereotype of the Negro is unclear.

Works Cited

Bogle, Donald. *Toms, Coons, Mulattoes, Mammies, and Bucks: An Interpretive History of Blacks in American Films.* New York: Continuum, 1989.
Howard, Moe. *Moe Howard and the Three Stooges.* Secaucus, N.J.: Citadel, 1977.

Lenburg, Jeff, Joan Howard Maurer, and Greg Lenburg. *The Three Stooges Scrapbook.* Secaucus, N.J.: Citadel, 1982.
McDonald, J. Fred. *Blacks and White TV.* Chicago: Nelson-Hall, 1992.
Reddick, Lawrence. "Of Motion Pictures." *Black Films and Film-Makers.* Ed. Lindsay Patterson. New York: Dodd, Mead, 1975.
"Supporting Cast for the 3 Stooges: Dudley Dickerson." Ed. O. T. Express and O. T. Packer. 20 Dec. 2005. http://members.aol.com/otpacker/support.html.
Thorp, Margaret Farrand. *America at the Movies.* New Haven: Yale University Press, 1939.

16

Hassan Ben Sober: Images of American Indians, Latinos, and Arabs in the Short Films of the Three Stooges

Peter Seely

Beginning in the 1960s, numerous papers, books, and articles were published aimed at revealing racial, ethnic, and gender stereotypes in Hollywood films and television programs. The changing political climate of the mid- to late sixties made such studies possible. Concomitant with societal protests over the treatment of minority groups in civil rights arenas were groundbreaking political and sociological studies investigating celluloid and fifth-estate portrayals of these groups.

The majority of these studies tended to be longitudinal and political. That is, most were addressed to long-suffering minorities and the cartoonlike portrayals of these people. There was also an overt political agenda: to bring about change in society, one would need to have these filmic stereotypes either minimized or removed from general media consumption. Most prevalent in the movement for media deconstruction toward political and social ends were those studies examining images and portrayals of African Americans, American Indians, and Latinos. In this regard, one could point to the years 1953 and 1966 — the years that the television show *Amos 'n' Andy* went off network television and left syndication — as watershed years, though perhaps dubious victories.[1]

A study of the short films of the Three Stooges from 1934 to 1949 reveals numerous portrayals of minority groups. The focus here is on American Indians, Latinos, and Arabs. African American images in Stooges films are examined in Chapter 15 and Europeans in Chapter 17.

Included in this chapter are representations by the Stooges themselves and by actors purporting to be members of these racial and ethnic groups. The following four dimensions, or characteristics, are of particular interest:

- Wardrobe used to portray the racial or ethnic group
- Dialogue, insofar as the accent, word choice, fluency in English, or what passes as authentic representation of the group is indicative of a broader portrayal
- Behavioral characteristics, indicating a positive or negative image of the group
- Motive, which may be exemplified through behavior but may also manifest itself separately

A reality that becomes painfully apparent when examining images in film is that filmmakers are far too willing to blend the differences within a group in order to smooth out the storytelling process. Groups become homogenized to make the process of telling the story easier. Within that dynamic, all Indian tribes are interchangeable, Latin countries are hardly important enough to distinguish any real differences, and all Middle Easterners are Arabs, whether or not they happen to come from any one of the 22 Arab states. These are part of our examination as well. In the case of the Arab group, there are some borderline, Middle Eastern "types" that are not considered in detail, as they represent marginal characters with a very loosely identified cultural background.

American Indians

The image of the American Indian was one of the earliest to emerge in the American motion picture industry. Dating back to the silent film era, the image of the Indian was crucial to many of the early American films. Perhaps it was the Indian's status as a Native American or, perhaps from a more ethnocentric point of view, the fact that, out of all minority representations, this group had the most profound influence on the lives and heritage of (mostly) European Americans in the first two hundred or so years of America's existence.

Jacquelyn Kilpatrick (1999, p. 22), in her book *Celluloid Indians*, notes that Indian images were commonplace in silent films from 1910 to 1913. While the early films were devoted mostly to the image of the Indian as a noble warrior, toward the end of the silent era the image of the American Indian as a bloodthirsty savage prevailed.

One of the earliest directors to fully exploit the image of the American Indian was D. W. Griffith, through films such as *A Pueblo Legend* (1912). Kilpatrick (1999, p. 24) claims it was Griffith's alternate images of the noble warrior and bloodthirsty savage that helped define early screen images of American Indians.[2]

As with most stereotypes, the portrayals of Indians have been historically simplistic. Some common themes portray Indians as wild but simple (especially compared with the white man) or as savages or noble warriors. According to Kilpatrick (1999, p. xvii), Europeans have nearly always viewed Indians as less intelligent; even when portrayed in the most benevolent light (through such adjectives as innocent, primitive, or unsaved), the Indian is almost always viewed as unequal.

As if to compensate for the Indian's less intelligent qualities in film, directors endowed the Indian with "desirable" animal qualities, such as a degree of bestial sexuality. And while in recent years Hollywood films have striven to portray the Indian in a more spiritual, celestial way, the alternate image of the ruthless savage has usually included an animal-like sexuality (Kilpatrick 1999, p. xvii), perhaps a precursor to a predominant stereotype that was later to characterize portrayals of African Americans.

Whatever the character of the American Indian in film, his trappings were unmistakable and were seen in abundance during the first half of the twentieth century. The Indian was nearly always seen in his "native" costume: headdress, moccasins, and suede breeches or shirt and pants. His face was painted in a manner that held little regard for authenticity and native customs.

The Indian's dialogue, especially in comedies or B-films, was predictable. The Indian grunted, uttered expressions such as "Ugh" or "How" or "Give 'em," a kind of abridged English and guttural sounds that gave credence to the Indian simpleton stereotype.

In addition to the film images, American Indians were generally a prominent part of popular culture in the United States, including many instances in popular music. Prince's Orchestra and Prince's Band, one of the most prolific recording entities in the early years of the two-sided 78 record, recorded for Columbia Records between 1908 and 1923. They made several titles designed to appeal to the exotic stereotype of the Indian, with songs such as "Powhattan's Daughter," "Indian Intermezzo," "Dream of the Ancient Red Man," "Signal Fire to the Mountain God," and "Hiawatha Melody of Love." In 1923, the Benson Orchestra of Chicago recorded "Oklahoma Indian Jazz."

During the period the Three Stooges were making films with images of American Indians, a number of popular songs were either novelty numbers or attempts to fuse a stereotype of Indian music with popular styles. In 1929, film star Fanny Brice recorded a comedy novelty titled "Yes, I'm an Indian." Most prominent was swing bandleader Charlie Barnet's 1939 theme song, "Cherokee," which was followed shortly by "Redskin Rhumba." The Western Swing artist Bob Wills recorded "Cherokee Maiden" in 1941, and in 1952 the country and western great Hank Williams recorded one of his most memorable songs in the Indian vein, "Kaw-Liga," about a love affair between two cigar store Indians (an Indian pop culture phenomenon unto itself).

The image of the American Indian has been cleaned up considerably for films of the past 30 years. The bloodthirsty savage is mostly a thing of the past. While the most negative stereotypes of American Indians persisted on television well into the 1960s, their image received an upgrade, like so many other minority groups. This change of image is perhaps best typified by a television public service announcement in the late sixties that featured a noble Indian shedding a single tear as he watched the unabated pollution of what was once his land.

While changes of this kind are rarely full and absolute, a new image of the American Indian did begin to appear in media portrayals in the 1970s. The highly successful novel *Bury My Heart at Wounded Knee* and popular films such as *Billy Jack, Little Big Man,* and *A Man Called Horse* offered contemporary and positive images of both nineteenth- and twentieth-century Indians.

Today, the Indian image is marketed much like a commodity (as it has been during most of the years since the Industrial Revolution). But instead of tomahawks, headdresses, and bows and arrows, the Indian is exploited today much more for his spirit, as a kind of symbol of new age spirituality.

American Indians in the Stooges Films

The three films of the Three Stooges that featured portrayals of Indians were all made early in the Stooges' career within a four-year span: *Whoops, I'm an Indian!, Back to the Woods,* and *Rockin' Through the Rockies.*

In *Whoops, I'm an Indian!,* the Stooges are con men who wind up on an Indian reservation. A French Canadian named Pierre (played by Bud Jamison) is outraged to discover that an Indian chief has stolen his wife. This portrayal is a common negative stereotype of the American Indian. The Stooges, fleeing from the law, coincidentally end up in Pierre's cabin. To hide from the authorities, the Stooges dress in mock Indian garb, complete with absurd war paint; Moe's face, for example, shows a tic-tac-toe game. When the authorities find the Stooges, they are on the floor, legs akimbo, smoking the obligatory peace pipe and offering only a series of what are supposed to be authentic native grunts in response to the lawmen's questions, including an exchange of the "shave and a haircut, two bits" refrain. In frustration, the sheriff says to his deputy, "These Indians are either drunk or crazy," simultaneously pointing out two common Indian stereotypes that are also quite applicable to the Three Stooges.

Producers apparently gave no thought whatsoever to authentic portrayals of Native Americans. Here the Stooges disguise as Indians to escape the hot-tempered Pierre in *Whoops, I'm an Indian!* (1936).

This film contains a great deal of interesting wordplay. The title was a play on the aforementioned Fanny Brice song, and a lot of additional wordplay underscores the Indian stereotyping. For example, Pierre discovers the Indian Stooges in his cabin. Curly, dressed as a squaw, is suddenly quite appealing to Pierre, who is perhaps out for a bit of revenge against Chief Rain in the Puss for stealing his wife. Pierre, speaking his best broken English, asks the squaw to "keep my wigwam," to which Curly replies in his best Brooklynese, "You keep your own wig warm!"

Both *Back to the Woods* and *Rockin' Through the Rockies* show many similarities in their portrayal of American Indians. While the usual combination of tomahawks, teepees, and war whoops are certainly present, these portrayals go far beyond the usual mixing of tribal customs, resulting in combining headdresses, clothing, and face paint without regard to authenticity.

Back to the Woods takes place in the days of the Pilgrims, who are trying to reach treaty agreements with a tribe of Indians. The Indians agree, in principle at least, to having "no more war." A cruel irony follows. The Indian has been acknowledged, even in American folklore, to having been cheated out of his land, the best example being the so-called $24 deal for Manhattan Island. But in *Back to the Woods*, in exchange for the promise of no more war, the greedy Indian wants a cash settlement from the benevolent white men and women. When the Pilgrim leader (played by Vernon Dent) stresses that they have a limited amount of money, the chief describes his terms, including a down payment and the rest of the payment on time, with an interest of 6 percent. When one of the Pilgrims rejoices that at last they can hunt, the chief replies, "No. Not until F.O.B. Fork Over Balance." In disgust, Curly utters the slur "Indian giver!"

The last of the Stooges films to feature prominent American Indian stereotypes was *Rockin' Through the Rockies*. In this film the Stooges are part of a road show working its way west to San Francisco. While traveling through the Rocky Mountain region, they encounter a tribe of Indians known as the Escrow Indians, another reference to the financial "concerns" of Native Americans. While the Stooges and company are undoubtedly frightened, the Escrows make a threat that, in the context of the period of the film, was not entirely unreasonable. The chief (played by Dick Curtis) warns that the troop must leave within two sundowns, or else they will be "scalped." The film also includes sexual stereotyping of the Indian. When one Indian comments on the attractiveness of the "paleface squaws," the chief warns his aide to "keep 'em mind on business" but acknowledges, "Not bad!" Yet in spite of what, on the surface, seems a fair warning from the chief, the three young women in the troop are chased later in the night by a band of sex-crazed Indians, apparently intent on seducing the white women.

Also worth a brief mention are the passing references to American Indians in three other Stooges films. In *Pop Goes the Easel*, Curly proudly displays a painting that he says is "Sitting Bull with his back turned." In *Healthy, Wealthy and Dumb*, one scene shows the Stooges dressed as a giant Indian and trying to sneak past a hotel detective. Moe, the head of the Indian, tosses out a few lines in mock Indian dialect. The detective, who is not fooled, steps on their wrap to reveal Moe, atop Larry, atop Curly. In one of the Stooges' last films, *Sweet and Hot*, Joe Besser refers to a psychiatrist, played by Moe, as an "Indian giver," after taking too literally the doctor's instructions to take a seat.

The three primary films *Whoops, I'm an Indian!*, *Back to the Woods*, and *Rockin' Through the Rockies* are striking and significant. The images of the American Indian in these films are the most important part of the films' impact, and they are upfront and unmistakable. In spite of the fact that these Indians are, for the most part, fearless, they also possess nearly every negative aspect of the Indian stereotype. Their manner of dress, their motives, their speech, and their behavior all reflect the majority of film images of their day.

Yet this conclusion must be qualified by one important fact: the Indians in these films do much more than say "Ugh" and know about much more than just scalping and whooping. Indeed, the Indians in *Back to the Woods* and *Rockin' Through the Rockies* are quite savvy about certain issues, especially financial matters. The dialogue in these films, with the Indians negotiating sophisticated financial deals, depicts the Indians bettering the white man at the game at which he considered himself vastly superior. Perhaps had the producers focused more in this area and less on the war whoops, these films would have actually been historically significant.

Latinos

Though many ethnic groups fit under the "Latino" umbrella, this term has generally been applied to what can simplistically, but descriptively, be called "south of the border": the United States border. This term includes people from Mexico, Puerto Rico, Cuba, and South America, as well as mythical hamlets such as Valeska.

As with American Indian stereotypes, the image of the Latino, particularly that of the Mexican, has appeared in film almost since the medium's inception. In his important book *Latino Images in Film* Charles Ramirez Berg (2002, pp. 68–77) describes six Latin stereotypes that have endured over the years in cinema:

El Bandido— The familiar Mexican bandit dating back to the early years of motion pictures, stereotyped by his unshaven appearance and greasy hair and his wicked, abusive behavior. A latter-day variant is the inner-city gang member.

Harlot— The lusty, hot-tempered, and sexy female, possessing few scruples.

Male Buffoon— A stereotype pervading just about every ethnic category. In television and film, this common stereotype is represented, for example, by Leo Carrillo as Pancho from *The Cisco Kid* and Ricky Ricardo in *I Love Lucy*. The humor comes from many sources but primarily the character's inability to speak clear English.

Female Clown—A character exuding a great deal of sexuality that is essentially negated by her over-the-top comic characteristics. Carmen Miranda perhaps best exemplifies the Latina female clown.

Latin Lover— A fiery, dangerous, and non–WASPish lover. This character probably goes back to Rudolph Valentino but survived in later years through such noteworthies as Ricardo Montalban.

Dark Lady—A mysterious, sensuous, erotic woman, typified by actress Delores Del Rio.

The image of the Latino in film has been much defined by dress. For men, the image that often comes to mind is the Pancho Villa look-alike, a Mexican bandido sporting white gauze clothing, sandals, a bullet belt, and sombrero. A film such as *The Treasure of Sierra Madre* conjures up a classic Mexican stereotype. For women, the image is usually of a beautiful *bonita*, recognizable by her haunting, dark beauty, accented by long, colorful skirts.

Moreover, the Latino image in general, like the other stereotypes, often emotes a sense of *noir:* a dangerous personality, with dangerous preoccupations or a dangerous sexuality.

Latinos in the Three Stooges Films

Of the Latin types identified by Berg, only two are prevalent in the early Three Stooges films: the bandido and the buffoon. We focus on six films: *Cuckoo Cavaliers, Saved by the Belle, What's the Matador?, Three Hams on Rye, Three Dark Horses,* and *Sappy Bullfighters*.[3]

Cuckoo Cavaliers portrays the Three Stooges as former fish salesmen in southern California, who have given up the enterprise to go into the saloon business. They find an office run by a Latino businessman, Pedro Ruiz. When Curly tells the man that they want a saloon with class and beauty, the man mistakenly thinks they want to buy a beauty salon, and he sells them one in the mythical Cucaracha, Mexico. When the Stooges discover that they've been "given the business" by Ruiz, they decide to make a go of it anyway. Their first customers are four young Latinas who are chorus girls in a nightclub run by Manuel Mosales (played by Bob O'Connor). Despite the fact they are in Mexico, the club is located at 1410 South American Way. He informs the Stooges that since "gentlemen prefer blondes," he wants the Stooges to bleach the dark-haired beauties' hair.

After the Stooges are introduced to the four young women, Curly jokes that "they must be hungry, they all end in *ita*." He is enamored with one of the young ladies, Pepita, who tells him that "(her) English is not so good looking, no?" to which Curly replies, "Your English is atrocious." She takes this as a compliment. Ironically, the Three Stooges had a very successful career "*moidering* the King's English," but Curly confidently corrects the young Mexican woman. However, when one of the ladies asks Larry if he can make her hair "henna color," he replies, "Henna color at all, kid."

As the Stooges venture into the uncharted territory of beauty care, they give the first customer (played by Dorothy Appleby) a mudpack made from cement and remove large patches of her hair. The outraged nightclub owner returns with a pistol, declaring, "For what you did to my Rosita, I'm going to *keel* you." The Stooges beseech him to wait and see how the other girls turned out. He waits, only to be shocked as the Stooges remove the towels from the

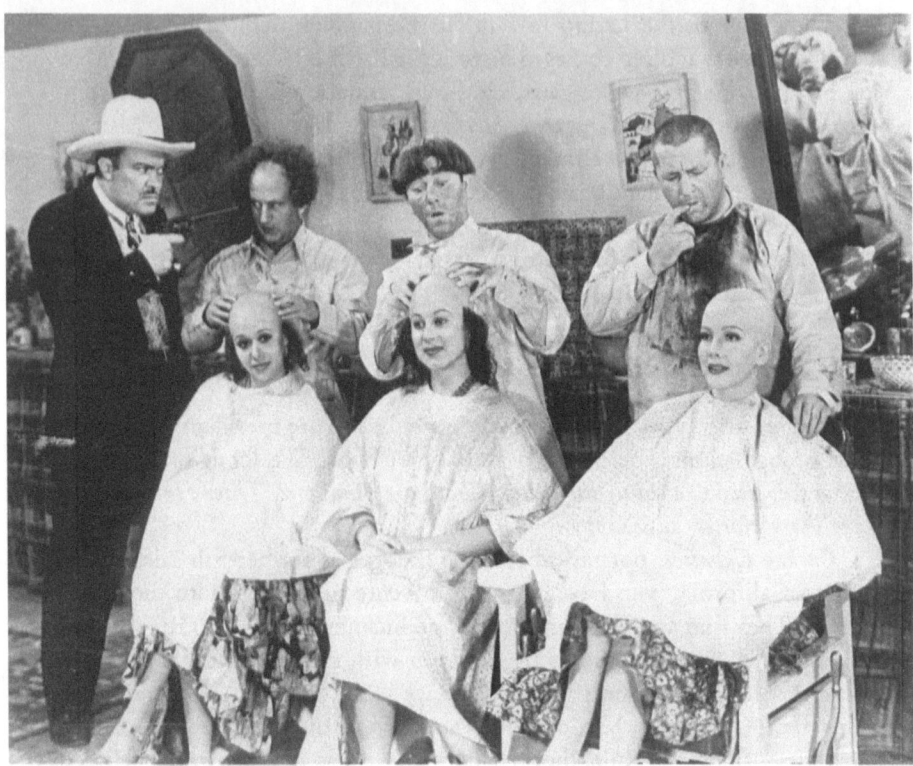

Stooges films often used non-ethnic types for ethnic roles. In *Cuckoo Cavaliers* (1940), actor Bob O'Connor portrays the angry Latin Manuel Mosales, who is incensed about what has happened to his daughters (uncredited) in the Stooges' beauty salon.

ladies' heads, revealing that they have made the women bald. The young women, all of who are bearing pistols, begin shooting at the Stooges as they try to make their getaway.

Several stereotypes are reinforced in this film. While the characters can be expected to speak English with accents, the thick "I'm going to *keel* you" is done for exaggerated effect only, and Pepita's broken English gives the Stooges perhaps their only chance ever to feel linguistically superior to another person.

Most significant, though, is the fact that the nightclub owner and the four chorus girls would rather resort to violence with guns than resolve their differences in some other way. This film thus reinforces the stereotype of the pistol-toting Mexican.

Cuckoo Cavaliers also reinforces some other common Mexican stereotypes. The Stooges' adopted town of Cucaracha bills itself as "The Busiest Site on the Map" on the sign as one enters the sleepy town. The four lovely young women are to be dyed blonde like American women. All five of the Mexicans whom we actually see in Cucaracha are wielding pistols.

But *Cuckoo Cavaliers* has perhaps a subtler but sinister subtext. The nightclub owner, Manuel Mosales, describes the young women in his employ as "chorus girls" and refers to gentlemen preferring blondes. Given the Hays Code that was in effect at this time, it is a short, logical leap to consider that these four young women in this border town were perhaps prostitutes and that their burly Mexican benefactor was more like a pimp than a boss.

Saved by the Belle takes place in the mythical city of Valeska, described in the opening credits as "a thriving kingdom somewhere in the tropics." It becomes clear early on, however, that Valeska bears a strong resemblance to the stereotypical film portrayals of Mexico. The Stooges are traveling salesmen who have been arrested as spies. Just as they are about to be released, the man in charge reads a telegram sent to the Stooges. He mistakenly infers that a message telling the Stooges that they will get no more money until they get rid of their present wardrobe means that they are being paid to assassinate the military dictator, Ward Robey. A young Valeskan woman named Señorita Rita befriends them and helps them to escape from prison. They arrive at a rebel military camp, only to find themselves bumbling a mission directed by the señorita. The Stooges manage to escape in an ammunition truck, which blows up and throws them onto a horse at the film's end.

This film features several examples of characteristics often used to perpetuate the Mexican stereotype, such as the broken English and the frequent siestas, revolutions, and Pancho Villa–like soldiers. Valeska is clearly a "banana republic," with a highly volatile and unstable political situation in which the Stooges find themselves unintentionally involved. It presents the largest number of Mexican stereotypes in a Stooges film, without actually taking place in Mexico.

What's the Matador? begins with the Stooges traveling to Mexico to perform a comedy bullfight. On the bus they befriend a young Mexican woman named Dolores and are confronted at the end of the trip by the woman's jealous husband, Jose. Like the nightclub owner in *Cuckoo Cavaliers*, he is also prepared to *keel* the Stooges. As they separate, the Stooges find they have switched suitcases with the couple. Most of the remainder of the film revolves around the Stooges trying to find the woman and return the suitcase, and the jealous husband trying to exact revenge on the Stooges for approaching his wife. During this adventure, the Stooges encounter two Mexican men. The first is angry when the Stooges interrupt his siesta and barks at them (in Spanish) to leave him alone. The second is a fat, comical character, a buffoon somewhat along the lines of Sergeant Garcia from the *Zorro* TV series. A long exchange takes place with the man, who speaks only two words of English, *hello* and *goodbye*, and has them confused with each other. The Stooges ask to "see Esther," which the man repeatedly mistakes for taking a siesta, giving the producers another chance to show a lazy, sleeping Mexican.

When the Stooges finally make it to the bull ring, they are introduced by a ring announcer who tells the audience, "We hope you like them too many." The comedy bullfight is supposed to feature Moe and Larry in a bull costume with Curly as the matador. But the evil Jose bribes a guard to release a real bull, which frightens Moe and Larry out of the ring. Curly eventually subdues the bull and is carried off by throngs of Mexicans shouting "Ole Americano, Ole Americano!" It is a strange ending because Curly did what only the greatest Mexican bullfighters could do.

What's the Matador? may actually be the most enlightened film of the group. It does contain some of the Mexican stereotypes found in films of the day: the reliance once again on the "siesta" gag, the broken English, and a hot-tempered man. But considering that the film contained nearly two minutes of mostly Spanish dialogue (punctuated by a few brief lines from the Stooges), the friendly and (mostly) nonsexual relationship between the Stooges and Dolores, and the comfortable, middle-class surroundings in which Jose and Dolores lived, one might conclude that this was a fairly bold step for creative people who were mostly used to grinding out quick and cheap films where there could not be much depth to the characters or to the story line.

Three Hams on Rye features the Stooges as actors who are backstage trying to trap a malicious stage critic who may be lurking in disguise. They don their own disguises, taken from the costume department, to fool him. This film offers a brief scene with Shemp Howard dressed in a Pancho Villa outfit, complete with a bullet belt and sombrero, and sporting a long beard. After donning the costume, Shemp feels compelled to get into character, saying in his best Mexican accent, "*Leesen*, Mr. Barker, don't you sneak in, or Ponch is going to shoot you, I *tink*. I'm a *bahd mahn*." The brief scene offers a chance at further exploitation of the bandido image.

Three Dark Horses includes a brief line by Shemp Howard, who claims to be the delegate "Gia Ronimo, from Rico Puerto."

Arabs

Despite the abundance of Arab images and stereotypes that date back to the same era as the earliest Indian and Mexican stereotypes, there is an inexplicable dearth of research in this area. One of the few exceptions is the research conducted by Jack Shaheen, a former Fulbright scholar whose study of Arabs in the media is something of a voice in the wilderness in the popular field of racial and ethnic stereotype study. For while most other sizable minority groups have developed political action groups and have effected significant changes in the way their people are depicted in celluloid images, the same is hardly true for Arabs.

Shaheen (2004) has characterized Arabs as "the other" in American film depictions. The term is not unique in defining the racial and ethnic stereotypes that proliferate in Hollywood. But the use of the term to describe Arabs perhaps rings with a greater truth than for the Latinos or American Indians, in particular because Arabs have no direct lineage to America through geographical boundaries or native status. Moreover, the Arab has not fared well in terms of positive images in film.

Film images of Arabs can be traced back to 1894 and the Kinetoscope short *Sheik Hadj Tahar Hadj Cherif.* *The Power of the Sultan,* the first film made in Hollywood, was another of the early Arab portrayals. These early images helped to solidify the images that American audiences would come to associate with the Arab, including the bastardization of the word *sheikh,* which actually means "a wise elderly person ... a head of the family" (Shaheen 2001, p. 19). Unlike many of the other stereotypes, societal pressure on Hollywood to cease stereotyping the Arab was not prevalent, and the practice continues today, relatively unabated.

Like the American Indian's portrayal, the image of the sand-riding camel-boy is one that has had its day in popular culture avenues other than film. Late in the nineteenth century, Tchaikovsky's "Nutcracker Suite" featured a movement titled "Arabian Dance," which set a tone for all popular depictions of Arab music composed by Western composers. Prince's Orchestra recorded Arab-flavored songs such as "Patrol over Hot Sands," "Afghanistan," "Mohammed," "Queen of Sheba," "Araby," "Omar Khayam," "Arabian Nights," "Cleopatra Had a Jazz Band," and "Allah's Holiday." In addition, a number of novelty big-band and jazz songs attempted to exploit this imagery, including "Shadrak," "The Sheik of Araby," and "A Night in Tunisia."

Shaheen (2001, pp. 14–27) identifies four predominant stereotypes of Arabs in film — villains, sheikhs, maidens, and Egyptians — each of which appears in Three Stooges films. A fifth type, Palestinians, is also identified, though this type is not found in the Stooges short films.

Villains— The Arab is often portrayed as a cutthroat: a ruthless, dagger- or scimitar-wielding scoundrel. Shaheen traces this image to the 1914 film *Imar the Servitor,* and it is one that continues to the present day (Shaheen 2001, p. 14). The Arab is also, to risk a pun, quite oily. He is frequently portrayed as a scoundrel, a slick and deceitful person who uses his villainous talents to steal and to cheat. While many stereotyped groups can complain that such portrayals of the villains in their group represent the worst aspects of the worst stereotypes of their people, the Arab can complain that the stereotype is unusually common; and unlike, say, the American Indian, there is seldom a redeeming quality.

Sheikh—The sheikh, one of Hollywood's most identifiable images, is another common stereotype. In contrast to the earlier definition of a sheikh as a wise elderly person, Hollywood portrayed another type (Shaheen 2001, p. 19). While a wise and elderly person of almost any other nationality evinces an almost omniscient aura, the sheikh of film is, above all, a "player." Having acquired material wealth commensurate with his position, he obsessively becomes a polygamist, searching for his next conquest. According to Shaheen (2001, p. 19), that "conquest" is often a fair, blue-eyed beauty of American extraction.

Maidens— Shaheen (2001, pp. 22–24) describes a number of stereotyped images of the Arab "maiden," including the belly dancer, beast of burden, bundle of black, and — beginning with the images in the 1917 film *Cleopatra*— the serpent and vamp.

Egyptians—The image conjured up by the "Egyptian" is one of "mummies and money," with the ever-present backdrop of pyramids and with a fair number of curses to accompany the storylines (Shaheen 2001, p. 25).

Arabs in the Three Stooges Films

The portrayal of the Arab in Stooges films is, unfortunately, much less complex than that of the Latino, or even the American Indian. We divide the film representations of Arabs into three categories: those portraying "actual" Arabs, those portraying characters disguised as Arabs, and those portraying Middle Eastern people of an indeterminate category.

Images of "actual" Arabs occur in *Wee Wee Monsieur, We Want Our Mummy, Mummy's Dummies, Malice in the Palace, Rumpus in the Harem,* and *Three Arabian Nuts. Mummy's Dummies* and *We Want Our Mummy* deal with stereotyping of ancient Egypt.

Wee Wee Monsieur presents the Stooges as part of the Foreign Legion, entrusted to guard Captain Gorgonzola. The Stooges are in usual form, finding ways to avoid their appointed duties. When two Arabs kidnap the captain from his tent, the Stooges are sent to the land of Tsimmis to rescue him from an Arab palace. There they encounter a guard, replete in a sheik's garb. The Stooges themselves are undercover, dressed in Santa Claus suits. The guard, in his best Brooklyn accent, declares, "Ahh, there ain't no Sandy Claus," but the Stooges succeed in subduing the guard and enter the palace. There an Arab royal (Vernon Dent) tries to persuade the captain to reveal the location of ammunition stores, offering him wealth, beautiful maidens, and his life.

The Stooges, meanwhile, encounter a harem den and woo the fair young maidens. Curly first meets a homely blonde with missing teeth but soon finds himself with a beautiful, exotic blonde. When Curly asks where she has been all his life, the Arab maiden replies, "Down at *Toity Toid* and *Toid Avenah*. I just came *ovah*." She is from the same New York neighborhood as Curly. Moe settles with a fair-skinned, dark-haired beauty who is eating garlic. The film concludes as the Stooges, dressed in harem costumes, work their way into a group dance and rescue the captain.

Wee Wee Monsieur recalls the "foreign legion in the land of the Arab" that was perpetuated in the films of Laurel and Hardy, among others. The Stooges' entry into Tsimmis in Santa Claus suits certainly raises questions considering the backdrop of the film, and the rescue of the captain from the clutches of an evil ruler is a cliché that has been followed in countless films.

This film, while following several conventions in the portrayal of Arabs, leaves many questions unanswered. For example, one wonders why the producers chose the name Tsimmis for the kingdom, as it is actually a Yiddish word that roughly translates to "a big mess." The New York connection, which occurs at least twice, is neither clear nor explained. Further, the unusual disguise of Santa Claus (reprised in two later films) forces one to wonder whether these films are offering a Christian subtext within the Arab surroundings. This is unlikely, though; the Stooges themselves were Jewish, as were many of the creative personnel on the Stooges' films.

We Want Our Mummy again sends the Stooges to Egypt to find a captured professor, who was there trying to acquire (steal?) the mummy of the ancient Egyptian King Rutentuten (likely a pun on King Tutankhamun). They miraculously take a taxi from New York to Cairo, Egypt. As they leave the cab, they hear a radio announcer (played by Moe Howard), saying, "You have been listening to the music of Ali Ben Woodman and his Swinging Bedouins. Do you need money? Borrow on your camel or elephant." Curly informs Moe and Larry that he'd like to go to Tunis so he can have Tunis sandwiches. The Stooges encounter a band of thieves who have captured the professor. Escaping the thieves' clutches, they rescue the professor and the mummified king. A casualty of the Stooges' ineptness, however, is the loss of the king's wife, Queen Hotsy Totsy.

This film includes no actual Egyptians. Its most notable feature is the blending of Egyptian and American cultures: the king and queen boasting names based on American references of the 1930s, Tunis sandwiches, and the radio station.

Mummy's Dummies, like *We Want Our Mummy*, takes place in Egypt, but this time in ancient Egypt. The Stooges are in the business of selling used chariots. After selling a faulty chariot to one of the king's guards, they are dragged before the king for an immediate trial. His Highness is suffering from a terrible toothache; and after a series of slapstick mishaps, the Stooges manage to pull the king's tooth and relieve his pain. The grateful king invests them as royal chamberlains, where they are fanned by servants and pampered with wine and grapes by beautiful maidens. In the end, the Stooges uncover a plot by the king's guards to steal tax money.

Malice in the Palace features the Stooges as proprietors of the Café Casbahbah. They serve two cutthroat Arab customers, Hassan Ben Sober and his partner, who are plotting to steal the King Rutentuten Diamond (a second reference to the mythical king). Both Arabs, though, are dressed in fezzes and more Western-style clothing. At one point, an Arab named Affah Dollah, dressed in a sheik's clothing, enters and warns of a curse on the first person who touches the diamond. Hassan Ben Sober decides that because of the curse, he will have the Stooges steal the diamond. He makes the Stooges an offer of a "thousand shilbleenas" and persuades the Stooges — at daggerpoint — to take the offer. Suddenly a dagger is thrown with a note attached, which reads: "Hassan Ben Sober You are late I Got the Diamond You got the gate. Signed, Omagosh, Emir of Schmow." Hassan Ben Sober confesses to the Stooges that he's just a doorman at the Oasis Hotel, and the Stooges escape his clutches. The Stooges then decide to pursue the valuable diamond themselves. They break into an Arab palace wearing their Santa Claus disguises for the second time on film. Shemp, acting as the head of a giant Santa Claus, scares the turban-wearing emir of Schmow, who had been amusing himself by reading the Sunday comics. The emir is forced to surrender the diamond. Two large, muscle-bound, black-skinned guards chase the Stooges, but the Stooges' cunning gets them out of this dangerous situation.

Malice in the Palace and the remake *Rumpus in the Harem* were essentially placing the Stooges in a different environment with the same kinds of nemeses they face in countless other films. These films are colored somewhat by the costuming and the language they use, but the "bad guys" in this film share a lot in common with their white counterparts in gangster-style films. Even in the scenes in the palace, with the ornate backdrops, the guards are essentially hapless in fighting the Stooges, just like the dozens of "five o'clock shadow"-laden white bodyguards from other Stooges films.

An interesting feature of this film is that an Arab, Frank Lackteen, plays Affah Dollah. Lackteen was born in Lebanon, and this is one of the few times in Stooges films that the producers had selected a member of the stereotyped group to play an ethnic role.

Rumpus in the Harem is one of four films that starred Shemp as the third Stooge but was made a few months after Shemp's death. Consequently, most of the film consists of stock footage, with a stunt double filling in for Shemp during a few scenes. The plot of *Rumpus in the Harem* varies only slightly from *Malice in the Palace*. One new scene is significant, however. Moe and Larry, dressed once again in Santa Claus suits, stumble into a harem, where two beautiful women beat up the Stooges (a recurring gag). One of the two maidens is blonde and is wearing what almost appears to be a business suit, giving her a distinctly nonethnic appearance. The other is a fair-skinned, black-haired woman, who mocks an Arab custom by crying, "and you caught me with my veil down."

Three Arabian Nuts, like *Malice in the Palace*, has the Stooges as proprietors; this time they own a warehouse and storage company. They are in charge of delivering a priceless collection of antiques and china for Mr. Bradley (played by Vernon Dent). As usual, the destructive Stooges are the last group that should be entrusted with anything of value. In this film, however, in addition to the mayhem that comes from the Stooges' incompetence in handling priceless objects, several twists occur in a highly farcical plot, with a situation that includes an Aladdin-style lamp.

The film opens with Moe examining a crate label written in Arabic. He reads gibberish (strangely reminiscent of his faux Chinese from the 1938 film *Mutts to You*) and concludes that the unfamiliar language translates as "knickknacks." In short order, two Arab thieves appear (played by the decidedly nonethnic Dick Curtis and Phil Van Zandt), clad in the kuffiyeh headdress and long, white robes. They are searching for a lamp and threaten to have the heads of the Stooges in order to get it.

While the Stooges are unpacking the crates, Shemp comes across the lamp that the Arabs seek. Noticing that it's dusty, he innocently rubs the lamp. A large puff of smoke appears and quickly disappears, revealing the genie (or as Shemp calls him, "the genius") of the lamp. The genie is a large, muscular black man, similar to the palace guards in *Wee Wee Monsieur*, *Malice in the Palace*, and *Rumpus in the Harem*. After two wishes are granted by the "genius," the remainder of the plot centers on the Arabs chasing after the Stooges in an attempt to procure the lamp and kill the Stooges.

Moe, who to this point has been skeptical of the "genius of the lamp," finds an artifact and wonders if it's the magic lamp found by Shemp. When he rubs it, the villain (portrayed by Van Zandt) enters the room. Believing him to be the "genius," Moe is persuaded to lay his head on the desk. As the Arab talks soothingly, he withdraws his scimitar from its scabbard and is ready to chop off Moe's head. Moe discovers the villain's motive in the nick of time and escapes. Later, Shemp instructs Larry to "smack anyone who's wearing a turban," incorrectly identifying the kuffiyeh headdress. The line is used so that a gratuitous piece of violence can occur: Mr. Bradley, who has a towel draped over his head, is mistaken for one of the Arabs and is smacked on the head.

The film climaxes as Shemp finds the lamp inexplicably burning in a fireplace. He retrieves it, and, after a "hot potato" toss of the burning lamp between the Stooges and the Arabs, he manages to cool it off, beseeching the "genius" (whom he now calls Amos, presumably after the character in *Amos 'n' Andy*), "Don't let me down." Suddenly, a great puff of smoke appears. When it clears, the villains are tied up back to back. The Stooges are surrounded by beautiful women, and a wheelbarrow full of money is brought in by Amos.

Three Arabian Nuts features more screen time for Arabs than does any other Stooges film. However, the two Arabs display the most prevalent stereotyped characteristics and the most evil motives. Throughout the film Van Zandt's and Curtis' characters are not content merely to procure the lamp; they must also kill the beloved Three Stooges. On the other hand, *Three Arabian Nuts*, with its far-fetched premise of a magic lamp, puts the negative stereotypes of the Arabs in full light. These Arabs, while ultimately not successful, succumb only because of a godlike power (the "genius" of the lamp). They are cunning, greedy, and cutthroat and will stop at nothing to get what they want. This is by far the most negative of all the Arab portrayals in the Stooges films.

Briefly mentioned in the previous chapter is one theme that runs through several of these films, including *Wee Wee Monsieur, Mummy's Dummies, Malice in the Palace, Rumpus in the Harem,* and *Three Arabian Nuts.* The darkest skinned of the Arabs — the Negro-appearing men with large muscles — are portrayed more like slaves than equals of the Arab. In all but two of the films, these men play guards protecting the higher-up, lighter Arabs. In *Mummy's Dummies*, the Negro is a male servant fanning Shemp, who is otherwise attended to by subservient women. And of course, Amos, the "genius of the lamp" from *Three Arabian Nuts*, is the ultimate slave.

In addition to portrayals of Arabs, several films of the Three Stooges include characters disguised as Arabs. In these films, also, the portrayals are fairly consistent, and the stereotyping is clear. Several other films of the Three Stooges feature a character who is from the Middle East but whose actual ethnicity and country of origin are unclear.

We Want Our Mummy briefly shows one of the thieves dressed as an ancient Egyptian.

The Hot Scots and *Scotched in Scotland* are virtually the same, with small changes in plot and scene made in *Scotched in Scotland*. The Stooges are hired as detectives to guard the valuables of a wealthy Scotsman living in Glenheather Castle. One of the castle's paintings features an Arab with a dagger in his mouth. The painting is soon cut out, and in its place stands one of the villains disguised as the man in the picture. In one scene, Moe is charmed by the lovely Lorna Doone (played by Christine McIntyre). She persuades Moe to dance a Highland Fling with her, while Moe invents his own dance.

While Moe is distracted, Lorna and the ersatz Arab are stealing valuable items from the castle. As Moe returns from his dancing demonstration, he finds not Lorna, but the Arab, and is so carried away that he attempts to dance with the man. The plot is revealed, and the thieves are captured.

In addition to "actual" Arabs and the disguised Arabs, Stooges films included Middle Easterners. *Pop Goes the Easel* contains a scene in which a detective, who has been pursuing the Stooges, manages to corner them in an art school. The quick-thinking Stooges each don a disguise. Larry is dressed as a robed and turban-clad mystic. As the detective attempts to speak to him, Larry recites a diatribe of gibberish and bows before the detective every few seconds.

I'll Never Heil Again is a World War II spoof in which the Stooges, as Nazis, are introduced to the Bay of Rum, leader of one of the Axis powers. This foreign leader sports a large, bushy beard and a turban and is smoking a water pipe.

Phony Express is unusual in that the setting is a medicine show in the old West. It involves a brief encounter between the Stooges and a white man calling himself "Dr. Abdul."

Three Little Pirates find the Stooges prisoners on an island. In one of the most famous of all Stooges scenes, Moe, Larry, and Curly are disguised in long, colorful robes and turbans. Curly portrays the non–English-speaking Maharaja of Canazzi. In an exchange between Moe and Curly, Moe basically speaks in rhymes and pseudo–English. Curly responds in a gibberish language and produces three cheap possessions that the governor mistakes for priceless treasures.

The Nature of Slapstick

As with many films of their day, those of the Three Stooges are fairly negative in their portrayal of American Indians, Latinos, and Arabs. All three groups have at one time or another been considered "the other," and to some extent that is a correct assessment. The Indian is depicted as a bloodthirsty savage, lustful in his desires and violent in the ways that he will fulfill them. The Latino is more moderately viewed as a lazy buffoon or a gun-toting bandit. The Arab is a ruthless cutthroat; unlike the Latino and to a lesser extent the Indian, the Arab shows no redeeming qualities whatsoever in the films of the Three Stooges. Even the "good guys" within their midst, such as harem girls, are not really Arabs but are actually Aryan types.

Any judgment of these negative portrayals should be tempered, however, by the knowledge that it is low-budget, slapstick comedy. This is not an excuse; rather, it is a context. The shooting schedules and the budgets for these films necessitated quick scripts and easily recognizable characters. Further, the very nature of slapstick is such that characters are going to be stereotyped; the supporting cast members are mostly foils for the main characters, who rarely change much. Indeed, almost every other group represented in the Stooges shorts was stereotyped as well.

The makers of these films deserve neither praise nor condemnation (for the most part) for the images that they created in these farcical, slapstick short films. But given the preponderance of Stooges shorts on television, in a period spanning 50 years, the time has more than come to set the record straight on the images of these minorities.

Notes

1. See Ely (1986) or Seely (1997) or the documentary *Amos 'n' Andy: The Anatomy of a Controversy* (1985). Some might argue that the NAACP's "victory" was a case of winning the battle while losing much of the war.
2. Kilpatrick (1999, p. 24). Today Griffith is better remembered for his overblown epic *Birth of a Nation*, with its highly negative portrayals of African Americans and its glorification of the Ku Klux Klan as the savior of parts of white America.
3. *Sappy Bullfighters* features a great deal of the script from *What's the Matador?* and also features a good deal of the original stock footage. Because of the similarity of the films, only *What's the Matador?* is addressed in this chapter.

Works Cited

Amos 'n' Andy: The Anatomy of a Controversy. Documentary. 1985.
Berg, Charles Ramirez. *Latin Images in Film.* Austin: University of Texas Press, 2002.
Ely, Melvin Patrick. *Holy Mackerel: The Amos 'n' Andy Story.* New York: E.P. Dutton, 1986.
Kilpatrick, Jacqueline. *Celluloid Indians.* Lincoln: University of Nebraska Press, 1999.
Kurson, Robert. *The Official Three Stooges Encyclopedia.* Chicago: Contemporary, 1998.
Seely, Peter. "Didn't I Disbar You Three Years Ago? Positive and Negative Portrayals of African Americans in Amos 'n' Andy." Paper presented at the Popular Culture Conference, 1997.
Shaheen, Jack G. "Address to the Washington Press Club." C-Span 2. 27 March 2004.
_____. *Reel Bad Arabs.* New York: Interlink, 2001.

17

Europeans and the Stooges: The Other "Other"

Peter Seely

They're the forgotten groups when it comes to ethnic studies: Europeans whose stereotypes the average viewer has come to accept. They include the British, Scottish, Irish, Germans, French, Italians, and Russians of Europe. These stereotypes have become ingrained in American consciousness through hundreds of motion picture representations, particularly for those who have never crossed the Atlantic. These are groups who, for the most part, are without a lobby to protest the stereotyping and labeling that have become so common. Perhaps it is because European stereotypes have not been nearly as egregious as those of other ethnic groups. In the case of the Three Stooges, however, these ethnic groups played a part in some of the Stooges' most memorable films.

British

Unlike some of the other ethnic groups examined within this chapter, such as the Irish, Italians, and Germans, the British are seldom portrayed as first-generation immigrants to America. Most motion pictures portray British people in their homeland of England, a country that allows for a wide expanse of roles and types, from the lower-class urchin of many Dickens tales to extremely wealthy lords and ladies. When British immigrants were portrayed in American films during the era of the Stooges shorts, they were nearly always the very wealthy or butlers for the very wealthy or, occasionally, detectives in the Sherlock Holmes tradition. The migrating Brit was not an urchin or a peasant; he was sophisticated, intelligent, and urbane, even when part of the working class.

The films of the Three Stooges were no exception to the stereotyping of Brits; indeed, all of the portrayals but two tilt toward the sophisticated version. The common stereotype of the English butler in American films has him portrayed as a proper gentleman, and the films of the Three Stooges used this type often. Of the nine portrayals of British people in the Stooges films, five of these are butlers. Vesey O'Davoren plays a butler in *Ants in the Pantry*, Bud Jamison plays the part in *Three Sappy People*, an uncredited actor becomes the Stooges' foil in *A Plumbing We Will Go*, Olaf Hytten succumbs to the Stooges' vices of smoking and gambling in *All the World's a Stooge*, and Herbert Evans plays the butler in *Vagabond Loafers*. Two other British roles involve an uncredited actor taking a shower (while wearing a towel and a monocle), who interacts with Curly in the famous bathroom scene in *A Plumbing We Will Go*, and a British countess (played by Ann Doran), who sits next to Curly at dinner in *Three Sappy People*. The two exceptions to the sophisticated British portrayals are a tough, gun-toting woman of the underworld (played by Barbara Bartay) in *Hot Ice* and a gorilla keeper (played by an uncredited actor) in *Crime on Their Hands* (and the remake *Hot Ice*).

Scots

The profile of the Scotsman includes several enduring aspects. The reputation of the thrifty Scot is largely born out of the country's Calvinist history, the corollary of the work ethic for which Scots are well known (Herman 2005, pp. 1–2). In film, the Scot is often featured as a kilted, bagpipe-wielding man or a kilted, attractive young woman in the mold of R. D. Blackmore's *Lorna Doone*. But while these accoutrements can be found in parts of Scotland and relate closely to the identity of a given Scottish clan, it is not the visage one would often see as a part of everyday life in Glasgow, Edinburgh, or other urban parts of the country. The image presented in American film was not representative of most of Scotland in the twentieth century.

Scottish roles were featured in three of the Stooges films. *Pardon My Scotch* has the Stooges mistaken for Scotch liquor distillers trying to sell the "breath of Heather" to Scottish distributors (played by Barlowe Borland and Scotty Dubsmuir). And in *The Hot Scots* and the remake *Scotched in Scotland*, the Stooges pose as detectives protecting the earl's treasures in Glenheather Castle. Christine McIntyre plays the crooked secretary Lorna Doone.

In all three films, the Stooges pose as Scotsmen, and much of the humor in these comedies revolves around the Stooges' fake Scottish dialect and attempts to do Scottish dances. In *Pardon My Scotch*, one of the genuine Scotsmen asks the Stooges if they are from Loch Lomond. Wise-cracking Curly replies, "No, we're from Loch Jaw." And when the Stooges are asked whether they can do the Highland Fling, Moe confesses, "We ain't much on the Highland Fling but we knock 'em dead with our Lowland Shim." The question arises again in *The Hot Scots* and *Scotched in Scotland*, giving Moe an excuse to do his own wild interpretation of the fling. In one other film, *Self-Made Maids*, the Stooges quickly don disguises as Scotsmen and play air bagpipes in an attempt to fool the father of their sweethearts.

The lingering stereotype of the Scot as cheap—indeed the logical and comedic exaggeration of the trait of thriftiness—is exploited in both Glenheather Castle films, in a scene where the earl is providing the Stooges with instructions for guarding his castle. The earl offers the Stooges a "wee snifter" of Scotch broth but merely allows them to sniff the cork. His Scottish butler McPherson (played by Ted Lorch) informs him that his cab has arrived and that the driver charges a "tuppence a minute waiting time," whereupon the wealthy earl streaks out of the castle to avoid these charges.

The two-and-a-half minute scene near the beginning of these films also features extended faux Scottish dialogue, as the Stooges try to convince the earl they are actually Scotsmen. This mostly involves the insertion of the common Scottish prefix "Mac" before both proper nouns and verbs, as the Stooges become MacLarry, MacShemp, and MacMoe, who are glad to macmeet the earl. Shemp breaks into his Southern dialect, and to cover the mistake, Moe informs the earl that the Stooges are "from southern Scotland, just south of the MacMason-MacDixon line." The Stooges even employ a famous Scottish line, "Hoots mon, it's a braw bricht moonlit nicht."

Irish

Of all the American immigrant groups in twentieth-century America, perhaps none were treated with as much hostility as the Irish. Like many other ethnic groups, the Irish tended to settle in enclaves in northern U.S. cities and, like those groups, emerged in American consciousness as possessing certain common ethnic characteristics. But the abject poverty that forced many Irish to move to America made them a perfect target for cruel parody. Invariably, in American culture the Irish were commonly portrayed as white trash drunks and criminals or, when the portrayal was of a more industrious Irishman, as a boxer or policeman.

Only three of the Stooges films feature Irish characterizations, but they are memorable. The first Stooges Columbia film, *Woman Haters*, included a brief scene with Irish-Americans. As part of the recitative, the future father-in-law of Jim (played by Larry Fine), who speaks with an Irish brogue, senses that Jim is dodging marriage. To stiffen Jim's resolve, the father tells him about what happened when his other daughter had a reluctant groom:

> Well, I took care of that guy,
> In a room I locked him and I socked him right in the eye,
> Then I turned him over to me brother the cop,
> He just picked him up, and spinned him 'round like a top,
> Then my other brother, who's a fighter, began,
> Son, I'm ashamed to tell you what he did to that man.

Woman Haters plays on the common stereotypes of the Irish-American boxer and policeman (the latter played by Stanley "Tiny" Sandford), but also portrays Jim's father-in-law (played by A. R. Haysel) as an upper-class Irishman, a highly unusual portrayal for the time.

Another Irish cop was portrayed by Bud Jamison in *Mutts to You*, in a scene where Curly is posing as a kidnapped baby's mother, Mrs. O'Toole. The cop, who is searching for the kidnappers, encounters the disguised Stooge and even engages "Mrs. O'Toole" in a brief conversation about the old country. When in drag, Curly rarely made an attempt to feminize the already-shrill voice of his screen character, but here he does change to an Irish accent. The cop is fooled until a water hose spraying on Curly's sponge-filled stockings exposes the masquerade. As the cop chases the Stooges, he is temporarily fooled by Moe and Larry posing as Chinese men (the one and only portrayal of Chinese in their Columbia shorts).

The only other Irish portrayal in a Stooges film is in *Pop Goes the Easel*. Moe sports a brief Irish accent as he poses as a half–French, half–Irish painter trying to escape a police officer.

French

A popular motion picture stereotype of the French people centered on the French Foreign Legion, which was often characterized as the roughest and most inescapable of all military units. The Legion was typified by movies such as *Beau Geste* (1939), *The Road to Morocco* (1942), and *The Desert Song* (1953). Other film stereotypes were less military-oriented and closer to that of the early Italian film images, with the French men most likely to be working as artists or policemen and the French women as maids or sexual temptresses.

Of all the European representations in the Stooges films, those of the French were the most abundant. At least 17 films featured French characters; and like most other nationalities featured in Stooges films, the portrayals of the French were fairly true to the predominant motion picture images of the day. For example, in one film, *Wee Wee Monsieur*, the Stooges are living in Paris, where they run afoul of an impatient landlord, shopkeepers, and the local *gendarmes*. As they try to escape their many adversaries, they wind up in the office of the French Foreign Legion. Thinking that it is a counterpart of the American Legion, Moe appeals to the fraternity: "You, Foreign Legion. We, American Legion. Brother Legionaires." The recruiting officer, who pretends not to understand or speak English, dupes them into signing commissions with the French Foreign Legion. The "French Connection" is thereafter dropped, as none of the soldiers in the legion speak French or even speak with an accent.

Two other French male stereotypes are explored in other Stooges films. One is the image of the huffy French artist. Leo White plays a frustrated painter who mistakes sunlight for a spot on his painting in *Pop Goes the Easel*. White also plays the temperamental decorator Omay in *Tassels in the Air*. A more unusual male stereotype is the French chef, played by a violent Emil Sitka in *Listen, Judge*.

Of course, French maids are also to be found in Stooges films, all speaking English with a French accent. This role was the French female counterpart to the British butler, and the setting was usually "high society." French maids were featured in the films *Ants in the Pantry*, *No Census, No Feeling*, and *Pest Man Wins*.

Probably the most interesting of the French characters were the women who were not maids: the gun molls, crooks, gold diggers, sweethearts, and others who came across the Stooges' path. Two actresses, who were either French or had French heritage, played most of these roles. French Canadian Nanette Bordeaux, a marvelous and attractive actress who appeared in many Stooges films, frequently played criminals or femmes fatales. She appeared in eight films, one as a maid (*Pest Man Wins*), as a gold digger trying to capture the Stooges' sweepstakes winnings (*A Missed Fortune*), as a jewel thief (*Hugs and Mugs*), as a gas station robber who keeps getting punched out (*Slaphappy Sleuths*), as a showgirl who tries to steal the Stooges inheritance (*Loose Loot*), as a stage actress (*Three Hams on Rye*), as the wife of an income tax inspector (*Income Tax Sappy*), and as a befuddled sweetheart (*A Merry Mixup*). Her character regularly displayed a mixture of sweetness, cunning, and toughness that made her a most worthy adversary for the Stooges.

In other films, Yvette Reynard appears as Shemp's French sweetheart in *Love at First Bite*[1]; Vanda Dupre plays Joe's French sweetheart and lost love in *Fifi Blows Her Top* (Hariette Tarler plays a flirtatious Parisian waitress in the same film); and Barbara Bartay plays a French gun moll in *Pardon My Backfire* and a beauty care expert attending to a cross-dressed Moe in *Blunder Boys*.

Germans

In his essay on German identity, Karlfried Knapp describes the university professor as the most important and influential individual in nineteenth-century Prussian society (Knapp 1995, p. 3) Indeed, the image of the German professor was co-opted by American comedians and vaudeville performers, including Groucho Marx, who dropped it from his stage routine after the sinking of the *Lusitania* in 1915 (Giddins 2000, p. 2). The image was a lingering one that pervaded motion picture portrayals of Germans at least until World War II. A complement of the positive image of the professor was the German psychiatrist, which was probably an outgrowth of the prolific image of Sigmund Freud, and a stereotype that lingers to this day.

As discussed elsewhere in this book (see, in particular, Chapters 12 and 13), Nazis were portrayed in several Stooges films. However, non–Nazi Germans also appeared in several Stooges films, including a Prussian-type officer in *Boobs in Arms*. The most prevalent German stereotype in these films was the German professor. In a case of mistaken identity, the Stooges take over academic appointments intended for three German professors (played by Eddie Featherstone, Al Thompson, and John T. Murray) at a women's college in *Violent Is the Word for Curly*; and Robert Williams plays Professor Tuttle looking for the mummy of King Rutentuten in *We Want Our Mummy*. Vernon Dent is a mad scientist wanting to steal Curly's brain in *A Bird in the Head*; and veteran character actor Benny Rubin, a master of many fake accents, is a rocket scientist in *Space Ship Sappy*. Moe Howard poses as German psychiatrist Dr. Hugo Gansamacher, who hopes to cure Muriel Landers' stage fright in *Sweet and Hot*.

Germans also appear in other Stooges films. Harrison Greene plays the role of A. Mouser, the Stooges' devious boss who orders the Stooges to infest houses with pests in *Ants in the Pantry*. Rubin also uses his best German accent as an internal revenue agent in *Income Tax Sappy* and as the Stooges' frustrated landlord Mr. Dinkelspiel in *Hoofs and Goofs*. And Christine McIntyre makes appearances as Moe's Viennese *Fräulein* in *Love at First Bite* and *Fifi Blows Her Top* (in stock footage).

Italians

Golden describes two early Italian stereotypes in American popular culture: the Italian immigrant as musical artist and the "second-generation off-the-boat" person as a nastier character with underworld connections. The image of the Italian-American as criminal was first created by Edward G. Robinson in *Little Caesar* (1930), and such criminal stereotypes endure to the present day (Golden 1980, p. 79). More benign images of the hardworking immigrant and the dark-eyed female beauty also existed.

It was these more innocuous images that were used in the films of the Three Stooges. In *Pardon My Scotch*, veteran character actor Billy Gilbert plays Signor Louis Bolero Cantino, an Italian opera singer, and Gino Corrado plays a similar and more memorable role as the Stooges' foil and enemy in *Micro-Phonies* as the out-of-control Italian nemesis of the Stooges. Corrado also plays the role of a berserk Italian chef in *An Ache in Every Stake*. The image of the Italian immigrant groundskeeper is exploited in *Three Little Beers*, as Harry Semels portrays the distraught man watching the Stooges destroy his golf course. Marie Montiel plays Larry's Italian sweetheart in *Love at First Bite* and in stock footage in *Fifi Blows Her Top*. Also featured in her scene was her father, played by Al Thompson, in a hilarious gag where a fan blows spaghetti off Larry's fork and into the father's mouth: Thompson pulls off the nearly impossible stunt of chewing spaghetti while he is sleeping. Benny Rubin reaches into his bag of accents in *Tricky Dicks* to portray an Italian organ grinder, whom the Stooges are grilling for a murder confession. However, when Rubin opens his mouth and speaks, he does so with a sophisticated British accent.

Russians

The first-generation European immigrant was generally portrayed in film as a hard-working, simple person. In the case of the Slav, this person was generally portrayed as also being a peasant (Golab 1980, p. 139). These dominant film portrayals had nothing to do with those in the Stooges films, however; the characterization of the Russian in Stooges films was strictly a by-product of the Cold War.

The All Powers Project (Pearson 1998) traces a rather notable history of Cold War and anti–Communist film portrayals dating back to *Bolshevism on Trial* (1939). These films hit their stride in the late 1940s and were quite abundant in the 1950s. The Cold War mentality in American cinema was apparent in well-known films such as *I Was a Communist for the FBI* (1951), *Trial* (1955), and *Rio Bravo* (1956). In the 1960s, this Cold War attitude was dealt with in a deadly serious manner, in films such as *The Manchurian Candidate* (1962) and *The Red Nightmare* (1962), or as hilarious satire in *Dr. Strangelove* (1964) and *The Russians are Coming, the Russians are Coming* (1966).

Russians were portrayed in three of the Stooges' films, each time by Stooges regular Gene Roth. Roth portrays Bortch, the nefarious Russian spy, in *Dunked in the Deep* and the remake *Commotion on the Ocean*. The role of Bortch is typical of the negative stereotype of the Cold War Russian in films from this era. Bortch is trying to smuggle secret film back to his country (which is not identified by name but is clearly Russia) and uses the Stooges as his unwitting dupes to get the film aboard a ship. Bortch is mean, selfish, and devious, and as with most bad guys, the Stooges prove triumphant over him in the end. Roth also portrays the high ruler of the mythical kingdom of Anemia, a thinly disguised Russian parody, in *Hot Stuff*, a Cold War remake of the earlier film *Fuelin' Around*. Roth even perpetuates another Russian stereotype in this role, as he drinks and clearly enjoys rotgut booze during his brief appearance.

The Stooges and Europe

Stereotyping of the European groups examined in this chapter is rarely challenged, save the occasional protests of Italian-American groups against television shows such as *The Sopranos* for the portrayal of the Italian gangster. In some cases, these groups even revel in the broad stereotyping. Indeed, the Scottish regularly lampoon their own brand of Anglo dialect. For example, a novelty single by Lord Rockingham in 1958 called "Hoots, Mon," features several jabs at the Scottish accent and was a popular U.K. hit.

Arguably the stereotyping that occurred with the portrayals of the British, Scottish, Irish, French, Germans, Italians, and Russians was not at the level of offensiveness as, say, the portrayals of American Negroes, Arabs, Japanese, Latinos, and American Indians, as described elsewhere in this book (see Chapters 14–16). Indeed, the epithets used with some of those types, such as *Jap* or the porter or blackface references, were almost completely avoided. Never does the viewer hear *Limey, Franc, Dago, Wap, Kraut, Russkie*, or any other of the somewhat milder derogatory terms used for the groups studied in this chapter. Only in the wartime film *Back from the Front* does Moe use the term *Jerries* to refer to Germans

In spite of the fact that the stereotyping of Europeans that existed in Stooges films was not nearly as derogatory or malicious as it was for some of the groups examined in this book, the portrayals described here were among the most memorable supporting ethnic characterizations in the films of the Stooges. By examining these European nationalities who have received much less attention than other racial or ethnic groups, we can see in an unbiased and unemotional way the real reasons writers and producers chose to stereotype groups so often. The Stooges shorts were only 15 to 18 minutes long, and what was needed in the scripts were individuals who could be quickly referenced and identified. And, of course, the portrayals of these people had to be funny.

Notes

1. The role of the Italian sweetheart has been alternately identified as played by Reynard and Marie Montiel. Our belief is that Montiel played the Italian sweetheart in *Love at First*

Bite and *Fifi Blows Her Top* and that Reynard played the French sweetheart in *Love at First Bite* only.

Works Cited

Giddins, Gary. "There Ain't No Sanity Claus." *The New York Times on the Web*, 18 June 2000. Book review of *Groucho: The Life and Times of Julius Henry Marx*, by Stefan Kanfer. Accessed 16 Dec. 2005. http://partners.nytimes.com/books/00/06/18/reviews/000618.18giddent.html.

Golab, Caroline. "Stellaaaaaa ... ... !!!!!! The Slavic Stereotype in American Film." *The Kaledioscopic Lens: How Hollywood Views Ethnic Groups*. Ed. Randall Miller. Englewood, N.J.: Jerome S. Ozer, 1980.

Golden, Daniel Sembroff. "The Fate of La Famiglia: Italian Images in American Film." *The Kaledioscopic Lens: How Hollywood Views Ethnic Groups*. Ed. Randall Miller. Englewood, N.J.: Jerome S. Ozer, 1980.

Herman, Arthur. "The Tobaccomen of Glasgow and the Myth of Scottish Thrift." *In Character*, Fall 2004. Accessed 27 Jan. 2006. http://www.incharacter.org/article.php?article=11.

Knapp, Karlfried. "What's German? Remarks on German Identity." EESE. October 1995, pp. 203–228. Accessed 16 Dec. 2005. http://webdoc.sub.gwdg.de/edoc/ia/eese/articles/knapp/10_95.html/

Pearson, Glenda, compiler. "The Red Scare: A Filmography." *All Powers Project*. 5 March 1998. University of Washington Libraries. Accessed 16 Dec. 2005. http://www.lib.washington.edu/EXHIBITS/ALLPOWERS/film.html.

18

"Hiya, Toots": Women and Gender in the Three Stooges

Kathleen Chamberlain

So powerful are many people's memories of the strongly male-centered world of Larry, Curly, Moe, Shemp, Joe, and Curly Joe that it can be easy to overlook the roles taken by women in the Stooges films. Yet female characters play highly visible parts in well over half of the team's 190 Columbia short subjects. Since the Stooges' universe is a microcosm of various 1930s–1950s social typologies, including sex-role definitions, women appear in a variety of female-specific guises, among them nurses, maids, society matrons, ballerinas, wives, mothers, widows, co-eds, dancing girls, landladies, and damsels in distress. And because the Stooges' comedy borrows from older modes,[1] their shorts also include the sexualized, stock female characters common to different earlier traditions: virginal girls, young women in love, man-hungry spinsters, *femmes fatales*, gold-digging predators, and those bathing beauties, saloon girls, and others whose highlighted bodies represent the focus of male heterosexual desire. Over the course of their film careers, the boys are shown having girlfriends, fiancées, wives, and even a mother.

A careful study of the Stooges' comedies reveals that women are thematically central to the cultural work performed by the team. In a variety of ways, the films reflect, epitomize, and rewrite many of the gender struggles that shape American society. By simplifying and universalizing these struggles through surrealistic exaggeration, farce, slapstick, caricature, and stereotype, the Stooges make complex issues of gender (and attendant issues of class) manageable and unthreatening for audiences. The shorts maintain the cultural status quo by reaffirming a world in which male and female roles are clearly delineated, the working class is largely ineffectual, and male autonomy is preserved. Yet at the same time that they reassure viewers, the Stooges also transgress and interrogate many of the gender categories that their films initially establish.[2]

In the Stooges' caricatured universe, women represent not realistic individuals but possible sexual and social types. At least two major patterns are at work simultaneously in the shorts: woman as other and woman as self. In the first paradigm, females in the shorts are presented as alien and unknowable, ultimately impenetrable despite their position as potential sexual objects. They are to be feared, fought, rescued, romanced, ogled ("Hiya, Toots," Curly often leers), but they are not to be understood or, in the end, even needed. Even in those episodes in which the Stooges are married or engaged, women are tangential to the series' central relationship: the comically perverse but united male trinity of Stooges. The female is ultimately unessential because the Stooges' world is homosocial; such community and intimacy as exist are male. Almost every episode ends by re-establishing the original male triumvirate.[3] Significantly, this triumvirate is separate, not only from women, but also from adulthood in general, as suggested by (among other ways) the childish directness of the Stooges' violence and by the tendency of critics, cast and crew members, and the Stooges themselves to refer to the team as "boys."[4] Such deliberate comic infantilizing further simplifies and streamlines the shorts, leaving space for the visual and narrative anarchy through which the Stooges dismantle, restructure, and affirm the indeterminacy of gender.

Woman as Other

Given women's extraneous positions relative to the boys, it's not surprising that "woman as other" is a dominant pattern in the films. As "other," women fit three broad categories: the good, the bad, and the ugly. The "good" women can be young or old, conventionally physically attractive or not, but they generally fit traditional gender roles: they are maternal, self-sacrificing, in need of rescue. The Stooges respond to these women in conventionally chivalric ways: they protect a young girl's ranch from a scheming villain (*Horses' Collars*), outwit swindlers who cheat a poor widow (*Oily to Bed, Oily to Rise*), and, in an unusually sentimental outing, unwittingly rob the U.S. Treasury to help a young woman finance her lame brother's operation (*Cash and Carry*). Female goodness is encoded visually as well as through narrative; in *Cash and Carry*, for instance, the loving sister can be recognized as good through her natural hair style (neither bleached nor overly set) and her demure checked gingham dress with its soft white collar. Good women are also often interested in and defined by heterosexual romantic roles; they accept a power dynamic in which males, even the Stooges, dominate.

The "bad" women also occupy a range of ages and physical types but are united by their access to forms of power. All the "bad" women offer some sort of threat to masculinity or the class status of the Stooges, which in turn calls into question traditional definitions of those qualities. The society dowagers, so admirably played by Symona Boniface, Bess Flowers, and silent star Clara Kimball Young, symbolize the sort of wealth and power that often threatens to emasculate the working, "common" man that the Stooges represent. The Stooges retaliate by ruining the emblems of such women's status — their houses, clothing, and social gatherings — with ordinary objects turned into weapons of class warfare, including deluges of water, exploding cakes, and a selection of pastry missiles of which pies are only the most famous. The boys may not be able to replace upper-class paradigms with new social visions, but their actions are nonetheless socially dangerous: they make clear that one alternative to a dominant cultural **con**struction is **de**struction. The Stooges' destruction may have no permanent consequences (the economic and social institutions represented by the dowagers remain in place), but the shorts at least give form to radical possibilities.

If the dowagers' power is economic and class-related, then sexual power is usually reserved for younger women. The "bad" category includes young women on the make who see the Stooges merely as meal tickets and who thus threaten men both sexually (by not acknowledging the authority of male sexuality and, instead, using sex to exert their own control) and economically (by threatening to usurp financial command). This type of sexual predator appears in several shorts, notably *Healthy, Wealthy and Dumb* (1938; remade in 1952 as *A Missed Fortune*) and *Three Dumb Clucks* (1937; remade in 1953 as *Up in Daisy's Penthouse*). In the first pair, Curly (and in the remake, Shemp) wins $50,000 in a radio contest. After the Stooges anticipate their windfall by checking into the Hotel Costa Plenty, three gold diggers try to separate them from their cash. Alternately flirtatious, admiring, and submissive, the girls thus manipulate traditional gender expectations to lure the boys into proposing marriage. When they learn that Curly's actual after-tax winnings will amount to $4.85, they respond with a physical attack. In a final assertion of female sexual power, they smash champagne bottles over the boys' heads, the bottles serving as possible phallic symbols of the women's usurpation of the male position. Yet the Stooges, penniless though they again are, have also asserted their own power by retaining inviolate their male bond.

In *Three Dumb Clucks*, the Stooges' father, Popsie, plans to leave their mother in order to marry a younger woman. Again playing with gender performance and expectation, this supposedly traditionally desirable girl turns out to be part of a murderous gang that plans to kill Popsie after the wedding for the inheritance. This short is a spoof of an Academy Award-nominated Deanna Durbin vehicle, *Three Smart Girls* (1936), in which a trio of sisters succeeds in saving their divorced father from marrying a woman who wants only his money.[5] In that film, the three girls leave boarding school to race to their father's aid; in the Stooges' version, boarding school is traded for jail as the boys break out of prison to stop Popsie from abandoning his wife for his con-artist girlfriend. Although this parody is obviously intended to capitalize on the popularity of the Durbin film, the context is significant. By replacing the genteel, upper-class female world of *Three Smart Girls* with its opposite — a rough, lower-class male world of prison that exists outside the border of cultural acceptability — *Three Dumb Clucks* blurs the boundaries between the apparent dichotomies. As a result, the short effects a gender and class substitution with at least two consequences: the exchange reveals, first, that the conventional categories are unstable constructs open to revision and, second, that the supposedly binary worlds are in fact linked: both the boys' prison and the girls' school are engaged in similar cultural work of control and dominance. Although in the remake *Up in Daisy's Penthouse*, the boys are no longer in jail, the ending of both shorts is the same: Popsie is dragged home to the wife he had hoped to leave, suggesting a prison of a different sort and reasserting both female otherness (in the person of the unwanted wife) and female control (the wife is essentially Popsie's jailer). Yet the boys' power is also asserted: they foil the murder plot and, for the time being at least, return the female characters to their proper social roles. The Stooges' mother remains a wife, and Daisy the gold digger is stripped of her gender artifice and revealed in her "true" guise.

The third category of women in Stooges' comedies — the "ugly" women — further extends the gender complexities of the films. In the superficial world of the Stooges, physical ugliness is its own crime, an unambiguous emblem of the alien and the undesirable.[6] Ugly women are often sexual predators as well, a further threat that links these female characters to the long-standing Western tradition of woman as the source of evil. In the shorts, ugly women are usually introduced in sexual terms. One common pattern finds the boys attracted to a woman they assume fits traditional gender expectations: because she wears a veil or is in some way hidden from view, she at first appears to be dainty, feminine, and appropriately available for marriage or romance. But the camera ultimately reveals a woman who violates acceptable standards of beauty: she has a big nose or buck teeth or some other visible, assertive token of her nontraditional gender status. *I'm a Monkey's Uncle* is typical. It features a trio of women, Aggie, Maggie, and Baggie, the first two of whom are conventionally lovely. Baggie, however, is leeringly unattractive, and the boys are comically horrified by her. Their horror is exaggerated, of course, as befits farce, but their reaction also marks the nature of Baggie's gender transgression: her physical appearance symbolizes the cultural consequences for women who do not accept a traditional gender position, who perhaps too forcefully assert their sexual desires, or who refuse to (or cannot) conform to expected aesthetic norms. The figure of Baggie suggests that such women are to be legitimately regarded as unnatural, as not "real" women, or certainly as undesirable women.

Although women's faces represent the most common locus for female ugliness in the shorts, other patterns are present as well, particularly weight and age. Like the facially ugly women, fat or older women who manifest sexual desire are also coded as unnatural. In *False Alarms*, for instance, the Stooges are supposed to attend a birthday party with Curly's girl and some of her female friends, one of whom, the amorous, man-crazy Minnie, is quite overweight. When the boys are late, one girl muses, "I wonder why Curly and his friends haven't shown up." Validating the weight-related comedy by creating it herself, Minnie answers, "It's me. I'm a Jonah. I guess the only way I can get a man to come and see me is to call a doctor." After Curly finally arrives, he is aggressively pursued by Minnie, who first pushes him to the floor and later chases him around. "I grow on people," she tells him, to which Curly replies, "So do warts." The "fat" humor continues as Curly, half-promising to get Minnie a boyfriend, phones Moe and says, "Moe, you better come right over here. You're missing the biggest thing of your life." Minnie, briefly made happy by the appearance of Moe with his car, shouts, "Come on, girls! Let's go places and eat things!" Her weight, her comic aggressiveness, and her appetites symbolize unnatural hungers, excess, unseemly desires — all the elements that create the unacceptable woman, the one whose inability or refusal to be contained by traditional gender expectations makes her culturally dangerous.

Age functions similarly. In *Some More of Samoa*, for example, the boys visit the jungle island of Rhum Boogie, where they are captured by cannibals who will eat them unless Curly marries the tribal chief's sister. When he sees that the sister is both old and plain, Curly chooses the option of becoming "roasted Stooge" (as the cannibals' handwritten menu proclaims), complete with an apple in his mouth and meat tenderizer on his chest. Much of the comedy derives from the supposedly inherent impossibility that an older woman interested in sex could be other than a figure of ridicule, an example of unnatural appetites that undermine her very identity as a woman.[7]

Woman as Self

The pervasive pattern of woman as other in the Three Stooges shorts is destabilized and rewritten by another important, seemingly oppositional pattern: woman as self. Many of the films contain scenes of simultaneous doubling and reversal, scenes in which the Stooges replace women with themselves or replace themselves with women. A sight gag from *We Want Our Mummy* offers a blueprint for this common trope, although it does not focus on gender. In *Mummy*, the Stooges are detectives who literally present false fronts to the audience when they enter a room in what might be called "backface"—they walk backwards but appear to be walking frontwards, since to their backs, heels, and heads are attached suits, shoes, facial masks, and deerstalker hats. This scene is emblematic of the patterns of gender otherness and doubling that mark the films: as the boys approach the camera, their alternative bodies and faces, which at first seem literal, are gradually revealed to be representations—false, in a sense, and yet not false, since the costumes are still part of the boys' physical bodies and still reveal their identities as detectives. The costumes are perhaps more properly described not as false fronts but as visual alter egos, part of and yet separate from the "real" faces and fronts that the boys reveal when they turn around.

The pattern of woman as self works in much the same fashion. The boys assume a gender position or identity that at first seems opposite to their "real" selves, as in Larry's substitution of himself for an unconscious woman in *Boobs in Arms*, Curly's classic turn as "Madame Cucaracha," the pseudo-singer in *Micro-Phonies*, the boys' drag scene in *Pop Goes the Easel*, and many similar examples. In plot terms, the gender switch is often motivated by the Stooges' need to hide their original identities: Larry is trying to fool a jealous husband in *Boobs in Arms*; the boys want the money they'll earn performing at a swanky party after they're mistaken for musicians in *Micro-Phonies*; and the trio is on the lam from a cop in *Pop Goes the Easel*. In each case, however, the assumed female identities complicate the boys' previously unquestioned categorization as male.

In *Boobs in Arms*, the Stooges are greeting-card salesmen who offer to help a weeping wife win back her husband by making him jealous. She agrees to their suggestion that they pretend to be her sweethearts, but she faints after one kiss from Curly. When the husband appears, Larry takes his place underneath the unconscious woman, moving his arms as if they were hers, while Moe and Curly pretend to make love to him/her. Since nothing can be seen of Larry beyond his hands and forearms, the female identity has momentarily become his — a suggestive usurpation of gender position. In *Micro-Phonies*, not only is Curly-in-drag accepted as female by the party guests, but he also internalizes the female identity by lip-synching a song so that "his" voice is a high, feminine soprano.

In *Pop Goes the Easel*, Curly extends his gendered performance into sexual assertiveness, flirting à la Mae West with the police officer who has been pursuing him. "I'm glad you came up to see me," Curly smirks. Thus he is no longer simply *being* a woman, that is, reacting as a woman might in particular circumstances; instead, he is actively creating his new gender identity, one that combines the male-female binaries. (A similar performance occurs in *Uncivil Warriors*.) Not content simply to appear in drag pretending to be Moe's wife, Curly acts out his part with gusto, calling to Moe, "Darling! Kiss me!"[8]

Staples of the Stooges' comedy, the many drag episodes are a main method by which the boys transform woman as other into woman as self. These scenes thus offer a number of complications to gender binaries. By blurring categorical boundaries, the shorts demonstrate the indeterminacy of gender; by inscribing "masculine" and "feminine" as attributes and outlooks not limited by a person's biological sex, the scenes reveal the constructed nature of the cultural dichotomies. While drag can also function to reinforce the tradition of woman as other by reducing the female to a joke and by comically emphasizing the contrast between the drag personae and the "real" boys, the scenes nevertheless offer the Stooges and their viewers one form of control over gender struggles: defusing the threat of otherness by transforming other into self.

In addition to writing the female onto their male bodies through drag and story, the Stooges often replace themselves with or recreate themselves and their gender identities through parallel trios of female characters. The three gold diggers in *Healthy, Wealthy and Dumb* provide a typical example, mirroring the Stooges right down to the wisecracking leader who is always ready with a flip nickname. Many shorts offer these doubled/reversed triumvirates: triplets of women, often of the same height and similar look, whose presence offers another form of gender deconstruction. Sometimes these trios are the boys' allies, sometimes their enemies, but they all symbolize aspects of Stooge identity, particularly the power of same-sex unity. The girls' tripled names reinforce this unity and emphasize its gendered nature. In addition to the previously mentioned Maggie, Aggie, and Baggie, there are Tiska, Taska, and Baska; Della, Stella, and Bella; Dorabell, Florabell, and Corabell; and Marybelle, Lulubelle, and Ringabelle. Such names further link these female trios with the boys, who also often have tripled names: Ziller, Zeller, and Zoller; Click, Clack, and Cluck; Duck, Dodge, and Hyde; Hook, Line, and Sinker; and so on.[9] Overall, these pairs of tripled characters reify the interrogation of gender categories that marks the shorts.

One final example of gender doubling and reversal involves the Stooges' trademark slapstick violence.[10] Long the subject of critical and parental debate, the boys' eye pokes, slaps, head bonks, and pie fights represent an important form of power, whether it be class- or gender-related. The threat (and actuality) of mob violence and revolt has always been one weapon that any oppressed group holds over its oppressors. Conversely, violence wielded by the state or by powerful individuals is also a weapon by which those in control maintain their control. And of course, violence is also a way of eliminating control altogether, of giving free rein to the carnivalesque forces of anarchy that are never far away in a Three Stooges film and that can offer radical opportunities for dismantling and rewriting prevailing cultural categories.

Slapstick Identity and Female Violence

The Stooges' comic mayhem demonstrates all these forms of the power of violence, a power that is also extended to the women. In a number of shorts, the boys are on the receiving end of comic violence from women. Throwing punches and pies, the women challenge stereotypes of femininity and passivity, indulging a direct physical expression of female anger and aggression that would not be possible in a more realistic setting. Violence becomes a gender equalizer, albeit one that is based on traditional male/female oppositions, in which comedy is derived from the members of each sex behaving in nontraditional ways—women battering men, men allowing themselves to be battered. But since the violence is balanced, traded equally among the Stooges and various dignified matrons and dainty blondes, each behaving like the other, the oppositions are again deconstructed; the Stooges again become the female selves they initially resist.

Overall, the slapstick violence can be read as emblematic of the way the Stooges' films address gender: throughout the shorts, the cultural constructions of gender are subjected to a form of textual slapstick. Through repeated patterns of opposition, merging, destruction, re-emergence, and reconstruction, the Stooges beat the traditional categories into new forms. They wrench "female" identities away from women and replace those identities with new ones; they relocate the gendered behaviors of one sex to the bodies and actions of the other. Just as they wreak havoc on social structures ranging from service institutions (schools, hospitals) to capitalist bulwarks (banks, beer factories, sports teams), from bastions of upper-class privilege (ritzy mansions, golf courses) to agencies of state power (the military), so, too, do they dismantle gender assumptions. But since the devastation is surreally comic and lacking in lasting consequence, viewers can be made aware of gender play without being threatened or having consciously to acknowledge the extent of the cultural challenges they have witnessed.

By the end of a Stooges episode, viewers sometimes parallel the boys and thus also become part of the film's narrative patterns of doubling and reversal. In the final scene of *Boobs in Arms*, Larry, Curly, and Moe, guffawing helplessly under the influence of laughing gas, ride giddily off-screen, not realizing or caring that they are traveling astride a live missile. As viewers, we leave a Three Stooges short in similar fashion: taking hold of the bombshell of gender deconstruction and laughing all the way.

Notes

1. For a brief study of the influence of the Renaissance Italian *commedia dell'arte* on the Stooges comedy, see Chamberlain (2002, pp. 53–59).

2. The issue of whether comedy is inherently radical or subversive has been widely treated by critics and theorists, but the theoretical implications of this topic are beyond the scope of this chapter. The Three Stooges shorts seem clearly to challenge cultural norms, but whether such challenges extend beyond the moment of laughter is still an open question.

3. A notable exception occurs in *Woman Haters* (1934), the Stooges' first Columbia short. In this episode, the ending separates Moe and Curly from Larry, who remains with his new wife. But *Woman Haters* is in almost all respects an atypical short, since it was conceived as part of an existing Columbia series called "Musical Novelties." The Stooges have different names; the dialogue is in (excruciating) couplets; the boys have not developed their recognizable later personae, nor are they yet a united team.

4. See, for example, Maltin (1972), Howard (1977), and material from cast and crew members cited by Okuda and Watz (1986). In this chapter, the term "boys" is retained to refer to the team's on-screen personae.

5. Creating a parody as a means of profiting from the success of a recent feature film was a ploy the Stooges used several times. For instance, their only Oscar-nominated short, *Men in Black* (1934), is a take-off on a popular medical drama of 1934, Clark Gable's *Men in White*, itself a version of Sidney Kingsley's Pulitzer Prize-winning play. Other examples parody film titles only: *Violent Is the Word for Curly* (1938) alludes to the 1936 film *Valiant Is the Word for Carrie*, starring Gladys George; *So Long, Mr. Chumps* (1941) recalls *Goodbye, Mr. Chips*; *Boobs in Arms* (1940) evokes Judy Garland's *Babes in Arms*.

6. The Stooges, of course, aren't exactly lookers themselves, but their appearance is so deliberately stylized and cartoonish that their ugliness does not function in the same way as does the ugliness of the conventionally unattractive women. Also, by exempting themselves from the "ugly" category, the Stooges continue their pattern of women as other by establishing separate standards for female and male appeal.

7. In this short, too, the age issue is complicated by the dimension of ethnic and racial otherness, symbolized by the cannibals of Rhum Boogie, who are played by African American actors decked out in headdresses, feathers, and nose rings. Significantly, the chief and his sister are white, a fact that both erases race as an element in the sexual relationship and makes race visible as a further aspect of otherness.

8. A not-too-subtle vein of homoeroticism runs throughout the shorts. The boys often share a bed, kiss each other, and make suggestive comments. When Moe and Curly embrace during a plane crash scene in *Dizzy Pilots*, Larry asks, "Do you guys go steady?" In *Movie Maniacs*, Curly ends up having to play the female lead in a film with Larry as his paramour. In *Three Missing Links*, Moe wriggles in tickled ecstasy when he thinks Curly is licking his feet (the licker is actually a lion). As happens with much of the gender comedy, the surrealistic absurdity of the Stooges' universe diffuses any threat in their homoeroticism and thus opens a space for same-sex possibilities that a more closed system of sexual imagery might block. However, a full-scale queering of the Three Stooges is outside the purposes of the chapter; it's enough to note that the comic homoeroticism of the films further destabilizes gender and sexual binaries.

9. Perhaps the most famous trio of names associated with the Stooges — lawyers Dewey, Cheatem, and Howe — was never actually used in a short, but only in a publicity shot.

10. For a theoretical study of the Three Stooges' violence and its consequences for narrative, see Brunette (1991, pp. 174–187).

Works Cited

Brunette, Peter. "The Three Stooges and the (Anti-)Narrative of Violence: De(Con)structive Comedy." *Comedy, Cinema, Theory*. Ed. Andrew Horton. Berkeley: University of California Press, 1991.

Chamberlain, Kathleen. "The Three Stooges and the *Commedia dell'Arte*." *The Film Comedy Reader*. Ed. Gregg Rickman. New York: Limelight, 2002.
Howard, Moe. *Moe Howard and the Three Stooges*. Secaucus, N.J.: Citadel, 1977.
Maltin, Leonard. *The Great Movie Shorts*. New York: Crown, 1972.
Okuda, Ted, and Edward Watz. *The Columbia Comedy Shorts: Two-Reel Hollywood Film Comedies, 1933–1958*. Jefferson, N.C.: McFarland, 1986.

19

Dames, Babes, Battleaxes, and Tomatoes: Women and the Three Stooges

Peter Seely

The Three Stooges' enormous popularity has always been considered a male-dominated phenomenon. Perhaps more than any other representatives of American popular culture, the Stooges are considered a "guy thing." The mention of classic Stooges lines can bring howls of laughter from the average male, and a look of puzzlement or mild disgust from the average female.[1] Conversely, there is a less sizable but substantial core of female Stooges fans, typified by a Web site titled "Women Who Run with the Stooges." The site features hundreds of testimonials from the boys' female fans, extolling the virtues of everything from their favorite episode to their favorite Stooges film to which Stooge is the sexiest one.[2] The fact that three of the eight authors in this book are women is an indication that Stooges fans are not necessarily a homogeneous lot. Nonetheless, the Stooges have always held a greater appeal for the male of the species.

However, the primary purpose of this chapter is not to examine why the Stooges may hold greater appeal for men than for women. While some may choose to view the Stooges' overwhelming popularity as a "men are from Mars, women from Venus" dichotomy, there wouldn't appear to be any great mystery to this difference in their appeal. The Stooges' ethos is loud, crude, violent, silly, vulgar, and obtuse. If these characteristics don't appeal equally to every man, it is fairly safe to conclude that men are probably much more tolerant than women of such qualities. The main purpose here, however, is to examine how women were portrayed in the short films of the Three Stooges. By examining these images, a clearer picture should emerge of one of the most controversial aspects of their films. Perhaps serendipitously, by reading this study, a woman may discover exactly what it is she doesn't like about the Stooges.

Feminism and the Stooges

Unlike many essays on the role of women in the arts and literature, this chapter is not heavily informed by feminist theory. This is not to say that feminist theories are not appropriate here, but the greater focus is more specifically on the work of the Stooges, who were part of a greater artistic construct, one that dictated a male-dominated hierarchy for most literary forms of expression. That is, the roles of women in the Stooges films likely were not all that different from the norms of the day in literature and film. For example, Boone (1991, pp. 961–982) has written on the latent *homosocial* messages in the writings of Herman Melville, Mark Twain, and Jack London. A greater examination of male-dominated media within the polemics of feminist theory is beyond the scope of our discussion; however, such a study may prove desirable to future scholars after reading this chapter.

All this is not to say, however, that feminist theory does not relate at all to the short films of the Three Stooges. Radical feminist theory, for example, is a useful reference point when studying the Stooges. According to Sedgewick (1985), the principles of radical feminism are such that "gender itself, and gender alone, [is] the most radical division of human experience." If one accepts that premise, then the Three Stooges would appear to be the apotheosis of radical feminism. As it is unlikely that most radical feminists would have the Stooges held to such an exalted status, then in the words of Shemp Howard, it must be something else.

This chapter will reveal tremendous differences between the treatment of the Stooges and an almost Marxist alienation at times of women in their films. In some shorts, women are so isolated from the rest of the cast of the film that their reality and humanity can be questioned. However, this certainly was not always the case, and there is not a simple hierarchical difference between a woman's existence and that of the Stooges, which was characteristic of women in many motion pictures in the first half of the twentieth century. Unlike, say, African Americans in their films, women were often superior to the Stooges, and to condemn these films as simply more examples of the dominant male dominating in a male-dominated society may miss the point of the role women often played in these films.

Women in Film in a Man's World

In the early years of the mainstream motion picture industry, the role for a woman was not often allowed a lot of breathing room. Save a few cultural icons such as Judy Garland, Katharine Hepburn, Mae West, and Marlene Dietrich, roles for women were largely confined to those of wives, girlfriends, or professional women working as nurses or teachers or unskilled service people. This is, of course, a generalization; motion pictures from the beginning of talking pictures have had their share of heroines as well, mostly figures from history, such as Cleopatra, Jeanne d'Arc, and Florence Nightingale. But at least for the first 50 years of talking pictures, motion picture studios were male-run businesses, with films written, produced, and directed mostly by men; it is therefore not surprising that the history of films can be accurately described as being male-centric. The films of the Three Stooges were also not very different in terms of the male-dominated creative personnel, and the gender hegemony was largely true with the supporting actors and their roles as well.

As for the portrayals of women in slapstick film, the very nature of the genre was such that the male stars were often inferior to or the foil of the women. In the case of Charlie Chaplin, Buster Keaton, Harold Lloyd, and Laurel and Hardy, and in the comedy films of Mack Sennett, the male comedians were often bested by their female supporting cast. Further, the short subjects field itself yielded a number of comediennes who were as adept as many of the men in the field of slapstick. Vera Vague, Thelma Todd, ZaSu Pitts, Patsy Kelly, and others starred in their own short series for a variety of studios. Indeed, the many supporting actresses in these shorts, in addition to turning in fine comic performances, were often the protagonists in these films.

The Women of the Three Stooges

The character portrayals by women in the Three Stooges comedies were many and varied, in spite of what one might assume as a dearth of types for women. This doesn't mean that women starred in the comedies; these were, after all, Three Stooges films. Nor were the majority of the portrayals necessarily positive or important. The women of the Stooges films could be wallpaper or background, or they could take roles front and center with the Stooges.

In American society, at any point in time, women make up approximately half of the adult population, and as such it is unfair to everyone to classify them as a minority. In the world of the Stooges, however, white males dominated, and those who didn't qualify could truly be called a minority. Viewed in this context, and compared to these other groups, the portrayals of women in the Stooges films were abundant.

In contrast to the other groups studied in this book, however, the portrayals of women cannot be grouped into a handful of overreaching categories. Women were not nearly as one dimensional as other types in these films and were not used simply to fulfill a handy stereotype that could act as a foil for the Three Stooges. Like every other group, including white males, women were subordinate to the stars of the film, but the types of women portrayed were many.

Society Dames

The most prevalent type of woman found in the films of the Three Stooges was the society dame. The role of the society dame was most often realized by Symona Boniface, who played this role in 22 different Stooges films. Boniface was to the Stooges what Margaret Dumont had been to the Marx Brothers in their films — the wealthy dowager who was occasionally bemused but mostly confused and foiled by the antics of the respective zany comedy trios. Don Morlan writes of the antiaristocracy themes (see Chapter 9) in many of the Stooges shorts (which was also apparent in Marx Brothers films), and Boniface was the brunt of most of the Stooges' abuse as they clumsily attempted to assimilate into high society.

Boniface is probably best remembered for her scene in the last Curly film, *Half-Wits Holiday* (in footage that was later used in the 1956 film *Scheming Schemers*). Boniface as Mrs. Smythe-Smythe approaches Moe to find out about the "amazing metamorphosis" that has transformed the Stooges from lower-class ragamuffins into society gentlemen. Moe panics, as he has just taken a pie away from Curly and tossed it at the ceiling, where it is now hanging precariously above their heads. Boniface, sensing Moe's fright, utters her most famous line: "Young man, what's wrong? You act as if the sword of Damocles is hanging over your head." As she looks up to find out what has Moe's attention, the pie lands directly on her face, which precipitates the most well-known pie fight in Stooges history.

Boniface played this same role in many other Stooges comedies as well. In some of these films, unlike the placid Dumont, Boniface would often turn the Stooges' violent behavior right back on them, as she does in *An Ache in Every Stake* and *Crash Goes the Hash*. Nonetheless, she was always in the unenviable and unwitting position of dealing with the Stooges' uncouth behavior. Occasionally she even found herself losing her clothes in films such as *Slippery Silks* and *No Census, No Feeling*.

Several other examples show society dames suffering at the hand of the Stooges, though occasionally it was the Stooges' lack of pretension in dealing with the upper class that resulted in happy endings for Boniface, such as recovering a valuable painting for her in *Vagabond Loafers* and exposing a confidence man posing as a prince (played by Dick Curtis) whom she is about to marry in *Crash Goes the Hash*.

Man Beaters

A fairly common role for females in Stooges films (and in most Columbia short subjects) was that of the abusive man-beater. Very often this behavior was combined into other, more pronounced behavioral types (such as the shrew, gun moll, or society dame), but often it was the single most identifying characteristic of the featured women. Short scenes include the Stooges being slapped by secretaries in *Hot Stuff*, punched by a showgirl in *Flagpole Jitters*, and slapped by a British gun moll in *Hot Ice*; and Larry is slapped by a crime witness for daring to look like someone she hates in *Tricky Dicks*.

One of the Stooges' most frequent female antagonists was Dorothy Appleby, who appeared in seven Stooges films. She was actually more prolific in the Columbia films of Buster Keaton, where she frequently played his wife or sweetheart. In the Keaton shorts, Appleby was able to display a fairly wide range of emotions and behaviors. In the Stooges films (with the exception of *So Long, Mr. Chumps*), Appleby was generally cast as the attractive, sassy nemesis of the Stooges, who would rather slap the Stooges than tolerate their juvenile flirting.

Gold Diggers

The Stooges' naiveté in love often resulted in their being taken advantage of by insincere, two-timing gold diggers. In the films *Three Dumb Clucks* and the remake *Up in Daisy's Penthouse*, the Stooges are trying to foil a plan by their father to marry a young, fortune-hunting woman. In *Corny Casanovas* and the remake *Rusty Romeos*, all three Stooges engage in mortal combat vying for the attention of the same woman (played by Connie Cezan). *Brideless Groom* (and the remake *Husbands Beware*) pits Moe and Larry as matchmakers for Shemp, who must be married in order to inherit his Uncle Caleb's fortune. Toward the end of the film several women create physical mayhem worthy of the Stooges as they try to become Shemp's wife. In *Healthy, Wealthy and Dumb* and the remake *A Missed Fortune*, the Stooges encounter three gold diggers eager to get their hands on the boys' newfound fortune. Other films feature this premise as a lesser part of the plot.

Gun Molls, Crooks, Con Artists, and Spies

Several Stooges films had the Stooges fighting or investigating the underworld. Their nemeses were primarily male, but of course any good leader of a gang has his gun moll or other female assistant. Female crooks are there at the ready in *Three Loan Wolves*, where a gun moll (played by Beverly Warren) leaves a baby with the Stooges. Con artist Mary (Mary Ainslee) enlists the unwitting Stooges to help her pull a fraud on an insurance company in *Hokus Pokus*. Another con artist, played by Greta Thyssen, helps her bosses swindle Joe out of his sweepstakes winnings in *Quiz Whizz*. And Flossie (Virginia Hunter) takes her boss's bankroll in *Sing a Song of Six Pants*.

Three films of the Stooges have women serving as spies to pry some secret from the hapless Stooges: Mattie Herring (Lorna Gray) is the Nazi spy in *You Nazty Spy!*, as is Delia Zwieback (Christine McIntyre) in *No Dough Boys*. Olga the spy (Phyllis Barry) threatens the Stooges at gunpoint in *Three Little Sew and Sews*.

Christine McIntyre appeared in 31 Stooges films, more than any other female actress. Her striking beauty and operatic singing voice, as well as her ability to be both tough and soft, made her the perfect female complement to the Stooges, and her appearances were much more diverse in nature than all other females and even most males who appeared in these films. McIntyre usually befriended the Stooges, but her ability to act tough also made her a perfect gun moll in shorts such as *Crime on Their Hands* and *Hot Ice*, a gold-digging crook in *Three Pests in a* Mess, one of three female jewel thieves in *Hugs and Mugs*, and the not-so-sweet Scotch lass cleaning treasures out of Glenheather Castle in *The Hot Scots* (and the remake *Scotched in Scotland*). McIntyre also manages to get her slaps and punches in against Shemp in one of the most famous of all Stooge scenes in *Brideless Groom* and *Husbands Beware*, as she mistakes the confused Stooge for her cousin Basil.

Shrews

Some of the most memorable female roles in Stooges shorts were women playing the role of the shrew: a nagging, verbally (and sometimes physically) abusive wife or lover. Yet these portrayals were few, turning up in only three of the Stooges films. The Stooges' wives had every reason to be shrewish to their lazy, no-account husbands in *Dizzy Doctors*. In *The Sitter Downers* and *Husbands Beware*, the Stooges discover when it is too late that the sweet women they think they've married are actually overdemanding, mean, and abusive women. While other women in the Stooges' films at times exhibited overbearing qualities, it is these three films where the female is a most complete shrew.

Uglies and Chubbies

Often the Stooges had encounters with women who were either very overweight or physically unattractive. The most common task for these women was to pursue one or more of the Stooges. Of the uglies, the most memorable was Dee Green, a wonderful comic actress who relentlessly pursued Shemp. When

Moe and Larry are searching in vain for a bride for the would-be heir Shemp in *Brideless Groom* and *Husbands Beware*, it is Shemp's tone-deaf and homely singing pupil played by Green who truly loves Shemp and wants to marry him, not knowing about his newfound fortune. She pursues Shemp in prehistoric days as Baggie, the sister of Aggie and Maggie, in *I'm a Monkey's Uncle* and the remake *Stone Age Romeos*. She plays the homely princess offered to Shemp as a reward by her father the king in *Mummy's Dummies*. Another homely princess (played by Louise Carver) pursues Curly, this time in *Some More of Samoa*.

In *Scrambled Brains*, Shemp, on the verge of a nervous breakdown, sees only a beautiful woman in his nurse Nora (Babe London, with some of her front teeth missing). A buck-toothed Miss Beebee (Margie Liszt) takes a shine to the Stooges in *The Tooth Will Out*. And the least attractive woman at a society party pursues Curly in *Hoi Polloi*.

Chubby women were sometimes used for comic relief for the Stooges, as in *Brideless Groom*, *Husbands Beware*, and *Slippery Silks*. In other films such as *False Alarms*, *The Sitter Downers*, *Sweet and Hot*, and *Muscle Up a Little Closer*, and also in *Husbands Beware*, one or more chubby women pursue or marry the Stooges. While sometimes the comedy of these films comes from the Stooges' attempts to escape these ladies, more often it is derived from the mere physical difference between these large women and the diminutive Stooges.

Strong Women

In several Stooges films, women exhibited some degree of emotional or physical strength, and not just the ability to beat up the Stooges. These were women who might have a profession or career, including a skeptical script girl (Hilda Title) in *Movie Maniacs*. Christine McIntyre is the brave and intelligent daughter of a rocket scientist in *Fuelin' Around* and its remake *Hot Stuff*. She also plays what would have otherwise been the role of helpless maiden until she demonstrates her physical and emotional strength in *Three Troubledoers*, and *Out West*, and its remake *Pals and Gals*. A brave woman helping to commandeer a space ship (Doreen Woodbury) keeps her cool while the frightened Stooges cause havoc in outer space in *Space Ship Sappy*. Even the character of Tiny (Maxine Gates) in *Muscle Up a Little Closer*, who becomes hysterical when she discovers that her wedding ring is missing, exhibits a far greater degree of physical strength and maturity than does her beau Joe.

One of the best examples of a strong woman in a Stooges film is the character of Señorita Rita (played by Carmen LaRoux) in *Saved by the Belle*. As the film's title implies, it is up to Rita to get the Stooges out of trouble. Rita is fighting an insurgency movement against the existing government of Vulgaria. With her help, the Stooges manage to break out of prison and deliver a crucial map to the head of the army. Rita is an attractive and affectionate woman, but she is also smart, savvy, and efficient.

Spinsters, Widows, and Divorcees

The Stooges frequently encountered elderly widows or spinsters in their different adventures. Sometimes these women played the role of a battleaxe, such as their landlady (Isabelle LaMal) in *A Pain in the Pullman* and Mrs. Magruder (Kitty McHugh) in *Gents in a Jam*, a fish customer (Dorothy Vernon) in *Booby Dupes*, and Nell (Kathryn Sheldon), the manager of a traveling show in *Rockin' Through the Rockies*. But most of the time the Stooges, in their unique way, became the benefactors of these kindly old souls. The Stooges help an elderly woman save her hotel in *Loco Boy Makes Good*, save a widow's oil-laden property in *Oily to Bed, Oily to Rise*, and try to save their mother's marriage in *Up in Daisy's Penthouse* and *Three Dumb Clucks*. They come to the rescue of an elderly woman whose husband is threatening to leave her because she has gotten old and lost her beauty in *All Gummed Up* and the remake *Bubble Trouble*. The Stooges, as druggists, discover a fountain of youth potion that restores her youth and beauty (Christine McIntyre plays the reborn woman). Their half-hearted attempts to do the same for the old man (Emil Sitka) backfire in both films.

Babes

As in most male-dominated comedies, the Stooges films often featured an attractive young lady who became the object of one or more of the male stars' affections. The first two Stooges films featured such a babe: Larry's fiancée Mary (Marjorie White) has a flirtation with all of the Stooges in *Woman Haters*, and Dorothy Grainger takes a shine to Curly in *Punch Drunks*. Larry's girlfriend Kitty (Claire Carleton) dumps Larry upon her first meeting with boxer Chopper Kane (Dick Wessell) in *Fright Night* and the remake *Fling in the Ring*. Shemp is attracted to both an angel and a devil in *Bedlam in Paradise*. In *Flying Saucer Daffy*, Joe rates the attention of two beautiful spaceship operators (Bek Nelson and Diana Darrin) and is reunited with his now-married former sweetheart Fifi (Vanda Dupre) in *Fifi Blows Her Top*.

Show People and Divas

Often the women who traveled in the circles of the Three Stooges were show-business people, such as actresses, song-and-dance ladies, and showgirls. Two films, *Gents Without Cents* and *Rhythm and Weep*, contain plots that have Moe, Larry, and Curly gaining the affections of three ladies who sing and dance, and the six of them then attempt to break into show-business. The women in *Gents Without Cents* are fittingly named Flo, Mary, and Shirley, and we are presented with Hilda, Wilda, and Tilda in *Rhythm and Weep*. A fan dancer (Susan Kaaren) named Gail Tempest becomes the object of attention to an entire courtroom in *Disorder in the Court*. Actresses play smaller roles with the Stooges in show-business in *Movie Maniacs* and *Three Hams on Rye*. And the Stooges run afoul of random showgirls in *Loose Loot* and *Flagpole Jitters*.

The film actress as diva makes three brief appearances in Stooges films. Mildred Harris is a leading lady disgusted with the Stooges' film direction in *Movie Maniacs*, Jane Hamilton plays a haughty actress in *Three Missing Links*, and Christine McIntyre portrays the cynical and pampered movie star who is kidnapped in *Studio Stoops*.

Wives and Sweethearts

The Stooges were featured at various times with wives and sweethearts. Most of the time, in films such as *G.I. Wanna Go Home, Shot in the Frontier, Pardon My Backfire*, and *Rumpus in the Harem*, these women play insignificant roles. But wives are featured prominently in *Pardon My Clutch* and the remake *Wham-Bam-Slam!* as the boys' taller and stronger wives elicit laughter with their physical punishment of the Stooges, and likewise in *Husbands Beware*.

Four Stooges films are otherwise notable for the portrayals of women. *I'm a Monkey's Uncle* and the remake *Stone Age Romeos* are set in the Stone Age. The Stooges play the roles of caveman protectors of Aggie, Maggie, and Baggie, setting the stage for thousands of years of portrayals of male-female relationships. In *A Merry Mix-Up*, Moe, Larry, and Joe are one of three sets of identical triplets, confounding their respective wives and sweethearts who are unaware of the existence of the other brothers. This provokes them into several acts of violence against their own husbands and boyfriends and other Stooge characters. And in *Love at First Bite* and the partial remake *Fifi Blows Her Top*, Moe, Larry, Shemp, and Joe reminisce about their exploits with their Italian, German, and French sweethearts.

Helpless Maidens and Belles

The helpless maiden was a motion picture staple from the beginning of the medium. In spite of the Stooges' general ineptitude, many of their films featured them as saviors or benefactors of helpless females. These female portrayals were completely unremarkable in films such as *Horses' Collars, Back to the Woods, Idle Roomers, Spooks!, Musty Musketeers*, and *Pals and Gals*. However, when the Stooges were providing their services to just one female, the results were more interesting. The pathos involved with the portrayals of the sister (Harlene Wood) of the handicapped boy in *Cash and Carry*, the depressed wife (Evelyn Young) of an inattentive army captain in *Boobs in Arms*, the sobbing wife (Dorothy Appleby) of a wrongly convicted sweetheart in *So Long Mr. Chumps*, and even the depressed young girl whose father has been kidnapped in *Nutty But Nice* provide somewhat deeper characterizations of women in need (see Chapter 7 for further discussion of this phenomenon in the Stooges films).

The Southern *belle* was a role for women in two Stooges films with a Civil War theme, *Uncivil Warriors* and *Uncivil War Birds*. Predictably, the female characters in these films were not at all noteworthy.

Ditzes and Props

It is surprising that only three films turn up showing the woman as ditz. The most famous of these portrayals was by Jeanie Roberts as the airhead nurse in *Men in Black*. Others included Phyllis Crane as the ditzy blonde opposite Lucille Ball's more savvy character in *Three Little Pigskins* and Lorna Gray as the spoiled and flighty wife of a rich man in *Three Sappy People*.

Quite often women acted as props for the Stooges, appearing primarily in nondescript and nonspeaking parts, usually where their physical attributes complemented the Stooges' craziness, such as showgirls in *Movie Maniacs* and *Whoops I'm an Indian!*; golfers and hangers-by in *Three Little Beers*; sexy co-eds in cute satin outfits playing basketball in *Violent Is the Word for Curly* (though some had speaking parts as well); various clothing models in *Slippery Silks*; secretaries in *You Nazty Spy!*, *He Cooked His Goose*, and *Triple Crossed*; and barflies in *Goofs and Saddles* and *Yes, We Have No Bonanza*. Unlike real life, where males are more attracted to the Stooges, the female prop is often bemused by the antics of the Stooges.

The woman as prop should not be confused with women as background or wallpaper. The latter are incidental parts for women, such as customers in a restaurant or people in a courtroom, parts that could just as easily be played by a man and are therefore of little concern in this chapter.

Maids

Seven maids were encountered in the Stooges films. While their incidence is relatively high, these roles are significant only because of the stereotypes they perpetuated. African American women portrayed maids in *Termites of 1938*, *Calling All Curs*, and *Income Tax Sappy*, and French maids appeared in *Ants in the Pantry*, *Pest Man Wins*, and *No Census, No Feeling*. The French maids were somewhat coquettish, while it is noted in Chapter 15 that the African American maids were portrayed as slow-witted or easily frightened.

Stooges as Women

The Three Stooges cross-dressed in many of their films. Sometimes this cross-dressing was done for burlesque comedy, or what feminist Mary Russo may have called the grotesque portrayal.[3] In some Stooges films, these men almost seem to be mocking feminine qualities, such as the Stooges dressed as little girls in *Nutty But Nice* and as ballerinas in *Rhythm and Weep*, and Larry as a homely maiden in *Knutzy Knights*. More often, though, the clothes were a disguise to help the Stooges escape from tight situations, such as eluding the police in *Mutts to You* and *Pop Goes the Easel* (which features Curly doing his best Mae West impersonation), fooling Southern military personnel in *Uncivil Warriors* and *Uncivil War Birds*, rescuing a captain while dressed as harem girls in *Wee Wee Monsieur*, and attempting to catch a crook in a ladies' sauna in *Blunder Boys*.

In some of their films, a single Stooge cross-dressed for purposes of deception, such as Curly's masquerades in *Mutts to You*, *Uncivil Warriors*, and *Uncivil Warbirds*, or the portrayals by Larry, who was a much more convincing female than the other Stooges, playing a young girl in *All the World's a Stooge* and Moronica in *Higher Than a Kite*. Much less convincing was Moe playing his own sister Birdie in *Hoofs and Goofs*. Probably the most effective and sincere portrayals of females by the Stooges came in the film *Self-Made Maids*, where all seven parts in the film are played by Moe, Larry, and Shemp (Moe actually played three parts). The Stooges portray themselves as well as their sweethearts, and Moe, Larry, and Shemp turn in somewhat convincing performances as female Stooges.

Four of the Stooges films have other men portraying women, and doing so more authentically than the Stooges. A midget with the stage name of "Little Billy," a man with a high-pitched voice, plays an annoying female patient in *Men in Black*. Joe Palma plays a maid who is trying to cheat Curly and his relatives out of an inheritance in *If a Body Meets a Body*. And Benny Rubin is a crook who disguises himself as an old lady in *Blunder Boys*.

The most significant portrayal of a woman by a man other than the Stooges was made by Monty Collins, who plays the Stooges' mother in *Cactus Makes Perfect*. Collins has several minutes of screen time and multiple lines of dialogue as the woman who spawned these three lunatics. Collins' portrayal of the alternately loving and violent mother is about as convincing a portrayal as one could ask for in the role of the Stooges' mother, much more so than the matronly portrayals by real women in *The Yoke's on Me* and *Up in Daisy's Penthouse*.

For Men Only

A close examination reveals that out of the 190 Stooges short films, 13 featured no (real) women whatsoever, even in crowds or other background.

Women did not usually receive a sympathetic portrayal. Here, the Stooges' mother is portrayed, rather effectively, by a male actor (Monty Collins) in *Cactus Makes Perfect* (1942).

These films are *We Want Our Mummy, Dizzy Detectives, Dizzy Pilots, A Gem of a Jam, Higher Than a Kite, Beer Barrel Polecats, A Bird in the Head, Malice in the Palace, Dunked in the Deep, Three Dark Horses, Creeps, Guns A-Poppin'!,* and *Oil's Well That Ends Well*. It is ironic that *Oil's Well That Ends Well* features no women at all, since it is a partial remake of *Oily to Bed, Oily to Rise*, a film whose plot revolved around women and featured them quite prominently.

The Stooges and Women

Comic actor John Cleese once offered that the reason the portrayals of women on episodes of *Monty Python's Flying Circus* were often so grotesque and bizarre was that most of the male actors doing the portrayals didn't actually know many real women, and therefore the characterizations were often quite askew. While the use of women in the comedies of the Three Stooges may not have been quite so strange as those of the *Python* troupe, one might argue that in many of their films the Stooges are striving for what Sedgewick

(1985, p. 470) has called a *homosocial* order. Most of the time the Stooges were existing without women, often living together in a platonic relationship, often even sleeping in the same bed. Even in several films where the Stooges were married, they were living with each other as well, under the same roof. And perhaps the best illustration of this order was that the Stooges' mother was most effectively portrayed by a man.

In examining the totality of the Stooges films, one sees that the Three Stooges exhibited an ambivalent attitude toward women. When the Stooges loved women, they did so in a most juvenile and even animalistic way. Their pet names for women, or those meant as terms of endearment, included *toots, babe, sweetheart,* and even *tomato.* But the Stooges' behavior was like that of lower life forms. When the Stooges pursued a woman, it was often without any sense of propriety whatsoever. When they were hoping to mate, the Stooges would often make howling or barking noises. As noted earlier, these unwanted advances frequently resulted in a face slap or a punch by the objects of their affection. Otherwise, the women would simply run away.

Conversely, the Stooges sometimes hated and despised women. Sometimes these feelings were with good cause, but at times they seemed almost pathological. Two films, for example, had as an overarching theme the hatred of women: the appropriately named *Woman Haters* and *Gypped in the Penthouse.* More typically, though, the Stooges' approach to women could be gruff, accusatory, and sometimes hateful. This was typified by their less-than-complimentary nicknames in these situations, which included *dame, tomato, beanpole, battleaxe, dragon, biddy, sister, gold digger,* and even *butch.*

Kathleen Chamberlain offers an explanation for this ambivalence. Says Chamberlain, "Since women always remain mysterious and even frightening to the Stooges, their presence helps emphasize the boys' position as oddballs who are never fully a part of the real world" (qtd. in von Busack 1997). Whatever fear or feelings of ambivalence the Stooges had toward women may be best typified in the surreal film *Cuckoo on a Choo Choo.* This short is replete with uncomplimentary references to the Stooges' traveling female companions. Larry, in a portrayal that has been compared to a young Marlon Brando (Okuda and Watz 1986, p. 72), demonstrates utter contempt for two sisters. A drunken Shemp hallucinates and falls in love with a giant canary named Carrie. Carrie is sweet and loving and, of course, sings like a bird. Carrie chirps, but cannot speak, and loves Shemp unconditionally. One might be led to wonder whether Shemp is visualizing his perfect female, even as one of the sisters is desperately seeking his attention and affections.

Chamberlain's position is that women are props in *all* of the Stooges' films, not just the ones identified as such within this chapter. In fact *everyone* is a prop to the Stooges in their films. She feels that their presence in these shorts is almost incidental. "Women are never fully realized as individuals," says Chamberlain (qtd. in von Busack 1997). But one would, in fact, be hard pressed to say that *anyone* in a short film is a fully realized individual, including the Stooges themselves. Only through the course of many, many films were the Stooges able to establish certain behavioral characteristics as palpable parts of their personalities. Women, perhaps more than other group of characters in the Stooges films (save white men and the Stooges themselves), approach some level of three-dimensionality.

Notes

1. Ed Williams, in his essay "Guys Love What Women Don't," lists the Stooges as the number one example of what men love and women loathe. 1 Jan. 2006. http://www.everydaybetterliving.com/understanding_women/guys_love_what_women_don't.html.
2. *Women Who Run with the Stooges.* 27 Dec. 2005. http://www.angelfire.com/ca4/stoogelovers/.
3. For example, see her carnival theory of cross-dressing males who appears as a pregnant woman (Russo 1986, pp. 213–227).

Works Cited

Boone, Joseph A. *Male Independence and the American Quest Genre.* New Brunswick, N.J.: Rutgers University Press, 1991.
Lehman, Christine A. *Women Who Run with the Stooges.* 1 Jan. 2006. http://www.angelfire.com/ca4/stoogelovers/.
Okuda, Ted, and Edward Watz. *The Columbia Comedy Shorts: Two-Reel Hollywood Film Comedies, 1933–1958.* Jefferson, N.C.: McFarland, 1986.
Russo, Mary. "Female Grotesques: Carnival and Theory." *Feminist Studies/Critical Studies,* Vol. 8, pp. 213–227. Ed. Teresa De Lauretis. Bloomington, Indiana: University of Indiana Press, 1986.
Sedgewick, Eve Kosofsky. *Between Men: English Literature and Male Homosocial Desire.* New York: Columbia University Press, 1985.
von Busack, Richard. "The Moe, Larry and Curly School of a Timeless Social Disorder." *Metro Santa Cruz,* 16–22 Jan. 1997. http://www.metroactive.com/papers/metro/01.16.97/cover/stooges1-9703.html.
Williams, Ed. "Guys Love What Women Don't." 1 Jan. 2006. http://www.everydaybetterliving.com/understanding_women/ guys_love_what_women_don't.html.

Appendix: Three Stooges Films for Columbia (1934–1959)

1934
1. *Woman Haters*
2. *Punch Drunks*
3. *Men in Black*
4. *Three Little Pigskins*

1935
5. *Horses' Collars*
6. *Restless Knights*
7. *Pop Goes the Easel*
8. *Uncivil Warriors*
9. *Pardon My Scotch*
10. *Hoi Polloi*
11. *Three Little Beers*

1936
12. *Ants in the Pantry*
13. *Movie Maniacs*
14. *Half-Shot Shooters*
15. *Disorder in the Court*
16. *A Pain in the Pullman*
17. *False Alarms*
18. *Whoops, I'm an Indian!*
19. *Slippery Silks*

1937
20. *Grips, Grunt and Groans*
21. *Dizzy Doctors*
22. *Three Dumb Clucks*
23. *Back to the Woods*
24. *Goofs and Saddles*
25. *Cash and Carry*
26. *Playing the Ponies*
27. *The Sitter Downers*

1938
28. *Termites of 1938*
29. *Wee Wee Monsieur*
30. *Tassels in the Air*
31. *Flat Foot Stooges*
32. *Healthy, Wealthy and Dumb*
33. *Violent Is the Word for Curly*
34. *Three Missing Links*
35. *Mutts to You*

1939
36. *Three Little Sew and Sews*
37. *We Want Our Mummy*
38. *A-Ducking They Did Go*
39. *Yes, We Have No Bonanza*

40. *Saved by the Belle*
41. *Calling All Curs*
42. *Oily to Bed, Oily to Rise*
43. *Three Sappy People*

1940

44. *You Nazty Spy!*
45. *Rockin' Through the Rockies*
46. *A Plumbing We Will Go*
47. *Nutty But Nice*
48. *How High is Up?*
49. *From Nurse to Worse*
50. *No Census, No Feeling*
51. *Cuckoo Cavaliers*
52. *Boobs in Arms*

1941

53. *So Long, Mr. Chumps*
54. *Dutiful but Dumb*
55. *All the World's a Stooge*
56. *I'll Never Heil Again*
57. *An Ache in Every Stake*
58. *In the Sweet Pie and Pie*
59. *Some More of Samoa*

1942

60. *Loco Boy Makes Good*
61. *Cactus Makes Perfect*
62. *What's the Matador?*
63. *Matri-Phony*
64. *Three Smart Saps*
65. *Even as IOU*
66. *Sock-a-Bye Baby*

1943

67. *They Stooge to Conga*
68. *Dizzy Detectives*
69. *Spook Louder*
70. *Back From the Front*
71. *Three Little Twirps*
72. *Higher Than a Kite*

73. *"I Can Hardly Wait"*
74. *Dizzy Pilots*
75. *Phony Express*
76. *A Gem of a Jam*

1944

77. *Crash Goes the Hash*
78. *Busy Buddies*
79. *The Yoke's on Me*
80. *Idle Roomers*
81. *Gents Without Cents*
82. *No Dough Boys*

1945

83. *Three Pests in a Mess*
84. *Booby Dupes*
85. *Idiots Deluxe*
86. *If a Body Meets a Body*
87. *Micro-Phonies*

1946

88. *Beer Barrel Polecats*
89. *A Bird in the Head*
90. *Uncivil War Birds*
91. *Three Troubledoers*
92. *Monkey Businessmen*
93. *Three Loan Wolves*
94. *G.I. Wanna Go Home*
95. *Rhythm and Weep*
96. *Three Little Pirates*

1947

97. *Half-Wits Holiday*
98. *Fright Night*
99. *Out West*
100. *Hold That Lion!*
101. *Brideless Groom*
102. *Sing a Song of Six Pants*
103. *All Gummed Up*

1948

104. *Shivering Sherlocks*
105. *Pardon My Clutch*
106. *Squareheads of the Roundtable*
107. *Fiddlers Three*
108. *The Hot Scots*
109. *Heavenly Daze*
110. *I'm a Monkey's Uncle*
111. *Mummy's Dummies*
112. *Crime on Their Hands*

1949

113. *The Ghost Talks*
114. *Who Done It?*
115. *Hokus Pokus*
116. *Fuelin' Around*
117. *Malice in the Palace*
118. *Vagabond Loafers*
119. *Dunked in the Deep*

1950

120. *Punchy Cowpunchers*
121. *Hugs and Mugs*
122. *Dopey Dicks*
123. *Love at First Bite*
124. *Self-Made Maids*
125. *Three Hams on Rye*
126. *Studio Stoops*
127. *Slaphappy Sleuths*
128. *A Snitch in Time*

1951

129. *Three Arabian Nuts*
130. *Baby Sitters Jitters*
131. *"Don't Throw That Knife"*
132. *Scrambled Brains*
133. *Merry Mavericks*
134. *The Tooth Will Out*
135. *Hula-La-La*
136. *Pest Man Wins*

1952

137. *A Missed Fortune*
138. *Listen, Judge*
139. *Corny Casanovas*
140. *He Cooked His Goose*
141. *Gents in a Jam*
142. *Three Dark Horses*
143. *Cuckoo on a Choo Choo*

1953

144. *Up in Daisy's Penthouse*
145. *Booty and the Beast*
146. *Loose Loot*
147. *Tricky Dicks*
148. *Spooks!*
149. *Pardon My Backfire*
150. *Rip, Sew and Stitch*
151. *Bubble Trouble*
152. *Goof on the Roof*

1954

153. *Income Tax Sappy*
154. *Musty Musketeers*
155. *Pals and Gals*
156. *Knutzy Knights*
157. *Shot in the Frontier*
158. *Scotched in Scotland*

1955

159. *Fling in the Ring*
160. *Of Cash and Hash*
161. *Gypped in the Penthouse*
162. *Bedlam in Paradise*
163. *Stone Age Romeos*
164. *Wham-Bam-Slam!*
165. *Hot Ice*
166. *Blunder Boys*

1956

167. *Husbands Beware*
168. *Creeps*

169. *Flagpole Jitters*
170. *For Crimin' Out Loud*
171. *Rumpus in the Harem*
172. *Hot Stuff*
173. *Scheming Schemers*
174. *Commotion on the Ocean*

1957

175. *Hoofs and Goofs*
176. *Muscle Up a Little Closer*
177. *A Merry Mix-Up*
178. *Space Ship Sappy*
179. *Guns A-Poppin'!*
180. *Horsing Around*

181. *Rusty Romeos*
182. *Outer Space Jitters*

1958

183. *Quiz Whizz*
184. *Fifi Blows Her Top*
185. *Pies and Guys*
186. *Sweet and Hot*
187. *Flying Saucer Daffy*
188. *Oil's Well That Ends Well*

1959

189. *Triple Crossed*
190. *Sappy Bullfighters*

Bibliography

Abate, Frank R., ed. "Surrealism." *Oxford Pocket American Dictionary of Current English*. Oxford: Oxford University Press, 2002.

Allen, Steve, and Jane Wollman. *How to Be Funny*. New York: McGraw-Hill, 1987.

Altman, Sig. *The Comic Image of the Jew: Explorations of a Pop Culture Phenomenon*. Rutherford, N.J.: Fairleigh Dickinson University Press, 1971.

Amos 'n' Andy: The Anatomy of a Controversy. Documentary. 1985.

"Andy Clyde Biography." Yahoo!Movies. 14 Dec. 2005. http://movies.yahoo.com/shop?d=hc&id=1800028008&cf=biog&intl=us.

Ausubel, Nathan. *A Treasury of Jewish Folklore*. New York: Crown, 1948.

Avisar, Ivan. *Screening the Holocaust*. Bloomington: Indiana University Press, 1988.

Baker, Robert K., David Lange, and Sandra Ball-Rokeach. "Mass Media and Violence: A Report to the National Commission on the Causes and Prevention of Violence," Vol. II. Washington, D.C.: U.S. Government Printing Office, 1969.

Balakian, Anna. *Surrealism: The Road to the Absolute*. New York: E.P. Dutton, 1970.

Bandura, Alfred, D. Ross, and S. A. Ross. "Imitation of Film Mediated Aggressive Models." *Journal of Abnormal Psychology* 66 (1963): 3–11.

Baum, L. Frank. *The Wonderful Wizard of Oz: 100th Anniversary Edition*. New York: HarperCollins, 2000.

Beckett, Samuel. *Waiting for Godot: A Tragicomedy in Two Acts*. New York: Grove, 1997.

Berg, Charles Ramirez. *Latin Images in Film*. Austin: University of Texas Press, 2002.

Bergman, Andrew. *We're in the Money: Depression America and Its Films*. New York: Harper and Row, 1971.

Besser, J. *Not Just a Stooge*. Houston: Excelsior, 1984.

Blocher, Henri. *Original Sin: Illuminating the Riddle*. Grand Rapids, Mich.: Eerdmans, 1999.

Bogle, Donald. *Toms, Coons, Mulattoes, Mammies, and Bucks: An Interpretive History of Blacks in American Films*. New York: Continuum, 1989.

Boone, Joseph A. *Male Independence and the American Quest Genre*. New Brunswick, N.J.: Rutgers University Press, 1991.

Boyer, Jay. "The Schlemiezel: Black Humor and the Shtetl Tradition." *Semites and Stereotypes: Characteristics of Jewish Humor*. Ed. Avner Ziv and Anat Zadjman. Contributions in Eth-

nic Studies 31. Westport, Conn.: Greenwood, 1993.
Brunette, Peter. "The Three Stooges and the (Anti-)Narrative of Violence: De(con)structive Comedy." *Comedy, Cinema, Theory*. Ed. Andrew Horton. Berkeley: University of California Press, 1991.
Bruskin, David N., ed. *Behind the Three Stooges: The White Brothers: Conversations with David N. Bruskin*. Metuchen, N.J.: Directors Guild of America, 1984.
Burr, Lonnie. *Two for the Show: Great 20th Century Comedy Teams*. New York: Messner, 1979.
Burtt, E. A. *Teachings of the Compassionate Buddha*. New York: Signet, 1955.
Cantor, Eddie, as told to David Freedman. *My Life Is in Your Hands*. New York: Blue Ribbon, 1932.
Carone, James (as told by Larry Fine). *Stroke of Luck*. Hollywood: Siena, 1973.
Chamberlain, Kathleen. "The Three Stooges and the Commedia dell'Arte." *The Film Comedy Reader*. Ed. Gregg Rickman. New York: Limelight, 2002.
Chaplin, Charles. *My Autobiography*. New York: Simon and Schuster, 1964
Cohen, Sarah Blacher. "Yiddish Origins and Jewish-American Transformations." *From Hester Street to Hollywood: The Jewish-American Stage and Screen*. Ed. Sarah Blacher Cohen. Bloomington: Indiana University Press, 1986.
Cole, Jeffrey, director. "The UCLA Television Violence Report 1996." Part III. Accessed 24 Jan. 2006. http://www.digitalcenter.org/webreport95/netfind.htm.
Culbert, David E. *Film and Propaganda in America: A Documentary History*. Vol. II. New York: Greenwood, 1990.
Dardis, Tom. *Keaton: The Man Who Wouldn't Lie Down*. New York: Limelight, 1979.
Dick, Bernard F. *The Star Spangled Screen*. Lexington: University of Kentucky Press, 1985.

Douglas, Mary. "Jokes." *Rethinking Popular Culture*. Ed. Chandra Mukerji and Michael Schudson. Berkeley, University of California Press, 1991.
Dumbrille, Erwin. Personal correspondence. 5 July and 27 July 1991.
Edelstein, David. "Moe Better Blues: Are the Three Stooges Martyrs, Demons, or Anti-Role Models?" *Slate Magazine*, 21 April 2000. Accessed 8 Oct. 2005. http://slate.msn.com/id/80966.
Ellis, Edward Robb. *A Nation in Torment*. New York: Coward-McCann, 1970.
Ely, Melvin Patrick. *Holy Mackerel: The Amos 'n' Andy Story*. New York: E.P. Dutton, 1986.
Epstein, Lawrence J. *Mixed Nuts: America's Love Affair with Comedy Teams from Burns and Allen to Belushi and Aykroyd*. New York: PublicAffairs, 2004.
Erens, Patricia. *The Jew in American Cinema*. Bloomington: Indiana University Press, 1984.
Eyles, Allen. *The Complete Films of the Marx Brothers*. Secaucus, N.J.: Citadel, 1992.
Feshbach, S. "The Stimulating versus Cathartic Effects of a Vicarious Aggressive Activity." *Journal of Abnormal Psychology* 63 (1961): 181–185.
Fineburg, Morris. *Larry, the Stooge in the Middle*. San Francisco: Last Gasp, 2001.
Fleming, Michael. *The Three Stooges: An Illustrated History*. New York: Random House, 1999.
Forester, Jeffrey. *The Stoogephile Trivia Book*. Chicago: Contemporary, 1982.
Freud, Sigmund. *The Ego and the Id: The Standard Edition of the Complete Psychological Works of Sigmund Freud*. New York: Norton, 1962.
_____. *Jokes and Their Relation to the Unconscious*. Trans. James Strachey. New York: Norton, 1960.
_____. *New Introductory Lectures on Psychoanalysis*. Trans. W. J. H. Sprout. New York: Norton, 1933.
_____. "An Outline of Psychoanalysis."

International Journal of Psychoanalysis (1940): 21–84.
Friedman, Lester D. *The Jewish Image in American Film*. Secaucus, N.J.: Citadel, 1987.
Friedrich, Otto. *City of Nets: A Portrait of Hollywood in the 1940s*. New York: Harper and Row, 1986.
Gabler, Neal. *An Empire of Their Own: How the Jews Invented Hollywood*. New York: Crown, 1988.
Galian, Laurence. *Beyond Duality: The Art of Transcendence*. Scottsdale, Ariz.: New Falcon, 1995.
Gerbner, George. "Toward 'Cultural Indicators': The Analysis of Mediated Message Systems." *AV Communication Review* 17, no. 2 (1969): 137–148.
Giddins, Gary. "There Ain't No Sanity Claus." *The New York Times on the Web*, 18 June 2000. Book review of *Groucho: The Life and Times of Julius Henry Marx*, by Stefan Kanfer. Accessed 16 Dec. 2005. <http://partners.nytimes.com/books/00/06/18/reviews/000618.18giddent.html>.
Golab, Caroline. "Stellaaaaaa ... ... !!!!!! The Slavic Stereotype in American Film." *The Kaledioscopic Lens: How Hollywood Views Ethnic Groups*. Ed. Randall Miller. Englewood, N.J.: Jerome S. Ozer, 1980.
Goldberg, Judith. *Laughter through Tears: The Yiddish Cinema*. Rutherford, N.J.: Fairleigh Dickinson University Press, 1983.
Golden, Daniel Sembroff. "The Fate of La Famiglia: Italian Images in American Film." *The Kaledioscopic Lens: How Hollywood Views Ethnic Groups*. Ed. Randall Miller. Englewood, N.J.: Jerome S. Ozer, 1980.
Graver, Lawrence. *Beckett: Waiting for Godot*. Cambridge: Cambridge University Press, 2004.
Hapkiewicz, W. G. "Children's Reactions to Cartoon Violence." *Journal of Clinical Child Psychology* 8 (1979): 30–34.
Hedley, George Percy. *The Holy Trinity: Experience and Interpretation*. Minneapolis: Fortress, 2004.
Helitzer, Melvin. *Comedy Writing Secrets*. Cincinnati: Writer's Digest Books, 1987.
Heller, Melvin S., and Samuel Polsky. *Studies in Violence and Television*. New York: American Broadcasting Co., 1976.
Herman, Arthur. "The Tobaccomen of Glasgow and the Myth of Scottish Thrift." In *Character*, Fall 2004. Accessed 27 Jan. 2006. http://www.incharacter.org/article.php?article=11.
Hodge, Robert, and David Tripp. *Children and Television: A Semiotic Approach*. Stanford, Calif.: Stanford University Press, 1986.
Howard, Moe. *Moe Howard and the Three Stooges*. Secaucus, N.J.: Citadel, 1977.
Huff, Theodore. *Charlie Chaplin*. New York: Henry Schuman, 1951.
James, Richard. "The Holy Fool." 28 Dec. 2005. http://www.haze.ca/fez/fool.html.
Jowett, Garth. *Film: The Democratic Art*. Boston: Little, Brown, 1976.
Kaufman, Rhoda. "The Yiddish Theater in New York and the Immigrant Jewish Community: Theater as Secular Ritual." Diss. UC Berkeley 1986; UMI Diss. Information Service, printed 1993.
Kaufmann, Walter. *Existentialism: From Dostoevsky to Sartre*. New York: Plume, 1988.
Kerr, Walter. *Tragedy and Comedy*. New York: Simon and Schuster, 1967.
Kilpatrick, Jacqueline. *Celluloid Indians*. Lincoln: University of Nebraska Press, 1999.
Kluge, Daniel. "Psychoanalysis and Film." Dallas Society for Psychoanalytic Psychology Fairhill Scholarship Competition 1999–2000. Undergraduate Division. Accessed 26 Dec. 2005. http://www.dspp.com/papers/kluge.htm.
Knapp, Karlfried. "What's German? Remarks on German Identity." *EESE*,

October 1995, pp. 203–228. Accessed 16 Dec. 2005. http://webdoc.sub.gwdg.de/edoc/ia/eese/articles/knapp/10_95.html.
Koppes, Clayton R., and Gregory D. Black. *Hollywood Goes to War*. Berkeley: University of California Press, 1987.
Kurson, Robert. *The Official Three Stooges Encyclopedia*. Chicago: Contemporary, 1998.
Langman, Larry. "Slapstick," "The Three Stooges," "Howard, Moe, Shemp, Curly." *Encyclopedia of American Film Comedy*. New York: Garland, 1987.
Lehman, Christine A. *Women Who Run with the Stooges*. 1 Jan. 2006. http://www.angelfire.com/ca4/stoogelovers/
Lenburg, Jeff, Joan Howard Maurer, and Greg Lenburg. *The Three Stooges Scrapbook*. Secaucus, N.J.: Citadel Press, 1982.
Letham, Robert. *The Holy Trinity: In Scripture, History, Theology and Worship*. Phillipsburg: P&R, 2005.
Lipman, Steve. *Laughter in Hell: The Use of Humor during the Holocaust*. Northvale, N.J.: Jason Aronson, 1991.
Lucie-Smith, Edward. *Art of the 1930s: The Age of Anxiety*. New York: Rizzoli, 1985.
"Malapropism." *The Compact Edition of the Oxford English Dictionary*. Oxford: Oxford University Press, 1971.
Maltin, Leonard. *The Great Movie Shorts*. New York: Crown, 1972.
_____. *Movie Comedy Teams*. New York: New American Library, 1985.
_____. *Of Mice and Magic: A History of American Animated Cartoons*. New York: McGraw-Hill, 1980.
Margolin, Victor. "Forward." *Propaganda: The Art and Persuasion of World War II*. Ed. Anthony Rhodes. New York: Chelsea, 1976.
Marx, Karl. *Karl Marx: Economy, Class and Social Revolution*. New York: Scribner, 1975.
McDonald, J. Fred. *Blacks and White TV*. Chicago: Nelson-Hall, 1992.
McElvaine, Robert S. *The Great Depression: America, 1929–1941*. New York: Times Books, 1984.
Minsky, Morton, and Milt Machlin. *Minsky's Burlesque*. New York: Arbor House, 1986.
Mitchell, Charles P. *The Hitler Filmography: Worldwide Feature Film and Television Miniseries Portrayals, 1940 through 2000*. Jefferson N.C.: McFarland, 2000.
Morlan, Don B. "An Analysis of the Three Stooges' Contributions to World War II Propaganda: Dictator Moe Hailstone, et al." Paper presented at the conference of the Popular Culture Association, San Antonio, 1991.
_____. "Slapstick Contributions to Pre–WWII Film Propaganda: The Three Stooges and Abbott & Costello." Paper presented at the conference of the Popular Culture Association, New Orleans, 1993.
_____. "The Three Stooges' Contributions to WWII Propaganda: Moe Hailstone and Adenoid Hynkel's Race to the Screen." Paper presented at the conference of the Popular Culture Association, Louisville, 1992.
Morreall, John. "Humor in the Holocaust. Its Critical, Cohesive, and Coping Functions." *Scholar's Conference Papers 1990–2000* (from the Annual Scholars' Conference on the Holocaust and the Churches). Ed. Marcia Sachs Littell. CD-ROM, Vista-Intermedia.
Motion Picture Herald, 27 Jan. 1940.
Nye, Gerald P. "Our Madness Increases as Our Emergency Shrinks." *Vital Speeches*, Vol. 7 (15 Sept. 1941), pp. 720–723.
Oehling, Richard A. "The Yellow Menace: Asian Images in American Film." *The Kaleidoscopic Lens: How Hollywood Views Ethnic Groups*. Ed. Randall M. Miller. Englewood N.J.: Jerome S. Ozer, 1980.
Okuda, Ted, and Edward Watz. *The Columbia Comedy Shorts: Two-Reel Hollywood Film Comedies, 1933–1958*. Jefferson N.C.: McFarland, 1986.

Olson, Kirby. *Comedy after Postmodernism.* Lubbock: Texas Tech University Press, 2001.

"Pathos." *American Heritage Dictionary.* New York: Dell, 1976.

Pearson, Glenda, compiler. "The Red Scare: A Filmography." *All Powers Project.* 5 March 1998. University of Washington Libraries. Accessed 16 Dec. 2005. http://www.lib.washington.edu/EXHIBITS/ALLPOWERS/film.html.

Perret, Gene. *How to Write and Sell Your Sense of Humor.* Cincinnati: Writer's Digest Books, 1982.

Pierce, Charles P. "Woise Guys." *The Boston Globe,* 27 Feb. 2005. http://www.boston.com/ae/movies/articles/2005/02/27/woiise_guys?pg=ful.

Plutarch. *Plutarch's Lives: Cicero.* Trans. Dryden; corrected and rev. Arthur Hugh Clough. Harvard Classics, Vol. 12. New York: P. F. Collier & Sons, 1909.

Reddick, Lawrence. "Of Motion Pictures." *Black Films and Film-Makers.* Ed. Lindsay Patterson. New York: Dodd, Mead, 1975.

Redfern, Walter. *Puns.* New York: Basil Blackwell, 1984.

Revel, Herschel. "Schlemiel." *Universal Jewish Encyclopedia.* New York: Ktav, 1943.

Robinson, David. *Chaplin: His Life and Art.* New York: McGraw-Hill, 1985.

Rogin, Michael. *Blackface, White Noise: Jewish Immigrants in the Hollywood Melting Pot.* Berkeley: University of California Press, 1996.

Rosenberg, Joel. "Jewish Experience on Film: An American Overview." *American Jewish Yearbook 1996.* New York: American Jewish Committee, 1996.

Russo, Mary. "Female Grotesques: Carnival and Theory." *Feminist Studies/Critical Studies,* Vol. 8, pp. 213–227. Ed. Teresa De Lauretis. Bloomington: Indiana University Press, 1986.

Samover, Larry, and Jack Mills. *Oral Communication: Messages and Response.* Dubuque: Wm. C. Brown, 1986.

Sandrow, Nahma. *Vagabond Stars: A World History of Yiddish Theater.* Jewish Publication Society of America. New York: Harper, 1977.

Saper, Bernard. "Since When Is Jewish Humor Not Anti-Semitic?" *Semites and Stereotypes: Characteristics of Jewish Humor.* Ed. Avner Ziv and Anat Zadjman. Contributions in Ethnic Studies 31. Westport, Conn.: Greenwood, 1993.

Sedgewick, Eve Kosofsky. *Between Men: English Literature and Male Homosocial Desire.* New York: Columbia University Press, 1985.

Seely, Peter. "Didn't I Disbar You Three Years Ago? Positive and Negative Portrayals of African Americans in Amos 'n' Andy." Paper presented at the Popular Culture Conference, 1997.

Shaheen, Jack G. "Address to the Washington Press Club." C-Span 2. 27 March 2004.

_____. *Reel Bad Arabs.* New York: Interlink Publishing Group, 2001.

"Shtik." *Oxford English Dictionary.* CD-ROM. Oxford: Oxford University Press, 1999.

Skeat, Walter W. *Concise Etymological Dictionary of the English Language.* New York: Cosimo Classics, 2005.

"Slapstick." *Oxford English Dictionary.* CD-ROM. Oxford: Oxford University Press, 1999.

Smith, Stacy L., Barbara J. Wilson, Dale Kunkel, Daniel Linz, James Potter, Carolyn M. Colvin, Edward Donnerstein, Jay M. Berhardt, Jane Brown, Shelley Golden, Ellen Wartella, Charles Whitney, Dominic Lasorsa, Wayne Danielson, Adrianna Olivarez, Nancy Jennings, Rafael Lopez, Joanne Cantor, and Amy Nathanson. "National Television Violence Study." Volume 3. 21 Jan. 2006. http://www.ccsp.ucsb.edu/execsum.pdf.

Snyder, Jane. *Puns and Poetry in Lucretius'*

De Rerum Natura. Amsterdam: John Benjamin, 1980.

Snyder, Robert W. *The Voice of the City: Vaudeville and Popular Culture in New York*. New York: Oxford University Press, 1989.

Sobel, Bernard. *A Pictorial History of Vaudeville*. New York: Citadel, 1961.

Sobel, Raoul, and David Francis. *Chaplin: Genesis of a Clown*. London: Quartet, 1977.

Spatt, Dave. "Stoogology, or The Stooge in You." OSLA Arts & Law Home Page. 1994. Accessed 26 Dec. 2005. http://www.artslaw.org/Stooge.htm.

"Supporting Cast for the 3 Stooges: Dudley Dickerson." Ed. O. T. Express and O. T. Packer. 20 Dec. 2005. http://members.aol.com/otpacker/support.html.

"Surrealism." *Phaidon Dictionary of Twentieth-Century Art*. New York: Phaidon, 1973.

Telushkin, Rabbi Joseph. *Jewish Humor: What the Best Jewish Jokes Say about the Jews*. New York: William Morrow, 1992.

Thomas, Bob. *King Cohn: The Life and Times of Harry Cohn*. London: Barrie and Rockliff, 1967.

Thorp, Margaret Farrand. *America at the Movies*. New Haven: Yale University Press, 1939.

Vaudeville. Video documentary, American Masters Series. WGBH-Boston, 26 Nov. 1997.

von Busack, Richard. "The Moe, Larry and Curly School of a Timeless Social Disorder." *Metro Santa Cruz*, 16–22 Jan. 1997. http://www.metroactive.com/papers/metro/01.16.97/cover/stooges1-9703.html.

_____. "Pure Slap Shtick." *Metro Santa Cruz*, 16–22 Jan. 1997. Accessed 26 Dec. 2005. http://www.ratical.com/ratville/3stooges75yrs.html.

Weiner, Richard. *Dictionary of Media and Communications*. New York: Webster's New World, 1990.

Wiley, Tatha. *Original Sin: Origins, Developments, Contemporary Meanings*. Mahwah: Paulist N.J.: 2002.

Williams, Ed. "Guys Love What Women Don't." 1 Jan. 2006. http://www.everydaybetterliving.com/understanding_women/guys_love_what_women_don't.html.

"Word play." 7 Dec. 2005. en.wikipedia.org/wiki/Word_play.

Yablokoff, Herman. *Der Payatz: Around the World with Yiddish Theater*. Trans. Bella Mysell. Silver Springs, Md.: Bartleby, 1995

Zettl, Herbert. *Sight Sound Motion: Applied Media Aesthetics*. Belmont, Calif.: Wadsworth, 1976.

Contributors

Kathleen Chamberlain is a professor of English and women's studies at Emory & Henry College in Virginia. Among her publications are essays on Lizzie Borden, Nancy Drew, girls' series fiction, and the Three Stooges. Currently, she is working on a book-length study of American girls' school stories.

Ted Levitt has a degree in comparative religion from Miami University (Ohio) and an MLS from Kent State University. He is a librarian in Alameda, California, an island in the Bay. Since writing a thesis about Yukio Mishima, he has pursued an interest in contemporary Japanese literature and culture. At about the same time, he discovered the Three Stooges Fan Club and has been researching, collecting, and convening with other fans for many years. He has lately been researching a vast array of written sources with an intention of compiling an extensive bibliography about the Stooges in American (primarily) literature. He also has an idea for a novel about the Stooges as they might have been had they been born in Japan, contemporaries of Mishima.

Don Morlan received his Ph.D degree in communication from Purdue University in 1969. He held academic positions at Indiana State University and Eastern Illinois University before joining the University of Dayton as department chair and professor of communication. His research and publication interests have been primarily in the area of popular culture with special emphasis in slapstick comedy film history and World War II film propaganda. After 25 years, he retired as professor emeritus from the University of Dayton in 2001 and currently resides in St. Germain, Wisconsin.

Gail W. Pieper is an adjunct professor at Benedictine University and a technical editor and writer at Argonne National Laboratory. She is coeditor of *A Heretic in American Journalism Education and Research: Malcolm S. Maclean*

(2001) and *Understanding the Funnies: Critical Interpretations of Comic Strips* (1997). She has also co-edited several books on artificial intelligence, so the transition to the Stooges seemed the logical next step!

Lynn Rapaport is a professor of sociology at Pomona College. She received her Ph.D. in sociology from Columbia University. She is the author of *Jews in Germany after the Holocaust: Memory, Identity, and Jewish-German Relations* (Cambridge University Press, 1997), which won the 1998 Most Distinguished Publication Award in the Sociology of Religion from the American Sociological Association. She is currently working on a project on how the Holocaust is portrayed in popular culture.

Faye Ringel is a professor of humanities and director of the honors programs at the U.S. Coast Guard Academy, New London, Connecticut. She is the author of *New England's Gothic Literature: History and Folklore of the Supernatural* (Mellen, 1995). The subjects of her articles and conference papers include the American Gothic, urban legends, demonic cooks, medievalism, Lovecraft, Tolkien, Yiddish folklore, and ballads. She is also a pianist and singer of popular and traditional music, having recorded the CD *Hot Chestnuts: Old Songs, Endearing Charms*. She is active in many scholarly organizations, including the New England Association of Teachers of English, the International Association for the Fantastic in the Arts, and the Northeast Popular Culture Association.

Peter Seely is a professor and the department chair of Communication Arts at Benedictine University in Lisle, Illinois. He has been a fan of the Three Stooges since he was old enough to talk, watching them daily on WGN-TV in Chicago. Professor Seely is also the former program director of the Media Workshops, a national program for high school and college students wanting to experience firsthand the inner workings of the mass media. He has published book chapters on the images of males in television advertising and on the future of communications education. He regularly participates in the conferences of the Popular Culture Association and American Culture Association, writing on the Three Stooges, non–Stooges Columbia comedians, the *Honeymooners*, *The Dick Van Dyke Show*, *Amos 'n' Andy*, Glam Rock, and budget-line records.

Brent Seguine first saw the Three Stooges at a young age, watching TV host Sally Starr televise their short subjects on Philadelphia's WFIL Channel 6, and was able to experience Stoogemania as it swept the country in the early 1960s. For the past 40+ years Brent has remained an avid fan. He has compiled a complete video library of their existing films, as well as all of the Stooges shorts and most of their feature films and cartoons on 16mm. A contributor to *The Three Stooges Journal*, he regularly travels to the West Coast to research the comedy team's scripts in the Jules White Collection of the Motion Picture Academy's library and to meet and interview Stooge costars. Brent's interest in film comedy also includes the work of Laurel & Hardy, W. C. Fields, Abbott & Costello, and Buster Keaton, and he is an active member of several film appreciation societies such as the Sons of the Desert. A 1980 graduate of James Madison University in Virginia, Brent works in corporate finance, currently as the controller and finance manager of Novus Fine Chemicals, a pharmaceutical chemical manufacturer.

Tim Snyder, a life-long Stooges fan, holds a Ph.D. in developmental psychology from the University of Akron. He is currently a professor of psychology at Lander University, where he has taught for 17 years. His research interests include cognitive and memory development in children and older adults, and the teaching of psychology. Dr. Snyder has been the chair of the Division of Behavioral Sciences and the Division of History and Political Sciences at Lander University, as well as the chair of the faculty senate.

Index

A-Ducking They Did Go 19
A Plumbing We Will Go: American Negro 186, 187; antisociety comments 125; British butler 218; Curly 125; Dudley Dickerson 186, 187; hole in the floor 91; jump cut 73; puns 17, 19; remakes 88; water stunt 37, 218
Abbott and Costello 138, 154
An Ache in Every Stake: 21, 126; Boniface in 239; chef 223; claims as experts 170n.9; ridicule of rich 126
actor miscues 79
actors in Columbia Studios films 90
African American in Stooges films 187
Africans, black 191
All Gummed Up 77, 213
All the World's a Stooge: acting errors 80; antisociety comments 126; British butler 218; Larry as young girl 246; puns 16, 20
America-first 150, 155
American Indians 199–204
Amos 'n' Andy 179, 193, 198, 213
animals in film 34, 79
antiaristocracy theme 120
Ants in the Pantry: animal set errors 79; boss 222; British butler 218; French maids 221, 245; Germans 222; pests 125; puns 17, 18
Arabs 208–215
automatic dialogue replacement 74

babes 243
Baby Sitters Jitters 24, 92
Back from the Front: cooked turkey stunt 32; Germans satirized 224; Hitler and Japanese satirized 158, 162, 165; military theme 145; Nazi references 164, 170n.6; wordplay 21
Back to Bataan 173
Back to the Woods: helpless maidens 244; Indians 201, 202, 203, 204; time distortions 35; wordplay 18
badkhen clown 131
bandido 204
Bedlam in Paradise: animal-like props 79; babes 243; McDaniel cut 106n.5; pictures alive 37, 38; Shemp invisible 34; wordplay 26
Beer Barrel Polecats: errors in remakes 75; illustration 4; jump shot 74; no women in 247; puns 16, 22
Besser, Joe 5, 102, 141
Beulah 196n.2
A Bird in the Head: mad scientist 222; no women in 247; puns 16, 22; storyline errors 74
Birth of a Nation 179, 181–182
black African vs. American Negro 190
black natives of South Seas 193–194
blackface 133, 191
Blake, Larry 152
Blunder Boys: beauty expert 221; man playing woman 246; Stooges as women 246; stunt double errors 78; wordplay 26
Bobo doll and violence 110
Boniface, Symona 57, 119, 120, 228
Boobs in Arms: depressed wife 245; gender deconstruction 233; military theme 145; parody of films 231, 234n.5; Prussian officer 222; soldier's walk Col-9;

265

violence 115; woman substitute 231; wordplay 20
Booby Dupes 22, 243
Booty and the Beast 77, 189
Breen, Joseph 149, 150
Brendel, El 88
Brideless Groom 23, 240, 241, 242
British stereotypes 217
Bubble Trouble 25, 77, 243
Busy Buddies 22

Cactus Makes Perfect 16, 21, 246, 247
Calling All Curs: American Negro maid 185, 194; Jewish elements 167; maids 245; pet costs and antisociety comments 125; puns 16, 19; vector changes 75
Cantor, Eddie 14, 124, 133
Capra, Frank 122
Cartoons, violence in 110
Cash and Carry: pathos 107, 227, 244; wall trap 92; wordplay 18
catharsis theory of media violence 112
censorship 156
Chaplin, Charlie: censorship of films 151; Great Dictator 152; Hitler depiction of 147, 152; pathos in films 102; surrealism in films 32
Chase, Charley 86
Clark, Bennett 150
clay fights 120
clowns 130, 204
Clyde, Andy 85–86, 89
Cohn, Harry 154, 158, 166
Cold War and film portrayals 223
Cullins, Monty 87
Columbia "difference" 84
Columbia Pictures 5, 42, 76, 78
Columbia Studios 87–89
comedy coexistence with tragedy 101
comedy shorts 82
commedia dell'arte 126, 233n.1
Commotion on the Ocean: military theme 145; post-Shemp 40, 78; remake errors 78; Russian spy 223; voice/motion mismatch 74; wordplay 26
continuity errors 51, 74
cops as Irish stereotype 220
Corny Casanovas 25, 76, 240
Crash Goes the Hash: antisociety comments 126; butler 90; script reused 88; society dame 239, 240; wordplay 22
cream puff fights 120
Creeps: creature's head alive 37; frog and hat gag 32; haunted suit of armor 91, 92; skeleton 33; women absent 247; wordplay 26
Crime on Their Hands: gorilla talking 28, 34; gun moll 241; plot from Clyde film 89; puns 16, 24
Cuckoo Cavaliers: hot towel 91; illustration 206; Latino stereotype 205–207; pathos 106; wordplay 20, 25
Cuckoo on a Choo Choo: ambivalence toward women 248; animal props 79; hallucinations 39; pathos 106; train stolen 35, 40; wordplay 25
Curly (Jerome Howard): cameo role after strokes 59; era 6–7; id-like behavior 95, 140; Mae West impersonation 231, 246; movie successes 134; pathos in films 104; pie fight scene 119; star soprano 126; switch with Larry 53, 57
Curly Joe (Joe DeRita) 8–9, 141

Dadaism and surrealism 31
Dalí and surrealism 31, 38
déjà vu and surrealism 32
democratic art 168
Dent, Vernon 90
Depression era 118, 121–122
DeRita, Joe 8–9, 141
dialogue errors 76
Dickerson, Dudley 186–189, 195, 196
dinner party mishaps 125
Disorder in the Court: actor miscues 79; fan dancer 244; puns 17, 18; talking bird 92
ditz 245
diva 243
Dizzy Detectives: malapropisms 14; no women 247; script reused 89; wordplay 18, 21
Dizzy Doctors 74, 241
Dizzy Pilots 22, 234n.8, 247
Don't Throw That Knife 24, 37, 40
Dopey Dicks 24, 34, 77
doubles, stunt errors with 77
dualism, Western 138
Dunked in the Deep: dialogue replacement 74; military theme 145; Russian spy 223; women absent 247; wordplay 24
Dutiful But Dumb 20, 34, 36, 40, 145

editing errors 73
Educational studio 85
ego 97, 140
Egyptians in film 210
European stereotypes 217
Even as IOU 21, 107

False Alarms: jump cut 73; pathos 105; ugly woman 230, 242; wordplay 18
Fascism 148
feminist theory 236
Fiddler's Three 23, 28, 35, 36
Fifi Blows Her Top: babes 243; guns 91; Italian sweetheart 223, 225n.1; military theme 145; pathos 105, 106; sweethearts 221, 222, 244; wordplay 27
film cost and mistakes 71, 80
Flagpole Jitters: continuity errors 74; flagpole stunt 91, 92; man beater 240; outwitted by furniture 91; showgirls 244; wordplay 26
Flat Foot Stooges 16, 19, 106
Fling in the Ring 26, 76, 90, 243
Flying Saucer Daffy 27, 34, 107, 243
For Crimin' Out Loud: continuity errors 76; last of Shemp films 8; puns 16, 26; stunt double errors 76, 78; water stunt 37; woman with man's voice 34
French Foreign Legion 220
French stereotypes 220
Freud 96, 140, 169
Fright Night: babes 243; continuity errors 76; puns 17, 23; Wessell 90
From Nurse to Worse 19, 187
Fuelin' Around; claims as experts 170n.9; military theme 148; puns 17, 24; remake 76; Russian ruler 224; strong woman 242; stunt doubles errors 778
fumbled lines 76

games with Allied and Axis powers 163
A Gem of a Jam: American Negro 91, 187; Dudley Dickerson 187–188, 196n.4; illustration 188; no women 247; wordplay 22
gender substitution 231–232
Gents in a Jam 25, 106, 243
Gents Without Cents: Niagara Falls scene 43; three women 243, 244; wordplay 22; World War II at home 158
German expansionism mocked 161
German stereotypes 222
The Ghost Talks: creature's head alive 37; frog and hat gag 32, 92; haunted suit of armor 33; production errors 77; skeleton 38; wordplay 24
ghosts and paranormal 33
G.I. Wanna Go Home 145, 167, 244
Gold Diggers of 1933 122
golf parody 125
Goof on the Roof 25, 78
Goofs and Saddles 17, 18, 79, 245

The Great Dictator 152, 155
Green, Dee 241
Griffith, D.W. 200
Grips Grunts and Groans 18
Guadalcanal Diary 173
gun molls 240
Guns A-Poppin'!: bear driver 34; pathos 106; remake errors 76; women absent 247; wordplay 27
Gypped in the Penthouse 26, 79, 248

Hailstone the dictator 153, 154
Half-Shot Shooters 89, 99, 145, 167
Half-Wits Holiday: Curly ill 7, 57–59; make-believe food 37; pie fight 119, 125, 239; society dames 239; wordplay 23
Hallelujah 190, 196n.7
Hallucinations 39
harlot, Latino 204
Have Rocket Will Travel 16
Hays, William Harrison 156
Hays Office 156
He Cooked His Goose: stock footage used 76; voice like a bird 34; women secretaries 245; wordplay 25
Healthy Wealthy and Dumb: antisociety comedy 125; bad women 228; gold diggers 232, 240; mock Indian dialect 203; sexual predators 228; wordplay 19
Healy, Ted: early work 4; leader of Stooges 4; straight man 140; use of wordplay 15
Heavenly Daze: American Negro 189–190; animal-like props 79; antisociety comments 126; pictures alive 37, 38; Shemp invisible 34; wordplay puns 9
The Heckler 86
Higher Than a Kite: Larry as girl 246; military theme 145; Nazis/Axis powers mocked 158, 162, 164; no women 247; wordplay 21
Hitler, Adolf: "death list" 170; Chaplin as 147; comic buffoon 160; common man 160; German attitude toward 157; Japanese version satirized 162; portrayal in *Man Hunt* 149; portrayal in *The Mortal Storm* 148
Hoi Polloi: jump cut 73; pie fight 125; ugly woman 242; wordplay 18
Hokus Pokus: flagpole stunt 92; gun molls 241; outwitted by furniture 91; vector change 75; wordplay 24
Hold That Lion!: American Negro 91, 189; Curly cameo role 7, 59; Dudley Dickerson 91, 189; fumbled lines 77; puns 16, 23

Hollywood and short films 83
Holy Fool 139
Holy Trinity and the Stooges 139
homosocial messages 237, 248
Hoofs and Goofs: landlord 222; Moe as sister 246; pathos 105, 106; reincarnation as horse 33; wordplay 27
Horses' Collars: helpless maidens 227, 244; radios 34; television 37; wordplay 17
Horsing Around 27, 33
Hot Ice: gorilla keeper 218; gun moll 218, 240, 241; man beater 240; plot from Clyde film 89; wordplay 26
The Hot Scots: Arab stereotyping 214; ghosts 32; gun molls 241; pictures alive 37; Scots stereotype 218, 219; skeleton 33; wordplay 23
Hot Stuff: experts 170n.9; man beater 240; military theme 145; remake errors 76, 78; Russian ruler 224; strong women 242; stunt doubles errors 78; wordplay 26
How High Is Up? 19
Howard, Jerome *see* Curly
Hugs and Mugs 24, 241
Hula-La-La: idol alive 38; mockery of Negro 190, 193; wordplay 25
humor, functions of 162
Husbands Beware 26, 240, 241, 242

I Can Hardly Wait 21, 91
id and Curly 97, 140
Idiots Deluxe 22, 76, 106
Idle Roomers 22, 33, 244
If a Body Meets a Body 7, 22, 32, 246
I'll Never Heil Again: bully 131; early release of 158; games of Allied and Axis 162, 163; Hailstone mocked 159, 164, 165, 169; homage to Chaplin 154; Japanese mocked 175, 177; Jewish elements 167; military theme 145; mockery of Negro 190; Thanatos 99; turbaned leader 215; wordplay 16, 21, 164, 169, 170, 170n.5
I'm a Monkey's Uncle: animal props 79; chimes 92; Stone Age women 242, 244; ugly woman 229, 242; wordplay 24
In the Sweet Pie and Pie: jump cut 73; malapropisms 14; miraculous appearance of saw 35; pie fights 119; puns 16, 21
Income Tax Sappy: American Negro maid 185, 194; dinner party mishaps 124; inspector's wife 221, 222; maids 245; neutral Negro 194; revenue agent 221; wordplay 25
inhuman beings 34
Irish stereotypes 219
Isolationists 146, 150, 157
Italian stereotypes 222

Jamison, Bud 90
Japanese stereotypes 172–174
Jewish humor: consolation of the victim 166; letz 129, 130; payatz 130; Purim plays 130, 166; Stooges "outed" 133; Stooges' relation to 129
Jews in film 166
jump cut 73

Keaton, Buster 86, 103
Knutzy Knights: animal-like props 79; helmet with dog's voice 37; Larry as homely maiden 246; wordplay 26

Langdon, Harry 86
Larry: comic foil 5; early career 4; ego-like behavior 140; existential Stooge 139; Holy Fool 139; Holy Spirit 139; superego-like behavior 98; switch with Curly 53; vaudeville origins 134; as young girl 246
Latino stereotyping 204–208, 215
letz 129
Listen Judge 25, 126, 221
Loco Boy Makes Good 16, 21, 106, 243
Loose Loot: actor miscues 80; pictures alive 37; show people 221, 244; wordplay 25
Lord, Del 87
Love at First Bite: German maiden 222; Italian sweetheart 223, 224n.1; pathos 106; puns 16, 24; sweethearts 221, 244
loving cup scene 89
luftmensch 131

maids 221, 245
Malamud, Bernard 132
malapropism 9, 13
Malice in the Palace: actor miscues 79; Arab stereotyping 210, 212, 213, 214; Curly scene omitted 7, 59–60; hotdog alive 37; Nubian guard 192, 210, 212; pathos 106; women absent 247; wordplay 24
Marx, Karl 140
Marx, Larry 140
Marx brothers 123
Matri-Phony 17, 21, 53–57

McCollum, Hugh 87
McDaniel, Sam 189–190
McIntyre, Christine 241, 242
Meet the Baron 15
Men in Black: doctor routine 135; glass door breaking 92; intercom alive 37; midget as female 246; nurse 245; parody of film 234; puns 16, 17
Merry Mavericks 25, 43–45
A Merry Mixup: surrealism 40; sweethearts 221; three sets of triplets 35, 244; wordplay 27
MGM short films 83
Micro-Phonies: antisociety comments 126; Curly in drag 231; as musicians 231; pseudo-singer 231; puns 22; Stooges' enemy 223; storyline errors 74
Minsky, Morton 132
minstrelism 191
A Missed Fortune: antisociety comments 125; gold diggers 221, 240; sexual predators 228; wordplay 25
mistakes in Stooges films 71
Mr. Noisy 86
Moe: attitude toward Negro 190; egolike behavior 97; Father 139; Hailstone the paperhanger dictator 159–160; legitimate theater roles 132; superego behavior 140
Monkey Businessmen 22
Movie Maniacs: Curly as female 234n.8; diva 244; script vs. film 60–70; showgirls 244, 245; strong woman 242; women as props 245; wordplay 18
Mummy's Dummies: Arab stereotyping 210, 211, 214; hallucinations 39; Jewish elements 167; ugly woman 242; wordplay 24
Muscle Up a Little Closer 27, 106, 242
Musty Musketeers 26, 244
Mutts to You: gibberish 213; Irish cop 220; Jewish elements 167; pathos 106; pets and antisociety comments 125; puns 16, 19; Stooges as women 246
My Man Godfrey 123

nar 129
Nazis: book burning mocked 161; *Confessions of a Nazi Spy* 148; Gestapo ridiculed 165; Hitler depictions in film 148, 157; Hollywood depiction of 157; Japanese compared with 172–173; negative portrayal in *Man Hunt* 149; Stormtroopers mocked 161; *see also* German stereotypes

Negro 181–182, 184–186
Nervous Shakedown 91
Niagara Falls scene 43
No Census No Feeling: bridge party mishaps 126; French maids 221, 245; puns 16, 20; unclothed 239
No Dough Boys: anti-Japanese 158, 162, 165; gun molls 241; illustration 176; military theme 145; wordplay 22
Nubians 192–193
Nutty But Nice: depressed girl 245; light bulbs and physics laws 36; pathos 107; pie fight 120; Stooges as girls 246; wordplay 19
Nye, Gerald P. 150

Of Cash and Hash: continuity errors 74; pathos 107, 227; wordplay 26
Oil's Well That Ends Well: no women 247; pathos 105, 107; puns 16, 27; wishes granted 35
Oily to Bed Oily to Rise: malapropisms 14; pathos 107; puns 16, 19, 27; widow 227, 243, 247; wishes granted 35
Our Gang and Negro image 182
Out West: physics laws distorted 37; plot reuse 88; strong woman 242; wordplay 23
Outer Space Jitters 27, 34

A Pain in the Pullman: American Negro 185; battleaxe 243; bull 92; train plot 89, 91; wordplay 18
Pals and Gals 26, 242, 244
paperhanger motif 159–160
Paramount Studio 83
paranormal 33
Pardon My Backfire: Italian opera singer 221; sweethearts 244; violence 114; wire dance 37; wordplay 25
Pardon My Clutch 23, 90, 244
Pardon My Scotch: claims as experts 170; dinner party mess 124; Italians 223; passages never filmed 45–49; Scots stereotype 218, 219; wordplay 25
pathos 101–109, 227, 244
payatz 130
PCA production code 150, 156
Pest Man Wins: French maid 221; pie fight 119; wordplay 25
pets and antisociety comments 125
Phony Express 22, 215
physics laws distorted 36
Pick a Peck of Plumbers 88
pie fights 118

Pies and Guys: actor miscues 79; make-believe food 37; pie fight 119, 125; wordplay 27
Playing the Ponies 18
Pop Goes the Easel: clay fight 120; French painter 221; Indian stereotypes 203; Irish accent 220; Middle Easterner 215; mystic 215; puns 16, 17; Stooges as women 231, 240
Prince's Orchestra and Band 200
production errors 77
properties and sets errors 78
Punch Drunks: babes 243; surrealism in 37, 40; wordplay 17
Punchy Cowpunchers 24
puns: definition 13; Eddie Cantor's use of 14; Edgar Allan Poe's defense of 15; etymology 14; mockery of Axis powers 162, 164; Oscar Levant defense of 15
Purim plays 166
Purimshpil 130

Quiz Whizz 16, 27, 241

racial aspects *see* particular ethnic or racial group
remakes and errors 78
Restless Knights 17
Rhythm and Weep: army induction 43; continuity problem 51–52; passage omitted in final 50–51; show people 243, 244; Stooges as ballerinas 246; storyline errors 75; undressing gag 89; wordplay 23
Rip Sew and Stitch 34, 74, 25
RKO sets 83
Road Runner cartoons 113
Rockin' Through the Rockies 19, 201, 203, 243
Rumpus in the Harum: Arab stereotyping 210, 212, 213; guard 192, 196n.9; hot-dog alive 37; pathos 106; post–Shemp 40, 78; sweethearts 244; wordplay 26
Russian stereotypes 223
Rusty Romeos: gold diggers 240; pathos 106; remake errors 76; wordplay 27

Sappy Bull Fighters: pathos 105, 106; production errors 77; script from *What's the Matador* 216n.3; wordplay 28
Saved by the Belle: Latino stereotypes 207; puns 16, 19; strong woman 242
Scheming Schemers: American Negro 186, 187; dinner party mishaps 125; Dudley Dickerson 186; footage used from earlier film 88; pie fight 119, 239; post–Shemp 40, 78; remake errors 78; society dames 239; water stunt 37; wordplay 26
schlemiel: characteristics of 131, 166; Curly as 131; Eddie Cantor as 132; Gimpel the Fool as archetype 131
Scotched in Scotland: Arab stereotyping 214; gun molls 241; men as ghosts 32; pictures alive 37; Scots stereotype 218, 219; skeleton 33; wordplay 26
Scots stereotype 218
Scrambled Brains: crooks tricked 92; fumbled lines 77; hallucinations 34; hand in fireplace gag 91; ugly woman 242; violence 114; wordplay 24
screwball comedy 122, 123
scripts, original 42–70, 88–89
Self-Made Maids: Scots stereotype 219; Stooges as women 246; stunt doubles errors 78
Senate Interstate Commerce Committee 150, 151
Shemp: complex character 141; death and film remakes 78; pathos in films 104; replacement of Curly 7; surrealism, postmortem 32
Shivering Sherlocks 23
Shot in the Frontier 26, 244
shrew 241
shtik, definition of 129
sight gags 77, 91
Sing a Song of Six Pants: continuity errors 74; gun molls 241; "legless" Shemp 34; puns 16, 23
Singer, Isaac Bashevis 131
The Sitter Downers: house misdesigned 39, 40; jump cut 73; pathos 106; shrew 241; ugly woman 242; wordplay in 18
Slaphappy Sleuths: illustration 115, 119; surrealism 35; thief 221; wordplay 24
slapstick 129
Slippery Silks: cream puffs as weapons 120; society dame 239; ugly woman 242; vanities as dresses 39, 40; women models 245; wordplay 18
A Snitch in Time 24
Snow White and the Three Stooges 16
Snowflake 184, 193
So Long, Mr. Chumps: continuity errors 75; illustration 51; man beater 240; parody of film 234n.5; passage not filmed 49–50; pathos 107; sweetheart 245; wordplay 16, 21
social commentary 120, 229

Sock-a-Bye 16, 21, 106
Some More of Samoa: old woman 230; puns 16, 21, 28; Snowflake 184, 193; ugly woman 242
sound effects 9, 90
Soup to Nuts 4, 15, 134
Soupault, Philippe 31
South Seas natives 193
Space Ship Sappy: Jewish elements 167; rocket scientist 222; space travel 34; strong women 242; wordplay 27
space travel 33
Spook Louder: antisociety comments 126; men as ghosts 32; pie fight 120; wordplay 21
Spooks! 25, 34, 91, 244
Squareheads of the Roundtable 23, 35
stereotyping in Stooges films 199; *see also* individual group
Stone Age Romeos 26, 79, 242, 244
stooging, definition 134
storyline errors 74
Studio Stoops 24, 92, 244
stunts 77
superego 98, 140
supernatural 30
surrealism 30
Sweet and Hot: German psychiatrist 222; Indian giver 203n.6; pathos 106; ugly woman 242; wordplay 27

Tassels in the Air 16, 19, 26, 221
Termites of 1938: American Negro maid 185, 194; dinner party mishaps 124; maids 245; puns 16, 18; script reused 89
Thanatos and death instincts 99
They Stooge to Conga: American Negro 187, 195; Axis powers mocked 164; claim as experts 170n.9; Dudley Dickerson 187, 195; Japanese mocked 175; jump cut 73; light bulb stunt 36; Nazis mocked 158, 162, 165; pictures alive 37; puns 16, 21; violence 114
Three Arabian Nuts: Arab stereotyping 213; Negro inferiority 195; Nubian 212, 214; wordplay 24
Three Dark Horses 25, 208, 247
Three Dumb Clucks: gold diggers 228, 229, 240; mother 243; parody of film 229; pathos 106; sexual predators 228, 229; wordplay 18
Three Hams on Rye: actress 221, 244; Latino stereotypes 208; puns 16, 24
Three Little Beers 18, 125, 245
Three Little Pigskins 17, 245

Three Little Pirates 23, 37, 38, 215
Three Little Sew and Sews: antisociety comments 126; gun molls 241; military threat 145; production errors 77; Stooges as flying angels 34; Thanatos 99; wordplay 19
Three Little Twirps 19, 21, 192
Three Loan Wolves 22, 57, 241
Three Missing Links: degrading representations of blacks 191; diva 244; homoeroticism 234n.8; Nubians 192; White's debut 80; wordplay 22
Three Pests in a Mess 22, 191, 241
Three Sappy People: British butler 218; cream puff fight 120; dinner party mishaps 125; spoiled wife 245; wordplay 19
Three Smart Saps 21, 106, 126
Three Stooges Fan Club 109
The Three Stooges Go Around the World 16
Three Troubledoers: Brendel/Langdon short as basis 89; pathos 106; strong woman 242; wordplay 25
time distortions 35
Tom and Jerry cartoons 113
The Tooth Will Out: scene omitted in filming 52–53; script shared with Merry Mavericks 43; teeth alive 37; ugly woman 242; wordplay 25
tragedy 102, 131
Tricky Dicks: Italian organ grinder 223; man beater 240; wordplay 25
trinities and the Stooges 138
Triple Crossed: remake errors 76; voice like a bird 34; women secretaries 245; wordplay 28
TV programs, fantasy vs. reality 111, 115
TV restriction of Stooges 109
two-person comedy teams 138

ugly women 241–242
Uncivil War Birds: military theme 145; Southern belle 245; Stooges as women 246; Stooges in blackface 191; wordplay 22
Uncivil Warriors: American Negro 184; darkie routine 185, 190; military theme 145; mockery of Negro 190; Negro baby 184, 194; pancake gag 92; Southern belle 245; Stooges as women 231, 246; wordplay 17
Up in Daisy's Penthouse: Collins as woman 246; gold digger 240; mother 242; pathos 106; sexual predators 228, 229; wordplay 25

Vagabond Loafers: dinner party mishaps 125; frightened African-American 91; hole in the floor gag 91; jump cut error 73; remake of 88; society dame 239; water through wires gag 37, 186; wordplay 24
vaudeville and Stooges comedies 133
vector field changes 75
violence 109, 233
Violent Is the Word for Curly: antisociety comments 125; film parody 234n.5; puns 16; sexy coeds 245

Warner Brothers 149
We Want Our Mummy: Arab stereotyping 210, 211; Egyptian 219; false fronts 230, 231; German professor 222; no women 247; puns 17, 19; storyline errors 75
Weber and Fields 133
Wee Wee Monsieur: Arab stereotyping 210, 211, 213, 214; French stereotype 221; military theme 145; Nubian servant 213, 214; soldier's walk 91; Stooges as women 246
Wessell, Dick 90
Wham-Bam-Slam!: McHugh 90; wives 244; wordplay 25
What's the Matador?: Latino stereotype 207, 208, 216n.3; production errors 77; wordplay 21
White, Jules: errors increased with 80–81; film files 42; Niagara Falls scene reused 43; responsible for Columbia style 84–85, 87–88; violence of films 88; wordplay 16

Who Done It?: American Negro 189; Dudley Dickerson 189, 193, 194; stunt double errors 76; water stunt 37; wordplay 24
Whoops I'm an Indian!: illustration 202; puns 16; stereotyping of Indian 201, 202, 203; women as props 245; wordplay 18, 202
Woman Haters: American Negro 184; atypical film 234n.3; babes 243; women barflies 245; wordplay 17
women in Stooges films 227–230, 236
wordplay 14, 16, 28
World War II 147, 158

Yablokoff, Hermann 130
Yes We Have No Bonanza: bikes in the Old West 36; first contract with Columbia 5; hatred of women 248; Irish cop 219, 220; puns 16, 19
Yiddish tragicomedy 130–133
The Yoke's on Me: Collins as woman 246; Gestapo ridiculed 158, 162, 163, 165; Japanese satirized 175; military theme 145; puns 16, 22; wordplay 22
You Nazty Spy!: bully 131; early release of 151, 153, 155, 158; games with Allied and Axis 162, 163; gun molls 241; Hitler satire 51, 152, 159, 160, 161, 165; id 118; Jewish elements 167; military theme 145; mockery of Nazis 97, 159; mockery of Negro 190; statue alive 37; Thanatos 99; women secretaries 245; wordplay 164, 169, 170, 170n.5

www.ingramcontent.com/pod-product-compliance
Lightning Source LLC
Chambersburg PA
CBHW021342230426
43666CB00006B/374